Revolution in China and Russia

Manchester University Press

ALTERNATIVE SINOLOGY

ALTERNATIVE SINOLOGY

Series editors: Richard Madsen and Zheng Yangwen

This series provides a dedicated outlet for monographs and possibly edited volumes that take alternative views on contemporary or historical China; use alternative research methodologies to achieve unique outcomes; focus on otherwise understudied or marginalized aspects of China, Chineseness, or the Chinese state and the Chinese cultural diaspora; or generally attempt to unsettle the status quo in Chinese Studies, broadly construed. There has never been a better time to embark on such a series, as both China and the academic disciplines engaged in studying it seem ready for change.

To buy or to find out more about the books currently available in this series, please go to: https://manchesteruniversitypress.co.uk/series/alternative-sinology/

Revolution in China and Russia

Reorganizing empires into nation states

Luyang Zhou

MANCHESTER UNIVERSITY PRESS

Copyright © Luyang Zhou 2025

The right of Luyang Zhou to be identified as the author
of this work has been asserted in accordance with the
Copyright, Designs and Patents Act 1988.

Published by Manchester University Press
Oxford Road, Manchester, M13 9PL

www.manchesteruniversitypress.co.uk

British Library Cataloguing-in-Publication Data
A catalogue record for this book is available from the British
Library

ISBN 978 1 5261 8275 3 hardback

First published 2025

The publisher has no responsibility for the persistence or
accuracy of URLs for any external or third-party internet
websites referred to in this book, and does not guarantee
that any content on such websites is, or will remain, accurate
or appropriate.

EU authorised representative for GPSR:
Easy Access System Europe, Mustamäe tee 50,
10621 Tallinn, Estonia
gpsr.requests@easproject.com

Typeset by Newgen Publishing UK

To my wife Hui Li and daughter Emily Ren

Contents

List of Figures	*page* viii
List of Tables	ix
Acknowledgments	x
1 Empires, nation states, and two revolutions	1
2 From an open union to an enclosed nation state	38
3 Reconciliation with traditional "Russia" and "China"	77
4 Revolution, nationalism, and multi-ethnic integration	131
Conclusion: Two revolutions in communist and world history	190
Appendix 1: Figures	213
Appendix 2: Tables	216
Bibliography	225
Index	249

Figures

1.1	This analytical strategy combines biographical analysis with comparative historical methods	*page* 26
App 1.1	The international overlapping of the two communist revolutions	213
App 1.2	Tradition, nationalism, and revolution	214
App 1.3	Communists' varied support for borderland self-determination	214

Tables

1.1	Differences between USSR and PRC national policy	*page* 4
1.2	Alternative accounts and their shortfalls	7
1.3	The thesis presented in this book	12
1.4	The three mutually independent differences between the two revolutionary leaderships	14
App 2.1	Bolsheviks' death dates, in total 104, all central committee members before 1917	216
App 2.2	CCP's death dates, in total 76, all central committee members before 1945	216
App 2.3	Arrests of the leading Bolshevik elites before March 1917	216
App 2.4	The CCP's overseas experiences in comparison with the KMT	217
App 2.5	The Bolsheviks and the Russian Liberals (Kadets), based on central committee members	219
App 2.6	The CCP and the KMT, based on central committee members in 1944 and 1945	219
App 2.7	The Bolsheviks' ages in comparison with the Liberals and Conservatives	221
App 2.8	The CCP's ages in comparison with the KMT	221
App 2.9	The places where the Bolsheviks studied or worked	223
App 2.10	The places where the CCP studied or worked	224

Acknowledgments

In the process of writing this book, I received substantial comments from many colleagues: Matthew Lange, Juan Wang, Barry Eidlin, Thomas Soehl, and Lorenz Lüthi from McGill University, Andrew Schrank, J. Nicholas Ziegler, Edward Steinfeld, Prerna Singh, Linda Cook, and Fabrizio Fenghi from Brown University, Liliana Riga and James Kennedy from University of Edinburgh, Mark Harrison from University of Warwick, Shizheng Feng from Renmin University of China, Andreas Wimmer from Columbia University, Xiaohong Xu from National University of Singapore, Peter Fibiger Bang from University of Copenhagen, Dingxin Zhao and Yang Zhang from University of Chicago, Jing Zhang from Peking University, Bill Kissane, Robin Archer, and George Lawson from London School of Economics. My greatest gratitude is dedicated to my doctoral thesis supervisor John A. Hall.

In writing this book I received support from many institutions, including the Watson Institute for International and Public Affairs at Brown University, the annual summer workshop on totalitarian regimes at the Hoover Institute of Stanford University, the Institute for Qualitative and Multi-Method Research at Syracuse University, the Center for the History and Sociology of World War II and Its Consequences at National Research University Higher School of Economics in Moscow, the Chiang Ching-kuo Foundation for International Scholarly Exchange, the Davis Center for Russian and Eurasian Studies at Harvard University, and the summer research laboratory on Russia and Eastern Europe at University of Illinois at Urbana-Champaign.

I am also grateful to the three teachers who taught me the Russian language for seven semesters at McGill University during my doctoral study: Zaure Kadyrbekova, Vladimir Ivantsov, and Liudmila Klimanova.

I thank the editing team of the Manchester University Press for its efficient work: Shannon Kneis, Katie Evans, Laura Swift, and Tanis Eve. It is my honor to publish my first book with Manchester University Press.

The Department of Sociology at Zhejiang University provided me a quiet space to write this book during the period of 2021–24.

1

Empires, nation states, and two revolutions

The nation state is the world's dominant political format. However, its foundational principle is volatile. "One nation, one state" can be understood in numerous ways, given that "nation" is defined by a variety of actions, ranging from merging, forging and claiming, to reducing and denying. Such vagueness gives rise to flexibility, as well as uncertainty, in how nation states are constructed. Over the past two centuries, the world has seen massive progress, setbacks, and frustration in building nation states. Cleansing, deportation, forced assimilation, territorial resettlement, manipulation in renaming, as well as recurrent secessionist movements, are all manifestations of the contestation around what a nation is. This ambiguity has also provided empires the opportunity to manipulate nationalism to their geopolitical advantage, often in combination with ideologies, e.g., imperialism, liberalism, communism, and religious universalism. This book is an endeavor to understand how revolution has created an opportunity for empires to manipulate the rise of nationalism.

Most modern nations trace their beginnings to a revolution. The Eighty Years' War, termed "the Dutch Revolt," was a protracted revolution which resulted in a united state independent of the Spanish. Oliver Cromwell's conquests of Wales and Scotland were motivated in part by a nationalist desire to unify Britain in the name of the republic. Both the American and the French nations were forged by revolutions as well. Within the pursuit of equality and the principle of "sovereignty resides in the people" lay the first step for forging a nation. These revolutions differed from each other, both in scale and in depth of mobilization, on the composition of leadership, as well as on their forefathers' consciousness of nationhood. However, in each of these cases, the revolutions out of which nation states would emerge were protracted, but not without retreats, truces, setbacks, and restorations. As revolutions were changing, the national models they created changed as well. The states they created not only differed from the ideal that spurred revolution but have remained in flux over time. Revolutions created confederation-like polities in the Netherlands, the British Empire, the Thirteen American Colonies, and the Jacobin National Republic in its transition into the Napoleonic Empire.

The Russian and the Chinese communist revolutions changed the world, not only by creating two distinct socialist models (Anderson 2010), but also by modeling ways for old empires to respond to waves of nationalism. They each transpired at crucial moments when nationalism was spilling over from the West to the East. Covering parts of both Europe and Asia, Russia had been exposed early to pressure from the European international system. Thus, its leadership had a clearer understanding of the modern nation state: they knew that sovereign states were equal, while China's leadership still viewed neighboring states as inferior tribute states. In contrast, China, at the eastern end of the continent and geographically separated from Europe, had a long history of unity, which led some sinologists to believe that it was a premodern nation state. For both polities, however, the transition from traditional empire fell behind and stuttered until, eventually, successive defeats convinced their leadership to reorganize into nation states. The ruling elite and intellectuals recognized that they had to acclimate to the international system, and also become more competitive geopolitically, by developing nationhood.

The transition was not easy. Neither polity was ethnically homogeneous. Rather, both covered vast geographical spaces with an array of ethnic minorities. This was common for early empires, but problematic for late-developers. While Russia and China were building nation states, many ethnic groups whom they had intended to incorporate into their nations-in-building had been awakened to their own nationhood. As unsuccessful modernizers, Russia and China, on the eve of revolution, had minimal glorifiable past to shape an ethnicity-transcendent national pride. This further reduced the cards they could play vis-à-vis Western competition. As social revolutionaries against minimalism and reform, neither the Russian nor the Chinese elite wanted to follow the Anglo-American path. Rather, they anticipated a Jacobin-style great revolution, which would create an ideal-typical nation that would eradicate all inequality from the outset. A fascist path of forced assimilation was equally undesired. For "revolutions from below" like those of the Bolsheviks and the CCP elites, ethnic minorities were the allies in the banner of national self-determination, not subjects to be conquered, as in "revolutions from above." Lastly, old regimes' conservative path of preaching traditional culture was loathed as well. Viewed as a carrier of toxicity, "tradition," at least in the formal program, was not to be celebrated; it was to be quashed by the revolution.

Adapting to the nation state model was crucial to both Bolshevik and Chinese Communist Party (CCP) revolutionaries. Any existing approach, be it ethnic, civic, class-based, or military, would have been insufficient. Thus, they had to maintain a dynamic balance across multiple fronts—ethnic relations, revolution, native tradition, and psychology—while navigating external interference. It was in this complicated configuration of ideology, structure, and process that the two national models took shape. Whereas the Soviet Union, an institutionalized internationalism, drew closer to the ideal type of a united world proletarian union, the People's Republic of China resembled a multi-ethnic nation state. However, beneath this distinction lay numerous subtle similarities.

The Bolshevik and the Chinese revolutions continued to be unique. The revolutions after 1945 signaled a new round of nation state making, with the falls of the British, French, Dutch, Spanish, and Portuguese empires. At this stage, great revolutions as protracted as the French, Russian, and Chinese revolutions were rare. Except for the proxy wars of superpower decolonization, most revolutions were coup-style, taking power with limited mass mobilization, and for short durations. Even the Iranian Islamic Revolution of 1979, which arguably ushered in a new era, had a simpler struggle of re-integration and social transformation than did the Bolshevik and Chinese revolutions; it was more of a restoration of previously suppressed tradition than the creation of an unprecedented one. This trend of expediency persisted throughout the collapse of communism at the turn of the 1990s, as nation states in Eurasia were liberated en masse from the Soviet Empire. Without major wars or prolonged guerrilla tactics, they were both unanticipated and abrupt. All these regime changes, termed "negotiated revolution," entailed fitting into a preexisting internal order, rather than creating a new one from scratch (Lawson 2005). Therefore, we must look back to the Bolshevik and the CCP revolutions to explicate the emergence of the modern world order.

China's deviation from the Soviet Union

The Soviet Union advised the CCP in establishing its national model, creating the impression that China, like other socialist states, had adopted the Soviet model (Connor 1984) without critique. In this model, ethnic minorities received nominal rights of autonomy in the name of eradicating national oppression. Under this territorial arrangement, minorities were entitled to economic and educational preferential treatment. Ethnic groups were recognized and identified as "nations," followed by efforts to create "national cultures," encompassing art, language, costumes, and lifestyles—this recognition transpired primarily in the 1950s and was complete by the 1980s. Related to this celebration of diversity was the ambiguous task of defining "China." Apart from a common territory and common past, officials were evasive in speaking of any cultural or biological essentials of "Chineseness." Rather, they emphasized that "Chinese" is not the equivalent of Han, even though the latter accounted for a supermajority of the Chinese population. This distinction resembles the Soviet model in its underplaying of Russianness and presentation of Russian chauvinism in contrast to Soviet internationalism.

Despite their outward similarities, there were important differences between the Chinese and Soviet models. By appearance, the PRC is a sovereign state with enclosed borders, whereas the Soviet Union was an open union which would theoretically keep accepting new members until it covered the entire globe. This difference was more than symbolic. The USSR was constructed through a process of adding new members, like Moldova, the Baltic states, Karelia, and the reorganized Central Asian republics. In Stalin's final years, he even considered allowing Eastern European states and Mongolia to join the Soviet Union when the appropriate moment arrived. In contrast, the PRC, despite its interference in anti-colonial revolutions in Southeast Asia, never formally annexed any territory. The Chinese model was one of a greater nation, where all ethnic groups are identified as subnational autonomous units of the Chinese nation through the ambiguous term "nation" (*minzu*). No ethnic group, regardless of size or economic importance, was entitled to a territorial republic, as was the case in the Soviet Union. Rather, CCP leaders openly rejected the Soviet model. There have been no equivalents of Soviet Ukraine, Soviet Kazakhstan, or the Soviet Transcaucasian Federation. In this sense, the PRC resembles the ideal typical nation state, i.e., it is not a union of nation states.

Table 1.1 Differences between USSR and PRC national policy

	The Soviet Union	The People's Republic of China
Openness of sovereignty and borders	A machine of world revolution that is supposed to continue accepting new members	A nation state claiming stable borders in spite of territorial disputes
The status of the former core nation	"Russia" decreased to one republic and denied core status	"China" highlighted as an overarching framework
Peripheral minorities	Socialist nations granted union republics and autonomous republics	Subgroups of the "Chinese Nation," with statehood rejected

Empires, nation states, and two revolutions

There is a subtle difference regarding the status of the dominant ethnic group—the Han Chinese and the Great Russians. Like the Bolsheviks who loathed Great Russian culture as an incarnation of corruption and the devil, the CCP saw conservative traits in Han Chinese culture, and claimed that the reactionary and outdated elements should be the target of revolution. However, this did not lead the CCP to negate "China" as the overarching frame of the socialist state and resort to a non-national Soviet concept; there was no institutional design to dilute "China." However, in the Soviet Union, the "Russian Socialist Federation of Soviet Republics" was not only merely one of multiple "union republics," but also a "decreased Soviet Union," not a Russian republic (Slezkine 1994). Aware that many cultural elements were at odds with revolution, the CCP sought to build an enlightened Chinese culture, which simultaneously would incorporate non-Han traits, elements of the Enlightenment, and a revolutionary path. This "Chinese national culture" is still under construction, but from the outset, its developmental goals diverged from those of Sovietism.

Why were the Soviet Union and China different?

Why did the Bolsheviks refuse to build Russia into a socialist Russian nation state, and instead opt for a union of nation states that eventually incurred a "revenge of the past" (Suny 1993)? Why did the CCP deviate from the Soviet model, despite its initial imitation of, and resemblance to, the latter? Demography provides a simplistic explanation. Ethnic Russians constituted a majority of the Soviet Union's population, but by a small margin. On the eve of revolution, they accounted for barely half of Russia's total population, whereas Han Chinese constituted nearly 95 percent of the PRC. This observation supports the popular opinion that the establishment of the Soviet Union was Russians' compromise with independence-seeking non-Russians. This made the Bolshevik Revolution one of "de-Russification," at least in form (Pipes 1964; Seton-Watson 1967). In a more recent development in this area of the literature, Andreas Wimmer adds that China's linguistic homogeneity, in the form of a common written script, enabled the Han-elite to maintain communication with each other, and preserve a unified country (Wimmer 2018). Apart from the demographic disadvantage, the Russians' structural weakness also manifested in that they were neither the most modernized, nor the most industrialized, people in the Russian Empire. Unlike in China where ethnic Hans have occupied most of the industrial and coastal areas, Russians inhabited the underdeveloped inlands, which positioned them as having less exposure to Western influence than their Ukrainian, Baltic, and Transcaucasian subjects. This factor, combined with Russia's shorter history, subjected ethnic Russians to images of barbarianism (Riga

2012). By contrast, it would be a stretch to say that ethnic Hans had such a relationship vis-à-vis non-Hans in China. Rather, a long line of scholarship has argued that the concept of a multi-ethnic China had been in place since the eighteenth century, under the Qing Dynasty. According to this argument, China was better prepared and more qualified to be a nation state than Russia in every regard and had been since antiquity.

A second major account regards the geopolitics which were intertwined with both polities' respective founding processes. As Mikhail Pokrovsky, George Plekhanov, and later Vladimir Lenin accused, Russia was a "prison of peoples." Ethnic Russians, having played the role of evil conquerors and colonizers, bore original sin vis-à-vis other peoples (Agursky 1987). Such a "prison" extends to the eastern and central parts of Europe, in playing the dirty role of oppressing European nationalist movements. This led Marx and Engels to accuse tsarist Russia of being a "European gendarme." On the contrary, CCP official discourse claims that all peoples of China, Han and non-Han alike, were the victims of Western imperialism, and thus should unite. This view manifests in explanations that attribute the CCP's Sinicization to the Sino–Japanese War (Liu 2004b; Wang 2001). According to this account, the CCP initially adhered to a Bolshevik-style policy of national self-determination. This led the Party to support China's peripheral minorities' reunification under a confederation. However, they eventually abandoned this route as the war with Japan commenced. In other words, the geopolitical account interprets Russia and China as two different types of anti-colonial united fronts—one against the imperial metropole within, and the other against an external imperialist power.

A third account considers interaction—the Chinese communism was far closer to Russian communism than the Russian revolution was to the French revolution of 1789. The Sino-Soviet split has been interpreted as evidence that these two cases are intertwined, and thus, methodologically incomparable. Sovietism is understood as a trick to facilitate the Bolsheviks' program of exporting revolution, termed the "Piedmont Principle" to Western countries (Martin 1998) and "national liberation" to the East (Pantsov 2002; Smith 1999). The PRC, as well as other socialist states in East Asia and Eastern Europe, were viewed as products of this Bolshevik-dominated creation. For example, Moscow forbade Yugoslavia and Bulgaria from developing para-Soviet federations as they had initially proposed. Sociologically, this thesis can be traced to the theory of a world culture template, which argues that once a nation state has become a model, all countries must accommodate it (Meyer et al. 1997). A more recent argument is that not only communist regimes, but also most imperial polities, shared the tendency to eventually learn to manipulate nationalism to advance their geopolitical agendas (Hall 2017). For such an account, it would be inappropriate to compare the boosters and the boosted, since the latter were manufactured by the former.

Empires, nation states, and two revolutions 7

Table 1.2 Alternative accounts and their shortfalls

Existing accounts or understandings	My argument
Demographically, China was far more homogenous than Russia, and thus conducive to building a Chinese nation state.	Not all communist movements in China were Han-centric. It was the Bolshevik-engineered ethnic Balkanization of China's revolution that shaped the CCP's Han-centric conception of the Chinese nation.
China was a semi-colonial society which had undergone a War with Japan. This eased a "One-China" discourse which overshadowed minorities' national self-determination.	The CCP's support for peripheral minorities' self-determination varied across regions and hinged on the CCP local branches' particular power relations with its foes.
The Comintern engineered the Chinese Revolution into a nationalist movement.	Nationalism could be presented in multiple ways. The CCP retained autonomy in establishing the variants of Chinese nationalism, depending on the depth and scale of revolutionary mobilization.

Each of these explanations has some element of truth, though none are definitive. With the demographic perspective addressed, the following question arises: as the Han Chinese had been in such a secure position, why did the CCP not choose a more generous stance by making a second union of nation states, even with a geographical title such as "Asian" or "Chinese"? Even if Russians had to compromise with non-Russians, why did the revolution go so far as to make Russia a federation within a federation, or in Yuri Slezkine's (1994) words, a "decreased Soviet Union rather than a republic of the Russian nation"? As for comparisons of social strength, the China of the early twentieth century suffered the problem of feeble infrastructural power—the premodern bureaucracy, mass illiteracy, the core and borderland areas mutually isolated by inadequate transportation, as well as the general absence of a *Gellnerian industria* to unify the entire domain. In parallel with Han elites' common written script, which Andreas Wimmer (2018) emphasizes, the separation between the core and the non-Han periphery was profound. The segregation and restriction on migration between core and periphery had been engineered by the imperial state, and it was maintained until the twilight of the Qing Dynasty. By contrast, in boosting a greater nationalism, tsarist Russia was more advanced. As an early comer to late development, the tsarist state had occupied a vast Eurasian territory which had been so geographically enclosed that external intruders had been unable to maintain stable rule. Further, this domain was covered by a tsarist bureaucracy mixing Mongolian and European experiences, which was more penetrative than that of most Eastern dynastical states. Via the efforts of the tsarist state, linguistic Russification, though inconsistent, had achieved impressive coverage by the end of the Romanov Empire. As a consequence, it created an elite group, many of whom had joined the Bolsheviks and other leftist parties who were ethnically non-Russian, but identified with Russian culture and envisaged a unified post-dynastical polity (Riga 2012).

Nation-building outside of the West shows that the ethnic composition and national model of a given country do not necessarily match each other either. Iran underwent two revolutions in the twentieth century, one from above by the Pahlavi dynasty, and the other from below by Khomeini. Through both Iran became a nation state, though its population was far from homogeneous: ethnic Persians only account for half of the population (Mojab and Hassanpour 1996). In Turkey too, the switch first from Islamism to Ottomanism, and then to Turkism was completed by revolutions. Though the territorial losses over the course of the Ottoman Empire's collapse relieved the tension of multi-ethnicity, the Kemalist nation state was one of assimilation against the Kurds and the broader Islamic population. The praetorian tradition of guarding modernization and development remained stable, but began to shake after the thawing of the Cold War (Sohrabi 2018). Nation-building in Egypt was intertwined with revolution, which affected Egyptian nation-builders' maneuvering between Great Egyptism, Islam, and Pan-Arabism. While early in his political career, Nasser adhered to the idea of a national Egypt, his revolution later expanded to the Middle East, and he co-founded the United Arab Republic with Syria (Jankowski 2001). The most salient example was India, whose nation-builders faced immense ethnic and religious heterogeneity, yet insisted on a secularized Hinduism as its basic national identity. This framework took shape in the National Congress Party's march to power, and survived attack from both liberal minimalists and Muslim Marxists (Sathyamurthy 1997).

Russia and China are not exceptional to these common experiences throughout the world. The socialist national model was not static but rather changed from revolution to revolution. For the CCP, most change occurred in the process of its protracted revolution, while for the Bolsheviks, change came after the founding of the Soviet Union. Given many disadvantages in nation-building, it is not surprising that the CCP's early program of nationality policy was almost a replica of the Soviet one. Up until the late 1930s, the CCP had preserved a formal program of self-determinism for non-Han peoples, allowing them to first establish nation states, and then decide whether to remain within China in a Soviet federation. This was more than rhetoric. For example, along the Long March, the CCP founded a Tibetan state at the border of Sichuan, as part of a general struggle against the KMT (Liu 2017). The CCP's attitude toward Mongolia was ambiguous as well. Early leaders such as Xiang Jingyu, Qu Qiubai, and Chen Duxiu claimed that Mongolia, even if returned to China, would fall into the hands of reactionaries to become an instrument of their repression of communists. In the Southern provinces where the CCP's forces were scattered thin, the support of ethnic minority riots was vital to undermining the power of the KMT, local warlords, and the Japanese. As argued by Sidel (2021), China, like other Asian polities, faced the universal problem of building a nationalist revolution without a clear and penetrative mass nationhood.

Equally important was the temptation of Russification in the Soviet Union after the Bolsheviks' takeover. This had started when Lenin was alive, as he railed against the danger of Great Russian chauvinism within the Party. The conflict between internationalism and Russianness culminated in his debate with Stalin on whether all non-Russian regions should be integrated into a Russian federation, not as national republics, but only as sub-national units (Fyson 1995: 77–78). This was merely the starting point. In Lenin's final words, he referred to Russian nationalism as the arrogance of Russian cadres and unspoken Russo-centric thought which had erupted over the course of revolution. However, beginning in the late 1920s, Russian nationalism had become an institutionalized official frame; Russian symbols and icons returned to textbooks, where they were glorified; the Marxist-style socio-economic narrative, which lacked any discussion of agency, was replaced by the celebration of a pantheon of Russian generals and governors who had "contributed to the progress of the country." Moreover, the conquest of the former imperial periphery was framed as a "necessary devil" (Brandenberger 2002). Such a restoration was limited, in parallel with the invention of other peoples' national culture in making Moscow a "Fourth Rome" (Clark 2011). However, it is indeed comparable to the CCP's reinvention of Han Chinese culture.

The insufficiency of demographics in explaining national models warrants examination of the other two accounts—geopolitics and Sino-Soviet interaction. Geopolitical war between major powers did have the effect of fanning the identity of nationalism, as Tilly (1994) has argued. The Bolsheviks did manipulate popular nationalist sentiment during the Civil War to present themselves as the defenders of the Russian motherland (Brandenberger 2002). Moreover, to win elite support, the CCP switched its rhetoric from class warfare to a united front of national resistance against Japan as an all-out Sino–Japanese War loomed in 1937. Nevertheless, under an untheorized war–nationalism frame, many events remain unexplained. Faced with the Allies' intervention, the Bolsheviks rejected a frame of international war, and continued to denounce nationalism, as they had done before 1918.

Though their covertness is debatable, their reluctance to embrace nationalism, and the overt rejection of traditional cultural symbols, diverges from Stalin's revival of traditional symbols in the 1930s and during the Soviet–German War. China's case is more open to question, as the definition of nationalism is stretched to the cultural dimension. The massive absorption of folklore and classics into revolutionary language had started long before the Japanese invasion, coinciding with the outbreak of the KMT–CCP Civil War.

A final issue is the Bolsheviks' labelling of the CCP as a nationalist party. This thesis has some validity, but it also raises several questions. Many scholars believe that the Soviet Union and China were incomparable, in that the former intervened too much into the latter's revolution. I argue that while there was intervention in China, Russia was subject to intervention as well. They were merely connected to the international socialist movement in disparate ways. Therefore, Russian socialists' supervision by European socialists and the CCP's mentorship under the Bolsheviks are comparable. Within this resettled framework, some European socialists, like the Bolsheviks, consented to a world revolution. This contrasts with how the Bolsheviks crafted the CCP's national revolution. The Bolsheviks claimed that the Chinese revolution had to fit the framework of internationalism as well, but their strategy was to "ethnically Balkanize" communist movements in geographical China. This was to be accomplished by dividing China into Xinjiang, the Northeast, the Southwest, Mongolia, and the Central provinces. The CCP's "Chinese" was in fact one of these many revolutions. The Comintern created many transnational revolutionary groups in other parts of China, many of which were non-Chinese, or multi-ethnic, or multinational, like the Bolsheviks themselves before 1917. Thus, an external intervention did not necessarily create a homogeneous national movement.

Revolution and nation-building

The shortage of alternative accounts calls for a more refined analysis of the role of revolution. In theorizing the impact of revolution on nation-building, Miroslav Hroch (Hroch 1985) suggests that the growth of nationalism undergoes three phrases—elite cultural invention, political awareness, and mass mobilization. He argues that how revolution crosscuts nation-building affects which phase a society can ultimately reach. Hroch suggests that nationalist movements often end during the primitive stages of cultural invention or small-group political agitation. Mass mobilization does occur in some societies, but not in the name of nation-building. However, Hroch's thesis has many blind spots. It assumes that all revolutions are independent.

It also implies a deterministic conception of a given territory's ethnic structure. He mentions the role of geopolitical conflict, but it remains unclear whether there is a unified mechanism between war and patriotism. The comparison of Russia and China provides an opportunity to overcome these shortfalls.

How do the two revolutions differ? This has been conceptualized by many scholars, as part of the general scholarship on the comparison of revolutions. In terms of process, these two revolutions shared their basic elements, encompassing urban labor movements, civil war, land reform and peasant mobilization alike, as well as resisting foreign interventions and exporting revolution abroad (Anderson 2010). However, these elements entered history in different ways across the two great events, in terms of pace, duration, timing, and sequence. At each stage, the magnitude of a certain element varied. For example, as Michael Mann observes, military power was central in the CCP revolution, but not as much in the Bolshevik takeover (Mann 2012: 211). These two revolutions also occurred in different international eras, one at the end of World War I and the other in the aftermath of World War II. The lag of three decades yielded social consequences, one of which lies in the fact that the CCP revolution unfolded while an established socialist state was already in existence.

In terms of explaining the national models, several concepts are noteworthy. One is Huntington's dichotomy of central and peripheral revolutions (1968). The Bolsheviks, closer to the prototype of the French Revolution, seized power first in central cities and industrial areas, and then quickly conquered the periphery. However, the CCP had long remained in rural areas, and gradually encroached the urban core. The other dichotomy is Skocpol's comparison, which conceptualizes the Russian Revolution as a top-down bureaucratic mobilization, and the Chinese Revolution as a bottom-up mass mobilization (1979). In Skocpol's comparison, the Bolshevik victory of 1917–1921 was a reversible and brief course. While the Civil War laid the foundation for later Stalinism, it left most real transformation to Stalin's revolution-from-above in the 1930s. Conversely, the CCP's protracted civil war, though local, was a profound mass mobilization which touched every aspect of the social structure.

Beyond Russia and China, an insightful typology is Arjomand's comparison of revolutions in the ancient world (2019). Arjomand claims there are two types of revolutions—Tocquevillian and integrative. The former is a decentralization, and follows the implosion of a despotic regime, while the latter is a process of re-integration, in which a fragmented society is transformed into a new social system. This dichotomy, applied on a worldwide scale, best depicts the vicissitudes of the imperial order, which alternated between global anarchism and cosmopolitan empire.

Table 1.3 The thesis presented in this book

Allegiance to a regular sovereign State	First and second successful revolutions	
	The Bolsheviks	**The CCP**
	Revolutionaries aspiring to a Europe-based state to replace the Socialist International	Disciplined by the Comintern to construct a "Chinese" national revolution
	Nationalism engineered as a device to spread revolution	Moscow-dominated ethnic Balkanization in China
	An expanding union of nation states	*A Han-centric "Chinese" national revolution in parallel with multi-ethnic revolutions in other parts of China*
Cultural reconciliation between tradition and revolution	Timing of mass mobilization	
	The Bolsheviks	**The CCP**
	1930s, inauguration after the foundation of the Soviet Union in 1922	1930s, long before the establishment of the PRC in 1949
	Revolutionary Russophobia is dominant around 1922	A revolutionary "China" had been invented before 1949
	"Russia" underplayed	*"China" highlighted*

Table 1.3 (Cont.)

Means of integrating peripheral minorities	Belief in the capability of steering self-determination	
	The Bolsheviks	**The CCP**
	Familiar with fused to borderland ethnopolitics	Unfamiliar and isolated from borderland ethnopolitics
	Feeling secure toward the end of the civil war in 1921	Feeling insecure through up to the 1960s
	Support for self-determination; claimed generosity was a revolutionary strategy	"One Nation" discourse invented to offset military and economic disadvantages
	Ethnic groups as nations in parallel with Russians	*Ethnic groups as subgroups of the "Chinese Nation"*

From an open union to an enclosed nation state

There was immense disparity in the two revolutions' external contexts. Both revolutions occurred in the first half of the twentieth century, in the course of the world's transition from empires to nation states. However, a subtle boundary, which demarcated two eras, lay between the Bolsheviks and the CCP. The Bolshevik victory of 1917 occurred in an avalanche of collapsing European land empires, when the wave of self-determination appeared overwhelming. The Bolshevik Party came to power upon the collapse of the Ottomans, Hapsburgs, Hohenzollerns, and Romanovs, when national self-determinist movements, fueled by Wilsonism, were sweeping the British and French colonies as well. Vis-à-vis this decentralizing momentum which Arjomand called "Tocquevillian," the Bolsheviks' odd union of nation states looks quite reasonable. Nor was there any great-power-based communist agency to impose its agenda upon the Bolsheviks. Yet, the same trend came

14 *Revolution in China and Russia*

Table 1.4 The three mutually independent differences between the two revolutionary leaderships

	Ethnic composition	Cultural tastes	Periphery control
Bolshevik Party	An endogenous but transnational group infused with European socialism	Adherence to revolutionary vigilance against old Russian culture as a corrupting legacy	Manipulating self-determination and multinationalism based on command of the peripheries
Chinese Communist Party (CCP)	A Soviet-selected Han-dominated group, in parallel with other Soviet-selected non-Han or transethnic groups	Transitioning from anti-traditionalism to a reconciliation between revolution and Chinese culture	Using the discourse of a multi-ethnic China to offset military disadvantage in controlling the periphery

to be reversed and displaced over the ensuing three decades. As the capitalist system re-stabilized, there were revivals in expansionism, irredentism, and ethnic purification, not only in the fascist Germany and Italy, but also in Japan, as well as in the Central European states which emerged after World War I; the Soviet Union was becoming an integrated sovereign state. Regardless of its federal model—Moscow was not only reversing the ethnic indigenization of the 1920s, but also annexing neighboring territories, and dictating disciple-parties in other countries to expand its sphere of influence, in the name of "defending the center of the world revolution." The CCP revolution, despite its temporal proximity to the Bolshevik revolution, occurred mostly in this period, while the world was recentralizing. Thus, it could not avoid integration as an external reference point.

The Bolshevik leadership of 1917 endogenously emerged from Russia's local political context, but at the same time was infused with the European socialists of the day. Their anarchist character was not at odds with the general trend of world decentralization before World War I. Unlike Russia's historical uprisers, the Bolsheviks, since their formative years, had lacked a commitment to building a typical sovereign state. Rather, their imagination of the course of revolutionary takeover was simplistic. The Bolsheviks anticipated that the cowardly, antiquated militaries around Europe would be quick to give up resistance, and thus power seizure would involve no serious armed conflict. Out of such expectations, the Bolsheviks had invested little in the military before the Russian Civil War, neither establishing officer schools, nor training professional combat groups. Instead, most of their combat focused on agitational work among soldiers and adventurist insurrections. Enmeshed with European socialists, they anticipated that a world revolution would sweep through Europe, and thus, there was little need to consider how to establish a separate Russian socialist regime. Many Bolsheviks imagined socialism as an open union which would continually accept new members. This was the original thought enshrined in the design of the Soviet Union.

The early Bolsheviks were a generation of restless border-crossers. This, certainly, was influenced by their members' transnational and transethnic backgrounds. Many Bolshevik leaders were born into one ethnicity, educated in a second language, and radicalized in a third national society, all the while struggling with the vagueness of their identities. To these persons, designing a socialist Russian state would further complicate their identity problems, and affect their association with their co-ethnics. Thus, it was less convenient than following a simplified solution of self-determination. The Bolshevik leadership was also staffed by many foreigners and cosmopolitan Russians who supported full integration with Europe, for various reasons. Certainly, some were counting on a worldwide revolution. These people, having resided outside of Russia for most of the pre-1917 years, rushed back to Europe to foment revolution. They viewed their residence in Russia as temporary, envisaging a life of retirement in a socialist Western Europe. Others, i.e., technocrats, valued European markets, capital, and technology as vital to Soviet Russia's development. Though opposing a world revolution, they spared no force in maintaining connections with the West, fearing that any loss of economic interdependence would engender adventurism from Russian invaders. Still, others who had lost substantial power were addicted to nostalgia for the earlier years in Europe, hoping to end up with a civilization with more gender equality, democracy, and civic spirit.

The genesis of the CCP revolution was nearly contemporaneous with the Bolshevik takeover—the turn of the 1920s. The imprint of decentralization was obvious. Upon the fall of the Qing Empire, Chinese elites were in collective confusion about how the successor state should be organized. Even the Beiyang government, the legally recognized successor to the Qing, expressed such uncertainty. Using a five-color national flag, it admitted a temporal lack of ideas about why "China" legitimately should include Han, Manchurian, Mongolian, Muslim, and Tibetan peoples. The early CCP elites' imagination of a socialist China, in this intellectual conundrum, was not that different from the Soviet model. As Mao had said in the late 1910s, self-determination was a worldwide fashion that China should follow. Not only should the border peoples have the right to self-determination, but the Han would also gain equal opportunity within the federation. Chinese radicals also considered a pan-Asian revolution, with China and Japan imagined as symbiosis analogous to Russia and Europe. Thus, the nationalist movement of the 1910s synergized with anarchism, Buddhist cosmopolitanism, and various concepts of local governance.

It is difficult to imagine what a CCP state would have looked like had they secured national power contemporaneously with the Bolsheviks in Russia. Yet, this did not occur. The CCP revolution persisted for the ensuing three decades, and into the next era of world history. Paradoxically, the most relevant factor locking the CCP into a regular nation-building track was the normalization of the Soviet Union. That is to say, it was no longer claiming to be a machine with the sole function of worldwide revolution. Under "socialism in one country," the Soviet Union had become a typical sovereign state in this regard. In advancing its geopolitical agenda, Moscow highlighted centralism and national liberation. This forced the CCP to distance itself from anarchists, cosmopolitans, and Trotskyists. Unlike the Bolshevik precursors before 1917, the CCP had no free period during which they could remain idle and factious abroad, debating the trivia of a blueprint. From day one, CCP members had to accept the Leninist norm of discipline and centralism, to fight for a China deprived of imperialist influence. Those who denied this goal were expelled.

The Soviet Union also locked the CCP into an enclosed space, isolated from neighboring Asian regions. This facilitated the CCP's transition to a national movement. The Chinese revolution had previously been a transborder affair—since the 1890s, it had been interconnected with Southeast Asia, Korea, Japan, and even the Americas, largely through overseas Chinese and their local associates. However, the 1917 Bolshevik victory changed this landscape. Amid the Red Scare aroused by the Bolshevik takeover, Japan, Dutch Java, British Malaya, Singapore, and Hong Kong each intensified their anti-communist repression, primarily by tightening border controls. The Chinese communists who fled abroad were either arrested and extradited or lost contact and disappeared from radical politics. Those who remained in China escaped to mountainous areas in Central or Southern China where they would start a protracted guerrilla war. Meanwhile, the center of the revolution would eventually shift from coastal metropolitan cities to rural inland areas. The foundation for a cosmopolitan revolution had been lost.

The Comintern did create a bloc of "internationalists" within the CCP, who were later disgraced as "dogmatists uncritically following Soviet experience." However, they were by no means the Bolshevik cosmopolitans. These people had no transethnic backgrounds. They had completed elementary education in Central or Southern China and had then traveled to the Soviet Union. Their position of supporting every instruction from Moscow had annoyed Chinese nationalists, but it would be a stretch to say that these

Empires, nation states, and two revolutions 17

people had cosmopolitan mindsets. Actually, when this group celebrated the Soviet Union's expansionism, every indication was that they had been disciplined by the Soviets to acknowledge the integrationist order. In defending Soviet wars in Poland, Romania, and Finland, and in mutual pacts with the Nazis and Japan, "internationalists" showed that they were thinking on the scale of sovereign states, viewing the Soviet Union's national interests as superior.

Moscow's most far-reaching arbitration was the ethnic Balkanization of China's revolutionary movements, which reduced the CCP's "China" to a Han-dominated concept. In sponsoring the Northern Expedition, the Soviets made Guangdong the starting point. This had a decisive impact on the CCP leadership's ethnic composition—mainly Han people from Central and South China. Meanwhile, Moscow established communist movements in other parts of China, which in many ways resembled the Bolshevik Revolution. One case was the Soviet-supported communists in Xinjiang, a cosmopolitan group. These people, born Uygur or Kirgiz, had studied in Soviet Central Asia, spoke fluent Russian, and had traveled across borders between Tadzhikistan, Afghanistan, Iran, and even India and Turkey. In the South, such trans-borderism also occurred among Indochinese communists, who were no less cosmopolitan. Ho Chi Minh's organizations covered Thailand, Malaya, Vietnam, Laos, and Cambodia, and Yunnan and Guangxi in China. At the same time, they were connected with the broad overseas French colonial world. Similarly, Korean communists centered on the Peninsula maintained a transborder network across Japan, Russia's Far East, and Northeast China. These peripheral and transnational communists, who were independent of the CCP, are indicative of Moscow's effect; it was the first established socialist state with a stable nationalist CCP.

Tension with "Russia" and reconciliation with "China"

While the Bolsheviks sought an open union in contrast to the CCP's pursuit of an enclosed nation state, it remains to be explained why the Bolsheviks underplayed "Russia," and why the CCP came to highlight "China." The CCP revolution differed from the Bolshevik revolution in terms of mobilizational depth, which had an effect on nation-building at the former imperial core. For the Bolsheviks, the victory of 1921 was a mass mobilization, but it occurred primarily in urban areas, where the industrial population shared affinity with the Bolshevik industrial ideology, exerting little pressure to extend its mobilizational frame. The urgent need to absorb traditional Russian symbols came as late as the turn of the 1930s, as the Bolsheviks were officially marching to conquer the countryside. However, this wave of Russification unfolded after the formulation of the Sovietist national model. It also exerted a restrained effect on the settled formal framework. By contrast, the CCP's pre-1949 mobilization was comprehensive, and penetrative among not only the peasantry, but also populations such as the urban uneducated and rural artisans. Over this course, the CCP's early anti-traditionalist leadership was displaced by a nativist leadership, who had a different mentality and educational background. Not denying the necessity of eradicating "reactionary elements" from Chinese culture, these CCP elites sought mediation between revolution and Chinese tradition. This was a calculated move, as they were cognizant that cultural tradition was vital to mobilization, especially among peasants.

The intellectual effort of inventing a popular and enlightened Russian nation pre-dated 1917, in historiography, literature, ethnography, and geography. Influential narratives highlighted the Slavic peoples' united struggle against the Mongolian Empire, the center–outward expansion into the Baltic states, Ukraine, and Transcaucasia, and the multi-ethnic background of the War of 1812 against Napoleon's invasion. Historians and historical writers were seeking a "Russia" broad enough to include all non-Russian peoples. Yet, the Bolsheviks appear to have not been swept up in this intellectual trend. This does not mean that they had no knowledge of the movement, but that they were more influenced by non-Russian and non-native thought. Except for Chernyshevskii and a few other "revolutionary democrats," the Bolsheviks rarely cited any native Russian sources. Rather, they were obsessed with the revolutionary lessons from Europe, even the failed ones like the Revolution of 1848 and the Paris Commune of 1871. In terms of literature, the Bolsheviks boasted about their outdated tastes, presenting the image of only reading Chernyshevskii, Pisarev, Herzen, and Nekrasov. In the arena of history, George Plekhanov and Mikhail Pokrovsky were the only authors the Bolsheviks were comfortable citing. These authors had depicted Russia as an enclosed vicious cycle, unable of developing high civilization without foreign intervention. The most radical faction, though not getting full recognition but reflecting official will, was the "Proletarian Culture School." Its adherents proclaimed a negation of all existing artistic forms, as a full break from the past. It is unlikely that these people would consider inventing a "new Russia" as an overarching coverage for the multi-ethnic Soviet state. There was a spontaneous exploration of the Russian culture, but these changes were latent at the moment of traditional Soviet Union's founding. They would blossom only when the Soviet regime entered the next stage of mass mobilization—industrialization, collectivization, and the Soviet–German War (1941–1945; World War II).

The CCP's protracted revolution fused Russia's two stages of mass mobilization into one. In the opening period, like that of the Russian Bolsheviks, the CCP disparaged the Chinese past. The writing of early CCP members is replete with radical language, such as "the traditional opera is toxic for the youth," "only Western trainees are qualified to study Chinese history," and "filial piety should be replaced by equal love between parents and children." This reveals the CCP leadership's influence. Most early CCP leaders were urban-based students and professors, who had vague boundaries with contemporary anti-traditionalist intellectual currents. A large number of them had been anarchists who had sought to eliminate restrictions from the state, the family, and traditional morals. Though most of this foundational generation had perished, this starting point yielded a far-reaching legacy, which kept the CCP in a state of self-restraint from a traditionally defined China; throughout the revolution, the CCP had never altered its anti-Confucian position, and continually called the KMT's cultural conservatism reactionary.

Reconciliation with Chinese tradition began in the late 1920s, when the CCP expanded its mobilizational scale to the peasantry. Like Stalin's revival of Russification, which preceded the Nazi invasion, the CCP's revival of Chinese tradition preceded the Japanese invasion of 1931 and cannot be viewed solely as a response to national crisis. As cadres were replaced by people from rural areas and the strategic need for mobilization increased, the feeling of shame over China's past faded. This was manifested in the CCP leaders' words, as well as in their behavior. These individuals, especially the generals, invoked ancient wars and military classics, and were enthusiastic about preserving heritage. This not only reflected a calculated attempt to win support from rural elites but also indicated the subtle change in their educational backgrounds. The instrumental use of Chinese history was no longer shameful, after the Civil War began. Many pamphlets and textbooks were published with CCP support to extoll ancient military wisdom and heroism in historical wars of resistance. This process also occurred in the Soviet Union beginning in the mid-1930s.

As this transition spread to the masses, reconciliation unfolded first and foremost in the folk approach, which had begun during the Jiangxi period. This was the most revolutionary way to equate the old culture with "elitism," and stake a claim to replace it with one created by the masses. No longer fearing disparagement as purveyors of "peasant backwardness," the CCP incorporated peasant cultural icons into its discourse, as a strategy for circulating revolutionary thought. Ballads were recomposed into revolutionary songs, termed "new wine in an old bottle"—a sharp contrast to the Soviet-imported symbols. Beginning in the late 1930s, nativism intensified and further displaced the alien Soviet culture. Writers who had been influenced by foreign operas and literature were sent to learn the language of the peasantry. New operas and plays were composed to draw inspiration as well as teach lessons from historical rebellions and transnational wars, such as the Late Ming resisters, Li Zicheng, the Taiping Rebellion, and the Opium Wars.

The CCP also felt the need to eliminate shame from the past for high-culture society. Like in the Soviet Union of the 1930s, a glorification of the past took place in China beginning in the 1920s and gradually blossomed as leftist intellectuals emerged. While at the end of the 1910s the leftists loathed Chinese history as a total failure responsible for China's defeats since the late 1800s, from the late 1920s onward, explorations to rediscover China gained momentum. By fitting China's past into Stalin's five-phrase formula, Marxist historians strove to demonstrate that China was a West-like system which was able to ascend from the primitive to the advanced stage without relying on external intervention. With Mao's support, beginning at the turn of the 1940s, experts on ancient philosophy began exploring the "revolutionary and democratic values" in Chinese thought.

Unlike the Bolsheviks' quick takeover, the CCP's long revolution provided a foundation for redefining "China." By the end of the 1940s, the CCP revolution had been underway for nearly three decades. Meanwhile, the Bolsheviks of 1917 had only the Decembrists, 1905, and spontaneous worker movements to speak of, none of which were its own history. As such, the CCP could evoke a richer autobiography of "revolutionary China," or even "the CCP's China." The work of writing the history of the Northern Expedition, the Civil War, and the Sino–Japanese War had started when the CCP's regime stabilized in Yan'an. Many festivals were invented to commemorate important days of the Party history, so many that there were three commemorative days in May alone—May 4th, May 9th, and May 30th. The Soviet Union would adopt this approach in the late 1930s and during the Soviet–German War, once the Bolsheviks had created a history which would be of use to shaping national glorification.

Control over peripheral ethnic minorities

Both Russia and China were multi-ethnic polities and revolutions which had to grapple with ethnic heterogeneity. In this regard, the Bolshevik and CCP revolutions' different paces caused differentiated learning about the nationality question. And yet, they faced the same fundamental challenge: how to legitimize the idea that Russia could include non-Russians, or that China could include non-Hans. Their revolutionary ideology provided an easy solution—avoid this question and simply invoke self-determination to undermine their enemies and liberate all nations. According to this theory, there was no need to study ethnic diversity, since class was all that mattered. However, the revolution soon offered a lesson. Both communist parties quickly recognized that a great revolution should allow no section of the population to remain outside its bounds, under any name. They also recognized that without consolidating their grip on their former imperial peripheries, the respective revolutions could not continue. This sparked a struggle between a retention of unity and maneuvering ethnopolitics.

The Bolshevik and CCP leaderships had differentiated fusion levels with borderland ethnopolitics. The Bolshevik leadership was more ethnically diverse than that of the CCP. However, ethnic roots do not determine political opinion. It is thus wrong to assume that a multi-ethnic leadership had to support the federation and a homo-ethnic leadership favored a unitary system. What mattered instead was how they interacted with other ethnic groups and engaged the entire imperial ethnic landscape. The Bolsheviks came from a vast diversity of ethnic groups, including Russians and Ukrainians, Jews, Latvians, Georgians, and Kazakhs. These people had intersected experiences with different parts of the tsarist empire. By contrast, the CCP lacked such experiences of all-imperial mobility and intersection. Remarkably few CCP elites had stayed in non-Han areas or spoke non-Han languages. Neither did the CCP deem they had a reliable "Fifth Column" among the ethnic non-Hans. Such a difference generated a massive gap between the Bolsheviks and the CCP regarding self-confidence in the capabilities of penetrating the borderlands. The Bolsheviks believed that they were skillful in maneuvering borderland national self-determination movements, while the CCP lacked such self-confidence. Once the CCP's regime began to touch the borderlands, they feared supporting minorities' self-determination would lead to real secessionism.

The CCP's borderland experiences led the revolutionary movement to an ambiguous position between self-determination and a "One-China" nation state. The CCP elites of the 1920s almost uncritically copied the Bolsheviks' nationality program to support peripheral peoples' self-determination. This stance came to be moderated in the ensuing two decades, displaced by the discourse that China should be a unified polity and that all Han and non-Han groups were part of the Chinese nation. The CCP viewed the nation as a multilayer identity, which did not have to be clarified on a biological, linguistic, cultural, or any other level; the CCP explicitly opposed all such efforts of defining a nation in its polemic with the KMT. For the CCP, nationality could be vague and not necessarily coherent. The CCP literati also openly commemorated legendary Hans in their resistance to Northern nomadic invasions as "model national heroes." This negated Chiang Kaishek's argument that "most interethnic wars in historical China were civil wars among sub-national clans." This flexibility is not present in pre-1917 Bolshevik theories on nationality.

Indeed, the CCP's attitude toward borderland self-determination was subject to regional variation, hinging on the communist party's evaluation of many factors: whether a potential (or real) nationalistic movement could threaten the CCP guerrilla state; if a secessionist group or riot could distract the CCP's enemies (KMT, warlords, local strongmen), whether there was a risk that these movements could be manipulated by great powers (Britain, Japan, and the USSR); and how the CCP's allies viewed the CCP's attitudes to the borderland affairs. In the border areas adjacent to Inner Mongolia, the CCP was cautious of its use of the slogan "self-determination," even though they simultaneously needed to counter the KMT's centralization among Mongolians. This was not only because the CCP relied on nomads for calvary techniques but also, more importantly, for the sake of security— Inner Mongolians inhabited the northern gates of the central guerrilla state. On Hainan Island, the CCP was less secure. Lacking a stable guerrilla base, there was less concern about the threat of ethnic riots. Local leaders highlighted the interethnic resistance to the local KMT and the Japanese. In the Northeast and Xinjiang, which had been beyond reach for most of the Sino–Japanese War, the CCP felt more conducive to vocal support for internationalism from afar.

Indeed, the two revolutions' courses were different. The Bolshevik Revolution was a swiftly concluded civil war that involved limited international interventions. Despite initial difficulties, the Bolsheviks quickly attained military superiority vis-à-vis the White Russians and then conquered the borderlands. Meanwhile, through skillful diplomatic maneuvers, the Bolsheviks successfully excluded the interventions from most foreign powers, blocking their attempts to manipulate the nationalist movements at the periphery of the tsarist empire. Believing that they had firm control, the Bolsheviks felt secure in propagating an ideology of national self-determination. By contrast, the CCP Revolution took a more complicated and multi-faceted course. It was a protracted war intertwined with significant foreign intrusions. The revolutionary war involved multiple forces whose alignments kept changing. Most of the time, the CCP was weaker than its foes in the homeland and the borderlands, faced with the KMT, the Japanese, and the Soviets (though the CCP would not make the influences of the Soviet Union explicit). The CCP's disadvantage at the borderlands was further accentuated by the factor that the elites had little knowledge, experience, and networks with minorities. Such a complicated power relationship made the CCP feel insecure to uncritically adhering to the Bolshevik-style discourse of self-determination.

From class and elite analysis to biographical analysis

The dialogue between agency and structure has intrigued sociologists for centuries: many have claimed to find a way to explain agency through structure, while others contend that structure can only be understood in terms of individuals. Thus, a dilemma has persisted since the inception of the discipline. On the side of structure, the problem is defining and measuring "structure"—for example, how do we describe what a certain class is thinking when it remains debatable who the members of the class are. In *The French Civil War*, Karl Marx accesses the calculation of Paris' dominant class by identifying several crucial individuals whose activities had received sufficient media exposure. Marx also infers the interests of an invisible class by interpreting promulgated policies as intentional devices to achieve certain goals. This entails a risk of conspiracy theory when information on intermediate linkages is missing. This problem has been mitigated along with the development of survey methods, as individuals' information has become available and codable by statistics. On the side of agency, although Max Weber identifies actors as the sole reliable starting point of social analysis, how to conduct this analysis remains uncertain. Access to individuals is as difficult as access to a defined and invisible "structure"—in his *The Protestant Ethic and the Spirit of Capitalism*, Weber approaches the psychology of historical Protestants who lived centuries ago by interpreting religious texts. As a method, this incurs critique. On the contrary, his research on the Russian Revolution was based on a more genuine agency study— Weber interviewed numerous Russian politicians and traced these prominent individuals' activities from Duma bulletins and Russian newspapers.

The methodology underlying revolutionary study has evolved over three generations, with focuses on, respectively, class, elites, and biography. The first generation centered on class analysis, as represented by Barrington Moore (1966). Moore's concern was questions such as whether an arising class possesses economic autonomy vis-à-vis the old regime, e.g., the English commercial landlords did, while the Prussian Junkers did not; and after the revolutionary takeover, whether this ascending class attains full control of state machinery and displaces the old dominant classes. Between the first and the second generations is Theda Skocpol (1979). Following Moore, Skocpol (1979: 192) continues to probe the class concept, such as how organizational solidarity facilitated peasant mobilization and how the eradication of the privileged classes shaped a meritocratic military bureaucracy. Meanwhile, she extends the analysis to state staff who retain autonomy which can counteract the dominant classes. Additionally, it was the self-justifying ideology and realistic organizational model that enabled the Jacobins and the Bolsheviks to defeat opposition from the bottom.

The second generation of scholarship deconstructed the crude concept of class into a more comparable unit (i.e., the elite), as represented by Jeff Goodwin and Ricard Lachmann. Goodwin (Goodwin 2001) highlights the internal variation among state elite, with respect to how their institutional inclusiveness, as well as their capacity for penetration and bureaucratization, affected the state capacity to prevent revolution. Likewise, Lachmann argues that a revolution did exert an effect, but that the effect varied across sectors, and even within states and classes. For example, the English Civil War and Glorious Revolution created an efficient bureaucracy and meritocracy in light of the Puritan discipline, but this efficiency was concentrated in the national treasury, Royal Navy, and settler colonies (Lachmann 2020: 180–88).

The second generation, despite its focus on the elite, is anonymous and vague. There are few names of historical figures, even the prominent ones, in the elite-centered narration. Most of the narration refers to a vague collective unit composed of anonymous actors and raises the question of how the authors extrapolate the internal worlds of these elites, and whether there was more detailed variation within them. It is based on this shortfall that the third generation arises, which transitions from elite analysis to the biographical method. In his volume on the French Revolution, Michael Mann offers a prosopographic overview of the leading revolutionaries' professional backgrounds. This is followed by an analysis of the emergence of ideologues (Mann 1993: 188–97). The pivot to the third generation follows the work of Liliana Riga and Stephen Mudge. Riga's (2012) research on leading Bolsheviks probes five or six Bolsheviks from each major nationality, providing a contour on how their ethnic backgrounds situated them within class politics, and led to their conversion to Bolshevism. Drawing comparisons over a broader temporal and spatial scope, Mudge (2018) traces the career development of party experts from the leftist parties of Germany, Sweden, Britain, and the United States to explain why this group evolved over time from socialists into neoliberals. Similar to Riga's research on the Bolsheviks, most subjects were either prominent socialist theoreticians or professional economists.

The biographical approach features a refined perspective on the nuance between structure, class, and the elite. Tsarist Russia's increasing ethnic heterogeneity is refracted in Riga's comparison of Bolshevik leaders of different nationalities. Even individuals of a single nationality had differentiated conceptions of ethnicity, which complicated the intersection of class and ethnicity. Mudge's approaches allow for a relational (rather than corporate) dynamics on how experts, Party organizations, and electorates were connected. It is also in Mudge's analysis that conventional key terms such as "ideology" and "organization" can be decomposed into specific intellectual

Empires, nation states, and two revolutions 25

trends and the professional statuses of Party experts. Both Riga's and Mudge's research allows for rich internal variation of discourse and frame in revolution. A second merit of the biographical method is that it fits revolutionary studies better than class- or elite-centered approaches. For example, in the English and American Revolutions, there was considerable overlap between the political and the economic elites. Though revolutionaries were not reducible to the puppets of landlords and commercial aristocrats, the two groups did have strong alliances and infusion. There was no clear-cut boundary between leaders, elites, rulers, classes, or the masses. However, in socialist revolutions, revolutionary elites tended to be more separate from interest groups. The schemes of social transformation stemmed not only from the population they faced, but also from the interaction between their backgrounds and imported ideas. Thus, it is important to recognize how such an insulated group mobilized and disciplined the rest of the population.

The conventional challenge to agency-based analysis is separating individuals from structure, i.e., convincing readers that particular actors exerted certain effects. This is a two-part counterfactual question: how can we show that a certain social consequence would not have occurred without the involvement of particular individuals; how can we show that these individuals were not passive reflections mirroring a preexisting structure. This problem is addressed, but not resolved, in Riga's and Mudge's work. Riga addresses the first part of the question: the overrepresentation of non-Russian Bolsheviks vis-à-vis the demographic structure of tsarist Russia reflected the empire's ethnic heterogeneity but reveals more. Her account of the Bolshevik leaders' internal course of radicalization explicates how multi-ethnicity was formally institutionalized into nationalities under a de-Russified Soviet Union. Mudge's "refraction" theory addresses the second part: the changing composition of Party experts over time—from the full-time partisan theoreticians of the 1890s to the university-based economists of the 1990s—was not a passive reflection of leftist parties' pressure to catch up with the popular mentality, but rather, a cross-section of political and cultural spheres that happened to shape broader social agendas.

Instead of an abstract discussion of the relationship between agency and structure, this book starts by identifying agency (the revolutionary leaders who had voices in shaping how nationalism was contained in the new socialist state) and the structure within which the revolutionary movement unfolded (the ethnic composition of a population, the cultural mentality of the masses, and the geopolitical pressure). I develop a heuristic approach, as shown in Figure 1.1, a chain paralleling many other chains in complicated historical processes. There is agency in such conditions: structure$_1$, from which actors take shape and with which they interact, cannot determine actors' knowledge, positions, and behaviors. Additionally, within a

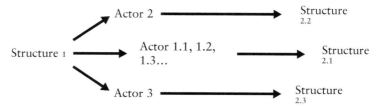

Figure 1.1 This analytical strategy combines biographical analysis with comparative historical methods

given structure, there are multiple actors. Meanwhile, over the course of revolution-making, actors externalize their features to the discourse. This becomes the institutional framework of the new state once power seizure is complete. Though such a framework could be "flawed," as many scholars of the Soviet and Chinese nationality institutions argue, once the new frameworks are stabilized, social consequences begin to emerge. Without such individuals, there could be different outcomes (Structure$_2$). Given the complexity (i.e., the duration and the participants) of the two great revolutions, it is possible to find actors and structure$_2$ other than communists to draw comparison, such as the Whites, the KMT, non-Han and non-Russian minority elites, non-communist federalists, and the local or temporal states they established. Moreover, it is also possible to compare communists over time, since the revolutionary dynamics were in flux, as were the compositions of their respective leadership (Actors 1.1, 1.2, 1.3, etc. in Figure 1.1).

A note on data and methods

Revolution and nationalism starts with the central committee members (hereafter the CCM) of the two communist parties, with a focus on those who completed the national takeover and subsequent state-building. For the Bolsheviks, this was the central committee members from 1917 to 1923. By the end of this period, the Soviet Union had been founded and its constitution inaugurated. For the CCP, the basic unit was the central committee from 1945 to 1956. This sample selection is based on the consideration that the emergence of a nationality framework is determined by elites in leadership roles. The case selection cannot be too broad. The rank-and-file revolutionaries had little influence on institutional design. Though their responses and pressure could exert an effect from below, it was the leading elites who filtered, presented, and interpreted this popular mood and demand. I also guarantee that case selection is not too narrow, i.e., I do not limit the biographical analysis to a few Party experts who specialize in the nationality issue. This is first and foremost because in the revolutionary period, the Communist Party had yet to achieve the level of organizational differentiation that it would later accomplish. There were some advisers who had more first-hand experience and were more well read with regard to the nationality question, but they were neither decision-makers nor full-time "nationality cadres." A more important reason for not adopting a narrow case selection lies in concerns over how to present evidence that nationalism in a socialist state extended beyond the reach of ethnopolitics and peripheral affairs. Rather, as this work's theoretical framework maintains, the institutionalization of nationality in a socialist state is shaped by how elites conceptualize the transformability of majority culture, and how they respond to geopolitical pressure, from counterrevolutionaries and international patrons alike. Thus, it is necessary to broaden the scope of the nationality issue, as this may reveal how knowledge and thought circulated among the revolutionary elites.

The two central committees are merely the starting point. Beyond this basic sample pool, this work offers one addition and one subtraction. The addition is an extension of the analysis to the elites who shaped the nationality frame, but who were not members of the central committee. These individuals included intellectuals who served as propagandists or research assistants, who did not specialize in the nationality question, but who were required to give advice. They could also be special delegates, diplomats, or military commanders who stayed at the forefront of the revolution and thus had control over information filtering and interpretation. Whereas some of them were seated in Central bodies before or after the state-founding period, others never were. In this work, I regard the Party elite, rather than the Party organizations, as the basic analytical unit. This is why I have incorporated many non-CCM elites into my analysis. Examples include Aleksandr Bogdanov, Anatorii Lunacharskii, Maksim Litvinov, Nikolai Podvoiskii, Georgi Chicherin, and Mikhail Pokrovskii, as well as Li Dazhao, Chen Duxiu, Li Weihan, Zhou Baozhong, Zhu Dehai, Saifuding Aziz, Deng Liqun, Qiao Guanhua, Fan Wenlan, Jian Bozan, and Guo Huaruo. During case selection, the availability of content was my primary consideration, i.e., I selected those individuals who hold extensive content on the nationality question in their biographies. Each of these non-CCM elites exerted influence on the issues that shaped the nationality question in their respective socialist states.

It is the principle of salience that determines how the subtraction is drawn. This work does not cover every elite in the state-founding central committees. For most CCM-level elites, some biographical data is available, thanks to the data that has accrued over the generations of communist elites, in both socialist states and in the West. However, the data is uneven. Some elites have detailed biographies, which record these revolutionaries' every career step, what they read, with whom they associated, and what challenges they faced. Other than biographies, the most fruitful ones are authored memoirs, diaries, and their own anthologies, which open windows into their outlooks on particular issues. Yet, many others only have minimal materials, such as an encyclopedia entry outlining their paths to radicalization. These materials give a contour of who their parents were, where they studied, and what drew them to communism, often with detailed self-narrations. Nevertheless, this work only traces those elites who exerted influence on the nationality question, who accounted for at least one-third of members of the central committee and most of the prominent leaders. This does not mean that this work omits the remaining elites. Rather, it addresses how their autobiographies and biographies evaded the nationality question.

This work's case selection adhered to the following protocol: First, the author read all of the available biographies of two central committee members. This covered 160 individuals and examined various types of available data, including secondary biographies, autobiographies, chronicles, diaries, memoirs, anthologies, and entries in biographical dictionaries and encyclopedias. These biographies were published over a wide range of time and place, spanning from the 1910s to the 2020s, and covering Russia, Mainland China, Hong Kong, Taiwan, North America, and Europe. In addition, there were two non-biographical approaches: when available, biographical information was collected from archives, mostly at the Hoover Institution; it was also collected from non-biographical publications, such as compilations of working documents, conference minutes, special pamphlets commemorating historical events, operational units, and institutions. These volumes were purchased from antique book markets in Russia and China. Most of the data used is in the original Chinese or Russian languages.

The first round of research consisted of screening biographies to identify any information relevant to the nationality issue. One objective of this screening was to collect basic demographics on the total population, including the ethnic and regional background, discover when these people started engaging in peasant mobilization, and evaluate their access to foreign counterparts. The results are summarized into tables, allowing readers to view the overall map in a numerical way. Beyond the initial screening, I narrowed the 160 individuals down to those figures who influenced issues pertaining to nationality. This was the interpretative component of this work, revealing the detailed perceptions, calculations, and misconceptions of leading revolutionary elites, as well as the contexts of their thinking. Meanwhile, over the course of biographical reading, I found the names of people who were crucial to the nationality question—their activities are mentioned and their words were often cited by their CCM colleagues—but who were not seated in the Central Committee. In a second round of screening, I extend the analysis to these non-CCM individuals. Where possible, small-scale prosopographic comparisons were drawn, for example, between the Bolshevik and the CCP elites who had extensive overseas experiences. To mitigate the problem of missing data, I added a third round of screening to ensure that communist elites with experience in significant peripheral regions were included, for example, those of any future republics of the Soviet Union, and China's major ethnic minority borderlands. This strategy, which combines a quantitative snapshot with in-depth single-case interpretations and small comparisons between individuals, certainly does not alleviate the potential for representation bias. However, it is the most technically practical approach. Within a universe of revolutionary elites, this approach exhausts every stream, though it does not cover every case of every stream.

Comparison with non-communist elites is brief, and in most cases, not systematic. Methodologically, the variations between communist elites were no smaller than the differences between communist and non-communist elites. For example, the KMT's assimilationist agenda of the 1930s was not far from the CCP's of the late 1950s, while the Ukrainian nationalists' agenda in 1918 was close to the national communist section within the Bolsheviks. The point of the comparison is to demonstrate the existence of alternative agendas and practices. In this way, I argue that macro-level social settings, such as ideology, geopolitical conflict, and ethnic structure, do not exert a deterministic effect on individuals' or groups' perceptions and prescriptions of the revolution. Likewise, this comparative strategy is not perfect, but it is technically feasible. The competing political parties, certainly, included diverse voices from within. It would be even harder to collect a complete sample of these political groups, since many were ephemeral, or they lacked a clear organizational structure.

Outcomes and implications

In terms of the outcomes of two revolutions Russia's and China's nation-building legacies are far-reaching. The vital difference between the Soviet and the Chinese model is more than merely name and title. "Soviet," though a hasty fabrication of 1905 and 1917, was detailed and concrete, with a short history, inseparable from Lenin, the October myth, and the Soviet Union's socialist system. Given that discrediting the tsar became an overarching frame, "Soviet" took over the function of legitimizing the bonds between nations. The Soviet model, as criticized by the theory of "revenge from history," was a self-negation, twisting an institutionalized invention of nations with an ideological restraint on nationalism. Yet, this combination, used against critics of the Soviet system, was not dysfunctional; rather it benefited Moscow in geopolitics and ethnic relations. It became problematic only when the ideological appeal of Soviet socialism had faded, which called into question the legitimacy of the international bond. Against the "revenge from history," Soviet leaders had been exploring how to blur the borders between "Soviet," "Russia," and "nation." In doing so, they were looking for ways to maintain control over the nations that they had invented, without formally rescinding these October-set categories.

The "Chinese nation" resembled the Soviet Union at the beginning of the revolution. "China" had previously meant little more than a geographical concept, and most components of "Chineseness" had been denounced as reactionary toxins, i.e., the targets of the revolution. Resembling the Bolsheviks' de-Russification, "China" had previously been constructed as a hollow container to create distance from Great Hanism. Nevertheless, "China," unlike "Soviet," was more vulerable to being manipulated into an array of political goals. It can be nothing, and it can be everything. As an organic concept, it is difficult to associate it with a narrow theory or foundational figure. It can be concrete enough when necessary, and abstract enough as well.

Whereas by 1949, the long revolution had become a grandiose manipulation of such flexibility, the history after 1949 added more restrictions. The "Leaning to One Side" during the Sino-Soviet honeymoon had fostered imitation of the Soviet nationality system. It was during this period that most of the modern-day fifty-five nationalities were invented. This left a far-reaching legacy with which Beijing is still reckoning today. This, and not the revolution or the communist ideology, was the most decisive step in creating a Chinese nationality system that would resemble that of the Soviets. After the Sino-Soviet split, a campaign of centralization and homogenization was unleashed. In the name of "equalizing the economic foundation," the ongoing Soviet-style celebration of ethnic diversity came to a halt. After Mao's death, the 1980s saw a revival of the 1950s nationality invention and diversity celebration, as the CCP attempted to rectify its "mistakes" from the Great Leap Forward and the Cultural Revolution. Yet, the next turn soon arrived. Amidst the collective collapse of Communism around the turn of the 1990s, the lessons learned from the collapse of the Soviet Union initiated a new momentum to give "China" more prominence. Given the resilience of "China" vis-à-vis the rigid Soviet Union, it is worthwhile to reflect on the two great revolutions to examine how "Chineseness" was utilized to exit the Soviet Union's shadow.

Under Xi Jinping's reign, China is reshaping its nation-building program. The official tendency has been for the state to switch its emphasis from ethnic diversity to one nation. This move has been visible in Xinjiang and Tibet, drawing concerns and criticism from the West. Existing understandings of this move, either via assimilation or integration, are unsatisfactory. Xi Jinping's reform has stemmed from reflections on the development of the PRC's national model after 1949. Though the PRC imitated the Soviet Union, the PRC self-identified as a Chinese nation state, rather than an international federation. The conception of Russia must be rethought as well. Whereas the Soviet model has been understood as a failure, a chronic self-harm that cultivated nationalism against the union center, this work shows that from the outset, the Bolsheviks had been manipulating nationalism. The seventy-year-long experiment was ultimately unsuccessful, but it did produce lessons and legacies. Furthermore, Putin's geopolitical tricks in the post-Soviet space have shown that the Soviet legacies were not lost. This work explicates this change.

Conversation with existing literature

This book engages with two clusters of scholarship: (1) communism and nationalism, specifically in a Sino-Soviet comparative context, when and where they were friends or foes; (2) the role of revolution in the transition from empires to nation states. The first contribution of this book is providing a deeper and wider description of the differences between the Soviet and Chinese models of nationalities, revealing that the federal–unitary distinction between them was not only about demographic compositions but also reflected two revolutions with different self-imaginations and trajectories. The relationship between the Soviet and the Chinese nationalities models has been discussed by political scientists and historians. Most Cold War-era scholars emphasize the antagonism between nationalism and communism. Their thesis is based on (mainly) the Soviet Union's repression of non-Russian minorities (Conquest 1986), as well as the nationalist disobedience of Moscow in Eastern Europe (Seton-Watson 1964). Scholars of this period also tended to contrast nationalism and communism not as complex political practices but rather as mutually exclusive intellectual doctrines (Szporluk 1988). Within this trend, however, Connor (1984) stands out as an exception, by providing a covering conception on how socialist regimes, the USSR, China, and others alike, recognized the nation state as a necessary stage on the path to communism, while at the same time strove to transcend them within a socialist framework. This thesis became influential after the global disillusionment with Soviet-model state socialism in 1989. Historians began to emphasize the fusion of national legitimacy and communist ideologies under communist/post-communist regimes, usually by elaborating how a single state/revolution at a particular state mobilized nationalist symbols to support the communist agenda (see Mevius 2009). A most relevant work in this regard is Liliana Riga's masterpiece (2012), which probes how the internal struggling between religious universality, ethnic particularity, and geopolitical nationalism shaped the Bolsheviks' comprehension of communist ideology.

With regard to the USSR and China vis-à-vis the revolutionary regimes' relationships with nationalism, several written works are significant precursors. These works suggest three potential perspectives when observing the nationalities problem, which this book synthesizes: to separate from a universal community (European hegemony, colonialism), to integrate multiple ethnic groups, and to develop a linkage between the nation(s) and the past. Rosenberg and Young (1982) suggest that both communist revolutions invoked nationalism for self-legitimization, mainly during international wars (the Soviet–German and the Sino–Japanese). Wright (1962) suggests that the Chinese communist revolution was more fused with nationalist salvation, whereas the Bolshevik Revolution, self-viewing as a revolution within an imperial power, lacked such concern. This thesis is later elaborated in S. A. Smith's (2008) comparison between the workers in St. Petersburg and Shanghai. Lastly, a comparison across Russia, Turkey, China, and Iran suggests that the Chinese Revolution didn't attempt to reshape the European civilization, as the Russian revolutionaries had aspired to, but strove to moderate the West-imported Enlightenment in an indigenous civilizational context. This also marked China's distinctions vis-à-vis the Iranian Islamic Revolution (Krejčí 2000). Yet, the literature on post-communist transitions all agree that the enormousness of the Soviet Union's ethnic heterogeneity was a barrier to an incremental route of marketization that the Chinese Communist Party adopted from the late 1970s. As the risk of ethnic separatism arose, Moscow dared not foster economic devolution, while Chinese leaders didn't have such concerns (Anderson 2010). A chronological overview of the CCP Revolution suggests that though regionalism threatened central power, ethnopolitics was not as central to the Chinese Revolutions as in the Bolshevik ones (Liu 2004b). Finally, Mullaney (2011) traces the PRC's significant revision of the Soviet approach of ethnic classification in the 1950s. According to Mullaney, whereas the Soviets defined nation through linguistic and other objective dimensions, the Chinese moderated this approach by introducing a subjective dimension, gauging an ethnic group's self-imagination.

A most refined and balanced transnational comparison is Matsuzato's (2017) comparative description of Russia, China, and India, the three polities that had, to different extents, adopted the Soviet ethno-federal legacies. One of the core arguments is that, in the USSR, the union republics had nominal sovereignties as nation states, whereas in China the minorities only had autonomous units within one nation state, a difference Matsuzato traces back to the moment of imperial collapse: the Bolsheviks seized central power alongside independent sovereignties in Ukraine and Transcaucasia, whereas the post-imperial Chinese government denied sovereignty claims from Xinjiang, Tibet, Inner Mongolia, and other borderlands. This book moves forward, arguing that the discrepancy between the Soviet Union and China was deeper and wider than Matsuzato describes: the USSR was formally designed to be an open federal system that kept accepting new nation states until the union covered the entire globe, while China institutionally denied such proclamations. While the bonding between Soviet nationalities was legitimized by a class-based internationalist ideology that rigidly defines an ideally socialist political economy system (though the Soviet leaderships at times attempted to ethnicize or even racialize this ideology), the PRC's master frame "Chinese Nation" left greater leeway for maneuvers between an invented community and historical legacies (languages, memories, rituals, and, importantly, historical patterns of interethnic interactions).

This book also speaks within the broader literature on the transition from empires to nation states. It argues that such transition involved uncertainties and reluctance, and the revolutionary process could play a significant role in shaping the final outcomes. Recent literature has noted that empires, struggling to survive, made adaptions to their appearances, so that they looked like nation states. Along this direction, several influential concepts have been coined, such as "imperial ethnicity" (Darwin 2013) "nationalizing empires" (Berger and Miller 2014), and "imperial nations" (Kolstø 2019). It was also apparent that there were tensions between the adapting to nationalism and maintaining empires. For example, Roman Szporluk suggests that whereas communist ideology could still barely disguise a triangular relationship between Russian, Ukrainian, and Belarusian identities, after 1991 as the notion of liberal democracy spread among the post-Soviet space, Ukraine's imperial subordination to Russia came into question (Szporluk 1993). In another comparison, Julian Go (2011) argues that though both the British and the US empires maneuvered liberal nationalism to their geopolitical advantages, the tension between liberal democracy and imperial hierarchy was significantly sharper in the British case than in the US one. This partly explains the US empire's takeover of global hegemony surpassing Britain. Drawing a five-case comparison, Kumar (2017b) mentions that as formal empires have ended, giant polities, such as the United States and China, have continued to exercise imperial power in the disguise of a nation state. Accordingly, he points out that many old empires, like the Ottoman, due to the sharp contradictions between their imperial ideologies and the principle of nationalism, were reluctant to adapt themselves to nation states (Kumar 2017a: 122–24).

The existing literature also explores the relationship between revolution and nationalism. Scholars find that revolution and nationalism, sharing common pursuits while emphasizing equality and integration respectively, could be friends or foes, depending on historical contexts. For example, Kumar's agenda-setting work (2015) finds that revolution could foster nation-building but at times contradicted the latter, as in the Revolution of 1848, when counterrevolutionaries finally sided with romantic nationalism. Malešević articulates the mechanisms by which revolution and nationalism reinforce each other: revolution was a mobilizational process whereby the penetration of ideology strengthened and organizational capacity developed, which could lead to a strong nationalism (Malešević 2017: 177–88). As Malešević (2019) further formulates, nationalism can exist as an ideological doctrine confined within tiny intellectual groups, as well as being a hyper-penetrative social force. Only the nationalism that seized the state and non-state organizational capacity and entered individuals' emotional world became "grounded," which could foster a mass mobilizational revolution and often appeared as the result of an overall social revolution. Lastly, George Lawson (2019) insists that revolutions must be analyzed in a transnational context. According to Lawson, revolutions can transform a national polity's status in the imperial domain, for example, making Iran a source of radicalist export while making Ukraine a battlefield of great empires (Lawson 2019: 195). Alongside this, positive empirical evidence is found with regard to the making of national community through the French Revolution (Keitner 2007), the post-Ottoman Middle East (Watenpaugh 2006), and Soviet nation-making in revolutionary Central Asia (Edgar 2004). In these cases, without revolutionary mobilizations, the imperial legacies would have remained in the way of nation-building. In other cases, like North America during the War of Independence, revolutions deterred nation-building, by provoking exodus, civil war, and legitimacy crises (Gould and Onuf 2005).

To summarize, this book offers two contributions to existing literature. First, it provides the most comprehensive description to date of the differences between the Soviet and PRC nationalities models, synthesizing international, tradition-inventing, and transethnic perspectives. Underneath the federal–unitary distinction were two alternative ways of reorganizing empires to nation states: transforming an empire into one enclosed nation state or an open union of nation states. This disagreement reflected two revolutions' imaginations of global missions and scales of social mobilization, as well as the judgments of the relative strengths of counterrevolutionaries. Such a conception involves a broadly defined understanding of nationalities.

Second, this book provides a general theory of how revolutions translated imperial legacies into the structures of nation states. Today there are no more formal-direct empires, and nation states dominate the world. In this sense, the transition to nation states was inevitable. Whereas many scholars have mentioned that the paths of transitions were multiple, this book suggests that revolutions could shape such multiplicity through inter-revolution relations, revolution–society relations, and revolution–counterrevolution relations. To understand how these relations worked to shape the empire–nation transitions, we must probe the individual leaders of the revolutions to see how they perceived and comprehended the "broader" nationalities this book identifies.

Preview of the book

This book includes one background chapter, three chapters that examine empirical evidence, and a conclusion. Chapter 1 provides the historical background of nationalism in Russia and China. It contrasts the two empires' ethnic structures and their respective geopolitical status, showing that conditions in China were more ideal than those in Russia for building a "one-nation-one-state" system. Having outlined these conventional statements, I reveal how Russia, in terms of infrastructural power and the nearby international system, had conditions more conducive to nation state building. Later in this chapter, by drawing comparisons with the decolonization process, I demonstrate the difficulty of empirically asserting whether a national model matches the structure of society. The remainder of the chapter is a historical review of post-imperial Russia and China. The examination of Russia covers the Provisional Government of 1917, the White states, various periods of the Soviet Union, and post-communism; the study of China covers the Beiyang state, the KMT, the CCP, the founding of the PRC through the conclusion of the Mao era, and the post-Mao era. This review shows that both regimes underwent enormous variation in terms of their national models, and how they attained agency in providing multiple interpretations of structure. It suggests that revolutionaries' perception of, and resistance to, structure were influenced by their backgrounds, knowledge, and experience.

Chapter 2 begins the book's empirical core. It explains why the Soviet Union was a union of nation states while the PRC was a single nation state, though largely only a name. It also elaborates upon the quintessential difference between the Bolsheviks and the CCP, i.e., their locations within international communism. Focusing on the leading elites who had broad experience of living overseas, I reveal that the Bolsheviks were far more embedded in an international and cosmopolitan network envisioned to create a Europe-centered socialist world, whereas the CCP was forced by the Bolsheviks to become a nationalist party. Several nuanced differences are added, which highlight the impact of the first successful revolution on the second. By composition, the Bolshevik leadership included many foreigners and transnational persons, who were acculturated to Europe, and thus had no serious state allegiance to Russia. Upon the conclusion of the 1917 power seizure, these individuals rushed back to Europe to foment a revolution. However, over time, this zeal faded. By contrast, the CCP, despite its early cosmopolitan network with revolutionaries in other East Asian nations, eventually lost its embeddedness. This was due to the Red Scare, as well as the Comintern's strategy of nationalization. By contrasting the CCP's ethnic composition to that of China at large, this chapter demonstrates that Han-centered Chineseness had been manufactured by the Bolsheviks—it was not a natural extension of the general demographic structure.

Chapter 3 explains why the PRC emphasized "China" (*Zhonghua*), while the Soviet Union negated "Russia" (*Russiia*) as its core. It compares how the timing of mass mobilization affected the two communist parties' reconciliation with national traditions. The narration traces how the revolutionary elites, especially the literati—historians, textbook-writers, composers, propagandists, as well as the supreme ideologues themselves—conceived of the tension between the revolution and the old culture that the revolution was supposed to eliminate over time. It shows that the commonality lies in that the elites of both parties came to figure out a way of how to mediate the old and the new, achieving reconciliation by reconstructing the old culture, and reshaping the cultural producers. I also show that reconciliation arrived sooner in the Chinese revolution than in the Bolshevik revolution. Long before the national takeover of 1949, the CCP had figured out a "revolutionary" way to present Chinese culture. Because of this, leading elites were more willing to associate with "China." By contrast, in Russia, the same course would emerge in the 1930s. When the Soviet Union was founded in 1922, the ideologues were dominated by a revolutionary Russophobia. This chapter argues that it was not international war with Japan or with Germany, but rather peasant mobilization that affected the treatment of traditional culture in the shaping of a revolutionary nation.

Chapter 4 addresses ethnopolitics in the revolutionary expansion to the peripheries of the old empires. I draw comparisons with military commanders, guerrilla leaders, and missionaries, as well as with the leading elites in charge of major peripheral areas, such as the Caucasus, the Baltic states, Central Asia, Ukraine, the Far East, and China's Northeast, Inner Mongolia, and Xinjiang. By presenting these people's perceptions of local conditions, I argue that formal autonomy tended to concentrate in a periphery where the revolutionaries believed that they had established control. Otherwise, when military

Empires, nation states, and two revolutions   37

strength and economic control were limited, CCP revolutionaries invoked a discourse of a multi-ethnic greater nation as a major weapon, even though this discourse was often of no use to hardliner separatists. Moreover, when a region was distant from revolutionaries' state apparatus, support for internationalism continued to work toward ideological and strategic purposes, merely to destabilize the foes of revolution. The CCP's influence over the three northern peripheries (the Northeast, Inner Mongolia, the Northwest) remained tenuous throughout the revolution, threatened by the KMT, Japan, and the Soviet Union. As the CCP's headquarters approached this region, they rescinded their support for self-determination to avoid fanning the fire of secession. By contrast, toward the end of the Civil War, the Bolsheviks stabilized control over their peripheries, with major rivals excluded. This chapter demonstrates that it is not ethnic composition, but revolutionaries' agendas that shaped how ethnicity was framed into a nation.

In the Conclusion, I summarize the book by applying the three theses to broader historical contexts. This chapter starts by situating the two revolutions to the world history of great revolutions, arguing that these two revolutions were at a threshold where nationalism and secular ideology were approaching their global dominance. They thus differed from the seventeenth- and eighteenth-century revolutions, which had been less self-conscious of nationalism. Russia and China also differed from the Iranian Revolution of 1979, where the world nation state system was taking shape. The chapter then compares two extended cases that enrich the Sino-Soviet comparison: communist Yugoslavia and Cuba. The three relationships of revolutions were at work in shaping these two systems' nationality models as well, though the historical context varied. Whereas Yugoslavia of the 1950s could be viewed as a nationalized Soviet Union, Cuba was a denationalized China where sub-national ethnic and racial divisiveness were denied. After analyzing Yugoslavia and Cuba, this chapter draws a brief comparative analysis of the other communist regimes. Though many regimes lacked clear revolutionary processes and political autonomy in shaping their nationality models, the three relationships that this book reveals were at work at certain conditions. Finally, this chapter concludes the book, arguing that the Sino–Soviet comparison has general implications in understanding nation-building that combined nationalism with secular ideology and strove for completion within a short period, which was typical for the twentieth century.

2

From an open union to an enclosed nation state

When the communist revolutionary movements grew in Russia and China, the world was in a transition from traditional empires to nation states. Empires faced a crisis in many regards: the monarchical imperial order was being delegitimized by the Enlightenment notions of popular sovereignty, scientific rationality, and representative democracy. Such a crisis led to the rise of the nationalist self-determination movement in every major empire. In reaction, empires sought to renew their forms of rule. Whereas the British and the French moved on the track of shaping "empires of liberty," the Germans and the Japanese resorted to a racist discourse, legitimizing their rule by a fabricated racial superiority. The common question all these various paths had to address was how to create a new imperial order that could incorporate nationalism.

Communist revolutions represented a unique path of reorganizing the empire. On the one hand, communists viewed nationalism as a weapon to undermine the world's imperialist and capitalist rule. Thus, they avoided naked racist language of denouncing the national liberational movement. Such language was often used by Nazi and Japanese racists. Instead, communists claimed they were fighting fascists in defense of "small and weak nations" and protecting these nations' linguistic and cultural rights. On the other hand, communists also viewed nationalism with vigilance, thinking of nationalism as a threat to a unified communist revolution. This concern restrained communists from claiming "liberty of all nations" as propounded by British and the French empires. Instead, communists, be they Russians, Chinese, or Serbians, adhered to transethnic uniformity. Such a contradicting dilemma led communists to cultivate "constrained nationalism." In the Bolshevik Revolution, nationalism was constrained by Soviet internationalism, and in the Chinese Revolution, nationalism was constrained within a revolutionary "Chinese Nation." Communists transformed empires into a group of nations with tight bonds.

From an open union to an enclosed nation state   39

The crisis of traditional imperial order

A core principle of nationalism was the inviolability of national sovereignty and national borders. The rise of nationalism thus put empire's expansionism, a course which used to proceed in the name of civilizing so-called "barbarian" people, into question. Today, there is little global tolerance for open attempts to change national borders or to annex sovereign states, either by great powers or secessionists. The United States overthrew the local regimes in Iraq and Afghanistan, but they reestablished their national sovereignties on the two territories, while Russia's overt annexation of Crimea in 2014 incurred harsh international sanctions, which continue to hold in 2024, and they have increased sanctions with their attack on Ukraine. Having internalized this principle of nationalism, the previous victims of imperialism have also viewed colonial rule as unacceptable. This makes it very difficult for great powers to sustain and stabilize their efforts in territorial annexation and rule, a threat the United States was recently observed in the Middle East and Afghanistan, as well as in the spheres of its conventional allies. It was in such a context that imperial powers eventually realized that the old way of building up colonies was a politically unaffordable solution, which propelled them to secure control by maneuvering the new trend, nationalism.

Toward the end of the nineteenth century, major European empires had recognized the strategic potential of playing the nationalist card in geopolitical competition. By boosting nationalism at the multi-ethnic rear of the enemy, empires counted on creating ethnic resentment, resistance, riots, and even secessionism to undermine their geopolitical rivals. In co-opting ethnic groups on the rival's territory, empires mobilized every strategy and social forces, such as sending missionaries to invent nations, recruiting elites for education and political training, and even offering military and financial aid (Hall 2017). Most importantly, major empires had come to the conclusion that nations were not natural and biological, but rather artificial and manipulalable. Making identity was important but not indispensable. Without substantial political organization and military aid, identity was nothing. By the same token, an ethnic group with scarce and disputed memory to imagine a community could still assert a powerful nationalism that sufficed to cause a shift of power balance between contesting empires. In such a situation, geopolitical competition entered a new stage, that of maneuvering nationalism.

Certainly, maneuvering nationalism was not easy. Empire's support for national liberation was a self-defeating concept. This tension appeared huge in empires that did not undergo any political changes but only invoked nationalism as a device. In the British case, for example, promising a liberal empire brought about the skepticism from colonial elites concerning the need for liberal colonies to stay within the British empire (Flint 1983: 398–99). Likewise, Japan's racist banner of liberating yellow Asia from the white went against itself when a Tokyo-dominated hierarchy remained unshakable in the Pacific Empire. By comparison, empires that had experienced internal revolutions were more open and consistent in maneuvering nationalism. The Americans, by claiming that anyone who identified with the foundational principles of the US could become a member of the American nation, promoted the Westward movement, a clear imperial course of annexing new territory from Mexico and Spain. Though the idea was never realized, the French revolutionaries proposed to unite the entire colonial world into a French nation state, with each colony transformed to an overseas province (Fieldhouse 1966: 308). The Portuguese Revolution of 1975 promised a great Portuguese nation as well. After revolutions, most empires, rather than seeking liberation, became more determined to integrate their colonies into a single power.

The Russian and Soviet approaches thus stood out. The tsarist empire underwent a radical social revolution that was incomparable with any other modern revolutions. The pre-1917 elite, institutional, and social compositions had been reshuffled and there was no longer a monarch. With a significant break in continuity, the Bolsheviks gained a flexible hand in dealing with the legacies of the imperial past and were able to move further in loosening the bars of the imperial "cage" that the British and the Japanese had to maintain in contrast to their nation-liberator image. In comparison with the French and the Portuguese, the Soviet regime was more overt in weaponizing nationalist movements. In most empires that claimed revolutionary liberation, peripheral nationalists, to their disappointment, came to find that the metropolitan support for nationalism actually meant integration into a greater imperial nation, be it French, or Portuguese. By comparison, the Bolsheviks' internationalist support for peripheral separation, though concentrated in formal and linguistic aspects, appeared more coherent. In the Soviet formula, most oppressed nations would become nation states in themselves, with the status of republics or autonomous republics, while united under the centralized proletarian dictatorship.

From the first socialist revolution to the second

It is absolutely mistaken to treat the Bolshevik and the Chinese revolutions as two mutually independent processes, though scholars often have to pretend to do so. Most prestigious comparisons of the two polities suggest an interaction, in terms of the subjects as well as the researchers. The comparative study of Soviet and Chinese communism originated in US scholars' search for a less evil alternative in the Marxist–Leninist world that was independent of Moscow's dominance. The search began with Mao's polemics with Khrushchev, which became known to the Western media in the late 1950s. The tension gained further momentum from Mao's "Cultural Revolution" (1966–76), which shocked the first generation of US sinologists; what occurred in China completely contradicted their previous understanding of Leninism (Whyte 2021). However, while most Sino-Soviet comparative scholars emphasize the CCP's growing impetus to depart from the Soviet model, which derived from the Russians' arrogance and the Chinese's dignity, very few have recognized how the Bolsheviks, consciously or unconsciously, had created roadblocks for other countries attempting to follow Russia's path to communism. It was exactly such a case in the sphere of nationality models.

The Bolsheviks' impact on the CCP speaks to a major difference between the two great revolutions—the Russian one was made when the world had not yet had an established socialist state, while the Chinese one was organized when the first socialist state was in existence and could exert influence. The comparison of these two revolutions can thus be asymmetrical as well as symmetrical. The Bolshevik revolution had no existing state model but had to rely on the texts of Marx on which to pattern themselves. However, the Bolsheviks were trapped in polemics with European socialists within the Social Democrats' International. This strained relationship, dating back to the late 1890s, had shaped the behavior of the Bolsheviks into a purposeful deviation to distinguish themselves clearly from the "corrupted" European socialists. The Bolsheviks' critique of the Second International was total, but one particular thread of criticism was of the European socialists' surrender to nationalism. As Lenin said, the leading socialist parties had been bankrupted since their decisions to encourage the working class to engage in the imperialist war to help the great powers oppress colonial peoples. To assert the long-existing claim that the Marxist torch had transferred from Western Europe to Russia, Lenin insisted in reorganizing the former Russian Empire into a format that supported national liberation.

This was in parallel to the CCP's purposive deviation from Moscow, a persistent effort that was covert during Stalin's reign and overt after his death. When Stalin accused Mao of being a "Mountainous Marxist," he was right that the CCP had deviated further from original Marxist thinking on nationality. The Bolsheviks professed Marxism seriously in transforming Russia into a union of states that would theoretically continue to accept new members until it covered the entire world. At the formative point, this model's major discrepancy from Marx's imagination lay in that such a union, if

42   *Revolution in China and Russia*

it had to exist in the first place, should have started with Europe, rather than the "backward" and "barbarian" Russia. Later, the discrepancy deepened, to Stalin's "Socialism in one country," where the Soviet state deviated from a workers' commission into a repressive bureaucracy. However, in comparison with the CCP, the Bolsheviks' deviation from Marxism was small. Aiming at "national liberation" and "socialism in one country" (many countries), the CCP created the PRC, which, in structure, resembled a regular nation state rather than a union. This state involved significant Soviet-style ethnoterritorial characteristics, with five autonomous regions and numerous small autonomous units assigned to "nationalities." However, it was officially recognized as a unitary entity, not a federal one. Whereas all minority nationalities were identified as part of the Chinese nation, the state's borders were firm, with no intention to extend. The CCP's revolutionary export to Southeast Asia after 1949 was not intended to annex new republics or provinces, but rather to establish anti-US and anti-Soviet buffers in the form of nation states.

The incorrect part of Stalin's judgment of Mao lay in the fact that he did not recognize that the CCP's nationalist tendency had a great deal to do with the Bolsheviks themselves and the Bolshevik Revolution. Stalin's judgment of "mountainous Marxism" carried a connotation that the CCP's deviation from the Bolsheviks' orthodox path grew out of China's local social conditions, such as a low level of industrialization, political division, and cultural enclosure. He missed that it was the first socialist revolution, which drew close to the internationalist model, that set the second on a track to become a nationalist one. It was also the geopolitical maneuver of the Bolsheviks that defined the "Chinese" of the "Chinese Communist Party" as it later transpired. A subtle connection thus rested in that it was the Bolshevik revolution's intention of extending revolution by maneuvering nationalism within an internationalist framework that set up the nationalist orientation and track for the CCP revolution. In Moscow's calculations, whereas China was one of many colonies that had the obligation of boosting nationalism to undermine the hegemony of the imperialist hegemony, the Bolsheviks had the obligation of supporting the CCP so as to ensure the nationalism they had released stayed in control to the Kremlin's advantage.

The Bolsheviks' weak state allegiance

The Bolsheviks' image of revolution and a post-revolutionary socialist state drew closer to the Marxist ideal type of internationalism than that of most socialists in the developing world. In principle, the core leaders did not anticipate "socialism in one country," which, as a concept, did not exist

From an open union to an enclosed nation state 43

in Marxist classics but rather expected a quickly concluded and bloodless power takeover followed by an immediate all-European spread of socialism. In the Bolsheviks' optimistic stance, there was no need to worry about how to run a well-bordered regular state, as such a state would never exist after the revolution had swept the European continent. Even if such a state existed, it would be temporary and expedient. Lenin's *State and Revolution* reduced the complicated work of state running to "basic statistics that any educated worker was capable of handling."

The weak state allegiance was evident in the leading Bolsheviks' indifference to affairs relevant to sustaining the function of a regular state with a fixed border. For example, the leading Bolsheviks collectively bore an anti-military psychology. Based on a structuralist Marxist belief that revolution came naturally, they speculated that the process of takeover as an easy step, one that involved no bloody conflicts but only worker strikes. They anticipated that the old military and police, consisting of oppressed peasants, would give up resistance and join revolutionaries. Alongside such optimism, the Bolsheviks had minimal interest in learning military skills. They devoted their attention instead to training in the event of terrorist attack, antiwar agitation, street battle, and the organization of worker guards. These skills caused disturbances to the old regime but had nothing to do with sustaining regular war against formidable rivalries. The Bolsheviks, paradoxically, believed that the old system would inevitably implode but it would never go away by itself. To strike the fatal blow, these revolutionaries did train themselves in certain combat skills—this refers to a broader circle of Bolsheviks, the "combat experts."

The Bolshevik leadership of 1917 involved few military professionals. While professional officers mostly came from officer families entering military schools after achieving a middle-school diploma, radical socialists were mostly sons of those in civilian occupations. Moreover, socialists stopped at the barrier of religious faith and ethnic exclusion. As nationalist reform unfolded in the military, individuals professing atheism had fewer opportunities to get incorporated. Not a formal group under the tsar, socialists in Russia also didn't feel as compelled to join the nationalists. A biographical survey shows that only one of the Bolshevik central committee members, Valerian Kuibyshev, had completed professional military education, but even he did not continue in a military career after graduation (Khromov et al. 1988: 8–11; Zhou 2019a: 5). It was very common for the Bolsheviks to escape from and openly reject military conscription with the excuse of poor physical condition or religious reasons, as occurred in the cases of Aleksandr Shliapnikov, Viktor Nogin, and Grigorii Petrovskii (Allen 2015: 33–34; Kliuchnik and Zav'ialov 1970: 18–19; Podgornyi 1966: 10). Not surprisingly, upon the power seizure of 1917, the Bolsheviks had no regiment- or division-level commanders, which differed greatly from the Chinese KMT, the Young Turks, and Meiji reformers. This meant the Bolsheviks of 1918 had no choice but to recall tsarist colonels and lieutenants to build the revolutionary military.

The indifference to state-building affairs was not confined to the military, but rather extendable to the entire establishment. No Bolshevik had ever been part of the Russian government. Whereas a few had been low-ranking staff, most came from workers, full-time agitators, and students. In this aspect, the Bolshevik was not only different from Young Turk and Meiji reformers, but unlike even the KMT. The KMT, after the end of the Qing Empire, transformed into a loose conglomerate, which was joined by local governors, senior bureaucrats, judicial professionals, literati, and landlords. The Bolsheviks, vigilantly safeguarding their organizational border against the former establishment, were separated from the latter. The most common connection between the Bolsheviks and the imperial establishment and Duma was the school alumni network, such as that on which the relationship between Lenin and Kerenskii was based. Many leftists served as administrative assistants, statisticians, and visitors at local zemstvos where they met with liberal leaders—it was known that Lenin used zemstvo statistics in completing his *The Development of Russian Capitalism* when he was spending his school vacation in the countryside. However, in general, not expecting to run a state, the Bolsheviks were not interested in the expertise of the old state function.

With no intention of establishing and safeguarding a regular well-bordered state, the Bolsheviks downplayed the severe geopolitical situation faced by Russia in 1917, and continued to focus on their domestic agenda before the February Revolution—boosting Trotskyist defeatism to make space for class struggle. Although Europe's first two decades of the twentieth century had been overshadowed by the threat and ultimately the reality of a major war, throughout the years prior to 1917, Lenin had been actively propagating antiwar propaganda among Russian soldiers and workers (Nation 1989). Central to the Bolshevik's agenda was the burning concern that war-driven nationalism would distract the working class from engaging in fighting against bourgeoise systems and would legitimize soldiers' repression of the laboring mass. The first Bolshevik "military activists" mostly started their radicalization as agitators within the old military, either from within or from outside. They gained knowledge of the military during World War I, when the tsarist army and navy massively conscripted workers to staff the rank-and-file roles such as soldiers, non-commission officers, or logistic staff. These people's antiwar agitation significantly weakened Russia's combat capacity, especially at the logistic sectors.

The freedom after the February Revolution allowed the Bolshevik military activists to transition into legal activities and upgrade the antiwar propaganda

From an open union to an enclosed nation state   45

to the organization of popular militia. Before their ultimate transformation into regular Red Army, one of their missions was to undermine the military morale and discipline, so that nationalist generals and officers would not be able to continue the international war. Usually, such agitation advocated at a transnational spread of revolution to countries adjacent to Russia. Grigorii Kotovskii, commander of the legendary Red Calvary Division, was such an example. Kotovskii was caught by the war in the Russian forces in Bessarabia. A senior leftist radical with extensive records of sitting in jail, he never received professional officer training. His revolutionary military career started by organizing militia to establish a soviet regime in Romania and to thrust General Kornilov's plan to gain support from the Entente (Anan'ev 1982: 60).

It was in the context of the anticipation of an open-bordered socialist polity that the Brest–Litovsk Peace became understandable, in the Bolsheviks' repression of leftist nationalists who insisted on continuing a "revolutionary patriotic war with Germany." To block these efforts of leftist nationalists, the Bolsheviks accelerated the demobilization of the tsarist military forces. According to Nikolai Podvoiskii, the Bolshevik's leading expert on "old-army transformation," Socialist Revolutionaries (SR) and Kadet elites were agitating soldiers to overthrow the Brest–Litovsk Peace to continue the war (Stepanov 1989: 275). The reorganization of the Cheka involved this consideration too. After being attacked and arrested, Felix Dzerzhinskii drew the lesson that the security department had to be exclusively controlled by the Bolshevik central committee, not allowing any nationalist-minded SR members to stay in control of this important agency (Tishkov 1985: 237).

The internationalists' request for unification with Europe

"Socialism in one country" was not a favored option before Stalin's rise. Rather, from the first day of the foundation of the Soviet regime, the struggle had been between making a socialist state in Russia and devoting the entire revolutionary force to the creation of an all-European socialist state. A bloc of internationalists was endeavoring to drive the revolution beyond Russian borders. These people shared a common background, having mostly left Russia at a young age, usually after arrest at home after involvement in radical politics. For a long time, they worked closely with European socialists, which gave them a deep belief that without integration with Europe, Russia would not be able to get rid of its backwardness. Once the Bolsheviks had seized power in Russia, these people actively sought to go back to the West to make a connection. Some counted on world revolution to conquer Europe, whereas others longed for a stable relationship, so that Russia could retain preexisting integration with the old capitalist world. Still others, pessimistic about blockage, strove to guarantee collaboration with at least one or two crucial capitalist countries, to ensure that Soviet Russia could receive aid for economic recovery and avoid becoming prey to an anti-Soviet extermination.

The Bolsheviks spent decades in political self-imposed exile and commanded clandestine movement from abroad. Fifteen core Bolsheviks had lived abroad for more than five years, including the best-known, such as Mikhail Bukharin, Ian Berzin, Lev Kamenev, Alexandra Kollontai, Leonid Krasin, Vladimir Lenin, Maxim Litvinov, Osip Piatnitsky, Aleksandr Shliapnikov, Leon Trotsky, and Grigorii Zinov'ev (Granat 1989b: 355, 406, 408, 582–83, 766–78; Piatnitsky 1925: 177–78). These figures had a pro-European mindset, in their gratitude to and admiration of Europe's freedom of association and expression. Living abroad, they had received wide support from Western socialists. Initiated by leading figures, such as Karl Liebknecht, the German, French, Swedish, Austrian, Belgian, Czech Social Democrats (SDs), and the headquarters of the Second International contributed hundreds of marks on a monthly basis.[1] In Britain, a group was founded as "The Society of Friends of Russian Freedom," which collected funds from the local public and published magazines to report Russia's domestic situation. Many British intellectuals volunteered for presentations and lectures.[2] Socialists also helped Russians to access media. For example, through the aid of a German medical doctor with socialist tendencies as a broker, the SD succeeded in publishing anti-tsarist essays in the *New York Times*.[3]

The liberal environment of Europe also allowed the Bolsheviks to continue their Party training. In the early 1910s, the Bolsheviks managed to establish Party schools in Paris and Capri (Gorelov 1990: 103–4, 120–22; Scherrer 1999). These training schools were not free from harassment by the agents of the tsarist secret police, but these troubles were balanced by international support. While Italian socialists called upon local police to drive out Russian spies, the French socialists—using their seats in parliament—attempted to strengthen anti-espionage laws to limit the activities of the tsarist Okhrana (Gorelov 1990: 106).[4] During the World War I, as European governments tried to contain antiwar socialist propaganda, many Bolsheviks began to be arrested; however, they acquired help from European colleagues who aided them by obtaining defense services or paying bail (Granat: 398–99; Haupt and Marie 1974: 54–59).

The most romantic Bolsheviks were the world revolutionists, who endeavored to start a world revolution with the aim of dissolving Russia's barbarianism and transforming Russia into part of an all-Europe civilization. Leon Trotsky was the representative and spokesperson for making a socialist revolution within the Russian border. Before 1917, Leon Trotsky had loathed Russia as a backward power that had for centuries been trapped in a system that persistently produced barbarianism (Baron 1974). His stance that socialism had no chance to grow from within Russia further strengthened during the revolutionary takeover. Arguing that the most conscious working class had vanished during the Civil War, Trotsky made the pessimistic assertation that top-down bureaucracy had usurped the revolution to make a Thermidor reaction. Such restoration was inevitable, stemming from bureaucrats who played no role in October as well as from the growth of productive forces that made privileges and hierarchies possible (Trotsky 1937: 41, 53–61). Trotsky was particularly against the idea of "Socialism in one country," which, he asserted, subjugated the Comintern as a submissive branch of bureaucracy (Trotsky 1937: 97).

In close alliance with Trotsky, Karl Radek was one of the most cosmopolitan Bolsheviks who impatiently sought to move the center of world revolution from Russia back to Europe. Even at the high tide of the Civil War, he downplayed patriotism, arguing that the risk of Russia's partition by the West was minimal. To invade Russia, Radek argued, the Entente powers had to re-arm Germany, which went against their geopolitical interests (Radek 1923: 70–71). Radek expected to open the way to spread communist revolution into Europe. He and other internationalist Bolsheviks want to conquer Poland in order to export communism to Germany and even further westwards. He attributed the setback of the Soviet–Polish War to the technical mistake of Budeny's divisions resisting unified coordination (Radek 1923: 62–63). In his service at Comintern, Radek was best at using the skills he and many Bolsheviks had developed during exile—manipulating the Western press and intellectual circles. He mobilized Western journalists to Soviet Russia to shape the image of the communist regime in the West. However, believing that Russia's backwardness would damage the reputation of the revolution, he seriously suggested a transfer of the Comintern headquarters to Germany. He was pessimistic in moderate economic collaboration, asserting that post-war Europe had neither the will nor the capacity to invest in Soviet Russia (Vatlin 2009: 257–58).

Other people were impatient to return to Europe to evoke a world revolution, if we consider that the Bolsheviks included many non-Russians and foreigners who felt more comfortable remaining in their home territory. Kamo, a Bolshevik who had conducted conspiratorial activities in Europe prior to revolution, viewed himself as "groom of revolution." During the Civil War he transferred his experiences to Transcaucasia, where he organized unsuccessful combat teams. Finishing his short-term study in Moscow, he asked Lenin to send him to Europe to continue revolutions— to persuade Lenin, he even proposed to assassinate Sergei Savinkov, the SR terrorist identified as a competitor threatening for the Bolsheviks. As a self-identified European-minded conspirator, Kamo seriously planned with his wife to spend retirement in Europe when the world revolution was completed. Finally, he was sent to Persia, where he continued to advocate for an aggressive revolutionary offense and marched into conflict with the moderate Soviet ambassador, Fedor Rotshtei (Matonin 2018: 243–57).

The impetus to return to Europe partly came from the foreigners at the Comintern, such as Robin Gud and Bela Kun. Originally a revolutionary from Germany, Robin Gud fought in both the Czech uprising and the German revolution of 1918. After being released from prison, he was invited to stay in the Soviet Union. However, having been a transnational fighter, he found it difficult to adapt to the already routinized political order after the Civil War. When he continued to propagate subversive ideas, he was sent into an honor exile in Siberia, where he fell into conflict with local authorities and was accused of unhealthy relations with women. He was finally permitted to return to Germany for agitation in 1930 (Vatlin 2009: 276–77). Also from Central Europe, Bela Kun, a Hungarian Bolshevik, suspected that communism had mistakenly taken root in Russia and should return to Europe, which was more civilized. To Kun, the French and German working classes were more civilized, though their souls were less penetrated by a revolutionary spirit (Kun 1971 [1919]: 7–8). Kun admired the Bolsheviks' centralized leadership, which was based on their rich experiences of revolution-making, but he thought it made sense only when such expertise applied to all of Europe (Kun 1923). Such conviction led to his stubborn enthusiasm for world revolution, even after he had been transferred to the Ural region to develop local industry (Zhelitski 1989).

Attachment to Europe also stemmed from a sincere admiration for its social equality and general civilization. Alexandra Kollontai is one example of such sentiment. Having spent her youth in Europe, she stated that she felt at home in Germany and did not see herself as a Russian patriot (Kollontai 1926 [2011]: 21–22). A prominent Bolshevik feminist, she was dismayed by the restoration of patriarchy within Russia during the New Economic Policy Period (NEP) (Holt 1978: 297–98). Sent into an honor exile in Norway, she was moved by the healthy democratic spirit of Scandinavian countries, where she experienced scant denial of women's capacities. As representative for trade negotiation, she felt motivated to set herself the task of recovering economic relations between Soviet Russia and Norway (Kollontai 1926 [2011]:40–41).

Realistic people sought integration with Europe too. Maxim Litvinov, who was against subversive agitation abroad on the whole (Haslam 1992: 17–18), viewed a close economic and technological connection with Europe as indispensable. He kept clarifying to the European media that the Bolshevik regime was doing no more than continuing the progressive program of the February Revolution, in order to win recognition by Western governments (Sheĭnis 1989: 119). With support from Lenin, throughout the Civil War, Litvinov

From an open union to an enclosed nation state   49

strove to keep lines of communication open. Seeing blockage as inevitable, he sought to secure open and normal relations with Estonia, so that Soviet Russia retained a strategic base to access Scandinavian countries (Sheĭnis 1989: 180). Litvinov also attended the Genoa Conference of 1922, hoping to normalize relations with capitalist countries (Phillips 1992: 31–32). While among European bourgeois governments, he focused especially on Britain. Based on his long experiences of residence in this country, Litvinov held that Britain, though rhetorically aggressive, was the most likely to reconcile with Soviet Russia (Phillips 1992: 53–56).

Two similar figures were Leonid Krasin and Dmitri Maiskii, who were incorporated into the Bolshevik regime to address its paucity of foreign-affairs cadres. Trained as an engineer, Krasin viewed diplomatic affairs from a technological perspective, which led to conflicts with the Secret Police and resulted in him being accused of making excessive concessions to imperialist governments. Krasin was opposed to exporting the revolution, but rather insisted that Soviet Russia should take advantage of the money-thirsty character of capitalism to absorb trade, investment, and technology (Matonin 2018: 156–57). Heading to the Genoa Conference, Krasin, argued—against hardliner Adolph Joffe—that Moscow should accept harsh conditions, including paying war redemptions, as long as it was allowed to reintegrate into Europe (Phillips 1992: 51–52). Dmitri Maisky, a different case, received a thorough European humanist education and completed a master's degree in Munich. He stayed abroad until the February Revolution of 1917 and viewed it as his mission to recover Russia's relationship with Europe. Sent to Britain as counsellor in 1925, he experienced exclusion and hostility from those who continued to count on a working-class revolution in Britain (Gorodetsky 2015: xxxii–xxxvii).

For Georgi Chicherin, Soviet commissar of foreign affairs, the necessity of maintaining friendly relations with European countries stemmed from his study of Russian diplomatic history. Born into the family of a Russian diplomat, Chicherin spent six years at the Imperial Foreign Service as an archivist (Trofimova 1973), during which time he wrote a substantial study of Goncharov, Russia's Minister of Foreign Affairs during the Crimean War (O'Connor 1988). Prior to 1917 and throughout World War I, Chicherin, residing in Britain, had been an antiwar internationalist who envisaged a unified European state as the ultimate solution to the abuse of violence. This led him to be arrested, and he coalesced with the Bolsheviks after release (Debo 1966). During the Civil War, in spite of his skepticism about the intention for peace on the part of the Entente, he strove to keep the line open, ensuring that some foreign groups—missionaries, the Red Cross, starvation relief organizations, diplomats, and war prisoners—remained in Soviet Russia so that the channel of communication with the West would

50   *Revolution in China and Russia*

not be entirely cut off (Chicherin 1920). The peak of his career was the reconciliation pact with Germany outside the Genoa Conference. He continued to appreciate Britain's great power and diplomatic skills.

The transnational connotation of the Soviet Union

The ideal of generating a socialist Europe was not realized. With revolutionary uprisings in Germany, Bulgaria, Romania, and Hungary repressed, the flame of world revolution faded out. Nevertheless, in its formative years, the Soviet Union maintained the intention of leading the worldwide trend of decolonization through the export of revolution. The Bolsheviks seized power at a moment of imperial decentralization—the Ottoman, German, Austro-Hungarian, and Romanov empires were collapsing, while the British and the French were seeing a growth of nationalist independence movements in their colonies. National self-determination, promoted by Woodrow Wilson as well as by socialists in Central Europe, was the dominant vision, and it gained the Bolsheviks' recognition in principle. However, when it came to how to technically combine socialism with national self-determination, opinion was divided among the loose conglomerate of 1917–22 Bolsheviks. The disagreement had to do with the variety of experiences and exposure to Western socialism. In this regard, there were multiple competing proposals on how socialism should deal with a world in transition to nation states. Four overlapping conceptions coexisted: cosmopolitan socialism, internationalist socialism, irridentist socialism, and pan-nationalist socialism.

In contradiction to the post-revolutionary propaganda that claimed the Bolshevik party as Leninist, before 1917 the Bolsheviks never coerced integration to promote ideological unity. Rather, since the organization's birth in 1903 as a faction within the SD, the Bolsheviks had been trapped in complicated relationships with various strands of socialists, and they had no unified vision for the post-revolutionary state. Many so-called Bolsheviks, including Leon Trotsky and Felix Dzerzhinskii, joined this faction in the last minute before the October Revolution. Others, like Nariman Narimanov and the Kazakh socialists, first joined the separatist movements in the course of World War I and the February Revolution and then came to be incorporated into the Soviet regime. Without any intra-Party purge or discipline comparable to the CCP's Yan'an Rectification, the Bolsheviks of 1922 were a loose group of individuals who retained great autonomy and a diversity of ideas about how the Soviet state should be organized. A wide spectrum of ideals extended from that of a unified nation state to full mergence with Europe. Some, notably Stalin, advocated for building a Great Russian nation state that incorporated all the ethnic non-Russian groups as autonomous

From an open union to an enclosed nation state · 51

regions. Others pressed for an immediate world revolution to unify Europe into a socialist stateless system or the United States of Eurasia. Still others, taking a middle ground, insisted in a federal system. While the radicals called for real political and economic power, as required by Bolsheviks from Central Asia, moderates raised the proposal of linguistic and cultural autonomy, which was echoed in Soviet Ukraine.

Ukrainians played a vital role in shaping the transnational concept of the Soviet model, cultivating national identity and language within an internationalist framework. Most Ukrainian Bolsheviks came from the Russified East and had less access to the ongoing cultural project intent on inventing the Ukrainian nation than the rightist Ukrainian nationalists did. By mobilizing, they worked closely with revolutionaries of Russian and other ethnicities. It would be difficult for them to imagine a Ukraine fully separated from the rest of the Russian Empire. In this regard, Nikolai Skrypnik was an exemplary case. By background an undereducated worker, Skrypnik maintained a clear Ukrainian identity. He did this through arduous self-didactic learning and informal mentorship from local intellectuals (Granat 1989b: 668–69). After the October takeover, he became an open supporter for cultural nationalism, self-identifying as a national communist. Skrypnik devoted himself to advancing the legalization of the Ukrainian language, which had been banned in tsarist Ukraine, leading to Eastern Ukrainians being educated in their native language. But this tolerance was short-lived. Ultimately, radical indigenization led to Skrypnik's purge and execution (Poleshchuk 1990). Once tamed by political repression, however, cultural nationalism became incorporated as a definitive cornerstone of the Soviet Union's nationality policy.

The cosmopolitan position of discarding all nationality, and merging Russian into Europe was embraced by Leon Trotsky. A Ukrainian Jew, Trotsky self-identified as a cosmopolitan who sought to erase national boundaries. While his claim that his Jewish identity had no place in shaping his radical trajectory appears exaggerated, it is certainly believable that he had little motivation to join a separatist Jewish nationalist movement. Trotsky came from a Jewish settler-farmer family in Eastern Ukraine. His father was almost illiterate. Scolding his son's engagement in the revolutionary movement as a blind attachment to a hopeless utopia, he expected Trotsky to become a doctor or engineer, which drove the latter to invest in academic work (Nedava 1972: 32–33). Trotsky briefly attended Hebrew school, where he received a shallow introduction to the Jewish religion. At the same time, he developed an antipathy toward the rigorous moral principles used to limit liberty and exert persecution. Like many other Russian Jewish socialists, his education was traumatic, due to the experiences of discrimination and racial bullying (Trotsky 1960: 39–42). Unsupported by a deep understanding of his faith, and subjected to ethnic abuse, he became disgusted by his own Jewishness, and throughout his radical path, he deliberately downplayed his Jewish identity in particular, and individual ethnicity more generally. For Trotsky, participation in the campaign against anti-Semitic pogroms was more about the struggle against tsarist tyranny and European capitalism than about Jewish liberation (Nedava 1972: 64–65). In essays commenting on the Romanian Jews, Trotsky invoked the Russian workers' struggle against anti-Semitism as a positive model, to elaborate his core argument that the Jews needed to join the internationalist socialist movement to protect themselves (Nedava 1972: 82–83).

There was a persisting tension in Trotsky's writings between cosmopolitan unification and the recognition of the Jews as a national group equal to other nationalists. Trotsky was opposed to the Bund, the Jewish socialist party, which only Jewish workers were allowed to join, citing Karl Kautsky's argument that such a small group would have limited exposure to the masses. Meanwhile, his unease with Lenin's personality and extreme centralism steered him back to seek a common language with the Bund (Nedava 1972: 95–96). Similarly, in terms of religion and culture, though Trotsky claimed to be indifferent to religion, he was opposed to Stalin's anti-religious propaganda, as well as to the corresponding excessive campaign against the Jews. This stand was derived from his vested hope on an all-European world revolution and the development of productive forces (Nedava 1972: 105–9). During the Civil War, as highest commander, Trotsky was in favor of the proposal to establish Jewish units, but he remained cautious for practical reasons: given the anti-Semitic stereotype that Jews were given to shirking conscription and battle, he wanted to avoid anything that might mar the centralized structure (Nedava 1972: 111–15). Trotsky himself was suppressed, but his ideals continued to inform the Soviet Union's ultimate goal: to create a nationless world after a thorough socialist revolution.

Although stopping short of nation-eradicating cosmopolitanism, an internationalist ideal in which borders were not confined to those of Russia, was prevailing among the Bolsheviks as well. The Latvian Bolshevik, Pyotr Stuchka, was the oldest central committee member of 1917. He left his homeland in early years to study at the Department of Law at St. Petersburg University, where he formed a solid personal friendship with Vladimir Lenin. From 1888 to 1897, Stuchka worked as a newspaper editor at the center of the Latvian peasant movement. Except for a few short trips to Switzerland and Russia, for most of the revolutionary years Stuchka was engaged with local Latvians, which led him to oppose Russian centralism (Granat 1989b: 127). On the other hand, Stuchka was the most internationalist Bolshevik. After Lenin made self-determination explicit in his April Thesis, Stuchka and his Latvian colleagues felt disturbed and directionless, which propelled them to seek a third International (Page

From an open union to an enclosed nation state   53

1976: 151). Later, at the thirteenth conference of the Latvian Social Democratic Party of 1917, Stuchka opposed any self-determination or federal separation from democratic Russia. He argued that the class struggle entailed territories and political unities being as large as possible; any creation of privileges for "folk" would obscure class consciousness. Nor did Stuchka see Russian imperialism to be as threatening as it had been in 1905, in that the Russian imperial center was collapsing (Ezergailis 1976: 146–47). As military units were heavily infiltrated by the Bolsheviks, the Latvian Rifle Brigades played a vital role in the Bolshevik success in 1917, in blocking the transportation line to Petrograd (Wildman 1976). Such a pan-European internationalism under Moscow's centralized control was enshrined in the Soviet Union's openness: it would continue to incorporate new members in the form of nation states.

Russified internationalism was another option, which emphasized that all nations of the former empire ought to be held together and transformed by Russia so that it achieved modernity. Stepan Shaumian, the founder of the first Bolshevik group in Armenia, argued that Armenia was too backward to independently formulate a modern political program. Studying at Riga's Polytech University, Shaumian formed an identification with the socialist movement within tsarist Russia as an entity (Granat 1989b: 765). He criticized Armenian writers for being people of emotion rather than people of reason. Immediately before 1905, Shaumian warned that without maintaining close ties with the Russian socialists, the Armenian nationalist groups would not be founded on political and economic views, but rather on mood and personal ties. Frightened by the censorship system of the tsarist state, he scolded, nationalist writers discreetly evaded public themes and abandoned their political project in favor of composing romantic histories (Shaumian 1978 1: 17–28). In an essay written in 1906, Shaumian argued that nations were not biological units, but dynamic ones, which could be accommodated flexibly under a socialist framework, taking the form of either federalism, national autonomy, or regional self-governance (Shaumian 1978 1: 147–62). Shaumian was murdered early on, but his ideas were incorporated into the Soviet model in the form of the idea that all nations had to be reshaped in the course of being invented. He raised the notion that indigenization was by no means a restoration of the past.

For nationalities with distinct identities, such as in Azerbaijan and Poland-Lithuania, the quest for creating a politically autonomic nation state was real. Nariman Narimanov, the sole Azerbaijan Bolshevik seated in the Central Committee of 1923, remained as a cultural nationalist until the October takeover. As an activist and teacher in pursuit of an enlightened Islam, he felt guilty about the status of Azerbaijan culture, which he thought of as stuck in the phase of medieval and barbarian. Narimanov sought to develop a modern

Muslim civilization to fit into the general process of the modernization of tsarist Russia. This process hinged on the assistance of and conversations with Russian progressive intellectuals, rather than on a break with the latter. Modeling his ideas on the Russian enlightenment movement, for a decade Narimanov directed dramas, compiled dictionaries, set up theaters and schools, and wrote columns. It was after these efforts had been frustrated by state repression that he switched to supporting the Bolsheviks, with the hope of further advancing his agenda (Akhmedov 1988: 22–24, 42–49,62–69, 75–77). Not surprisingly, Narimanov later insisted on playing an independent Azerbaijani role in the incursion into Northern Iran (Chaqueri 1995). Under Narimanov's leadership, Soviet Azerbaijan acted as an autonomous connection, controlling the transportation between the Eastern Mediterranean and Black Sea (Gasanly 2013: 527–33). Narimanov believed that by monopolizing oil production, Azerbaijan would be able to retain economic independence, an idea that was destroyed by the Soviet central plan of transforming Azerbaijan into a comprehensive economy dependent upon the entire union (Baibakov 2016: vol. 3, 13).

There was also a "dangerous" understanding of the Soviet model, irridentist socialism, which advocated for a polity that transcended Russia and European borders to incorporate and embolden small nations against a geopolitical foe, reminiscent of Pan-Slavism. This idea was clearly expressed by Christian Rakovskii, Trotsky's closest ally within the Bolshevik party. Rakovskii's father was a Bulgarian businessman who regularly traveled to Constantinople, whereas his mother came from a pro-Russian Bulgarian family. Family members from his mother's side viewed Russia as a giant who was able to liberate Bulgarians from the Turkish yoke (Conte 1989: 25). During World War I, Rakovskii was conscripted as a military doctor and sent to the front close to Romania. As an educated man, he had an erudite knowledge of the region's past, which was elucidated in essays he authored on the history of the Byzantine Empire and the Balkan's fight in the broad confrontation between Russia and Turkey (Conte 1989: 25–26). Rakovskii participated in the 1905 Revolution by agitating the Russian sailors in Romania. While viewing the integration with a socialist Russia as necessary, he also thought of a Balkan socialist federation as inevitable, given the complicated ethnopolitics in this region and this region's general weakness vis-à-vis the Ottoman Empire (Conte 1989: 53–54). Rakovskii's vision would be realized in Moscow's annexation of Bessarabia in 1940.

A more "dangerous" understanding of the Soviet Union was to use it as a protector and booster for pan-nationalism. This occurred to Kazakhstan and Central Asia, a region historically associated with Pan-Turkism. Turar Ryskulov, an ethnic Kazak from a nomad-employee family in Bishkek, started his revolutionary career as a Kazakh nationalist. Ryskulov's early

From an open union to an enclosed nation state   55

education was bilingual, covering both national literature in Kazakh and modern subjects in Russian (Ocadchii 2005: 6–7). This led him to become involved in the fight against the tsar's colonial rule in Turkestan in 1916 (Ryskulov 1927). Before his meeting with Lenin, Ryskulov aspired to build a Turkic socialist republic through his program. After the February Revolution, Ryskulov insisted that Russia should be a democratic federation, which a separate Kirgiz republic would join (Ocadchii 2005: 8). After relinquishing the post of the chairman of the Muslim Bureau (Musbiuro) of the Territorial Committee of the Communist Party of Turkestan, he briefly worked in Azerbaijan, Moscow, and Mongolia, where he insisted that all Turkic peoples should be integrated into one nation and have a separate Turkestan Republic. This led him into conflict with Stalin. Ryskulov, certainly, was not a separatist. He defended the Siberia–Turkestan railway project, claiming that the development and prosperity of Kazakhstan depended on transportation links with other parts of Russia (Ocadchii 2005: 12). Ryskulov's Turkic tendencies were not fully negated with his own purge; the transformation of the Transcaucasian and Central Asian republics became a model for further attempts to bring communist revolution to other Muslim regions.

Incorporating new members into "socialism in one country"

The Soviet Union did not, of course, become a union that constantly incorporated new nation states and expanded to the end of the world. Rather, it eventually transitioned into a regular international sovereignty equivalent to other nation states. However, the openness of its ambitions was not a myth. A course of creating and accepting new members persisted. It first came in the form of establishing new union republics and accepting them as members of the Soviet Union. This wave continued into the mid-1920s, with three Transcaucasian republics taken in and then the Kazakhstan and Central Asian republics demarcated. They, together with RSFSR, Ukraine, and Belarus, were identified as the foundational republics of the Soviet Union. The second wave started on the eve of the Soviet–German War, with Karelia, three Baltic states, Moldavia, Western Belarus and Western Ukrainian incorporated, immediately expanding the number of union republics to sixteen. There were a few annexations during the World War II, including the incorporation of Tuva and the recovery of Southern Sakhalin Island in the August Storm of 1945. After 1945 the Soviet Union controlled all of Eastern Europe, but the newly created socialist states were not incorporated into the USSR as new union republics, though it was claimed that this would take place at some point in the future. In the 1940s, Moscow received applications to join the Soviet Union as union republics, for example, from Sheng Shicai of

Xinjiang and Gao Gang of Northeast China, but they were declined. There were also attempts in the Soviet sphere of influence to replicate the Soviet model, as in Yugoslavia, Bulgaria, and Indochina. Yet Stalin continued to emphasize the concept of union states. At his insistence, Soviet Ukraine and Belarus were both voting members of the United Nations. Soviet internationalism never faded: it was institutionalized, as in the Comintern and the CPSU's International Department; it could be overt, as stated in the Brezhnev doctrine, "each country has a limited sovereignty," or covert, as exemplified by Khrushchev's intervention into the Middle East, as well as Gorbachev's installing of Perestroika in Eastern Europe; in this sense, the Bolshevik Revolution continued to the end of the Soviet Union.

The makers of the world's first socialist state and their followers

The late nineteenth century was a period of transition, confusion, debate, and chaos. During this period, the transition to a system of nation states had swept Europe, with nationalism arising to undermine the Pan-European workers' movement and threaten old empires. Major European powers like France and Germany were establishing universal education and conscription, which created a nationhood to displace the international class identity of the 1860s (Anderson 2002: 12–13; Joll 1956: 4–22). Meanwhile, old transborder ties retained their robustness. The dynastic transnational imperial structure was shaken but remained intact, thus presenting nationalists and national socialists with a question of how to deal with the imperial structure if the revolution succeeded. What was fashionable was not "socialism in one country" but rather "socialism in one empire." On the other side, the workers movement—a form of internationalism that succeeded dynastic alliance—gained a new momentum by spilling over into the colonies, and showed a tendency to form alliances with the resistance movements in colonial societies. The general direction of the world appeared perplexing, leaving revolutionaries puzzled.

Most importantly, prior to the Bolshevik takeover in 1917, there was also no established socialist state to play the role of "big brother" outside of Russia. Europe between the Franco-Prussian War and World War I was undergoing democratization and the transition to nation states; both of which caused enormous confusion within socialist movements. While the expansion of suffrage showed the possibility of improving workers' welfare without violent revolution, the foundation of a tariff system and universal conscription divided the international proletariat in a nationalist direction (Anderson 2002: 12–13; Joll 1956: 4–22). This triggered the debate on "revisionism" (Hamilton 2000). In terms of institutions, the Socialist

International (1889–1914) did not bear any real power over its constituent members. Instead, it served only as a platform to share information (Halliday 2008: 77–79). Nor were any leading parties, neither the French nor German, were able to dominate this organization; as nationalism arose, their conventional power became increasingly undermined by small socialist parties of South and Eastern Europe, who still engaged with manual laborers of rural origins. Such pluralism allowed for Russian socialists of various ideological orientations to find overseas supporters. Working closely with socialists of the Second International, many Bolsheviks joined factions for parliament struggle and trade unionism (Allen 2015; Cliff 2010: 241; Piatnitsky 193[?]; Porter 2013). Some even personally joined the French or German parties (Piatnitsky 193[?]: 175–76).

The Bolshevik Revolution created the world's first—and for a time only—socialist state. Though many communist parties were similar to the pre-1917 Bolsheviks and strove to imitate the Bolshevik precedent, from 1917 on they had to make revolution in a world where an established socialist state had been in command. This shift was fundamental and irreversible. For over the three decades following the October Revolution, no matter how unsatisfied these communist movements felt with Moscow's arrogance, most of them had to respect Moscow's authority, until they attained sufficient power to break away, which came as late as the turn of the 1950s. In terms of nationality policy, the relationship between the first revolution and those that followed was more paradoxical. The Soviet Union was a special starting point. The USSR itself was not a regular nation state, but rather a cultivator of (pro-Soviet) nation states. Its internationalist structure of promoting nationalism began by reaching out from the Russian core to the former imperial periphery, then extended beyond those borders, creating a transnational continuum. Eventually, this approach to world revolution shaped most communist movements into nationalist ones, some of which even, unintentionally, became Moscow's foes. Meanwhile, the idea of "nation," in this context was heavily manipulated by Moscow in service of its own interests. As in the formation of the Soviet Union itself, the arbitrary definition of "nation" let to the creation of multiple national communist movements within a single society.

The CCP revolution started almost at the same time as the Bolshevik one, at the turn of the 1920s. The CCP of the 1920s resembled the pre-1917 Bolsheviks in every regard. Taking shape at a time when old empires were either collapsing or reorganizing, the early CCP elites envisioned a revolution transnationally and internationally. Their imagination of a socialist China was not that different from the Soviet model. As Mao said in the late 1910s, self-determination was a worldwide fashion that China should follow (Wang 1968). Not only should border peoples be self-determining, but the Han themselves would gain from a federation. Li Dazhao, the co-founder of the CCP and professor at Beijing University, was vague about the nationality question. While criticizing the fashion of Pan-Asianism as a plot of Japanese imperialism, he also contrasted Soviet Russia to Britain, as two models representing an open and equal federation and a coercive empire (CDUF 1991: 53–55). Developing a pan-Asian revolution was considered, with China and Japan imagined as a potential symbiosis analogous to Russia and Europe (Jiangsu sheng dang'anguan 2014: 48).

The CCP came into being at the turn of the 1920s, a period of decentralization when the post-World War I world was celebrating transnational brotherhood. Such a trend spread across an ideological spectrum, including ideals and institutions such as Pan-Islamism, Pan-Turkism, the League of Nations, the League Against Imperialism, and Comintern, all promoting similar ideals, including love, peace, solidarity, and anti-imperialism (Duara 1998; 2001). In China, the KMT, modeling itself on the Soviet Comintern and Japanese pan-Asian movement, was actively proposing an International of Nations to coordinate Asian "weak and small nations" to counteract the colonial Western powers (Smith 2017). This strategy had a long tradition, dating back to China's intellectual obsession with Pan-Asianism at the beginning of the twentieth century among overseas diaspora (Karl 1998). This internationalist instinct was reflected in the arts as well. Cosmopolitan drama arose in the 1930s, especially among leftists. This thread was at odds with assimilationist-militarist nationalism and thus suffered repression, but it persisted until the national takeover by the CCP (Levenson 1971).

Related to internationalism was the widespread anarchist movement, which believed that interests, including national interests, could be discarded (Dirlik 1991: 145–47). Liu Shipei, an anarchist scholar, advocated for the creation of a socialist Asian entity. Formulating a critique that imperialism was based on racism, Liu claimed that weak nations had to abandon narrow national self-interest to strengthen themselves through unity. International war, as Liu said, benefited power holders and hurt the common people of both sides (Zarrow 1990: 175–77). A philologist, Liu advocated that schools should teach both Chinese and Esperanto as complementary languages (Zarrow 1990: 169). Another leading anarchist scholar, Li Shizeng, argued that the purpose of revolution after the revolution itself was to achieve the transition from nationalism. He rejected the dichotomy between China and the West, arguing that truth belonged to neither. An anarchist, he argued, could only ridicule the conservative concern with ethnicity, nation, and identity, which would have no place in a stateless world (Zarrow 1990: 179–80).

The CCP was not immune to internationalism. Inspired by Soviet Russia, it sought to extend local communist movements to the peripheries of the

From an open union to an enclosed nation state   59

former Chinese empire. From 1923 onward, for example, the CCP maintained continuous efforts among the Chinese diaspora in Southeast Asia to build a Communist Party of Malaysia. Such an active outreach stemmed partly from the internationalist ideal of a world anti-capitalist revolution and partly from a geopolitical strategy to add credit to China's national liberation (Belogurova 2014). More broadly, based on the network of Chinese international students and diaspora, the CCP also exerted influence outside of Asia, in an effort to win support from leftist parties in Europe and America to counter their native governments (Belogurova 2017). Inspired by the Comintern, the CCP was deeply involved in organizing and helping the Japanese Communist Party, as Chinese faces were less likely to stand out in Japan than Caucasian ones (Tu 2019: 214). In the Americas, local CCP activists, based on the platform of the "Chinese Anti-Imperialist Alliance," provoked agitation among Chinese laborers (Belogurova 2019).

The CCP was inseparable from anarchists and cosmopolitans in its formative years (Xu 2013). At the turn of the 1920s, some CCP literati, such as Qu Qiubai, affected by anti-colonial ideas, had developed ideas that modern scholars would find rather similar to the theory of dependency. Qu argued that the oriental world had fallen behind the occidental world, but the patriarchal East had no hope of transitioning to the capitalist West, as the latter was deliberately keeping the former stagnant at a primitive stage—he offered the example of the US-sponsored missionary school, where Chinese students were taught to play soccer, but not allowed to win over their American classmates (Qu 1985 1: 11–15). In a few years, Qu deplored the fact that Chinese nationalism was an outdated movement, in that the world had moved forward into a post-nationalist stage (Qu 1985 1: 55). Accordingly, Qu argued that what China should pursue was an internationalist agenda to entirely abolish imperialism worldwide (Qu 1985 1: 143).

The early CCP's aspiration for transnationalism was more than rhetoric. The internationalist and anarchist origin partly explains the overlapping of CCP founders with Japanese collaborators in the 1930s, which also occurred to non-CCP anarchists. Two of the thirteen delegates who attended the CCP's foundational congress of 1921, Chen Gongbo and Zhou Fohai, became high-ranking Japanese collaborators. Zhou spent eight years studying in Japan, where he dreamed of becoming a leftist leader like Lenin and Trotsky. As Zhou recalled, he devoted himself to reading the history of the Russian revolution and pamphlets on socialism. Zhou was the translator of Petr Kropotkin's *Mutual Aid* (Zhou 2015: 48–52). Compared with Zhou, Chen Gongbo's trajectory shows a volatile switch from one ideology to another. Son of a Qing governor, Chen joined the anti-Qing uprising as a Han-nationalist, believing that China lost wars because it was ruled by Manchurians (Wen 1994: 10–14). When attending the CCP's first congress,

60   *Revolution in China and Russia*

Chen expressed loathing toward the party's hierarchy and factionalism, which led to his later alienation and disobedience—the CCP expelled Chen by accusing him of defying the party's discipline (Miao 2011). After joining the KMT, Chen actively sought to reorganize the party's structure in line with Wang Jingwei to weaken Jiang Jieshi's dictatorship (Zhu and Yang 2006 9: 624–28). Chen was depicted as a person who valued personal friendship over political ideology and national identity.

The anti-militarism and anachronism of early communists

Not surprisingly, before the Comintern's buildup of the united front with the KMT, the anarchist CCP leadership of the early 1920s had a weak state allegiance, similar to the Bolsheviks before 1917. They had minimal involvement in the old military. Almost none of the members of the first five central committees served in the army or participated in warlord warfare. Most of these members were workers, intellectuals, and students. Also, like the Bolsheviks, the CCP of this stage had an anti-military psychology, denouncing militarism as responsible for China's warlordism. Accordingly, the CCP first brought non-military tactics to the task of social reconstruction: mobilizing workers and peasants, distributing propaganda among students, and discussing polemics within narrow intellectual circles with regard to designing a post-revolutionary blueprint. A revolutionary civil war was considered to avert the risk of China falling back into its historical cycle of dynastic change. Yet, as party leaders reflected afterwards, the real focus had been on socializing with local strongmen, mafia leaders, and officers, which proved fragile if not useless. There were attempts to penetrate the KMT military, mainly through the Soviet-sponsored Huangpu Academy in Guangdong, but the depth of penetration was limited. In the best cases, CCP members reached battalion level, while most played the role of political commissars or students.

The CCP leaders' reminiscences of the years before 1927 were not military centered, though they defined the China of this period as an oppressed semi-colonial society. Unlike the Beiyang warlords who started their career paths in the Sino–Japanese War, the Boxer Rebellion, and the Russo–Japanese War, no CCP elites had ever participated in China's major conflicts with foreign powers. This pattern differed from their Bolshevik counterparts, many of whom had experiences of the Balkan War and the World War I. Most CCP pupils perceived China's wars through elementary education, where wars with Japan and Russia were presented as a memory of "national humiliation" (Xie 1991: 2). Prior to the breakout of the Second Sino–Japanese War, most CCP elites had participated in only three major nationalist confrontations: the protest against Japan's

"Twenty-first demands" of 1915, the May Fourth Movement of 1919, and the May Thirtieth Movement of 1926. Whereas the first two were mainly street marches and cultural protests, the third involved skirmishes with the British authorities. However, the 1926 wave of nationalist protests began with Moscow's intervention in the Chinese Revolution, and it was largely a product of this intervention. It was from this point on that the CCP and Chinese leftist cosmopolitan and anti-military orientation began to be re-disciplined into a national one.

The ethnic Balkanization of China's communist movement

Ironically, it was the Soviet Union, the "Internationalist movement" with the ultimate goal of eliminating nationality, that transformed the multiple-directional Chinese leftist movement into a Leninist anti-colonial nationalist revolution. As Yang Kuisong (2021) notes, while the program promulgated by the CCP's first national congress identified no national missions, the second congress, more closely supervised by the Comintern, progressed significantly in this regard. However, most scholars of "Sinicization" have neglected that in Moscow's agenda, "nationality" was a highly subjective concept subject to arbitrary manipulation. When the Soviet Union exported revolution, it was Moscow that defined the "nation" of a "national" communist movement. In some regions, Moscow closed its eyes to transnational mobilization. In Southern Europe, for example, the Yugoslav communists provided secret support for Albanian and Greek guerrillas, while at the same time striving to unify the communist groups of Southern Slavic nations into one. Though Tito's ambition to create a Balkan socialist federation was finally thwarted by Stalin, the Soviet Union did not push Yugoslav communism to disintegrate into separate Serbian and Croatian ones as these "nationalities" could have been defined. In Southeast Asia, by contrast, though the Vietnamese communists traveled across borders between Laos, Thailand, China, and Cambodia, their request to redefine the small pan-Indochinese world into one nation was never approved, either by the Soviet Union or by the PRC (Singh 2015: 627).

In China, unlike the Balkans and the Indochinese peninsula, Moscow's intervention, in the name of liberating the "Chinese nation," actually confined the Chinese communist movement to a sub-national level. In Moscow's geopolitical agenda, geographical China was divided at least into five national regions: inland China, the Korean borderland, the Mongolian belt, the Southeast Asian corner, and the Xinjiang enclave. Except for inland China where the CCP was created and active, each of the other four was transnationally connected with radicals abroad, thus more or less independent of the CCP movement. Whereas Mongolian, Vietnamese, and Korean communists sustained some contact with the CCP, Xinjiang communists remained separate until 1950. Moreover, unlike the Han-dominated CCP, communist movements in each of the four border regions were homogeneously non-Han, or entirely diverse. The Inner Mongolian group, which traveled back and forth between the USSR and China and passed through the Mongolian People's Republic, was ethnically homogeneous, but non-Han, and it carried a transnational character. The Soviet-supported leftists in Xinjiang, the makers of the "Three-Region Revolution," was a multi-ethnic and transborder cosmopolitan group. These people, born Uygur or Kirgiz, studied in Soviet Central Asia, spoke fluent Russian, and traveled across borders between Tadzhikistan, Afghanistan, India, Persia, and even Turkey (Saifuding 1993). Similarly, Korean communists, centering their activities around the peninsula, maintained a transborder network across Japan, the Soviet Far East, and Northeast China. Whereas some of them kept close ties with Moscow, others developed an alliance with the CCP (Shen 2015). It was the first socialist state's strategy of division, rather than China's demographic structure, that created a Han-dominated "Chinese" communist revolution.

Inner Mongolian communists marked the multinationality of China's revolution. These people, speaking fluent Mandarin, retained their distinct ethnic identities and languages, which located them at a subtle intermediate belt between the Soviet Union and China. In the course of power seizure, they sought to secure an equal status of their mother nationality by drafting a concept of multinational China. Such a transnationality is revealed in the biographies of Kui Bi and Ji Taiya, two close associates with Ulanhu, the CCP's governor of Inner Mongolia. Whereas Kui Bi was one of the two ethnic Mongolians in the CCP's Eighth Central Committee, Ji Taiya was the CCP's ambassador to Mongolia. Both Inner Mongolians attended the Tumote Elementary School and Beijing Mongolian–Tibetan Middle School, where they learned fluent Mandarin. However, their revolutionary paths retained geographical separation with the CCP's as well as the Ulanhu's personal one for a longer time. After brief training in Moscow, Kui Bi and Ji Taiya worked in Outer Mongolia for years. Kui Bi returned home after the breakout of the Sino–Japanese War, organizing guerrilla war in Inner Mongolia, with the assigned mission of securing a buffer on the steppe between Yan'an and the Japanese. Ji Taiya stayed in Outer Mongolia from 1938 to 1946, functioning as a leading reporter on the CCP's performance in the War (Fu 2014: 291–94). Mongolian nationality as a distinct entity did not disappear. The Inner Mongolian communist group continued to request autonomy after the CCP had officially abandoned the confederal program, and would continue to do so until the ultimate foundation of the PRC (Gong 2002: 49–51).

From an open union to an enclosed nation state   63

The Xinjiang and Korean communists better exemplify how Moscow's arbitrary way of nation-defining determined the ethnic Balkanization of the Chinese revolution. Saifuddin Azizi, the chairman of the PRC's Uygur Autonomous Region, was born in 1915, when Xinjiang was under a de facto separated rule from the Beiyang Beijing government. Saifudin's early education was Muslim-style—Koran, prayer, with Islam as a subject in parallel with mathematics and language. As Saifuding recalled, some texts were inaccessible for natives because they were Persian and Arabian. Saifuding's father was a factory owner, with broad overseas connections, in cooperation with Armenian and Afghanistan businessmen. He had a four-year-long exile in Russia, the most northern spot of which reached Finland and Arctic (Saifuding 1993: 9–11, 21). In 1934, Saifuding attended a secular training school operated by twelve Turkish exile educators, where he first encountered ideas about enlightened Islam and socialism (Saifuding 1993: 207–11). After graduation, the connections generated through this experience led him to Soviet Uzbekistan for two years' further studies in Tashkent, which transformed him into a Soviet communist party member (Saifuding 1993: 223–43). With Mao Zedong's approval, Saifuding switched his affiliation to the CCP in October 1949, right after the foundation ceremony of the PRC. His letter of application received Mao's signed approval immediately. This visit was Saifuding's first entry to inland China.

A less typical case was that of ethnic Koreans. After the Revolution of 1911, Koreans were not recognized as any of the five constituent nationalities of China, instead viewed as a migrant people. Struggling with their dispersal among Russians, Japanese, and Chinese, they diverged into multiple political forces—Chinese communists, Soviets, Korean nationalists, and Japanese collaborators. The trajectory of Zhu Dehai, the CCP's future state governor in Yanbian and the highest-ranked Korean within the Party prior to 1956, overlapped with the first three of these streams. Zhu was born in Russia's Far East, with a Korean genealogy. Escaping from war-caused banditry, Zhu's family moved back to Korea after 1905, where Zhu completed his elementary education under the close instruction of Korean national communist, Jin Guangzhen (Cui 2012: 3–4). Zhu's early radical path was thus closely associated with the Korean Communist Party, until the latter was disbanded in 1930. After that, by the Comintern's "one country, one party" rule, Zhu, like other Korean communists active in China, switched his organizational affiliation to the CCP and was sent to Moscow Eastern Toilor University for revolutionary training (Cui 2012: 4–5). Zhu could barely speak Chinese, for which he was soon transferred from the CCP class to the Korean communist class. After graduation from Moscow, Zhu was sent to Yan'an, where he held a position that gave him responsibilities for the management of Korean communist emigrants. During this period, Zhu still retained his distinct Korean identity, viewing his mission as preparing for a return to the homeland to foment a Korean anti-Japanese communist revolution free of foreign intervention. This thought persisted until 1945, when the Soviet Union invaded Korea. From then on, Zhu changed his stance and he aimed to transform Koreans in China into a Korean nationality as part of the Chinese nation (Cui 2012: 9–14).

The Vietnamese case is unlike the others, in that there was no bloc in the CCP leadership closely associated with Indochina as there was for Inner Mongolian, Xinjiang, and Korean. However, it was still informative. The Vietnamese revolution benefited from close assistance by the Chinese. It did not gain recognition from Moscow until 1950, following repeating endorsements by the CCP (Goscha 2006). Yet, in many aspects, the Vietnamese communists were more like the Bolsheviks than the CCP. The decades-long French colonial rule of the country shaped a transnational Indochinese identity entrenched among the youths in opposition to the Annam identity of elder generations. By the mid-1940s, they had actively recruited cadres from Laos and Cambodia, while at the same time overseeing the foundation of communist groups in the two countries. Moreover, like the Bolshevik revolution, the Vietnamese revolution was also a transborder one. Communists traveled extensively between French Indochina, Northern Thailand, Malaysia, and Southwest China (Vu 2016: 277–81). The blurring of a national homogeneity was evident in the leaders' experiences. The Vietnamese communists were broadly connected with the anti-colonial movement of the French-speaking world. Unlike the CCP leaders, whose writings were overwhelmingly China-centered, a significant part of Ho Chi-min's early works were devoted to his observations about French colonies in Africa, the Pacific islands, and South America. They discussed the decline in the health of the populations, forced trade, sole-lateral export, racial persecution, military conscription and trans-colonial deployment, de-professionalization of colonial officials, and institutional barriers to immigration (Hu 1964 1: 31–32, 37–38, 53–54, 103–4). Another pro-Chinese leader, Hoàng Văn Hoan, spent his radical years across the societies of Southeast Asia, and the most intensively among the Vietnamese compatriots in Northern Thailand, China, and Laos (Huang 1987).

All these peripheral and transnational communists, who were more or less independent of the CCP, indicated the long reach of Moscow. It was the first established socialist state, not China's ethnic composition or cultural essentials, that defined what "Chinese nation" meant. Ethnic composition and cultural character, as overarching structures, were not consistent among the individual parts of a national society that covered a vast geographical space. Rather ethnic composition varied greatly from region to region, and revolution-makers had to start with such particular regions. For example, in

From an open union to an enclosed nation state   65

sponsoring the Northern Expedition of 1926, the Soviets made Guangdong the starting point. This had a decisive impact on the CCP leadership's ethnic composition of mainly Han people from Central and South China: Hunan, Hubei, Guangdong, and Jiangsu. If Moscow had started its military action in Northwest or Sino-Mongolian borders, as Sun Yat-sen first proposed and then Mao, the communist movement would have been entirely different, very similar to the enclaves in Xinjiang, Korea, or, more straightforwardly, like that propounded by the Bolsheviks themselves. Whether it would have been called the "Chinese Communist Party" is uncertain.

Geographical isolation from Japan, Southeast Asia, and Europe

Though the Soviet Union aimed to confine China's communist movement to a national cage, there was resistance, which gained momentum from China's native revolutionary traditions, as well as from Moscow's internal division. In its exportation of revolution, the Soviet Union aroused a world-wide anti-Bolshevik red scare, which, unintendedly, diminished the overseas connections for the CCP and other radical groups. This shift enclosed communist movements within a small world, and thus significantly changed the composition of their leaderships from cosmopolitan and transnational into a native, rural, and nationalist core. As the red scare spread, states surrounding Russia hardened their border control and intensified anti-communist repression, which limited the success of the Bolsheviks to Russia and left its followers outside Russia stranded. This occurred first in Europe with its tight borders. Whereas, in the two years after 1917, communist revolutions broke out and immediately perished in Germany, Bulgaria, Romania, Hungary, and Czechoslovakia (Pelz 2018; Tökés 1967; Weitz 1997), Moscow's support for Kemalists as well as the for Turkish communists ended up with Kemal's bloody anti-communist repression in 1926, which forced the Turkish communists underground (Gökay 2006; Harris 1967: 8–9, 141). It was only in Northern Iran and Mongolia that Moscow, backed by direct military support, achieved the establishment of local Soviet regimes, though the Soviet republic in Northern Iran was abolished according to an Anglo-Soviet Agreement (Chaqueri 1995).

   In East Asia, the Bolshevik Revolution aroused strong reaction from Japan and from British and Dutch colonial authorities. A wave of border tightening and increased repression blocked Chinese radicals' outlets to their conventional overseas shelters, and thus changed the power balance between the internationalist and native factions within the CCP movement. As already noted, the long Chinese revolution, since its inauguration in the 1890s, had a tradition of transnational mobilization. Like the Bolsheviks before 1917, Chinese radicals stayed overseas to avert domestic repression. Japan, for example, was a stronghold of the KMT in the fight against the Qing Dynasty and Yuan Shikai. Given that studying in Japan became an intellectual trend after 1895, many radical students used their education in this country as a platform to prepare for revolution. Here, they continued their education, recovered their network, published newspapers and periodicals, and allocated money. Such a route remained open after the collapse of the Qing Empire, until the Bolshevik Revolution aroused the red scare. Chinese radicals of this period even often gained aids and instructions from Japanese sympathizers (Xue 1935[1996]: 467).

The CCP's early elites also spent time in Japan. CCP senior leaders, like Wu Yuzhang, Lin Boqu, Wang Ruofei, and Zhou Enlai all had brief experiences of studying in Japan's crash schools before they encountered the Comintern (Chen and He 1986; Li 1978; Lin 1984). But after 1917, the Japanese authorities removed preexisting freedoms. Galvanized by the anti-communist panic, a consensus between the army and liberals quickly took shape to form an anti-Soviet firewall against Bolshevik expansion (Linkhoeva 2020). One year after the massacre of 1927, Tokyo and the KMT Nanjing government reached an agreement, which stipulated that any captured CCP activists would be sent back to the KMT government (*Riben gongchandang de sishinian* 1962: 10–12). In the late 1920s, some CCP members, who had escaped to Japan in the hope that they could enroll into local colleges as their radical precursors had in the 1910s, found upon boarding that they had been added to the police blacklist (RMA 1985, 4: 57, 105, 112–14). The CCP's Tokyo branch did contrive to survive until the outbreak of the Sino–Japanese War in 1937, but due to intensive repression, their activities eventually decreased to apolitical intellectual entertainments such as Esperanto, woodblock painting, and foreign drama (RMA 1985, 4: 125–26; RCCCPH, Research Committee of CCP History, 10: 169–80).

Another overseas outlet ruined by the Bolshevik Revolution was British Southeast Asia. Since the 1890s, Singapore and Malaya had been a major base for the KMT radicals, owing to the large Chinese population and the geographical proximity to China's mainland. The KMT branch at Singapore was once a legally registered organization under British rule. However, after the Bolshevik takeover, control tightened. At the height of the 1927 massacre, the CCP attempted to make Hong Kong a temporary base, but the ability to reject visas proved problematic (RCCCPH 1980–86: 43–45; RMA 1985, 4: 3–4, 210; 7: 151–52, 329). The CCP leaders who escaped to Malaya and Singapore founded a "Communist Party of the South Seas" (Yu 2015), but the British authorities quickly uncovered this. With all core leaders arrested, the party disintegrated. CCP activists, Luo Zhu, Tan Pingshan, and Wang Yazhang, escaped to Southeast Asia and then lost connection because they had no local networks to join (RMA 1985, 6: 61; Wang 2007, 1: 355).

The Soviet Union also cut off the CCP's relation with Western Europe, a place denounced by Moscow as the degraded former center of world worker movements. Since the CCP's historical relation with Western European socialism had been thin before 1917, Moscow's action involved a preemptive consideration to block the CCP from the influence of Trotskyists in exile. Many senior CCP elites, at the turn of the 1920s, joined the "Work-Study" program in France and Belgium, a program crafted by three Chinese anarchist educators who bore the Tolstoyan illusion that, with half funding from the Chinese government, these students could study in France and gain enrollment in local educational institutions. This illusion collapsed within two years, owing to the limited financial resources of the Chinese government, while the program eventually became a hotbed for student radicalism, creating an opportunity for Chinese students to access the Comintern agents in Europe (Levine 1993).

After the Bolshevik takeover, Western Europe became inaccessible for Chinese radicals. One reason was that Chinese students were involved in Moscow-backed socialism and they aroused the vigilance of the French police, which led to increasing antagonism. The other factor was domestic. To secure its absolute control over international communism, Moscow banned its foreign followers from contacting each other without the Comintern's supervision. Traveling across Europe was thus forbidden for the CCP, as well as for many other communist parties. Liu Renjing, a Trotskyist and one of the thirteen attendees at the CCP's founding congress, met with Trotsky in Turkey. Their meeting drew explosive media attention and thus irritated Moscow. Emel'ian Iaroslavskii, then the member of the Central Inspection Committee, pressed for further tightening of travel control and for banning anyone from crossing Europe to leave or enter the Soviet Union (Liu 1997: 246–47).

A national revolution by Soviet-made internationalists

The CCP revolution, self-framed as an anti-colonial nationalist movement, never abandoned its other facet, internationalism. According to the CCP's official discourse, China's weak national strength vis-à-vis colonial powers created the need to build alliances with other liberation-seeking nations and liberation-supporting states. Yet, the CCP's internationalism fundamentally differed from that of the Bolsheviks, which, paradoxically, resulted from the Soviet Union's transformation of the Chinese leftist movement in a way that separated it from cosmopolitans, anarchists, and Trotskyists.

When it originated, the CCP had a strong continuity and overlapping with the anarchist socialists. While the phenomenon of individuals joining the CCP has been explained as the elective affinity between one's early ideology and Soviet-style Leninism (Xu 2013), what is often overlooked is the role that Moscow's policy of selection and purge played in shaping the CCP's understanding of an anti-colonial national movement. National liberational movements could be organized in multiple ways, from an elitist approach, involving minimal mobilization, to a totalitarian one that mobilized the masses from the bottom up (Slater and Smith 2016). In CCP's case, the Soviet Union set up the concept, modeled on the Bolshevik prototype, that a national movement had to be organized by a party seeking to create a strong and centralized state. It was by following such a standard that the CCP eventually purged all elements that were at odds with Bolshevism.

A main stream of such transformation was the CCP's perennial campaign, encouraged by the Soviet Union, to purge so-called Trotskyists. Originating as a student faction formed in 1927 after the massacre, Chinese Trotskyists deemed that Trotsky's opposition to the united front with the KMT had proved correct, and it was Stalin's mistake that caused the counterrevolutionary massacre. As Stalin's power became consolidated, most students who held such a position were labeled as Trotskyists and expelled from the Soviet Union. In the ensuing two decades, it was undisputedly correct political practice for each Soviet-following communist party to seek and purge Trotskyists, though who actually qualified as Trotskyists was not universally agreed. With a reference to Moscow's guidance, the CCP defined "Trotskyism" as two stable components: "defeatism" and "permanent revolution." Defeatism was the view that all international wars were conflicts between imperial powers in which communists should not participate under any conditions or for any purpose. Permanent revolution was manifested in an opposition to any united front or to reconciliation with the non-proletarian classes; instead, it made use of every opportunity to advance class revolution against the enemy of proletariat.

Whereas Trotsky's conflict with Stalin unfolded in every direction, defining Trotskyism by these two particular elements reflected the Soviet Union's national interests and security issues of the 1930s and 1940s. As the Sino–Japanese War escalated and the Soviet–Nazi War started, Stalin's plan that Moscow must keep China fighting to its full strength so to trap Japan from assaulting the Soviet Union from the east became clear. The maintenance of a united anti-Japanese front was to Moscow's advantage, even if the CCP was inferior to the KMT. To this end, the anti-Trotskyist movement during the war accused Trotskyists as "national traitors." In a speech to the KMT officers, Wang Ming claimed that the Trotskyists desired the defeat of the Chinese fatherland, so that an opportunity could be created for them to seize power. He asserted that "Trotskyists had been in opposition to the Brest Peace in 1918 against Lenin ... in 1936 they wanted to kill the mediator to drag the KMT and the CCP into a civil war ... Trotskyists bear the illusion that China could fight national and class wars simultaneously, a dangerous idea only to the Japanese's advantage ... they had no principle and would even receive subsidies from the Japanese invaders ..." (Wang and Xu 1940: 3–5, 8–9, 10–11).

The CCP persisted in its repression of Trotskyists, normalizing the repression, and in December 1952, the sweetest moment of the Sino-Soviet honeymoon, a nationwide arrest was carried out, with all active Trotskyists in mainland China jailed (Wu 2008: 162–63). In a demonstration of its respect for the Soviet Union, the CCP was fighting with all its strength to safeguard the Soviet Union's eastern borders from Japan. The Comintern did create a bloc of "internationalists" within the CCP, who, upon the rise of Mao, were disgraced as "dogmatists uncritically following Soviet experiences." However, these people were by no means like Karl Radek or Felix Dzerzhinskii. Like Wang Ming and the "Twenty-eight and a half Bolsheviks," they had no transethnic backgrounds. They completed elementary education in central and southern China and then traveled to the Soviet Union. "Born in one nationality, educated in a second language, and making revolution in a third and fourth countries" was not their trajectory. Their tendency to support every instruction from Moscow was annoying in the eyes of Chinese Russophobic nationalists, but it can hardly be said that these people were cosmopolitan by mindset. Actually, when this group celebrated the Soviet Union's expansionism, it was clear that they had been disciplined by Stalin's Soviet Union to view the world through the lens of the nation state, in defending Soviet wars in Poland, Romania, Finland, and in their secret pacts with Nazi Germany and Japan. These internationalists' claims of the superiority of Soviet Union's national interests can hardly be taken seriously, in that such a claim largely stemmed from a strategic calculation with the purpose of pleasing Soviet supervisors to gain an upper hand in the power struggle.

Apart from purging "Trotskyists" and creating "Internationalists," the Soviet Union channeled the CCP into a national movement by training the latter's foreign-service men, a group with substantial transnational background, but profoundly engaged in China's indigenous revolution. Like Moscow-trained communists from other countries, these CCP elites spent the years of their political education in Russia. They spoke fluent Russian, appreciated Russian arts, maintained close connections with Soviet colleagues, and viewed the Soviet Union as a utopian ideal for the future. Nevertheless, these CCP elites were all pushed back home early, which enabled them to participate in the entire course of the Chinese Revolution and to form a strong attachment to the Chinese national cause. Self-identifying as internationalist fighters, they showed a national face, in that they were not the Bolsheviks, who dreamed of moving back to Europe, like Leonid Krasin, Alexandra Kollontai, Karl Radek, and Alexander Shliapnikov. Such a national face also differed from, for example, most of the Moscow-trained Eastern European communists, who spent most of their time in Russia and continued to view the Soviet Union as their spiritual fatherland.

The three most prominent Russia-returning diplomatic leaders, Wang Jiaxiang, Wu Xiuquan, and Zhang Wentian, all spent nearly ten years in the Soviet Union in the 1920s and 1930s. Their engagement with Russia was profound. After graduation from Moscow's Sun Yet-san University, Wang taught Chinese politics at the Comintern. He returned to Moscow in 1936 as the CCP's delegate to the Comintern and spent another two years there. During his first sojourn in Russia, Wang also admired the modernity and openness of the NEP-period Soviet Union, which led him to date a Ukrainian woman (Xu 2001). Yet, Wang viewed the Soviet Union as a regular sovereign state and never lost his ambition to make the CCP-led China a power equivalent to Russia. Back in China, Wang participated in the Long March, where, in the historic Zunyi Conference, he sided with Mao. During the Civil War, he was sent to Manchuria, as chair of the department on urban work, which was central to Manchuria's industrial context. In the fall of 1949, Wang was appointed as the PRC's first ambassador to the Soviet Union, a position vital to the establishment of the CCP's "Leaning to One Side" pro-Soviet stance. His ambition to retain a national China persisted, and it was recorded that when meeting in person with Stalin, Wang declined the latter's proposal that China should organize a Union of Asian Socialist Republics (Xu 2001: 335).

Wu Xiuquan, the PRC's ambassador to Yugoslavia and later Minister of Foreign Affairs, spent six years in the Soviet Union. Unlike many CCP students at the time, he did not confine his activities to polemics in the classroom. Rather, Wu was selected for special military training in an infantry camp in Moscow, where he was impressed by the Soviet Union's military forces and came to see the importance of military superiority in defeating the domestic and external foes of the Chinese Revolution (Wu 1998: 38–39). Speaking fluent Russian and completing a comprehensive military training course, he participated in the 1929 conflict over the Chinese Eastern Railway, fighting against the Chinese warlord Zhang Xueliang, which earned him credit having for an "internationalist mindset," since the foe was an ethnic compatriot. Like Wang Jiaxiang, Wu Xiuquan returned to China in 1931 and observed every important stage and event of the CCP revolution. During the Sino–Japanese War, he directed the CCP agency in Lanzhou, ensuring that Soviet aids to the KMT could be delivered without losses from China's Northwestern borders. After 1945, Wu was sent to Manchuria, first to establish contact with the Soviet forces and then to direct the buildup of local military industry (Wu 1998: 146–48). In the wake of the Beijing–Moscow split, Wu's expertise in language and ideology made him a leading organizer of the CCP's polemics with Khrushchev.

Zhang Wentian, who succeeded Wang Jiaxiang as PRC's ambassador to the USSR, had been a freelance literature researcher and translator. In the 1920s, Zhang, residing in California as a non-registered student and Chinese journal editor, advocated the displacement of toxic traditional Chinese classics with enlightened Soviet literature. Such a cosmopolitan mentality would continue to define Zhang's later revolutionary path. From 1924 to 1931 Zhang studied and taught in the Soviet Union, where he was involved in the factionalism among Chinese students. After returning to China, Zhang participated in the guerrilla war in Jiangxi as a standing member of the CCP's central political bureau. Supportive of Mao at the Zunyi conference, Zhang was promoted to be the CCP's general secretary, which was the peak of his personal political career. Zhang lost power in Yan'an and became a target of Mao's anti-dogmatist campaign. As the return for his show of softness, Zhang was appointed as the party secretary of Liaoning, the first province occupied by the CCP. When managing the economy in Manchuria during the Civil War, he insisted that China should not force a Stalinist socialist transformation (ShShDY 2010:75–78).

The creation of the PRC in Moscow's shadow

As the CCP revolution moved toward success, a looming option to develop real internationalism surfaced. There were two potential directions for "internationalism": integration into the emerging Soviet-led socialist bloc as a member republic, rather than establishing a Chinese nation state, or federalization into an Asian-version of the Soviet Union, which covered the entire Eastern Asian continent. There were signs of such a trend. Becoming a revolutionary giant in the East, the CCP was entrusted by Stalin to play a leading role in communist movement in East Asia and, more broadly, the entire colonial world (Chen 2010: 14–15). To convince Stalin of its willingness and capacity of "Leaning to One Side," the CCP engaged military operations in Korea and Vietnam. However, these performances did not convert to an internationalist structure. The first option, to become a member of an expanded Soviet Union, was easy to exclude. When the CCP approached power in the late 1940s, the term, "socialist bloc" was still an emerging and vague concept. Fearing to project a provocative image on to the US and the West, Stalin, up until 1947, had been hesitating to Sovietize "popular

72 *Revolution in China and Russia*

democratic polities" in Eastern Europe and Asia (Zubok 1996). Even after Sovietization had officially started, his focus was mainly on expropriating economic benefits to recover the war-devasted economy at home, rather, it than developing an EU-like integration and community. In the final years of Stalin's reign, the socialist bloc lacked institutional integration; rather maintained unification through coercion, terror, and personal authority (Gati 1990: 25–28).

When it came to China, Stalin firmly declined a proposal for transnational integration, first from Sheng Shicai and later from Gao Gang. When Mao showed his eagerness for rapid Sovietization of the Chinese economy and politics, Stalin suggested that China should remain a "popular democratic" nation state, clearly separate from the Soviet Union (Li 2006: 40–45). Stalin's plan was to extract resources, such as rubber in South China and Japanese industries in Manchuria, and to use China as an amenable geopolitical buffer. His distrust of the CCP did not begin to decrease until 1952, when the CCP demonstrated its loyalty by having been trapped in Korea for two years—it was in August 1952 that the CCP was allowed to send its first delegation to negotiate economic aid from Moscow (Kong 2010). To deflect the US's suspicion, Stalin also kept the relationship vague and shallow, so that Moscow would be in a position to cut off its alliance with Beijing if a reconciliation with the US was needed.

Rather than the option of joining the Soviet Union, a more likely scenario was that the PRC could have lost three "Norths"—Xinjiang, Inner Mongolia, and Northeast—and confined "China" to a small territory tantamount to the domain of the Ming Dynasty. With the annexation of Tuva in 1944 as a precedent, Moscow had expressed an interest in retaining Soviet influences in China's three Norths, and what remained open was how to achieve this goal. An attempt was made in October 1945 by the Soviet occupational forces to create an Inner Mongolian People's Republic and later a Northern Rehe Autonomous Republic, an action that was reminiscent of the Soviet Russia's creation of the Northern Persian Soviet Socialist Republic in 1920 (Chaqueri 1995). Claiming that these border states were to replace the overthrown Japanese-collaborating Mongolian duchies, the Soviet forces demarcated clear borders banning the CCP from entering. These states also began to prepare their diplomatic delegations to visit the Mongolian People's Republic, conveying an interest in a merger. This stance, certainly, was met with resentment and opposition from the CCP. Later on, upon orders from Moscow, the Soviet forces reduced their support for these states, allowed CCP members to join, and finally abolished these border de facto states (CDUF 1991: 966–73).

In Xinjiang, the Northern Iranian model was applied. Backed by Moscow, Islamic nationalists plotted a "Three-Region Revolution" in 1944, which

From an open union to an enclosed nation state   73

created an "Eastern Turkestan Republic." Then Stalin used this state as a leverage to channel the KMT's and later the CCP's entry into Xinjiang. Moscow banned the Xinjiang republic's separate contact with the CCP, which caused Abdulkerim Abbas, a Uyghur revolutionary born in Kirgiz, to be warned in person. Having achieved the goal of preventing the British and US from penetrating this region, Moscow eventually stepped back, withdrawing its support for founding any independent state in Xinjiang. Such an acknowledgment of an "intact" China, however, was preconditioned by the promise that Soviet influences had to be guaranteed. Therefore, Xinjiang's status was different from other parts of the PRC. For example, the Soviet Union signed the agreement of cultural development not with the Beijing government, but rather with the local Xinjiang delegation (Shen 2020: 21–22). Such a status persisted until the Sino-Soviet split in the 1960s. Similarly, in Northeast China, though the entire region was finally defined as the PRC's provinces, Soviet forces and commercial agencies stayed until 1955, after Stalin's death. Mao's bargaining led Stalin to agree to return the Lvshun-Dalian port, but this soon involved China in the Korean War (Shen 2014, 2: 421–27). This flexibility in border demarcation in the name of supporting national liberation reflected Moscow's arbitrary willingness to determine what a nation was and where its domains and rule ended.

Summary and conclusion

This chapter has demonstrated how Bolshevik revolutionaries maneuvered and manipulated the trend of nationalism to preserve the Russian Empire domestically and extend its influence in Asia. The turn of the twentieth century saw a crisis for traditional empires as they legitimized their expansionism. Empire as a term had been associated with a glorious mission of civilizing the "barbarian" world, but by this time it had been denounced as an evil violation of the principle of sovereignty and national dignity. Yet, given the vagueness of the concepts of "nation" and "nationality," these features of anti-imperialism once again became the tools of empire building. But rather than recreate the old world of empires, in this new phase, ancient empires fell, while others survived by changing their faces. In this wave of transformation, Russia and China represented two unique paths: the former self-adjusted to an internationalist union of nation states, which, at the same time, the latter came to self-reframe as a national state. In both cases, social revolutions played a vital role in the empire's transition to nation states. Equally significantly, by maneuvering nationalism, the first successful socialist revolution heavily impacted the second. The CCP's adherence to Han-centric Chinese nationalism (though they didn't always recognize it) resulted from the USSR's intervention rather than being merely a function of China's ethnic and linguistic homogeneity.

The Russian Revolution was the most serious of the attempts to approach a Marxist imagination of internationalism. The Revolution translated such an imagination into an institutionalized effort to maneuver nationalism with the aim of fomenting a world revolution. The Bolsheviks' weak state allegiance led them to envision a pan-European socialist world. Admiring the civilization of the West, as well as loathing Russia's backwardness, many European-minded Bolsheviks anticipated a full merging of Russia into Europe after the revolution, rather than the development of a separate Russian socialist state. Alongside this expectation was a strategic consideration to formally break down the former Russian Empire into a union of nation states. The Bolsheviks expected that such a move would create a continuum to connect Russia into Europe and the Eastern colonial world where the nationalist volcano was erupting. The Bolshevik leaders had competing conceptions of how the former empire should be reorganized, but their disagreement suggested that nationalism could be steered to serve the advancement of revolution. They also shared the consensus that their alliance with nationalism was temporary. The Soviet Union was more a movement than an eternal state, open, though conditionally, to accept new member republics.

The Bolsheviks did not want to see a second communist party that was as cosmopolitan as they were, be it in China, Yugoslavia, or elsewhere. They wanted to be the first and the last world communist party. All other communist movements could only be national. In exporting nationalist revolution to the East, the Bolsheviks pressured the CCP into a national track in four ways, some intended and others unintended. First of all, the Bolsheviks divided geographical "China" into five ethnic regions: Inner Asia, Inner Mongolia, Northeastern Asia, Indochina, and China inland, and the CCP was granted control of only the last of these. Under Moscow's dominance, pro-Soviet movements in these five "Chinas" were independent and isolated from each other. In such an ethnic Balkanization, the CCP attained its Han-dominant "homogeneous character." Second, in exporting revolution, the Bolsheviks triggered a red scare around China. As Japanese, British, and Dutch authorities tightened their anti-communist border control, conventional exile outlets for the Chinese revolutionaries were blocked, making the revolution less transnational. Third, Moscow also instilled a nationalist ideal into the CCP through organizational transformation. In the 1920s, this separated the CCP from Chinese anarchists and China's native cosmopolitans. During the Sino–Japanese War, in the name of purging Trotskyists, Moscow pressed the CCP to engage in national wars with the Japanese. This significantly displaced the CCP's inner universalism, which viewed winning "all under heaven" as the top priority. Lastly, with his geopolitical considerations at the end of the

From an open union to an enclosed nation state 75

protracted revolution, Stalin stepped back from the previous stance of building de facto states at China's northern borders. Without this compromise, the CCP regime would have possessed only the territory of the Song-Ming Dynasty rather than a larger, multi-ethnic China.

The manipulation of nationalism, however, was not always well-designed; nor was it always successful. Despite the Soviet Union's engineering of CCP nationalism, Moscow's long arm was not without limitation. Even in the most "dogmatic" period of the 1930s, the Soviet Union never achieved absolute control over the Chinese revolutionary movement. Despite the outer display of a purge of Trotskyists, the Trotskyist tendency within the CCP remained strong. There was a robust impetus to engage in class struggle as the first priority and a persistent belief that national war and class struggle could proceed in parallel without harming each other. Many CCP elites, having fought the KMT for nearly a decade by 1937, refused to create a united front with the KMT. These people viewed negotiation and collaboration as betrayal (Liu 1990: 100–101). Refusing to join the KMT-led national government, many even threatened to quit the CCP and go home (Liu 2004: 88). This was especially true among those who had joined the CCP after 1927 from rural guerrilla bases. These people had not experienced the CCP's cooperation and friendship with the KMT of the early 1920s. In their recollections, the KMT was equated with atrocities, massacres, and hostility. Having fought guerrilla wars for ten years, these partisans found the switch to a united nationalist front too drastic a change to accept (Zhou 1991: 70). Furthermore, Moscow's manipulation of nationalism was often returned by the CCP. In the mid-1930s, for example, Mao attempted to drag the Soviet Union into war with Japan, to create a state of chaos that would facilitate the CCP's seizure of power (Titov 1981: 78–92).

Resistance to the switch to nationalism also reflected their fear. This was another factor that the Soviets could not overcome. Many cadres who completed training during the civil war had a narrow understanding of the revolution. They lacked skills, other than redistributing and expropriating land, persecuting landlords, and carrying out civil wars. They couldn't imagine how a "national united front" should work if the work of class struggles had to be suspended. Nor did these cadres possess the diplomatic skills to maintain an alliance with their erstwhile enemies—bandits, local strongmen, KMT officers, and businessmen (DUFYC 2010: 32, 89, 200–201). This collective concern was so pervasive that Moscow could not dismiss it through pro-Soviet CCP leaders; it impeded the CCP from switching to anti-Japanese nationalism. As a report of 1944 stated, people tended to view the department of the united front as a non-substantial sector irrelevant to revolution. Because of its liaison with non-communist forces, staff of this sector were the first suspects when anti-spy investigations were carried out (DUFYC

2010: 1944–09). The deep fear of being polluted by "nationalists" thus led to self-isolation, which the CCP termed "closed-doorism" (guanmen zhuyi).

Over the long term, a profound crisis for Moscow's maneuvering of nationalism surfaced. As the CCP's relative power increased, Moscow became unable to confine the CCP revolution within a "nationalist" track under the control of Soviet internationalism. Beijing showed a tendency to develop into a new center of a universal world revolution that offered a path in competition with Moscow's universalism (Friedman 2015). An empire whose anxiety had stimulated a nationalist movement for decades, now suffered the anxiety of watching the rise of a new empire. The same history would be repeated between Moscow and Belgrade and between Beijing and Hanoi.

Notes

1 HIAPO (Archive of the Tsarist Secret Police, Okhrana), Box 190, Index XVIb (2), Folder 1.
2 HIAPO, Box 205, Index XVIIs, Folder 2.
3 HIAPO, Box 205, Index XVIIt, Folder 1.
4 See also HIAPO, Box 212, Index XVIVe, Folder 2.

3

Reconciliation with traditional "Russia" and "China"

As traditional imperial notions declined, the creation of nationalist legitimacy became a critical mission. Without the successful invention of nation(s), the end of the empire would lead to a chaotic situation similar to the Durkheimian "anomaly." However, nation-inventing is not easy. As Rogers Brubaker (1992) says, inventing a nation always involves a hybrid of civic and ethnic definitions. Even the most civic nation must produce ethnic definitions, and the most ethnic nation must involve civic definitions. Meanwhile, these two coexisting dimensions are always in tension. While the civic aspect of nation-inventing looks forward to the future and the general, the ethnic dimension speaks to the past and the concrete. In theory, as both the future and past are endlessly rich supertexts, it is thus always possible to find a crossroad where these two dimensions can be mediated. Yet, for specific nation-builders, not all possibilities are attainable. Nation-builders are restrained by many factors, such as ideologies, the availability of cultural experts, and the audience of their mobilization. The available choices can be so limited that, in some cases, nation-builders pause nation-inventing work.

With regard to reacting to the decline of traditional empires, both the Bolshevik and CCP revolutionaries were active nation-builders. Their difficulties lay in their nation-building project; the civic dimension was in sharp contradiction with the ethnic dimension. In the eyes of the communist elites, there was an enormous gap between revolutionary/socialist ideologies and Russian/Chinese national traditionalism. They believed that the former were more progressive than Anglo-French liberalism and the latter, in its rejection of modernity, fell beneath even German and Japanese fascism. At the earlier stage of the revolutionary movement, they thought it was impossible to base the future they envisaged on the past that they had vehemently criticized. This is why the first generations of the two leading groups carried a strong anti-traditionalist mentality, to the extent that many wanted to abandon the idea of the nation.

But this attitude changed over time. The two supertexts were so rich that it was always possible to find places where they overlapped. When the composition of revolutionaries changed, breakthroughs took place. The Bolsheviks and the CCP elites came to find ways to infuse these two dimensions. At least they began to believe that the contradiction was not as irreconcilable as they had deemed. This change stemmed from many factors. When mobilization expanded, revolutionaries faced a broader audience. To address the changing audience, revolutionaries had to compromise, whether they wanted to or not. As the revolution progressed, an increasing number of intellectuals were drawn to communism, and their skills in disciplining these intellectuals were advanced. Revolutionaries had more accessible access to cultural experts who had better skills in infusing socialist ideologies and national traditions. Moreover, as the revolution's recruitment pattern and generation changed, the revolutionaries adapted to a new habitus and taste. Accepting traditional culture was not morally and aesthetically unacceptable to this new group.

The politics of culture and nationalism

There are multiple ways to invent a nation, but historicity is a central one. Such centrality gives rise to the subarea of cultural nationalism. Scholars view the making of nationalism and national identity as a process of construction, where native languages, folklores, traditional icons, and symbols, as well as popular cultures, are discovered, recovered, or fabricated to shape a common past with which members of a nation collectively identify (Hobsbawm and Ranger 1983). It is a process in which traditional elements, in the formats of folklore, material culture, and performance, are salvaged, inventoried, produced, and propagated (Leerssen 2006). The drives of cultural nationalism stem from multiple sources, but they can be roughly categorized into two: regeneration and vernacularism, which respectively shape the motivation and format (Hutchinson 2013).

While most scholars explicitly explain why cultural nationalism is needed and how it contributes to the shaping of a national identity, the difficult facet of tradition has received less attention. It is noted that the invention of tradition is neither arbitrary nor inevitably successful. Rather, in many places, such efforts are distracted from, competed with, undermined, or even thwarted. Factors that obstruct the making of cultural nationalism cover a wide range. The availability of cultural materials for memory and identity shaping is often emphasized as relevant. Peoples of limited historical memory and linguistic basis encounter more difficulties in inventing their history as one of a nation (Hroch 1985). A common historical memory imbued with heterogeneity, infight, and interethnic killings can hardly serve to cultivate the sense of a national solidarity (Wimmer 2018). By the same

Reconciliation with traditional "Russia" and "China"   79

token, a state-forged national identity that bluntly goes against mass culture can hardly take root (Lord 2017). It is more difficult for some nations to fabricate a coherent and rich image of the past than for others (Spillman 1996), and some historical memories are better suited to arousing patriotic feelings of solidarity than others (Debs 2013).

A second challenge is concerned with agency: that is, the individuals who operate or resist the invention of tradition. This makes sense in that, even a tradition supported by rich cultural materials had a primitive stage, and the task of developing a tradition that bridges the gap between the primitive stage and modern cultural pride requires professional expertise. In terms of agency, the obstruction to the cultural invention of a nation often comes from external pressure, from colonizers-conquerors or domestic oppressors. Cultural nationalists may encounter hard repression or soft discipline from colonial powers (Chatterjee 1986; Said 2003). Finally, and to be further discussed in the following section, the effort of building a national culture based on a community's past can suffer resistance and failures from inside too, which may be caused by internal technical competitiveness to achieve market popularity and internal resistance based on a rigidly understood concept of modernity (Hutchinson and Aberbach 1999).

Tradition, modernization, and revolution

The relationship between revolution and tradition is complicated. It is easy to place the two in contrast with each other. Revolution is certainly a process of breaking tradition, in that it replaces old ethics, lifestyles, and aesthetics with new ones, and even persecutes the individuals who carry the old values. A stereotype of revolutionaries is that they are youths who loathe old trends, viewing tradition as a justifier and symptom of patriarchy, despotism, patron–clientism, ignorance, and other corruptions that a revolution must eradicate. These youths have a good understanding of the past but they loathe it, or they have received no education in the native tradition at all. Yet, more accurately, revolution should be viewed as a reconfiguration rather than an entire negation of the past. Several factors work against a full negation of tradition. One is the need for mass mobilization. No matter how much revolutionary elites reject tradition, if the revolution is to be successful they must mobilize people other than themselves. Traditional cultural icons and symbols are facilitators for mass mobilization from below. They are more successful in evoking psychological echoes among peasants than alien language. Certainly, such use of tradition can be mixed and covert. It can be a simple transfer of original traditional icons, in their most intact state, into the radical arsenal to express a revolutionary idea. Or it can take only some elements from the old repertoire and mix them with new ideas. But either way, the use of tradition must appeal to the mass mentality. According to this thesis, those revolutions that involve minimal mass mobilization have a lessened need for tradition than the ones that involve heavy participation from below.

A second restraint on anti-traditionalist radicalism lies in the revolutionaries themselves. Not only the masses but also revolution-makers may have a resistance to foreign symbols. This stance can be a result of early socialization, education, and living experiences. To be familiar with a nonnative culture, one must reside long enough and engage deeply enough in a foreign community. Yet, very few revolutionaries have actually achieved this. Some of them stay in exile abroad and maintain a transnational network, speaking multiple languages, forcing themselves to only read foreign literature. But even these people continue to engage in local communities comprising people coming from the homeland—using James Scott's term, their knowledge of external societies is mainly of "great tradition," not a "little" one. Some others travel abroad only briefly, for conferences or as short-term political refugees. It is hard to say how such brief experiences shaped these travelers' perception of tradition. However enthusiastically they embrace an advanced world, they often find themselves pushed back, by their arrogant and condescending comrades, to a love of native tradition. Still other revolutionaries, never living outside of their home countries, receive revolutionary ideas only through secondary channels—books, newspapers, dramas, and people returning from abroad. These people, despised by the traveling community as ignorant natives, often fall into conflict with the returnees from abroad, leading to infighting. This category of revolutionary is the most common, owing to factors such as financial resources and linguistic capacity. As a revolution expands and requires increasingly large forces, the proportion of homegrown revolutionaries enlarges. While some revolutions manage to seize power with a relatively small revolutionary force, others must draw on a wide range of potential revolutionaries to achieve their aim.

One more restraint, no less important, comes from the enemies of the revolution. Counterrevolutionaries invoke traditional culture as well; how they invoke it affects the position of revolutionaries. It is usual that enemies of revolution depend on conservative values, though they are not necessarily hardliners in defending everything from the past. They advocate drawing on the past in a reformist way, rather than totally negating it. This position leads them to criticize revolutionaries' radical break with the past. A commonly used strategy in this regard is to accuse revolutionaries of "vandalism" and "barbarism," in order to evoke an alienation from revolution among both the elites and the masses. Such attacks need not be fully addressed, but they must be reckoned with. They do have the effect of moderating revolutionaries' attacks on traditional culture. Revolutionaries come to realize that endless and indiscriminatory destruction of everything about the "past" might alienate them from sympathizers at home and abroad, and incur more enemies. The effect of an attack by "reactionaries" hinges on their way of invoking traditions. An intellectually crude and exclusive attack is less worrisome for revolutionaries, as such traditionalism has been in itself sufficient to arouse popular antipathy. On the other hand, a reformist traditionalism preached by a well-established regime, can be highly effective in winning hearts and minds against revolutionaries.

A more complicated issue is the availability of qualified framers—experts able to frame the past as part of revolution. However well led and widely supported, revolutions must involve traditional elements—it is impossible to fully dis-embed from a given society. In the course of absorbing existing elements, a technical problem surfaces in how to ensure that this process unfolds in a legitimate way, maintaining a balance between efficient mobilization and ideological rightness. This requires knowledge and skills. Sophisticated literati, aware of the tension between revolution and the past, matchmake the two in a way that may be covert or open, while being aesthetically elegant. In contrast, crude ideologues lack such capacity, either refusing to make such a match or making it in an illegitimate manner. For radical groups without skilled literati, the most secure strategy is to assert a resolute break with the past, in order to avoid the framing work that they are unable to handle adeptly. The availability of qualified framers stems from multiple factors, ranging from a society's general intellectual development to the level of participation by intellectuals in radical politics. In a society where intellectuals are distant from radical politics, revolutionary movements are more likely to undertake an openly anti-traditionalist stance.

The Great Retreat theory

The "Great Retreat" thesis argues that communist movements in the process of enlarging social mobilization would retreat from their early anti-traditional position to reinvent tradition. It started with Leon Trotsky's thesis on "the revolution betrayed," which argues that the bureaucrats had usurped the communist party during the Civil War (Trotsky 1937). Later, in George Orwell's *Animal Farm*, a similar thesis was formulated that revolutionary regimes, in the long term, tended to retreat back to normal and reconcile with the foes they had intended to overthrow (Orwell 1946). In Orwell's writing, the retreat mainly referred to a failure to overcome the emergence of stratification and hierarchy in pursuit of a revolutionary social transformation. The scholar who formally coined the term "Great Retreat," in writing about the Soviet Union, was Nicolai Timasheff (1948). His theory was that the communist regime had retreated from its original internationalism to a revival of Russo-centric national traditional symbols, while reneging on revolutionary promises by adopting policies such as bureaucratization, terror, and a restoration of hierarchy, centralization, and coexistence with capitalism.

Since Timasheff, a great deal of scholarship has been produced to explain why this retreat occurred. Most literature highlights four factors. First and foremost, the revolutionary program was unworkable, and it was soon or later to be replaced or displaced by traditional ethics and behavioral patterns, which were named "neo-traditionalism." Second, communist regimes had to confront geopolitical pressures and international competitions, which compelled them to switch to nationalism as a supplementary mobilizational frame. Third, from a Weberian perspective, retreat means routinization. The completion of socialist transformation made the old frame of class warfare pointless, and the endless use of terror to control society was unaffordable. A bridge over the vacuum that this produced was found in the language of national solidarity. Nationalism, which involved traditional and folk symbols, was more efficient than internationalist-cosmopolitan culture. Fourth, reconciliation with native language, schemes, and cultural symbols facilitated administration and mass education by providing a streamlined and clear-centered narrative (Brandenberger 2002; Brandenberger 2016; Dubrovskii 2018: 24–25; Fitzpatrick 1992; Janos 1991; Jowitt 1983; Yilmaz 2015: 13–14).

The Great Retreat theory's main blind spot is the risk of retreat. Moving to routinization involved not only the opportunities for regime survival but also the risks of losing revolutionary momentum, since counter-tradition action had been a cornerstone to the legitimacy of revolutionary movement. There were benefits to returning to a normal way of running the state, army, social economy, and cultural life, but using old legacies without any innovations blurred the boundary with the enemy and obscured the necessity of a revolutionary takeover. This was not a secure signal in a situation where reactionaries and counter-revolutionaries were more infused with and defensive of the old social structure. Even after domestic enemies had been smashed, a revolutionary regime still faced the pressure to demonstrate that the revolution had created something new, and such inventions were necessary. This may apply to industrialization, economic development, and the improvement of human health and education, as well as general psychological status. For all these concerns, the actual process of retreat was not like a smooth free fall, but rather a struggle and arduous exploration in inventing a new tradition.

Reconciliation with traditional "Russia" and "China"   83

The relationship with nationalism was a major and most visible aspect to which scholars of "Great Retreat" theory refer. Most communist regimes, early or late, returned from a past-breaking ideology to a refined nationalist tradition-invention, that is, "national communism." Retreat in the form of national communism might occur at multiple levels, from covert support for irridentism to discreet emphasis on "national interests of socialism" and then to overt celebration of ancient heroes (Banac 1992; Brunnbauer 2011: 358–59; Chandler 1999: 165–70; Deák 1992; Kořalka 1992; Ladwig 2017: 287–88; Stuart-Fox 1983: 448–52). The variation among the multiple revolutionary movements of the twentieth century suggests that the retreat could also occur at different times between power seizure and consolidation. For some revolutions, mainly the Chinese, it came rather early, when communists were still amid the struggle for national power. For some other revolutions, the Russian and most Eastern European ones, retreat arrived late, only after the consolidation of power had been established for a while. Still other revolutions were so unsettled and short-lived that they ended before the retreat could get started. Examples of this are the German Revolution of 1923 and revolutions in the Indochinese Peninsula. Such a variation indicated that there was no fixed relationship between nationalism and communism in terms of dealing with a nation's cultural tradition—diachronically within each revolution this relationship changed, and the difference over timing requires an explanation.

Both the Bolshevik and Chinese revolutions underwent "great retreats," but in different ways, and each represented an archetype. For the Bolsheviks, the attacks and the retreats occurred in two relatively separate stages. The Bolsheviks first took power with the original revolutionary ideology of breaking with the past, creating the Soviet Union, before eventually retreating to a reinvented "Russianness." For the CCP, these two stages were intertwined and shaped one another. Though the early period, in terms of attitude toward "Chineseness," resembled the Bolsheviks' attitude to "Russianness" before Stalinism, a process of retreat and reinvention unfolded throughout the ensuing two decades. By the end of the protracted revolution, "Chineseness" remained vague in terms of concrete substance but had been imparted by revolutionaries with a likelihood of becoming progressive. The outcome was that, when founding a national regime, the CCP was far less reluctant to embrace "Chineseness" than the Bolsheviks had to engage "Russianness." This had a great effect on how the two communist parties imagined the reorganization of the former imperial territories: the CCP revolution was a process of Sinicization and the Bolshevik revolution was one of de-Russification. "Russia" as the overarching title of the former empire was removed.

84 *Revolution in China and Russia*

Russia's transcendence to overcome inferiority vis-à-vis the West

With its earliest state created in the ninth century, much later than most European countries, Russia had been playing catch-up since its birth. Accordingly, a sense of inferiority was perennial in Russia's cultural development, with first Byzantium and the West as advanced others to look up to. A pervasive contempt of native Russian culture stemmed from several sources. One, according to Max Weber (Pipes 1955), was Russia's general primitive and underdeveloped stage of a civic culture, in comparison with Western Europe and North America. As Durkheim argues, in Russia the society was organized by the state, not the other way around, as in the West (Durkheim 2003). Russia did have cultural elements on which to build the foundation of a nation: the Russian language did not vary by region, and there was a shared memory of historical figures and entities such as Ivan the Terrible, Dmitri Donskoi, the early Rus states, and the Eastern Orthodox church; but these elements were not sufficient for the development of a national consciousness strong enough to drive political nationhood (Brandenberger 2002). Aware of this problem, tsars and intellectuals sought to learn from the outside how to make the barren soil fertile. This endeavor forged a second source of antipathy: Russian nationalism was closely tied with tsardom and thus incurred attack, which gained a new target when the tsarist state openly switched to grab the banner of nationalism in the late nineteenth century. Russian state nationalism, self-identifying with autocracy, Orthodoxy, military expansion, and rural ethics, was criticized from every progressive perspective. In historians' writings, the official effort of forging a Russian nation was described as inefficient and subject to backlash; rather than diminishing social gulfs, it stimulated peripheral nationalism and it excluded social groups (Brandenberger 2002; Kappeler 2001: 348–53, 362–66; Lieven 1999; Moon 1996).

On the other side of the coin, there was a persistent effort to create a unique framework to separate Russia from tsardom. Various efforts to forge a non-monarchial Russian identity had been ongoing before the revolution of 1917. As is well known by historians, an anti-tsarist consensus had taken shape among the middle class and intellectual circles in the years prior to the outbreak of World War I, and this was further fostered by the setbacks during the war. In the military, for example, a professional ethics to safeguard the Russian nation against the danger of civil war and foreign occupation significantly grew in the course of World War I among the officers who supported a republican or restrained-monarchial replacement. The imperial family's performance disappointed many frontline officers, engendering a nationalist discourse that the House of Romanov was more a German ally than a Russian monarchy. It was also in the military that nationalist propaganda got started, mostly in the form of misinformation and demonization of the foe rather than glorification of the self. The emotional contest with the West culminated in the Civil War, when Allies intruded the core of the Russian territory and even proposed to partition Russia as they divided the Hapsburg and Ottoman empires. It is thus incorrect to assume that in 1917 there was no "healthy" Russian nationalism that revolutionaries could speak to.

An alternative approach to making a Russian nation—equally significant and persistent, and intellectual as well as political—was to develop an identity that transcended the narrow and indeed problematic ethnic concept of Russia; once all of Europe and the world had been included, the "Russian Problem" would surely be addressed. Such an endeavor was supported by the tsar, the intelligentsia, and the middle class, as well as by the revolutionaries, and a clear distinction from the experiment to forge a Russian nationalism was always maintained. The most visible and consistent attempts were Orthodox messianism, Pan-Slavism, and Eurasianism. Orthodox messianism believed that Russia was the chosen nation obliged to extend its own salvation to the ends of the world. It was preached by leading Slavophile thinkers and strategically invoked by the tsarist state in geopolitical operations. Russian messianism involved many ethnically non-Russian thinkers and church scholars that the "Russian" had to be defined in a transcendent way (Shevzov 2020: 42–43). However, it would be misleading to deem that such a transcendent endeavor was intrinsically dependent on the tsarist state. Toward the end of the Romanov dynasty, during the reign of Nicolas II, the Orthodox Church, navigating the turmoil of Russian society, came to seek a more independent position in relation to the state. This shift posed a serious challenge to the state–church relationship that had been in place since the reform of Peter the Great (Kizenko 2020).

Two transcendent ideals that were more separable from tsardom and Eastern Christianity than Orthodox messianism were Pan-Slavism and Eurasianism. Pan-Slavism was preached among intellectuals, envisioning a pan-Slavic polity encompassing the western Russian borders, Baltic Region, Poland, and Balkan Peninsula. It was appropriated by the tsarist state as a strategic discourse to support overseas geopolitical operations, but the political influences faded after the Russo-Turkish War, and the movement degraded into a cultural one (Gleason 2004). The major thrust of Slavism applied to the empire's western front, inhabited by Slavic peoples, and had less value in supporting the expansion into the Caucasian South and Asian East. In the ensuing three decades, Pan-Slavism was succeeded by Eurasianism, an intellectual endeavor to reinterpret Russia's separateness from the West. Eurasianists identified Russia as an amalgamation of

86   *Revolution in China and Russia*

multiple ethnic groups distinct from both East and West. The cultural effort of building a transcendent policy was popular among archeologists, anthropologists, philologists, literary critics, historians, ethnographers, and public writers. The primitive nomads and mountaineers unpolluted by industrial civilization, argued Eurasianists, had preserved the original source of human revival, which the West had lost. After the Bolshevik takeover, leading figures began to think of Soviet Russia as a new civilization that played an indispensable role in defending the West from the "yellow peril," and civilizing Asia (Duncan 2000).

Compared with Pan-Slavism and Orthodox messianism, Eurasianism was the most compatible with revolutionaries who looked forward to an all-imperial revolt, given that intellectually, Eurasianism did not assert any biological determinism or religious exclusivism to confine itself. The "peoples of Eurasia were united not by a race, but rather by a common historical faith" (Tolz 2015: 32). Eurasianism's attack on the West was deeply affinitive with revolutionary thought. Articulated by Alexander Herzen, it criticized materialism, democratization, and colonialism as the sins of the West, and claimed that a Eurasian civilization would offer a superior alternative by preserving the "barbarian" energy inherited from the Mongolian Empire and Asian neighbors. The revolutionary thrust thus extended to accuse the Romanov House of being a Western agent in corrupting Russian society from above (Maiorova 2015: 22–25). All these major factors—national liberation, anti-materialism, rejection of representative democracy—came to enter the Bolshevik Revolution in a complicated manner. The Soviet Union was a project that fostered de-Russification, de-territorialization, and de-imperialization at an open institutional level while in practice, it often acted against these ideals.

The early generation of Bolsheviks were both inheritors of and contenders with Russia's tradition. They inherited Russian intellectuals' conventional anxiety about Russia's cultural inferiority vis-à-vis the West, and accordingly looked forward to a unified Europe that would accept Russia as its member. They did not think that Russia could survive by self-isolating from Europe. Unlike imperial missionaries, scholars, and statesmen, however, the Bolsheviks appeared to be less obsessed with creating a unique Russian road in an effort to surpass Western civilization. Their contempt of Russia's backwardness and barbarism was real, at least among those who had lived in the West for a long period. The Bolsheviks merely requested a pan-European revolution, in which Russia, at most, would play a leading role in igniting the fire. Once the old regime had been swept away, as the early Bolsheviks imagined, Russia's disparity with Europe in every regard would finally return the leading power to the industrial Europe, and Russia would obtain an equal position by virtue of its contribution to the revolution.

The Bolsheviks' low estimation of Russian culture

The Bolsheviks' backgrounds made them oppose almost all existing efforts to invent a Russian nation. Their collective biographies suggest three common features. First, most of them self-claimed as atheists, having become detached from Orthodoxy through their reading of Darwin, Buffon, and Lavoisier. Some boasted in their autobiographies of their conflicts with the clergy, their refusal to swear an oath at military conscription, and their participation in iconoclastic campaigns (Allen 2015: 29–32; Davidov 1961: 8; Khromov et al. 1988: 13; Levidova and Salita 1969: 26). Second, unlike certain socialist parties such as the Laborists, who considered constitutional monarchy acceptable, the Bolsheviks rejected this idea. Reading Pisarev, Shedrin, Belinskii, Chernyshevskii, Tolstoy, and Dubroliubov, most Russian Bolsheviks regarded the tsarist state as a barbarian regime that exerted brutal punishment and valued old-fashioned nobility aesthetics and patriarchal structure (Fateev and Korolev 1988: 75). There was also a generational factor in the republican attitude of most Bolsheviks. They had been radicalized between the 1905 revolution and World War I, a period during which the tsar's legitimacy was challenged. The Slavic movement, as a "cultural nationalist response to Russia's failure to become part of Europe," opposed the socialist movement, criticizing the latter of neglecting individual self-improvement, of having an over-commitment to written constitutions, and a materialist worldview lacking in spiritual values (Rabow-Edling 2006: 141).

This doesn't mean that the Bolsheviks-in-making had no knowledge of what was going on. The early experiences of some prominent Bolsheviks exemplify what a Russian pupil in the 1890s would study. Having passed exams in basic Latin and Greek, in a history test, Lenin wrote answers on medieval Slavs, the Khemernistky Uprising, the annexation of Ukraine, and Church schism (IMTsK 1971, 1: 24–25). Bukharin recalled that at school students were divided into two streams. The highbrow ones carried the volumes of Solov'ev, Niche, and British and French novelists, pretending they had read them all. The radical ones, on the other hand, read native writers such as Pisarev and Gorky. The latter group approached Russian history from the very practical perspective of how to make a revolution (Slezkine 2019: 27). Elena Stasova, from a family of lawyers, recalled her musical education listening to Glinka, Mussorgsky, Borodin, Rubinstein, Kologrikov, and Balakirev. Her leisure reading at school covered Karyshev, Uspenskii, Zlatovratskii, and Vorontsov-Vel'iaminov (Levidova and Salita 1969: 16–18).

The subtle fact was that the Bolsheviks claimed that they were more influenced by non-Russian and non-native thought. Vladimir Lenin, for example, completed his school education with extensive knowledge about medieval Russia (Startsev 1970). Not an anti-traditionalist as radical as the "Proletarian Culture School," he insisted that classic literature should be circulated to eradicate illiteracy and that historical heritage had to be preserved (Lenin 1956: 12–14, 43–44). Nevertheless, except for Chernyshevskii and a few other "revolutionary democrats," Lenin rarely cited any Russian native sources. In his writings there was no place for the military science of Alexander Suvorov or Mikhail Kutuzov, the political wisdom of Ivan IV or Catherine II, or even Stepan Razin's and Yemel'ian Pugachev's skills in leading peasant rebellions. What he was obsessed with was revolutionary lessons from Europe, even the failed ones. As Krupskaya recollected, Lenin was not interested in ordinary museums, spending only ten minutes in the British Museum in London. But he loved the Museum of the 1848 Revolution in Paris, closely examining each exhibit and making notes (Krupskaya 2015 [1933]: 55).

As the supreme leader of the Bolsheviks, Vladimir Lenin had never stopped warning against the danger of Russian nationalism (in his words, the "Great Russian chauvinism"). In the years before 1917, Lenin had argued that the level of capitalist development in Russia proper was lower than that at the peripheries, which disqualified Russia's assimilation of the other nations (Lenin 1971: 51–52). In principle, Lenin was not against the use of Russian classics to expand literacy and education, which was the precondition to moving on to communism—he was critical of the School of Proletarian Culture for the latter's futurism inaccessible to the masses (Lenin 1956: 12, 19–20, 48–49). Lenin insisted that the legacies of the past were mixed, and time was needed to separate the progressive from reactionary ones. According to Lenin, most Great Russian writers had reactionary elements in their thinking, required rectification before being introduced into socialist teaching (Lenin 1956: 15–16). To dilute the toxic Russian legacies, Lenin insisted that the Soviet Union should be a cosmopolitan inheritor of all world civilization, which would function as a guarantee that the socialist regime would not degenerate into chauvinism (Lenin 1956: 23). Lenin saw this threat as real. In December1922 he asserted that the Bolsheviks had been so preoccupied with the civil war that they had simply accepted the apparatus of the tsarist Russian state, without recognizing that it had been polluted by Russian chauvinism (Fyson 1995: 194).

This indifference and even hostility toward Russian native culture was prevalent among the Bolsheviks who led the revolution. In terms of literature, the Bolsheviks boasted of their outdated taste, rarely invoking any contemporary writers and presenting the image of reading only Chernyshevskii, Pisarev, Herzen, and Nekrasov (Zhou 2019b: 12–13). Bukharin, for example, claimed that he had been a fan of Pisarev and Saldykov-Shchedrin since childhood, receptive to the latter's assertion that Russia was a culturally

Reconciliation with traditional "Russia" and "China" 89

bare soil that could only produce evil flowers. Even so, Bukharin did not forget to qualify that "Saldykov-Shchedrin was after all a Russian native writer, without the worldwide influence Heine had" (Bukharin 1924: 25). In the area of history, the only sources cited by the Bolsheviks were George Plekhanov and Mikhail Pokrovsky, who had influenced one of the most important Bolshevik leaders, Leon Trotsky. Plekhanov depicted Russian society as an interlocked system that had no internal momentum to move upward into capitalism, which indicated the absolute necessity of inviting a world revolution for rescue from outside (Baron 1974). Pokrovskii, a Marxist historian, wrote of Russia as a prison of peoples, where commercial capital, in close alliance with international powers and the tsarist state, traveled over Russian land as well as across borders, in perpetuating brutal exploitation at will (Pokrovskii 1915). Pokrovskii's most popular two-volume textbook on Russian culture included a small section, less than eighty pages of the total six hundred, to pre-Petrine Russia. Even such a small section had little description of Russia's cultural achievement, but rather was devoted to articulating the story of how "commercial capital" drove Novgorod and Moscow Duchies to open and maintain transportation for business (Pokrovskii 1933). Pokrovskii's style of writing Russian history as a tragedy of the cultivation of transnational capital was in sharp contrast with contemporary non-Marxist textbooks that admired early Rus's endeavor to absorb all advanced cultures even when they came from the enemies and oppressors. It is thus not surprising that in the 1930s he came under fierce attack by a young generation of scholars for the absence, in his socioeconomic history, of positive research on the nationhood of Soviet peoples, either Russian or non-Russian (Amacher 2018).

The Bolsheviks' vocal negation of Russian culture doesn't mean that the past left no imprint on them. Rather, revolutionary thinking had a profound affinity with traditional Russian cultural elements that the Bolsheviks denounced rhetorically, but only in indirect, covert, and unconscious ways. In the early 1920s there were no institutionalized efforts, comparable in depth and magnitude to the neo-classicism of High Stalinism, to glorify the cultural icons of the Russian past. The things of the past could be 're-purposed' to suit the revolutionary cause, and the main ideological thrust was future-oriented. Anatolii Lunacharskii openly saw an analogy between socialism with Christianity, celebrating socialism as a new citizen religion, which devoted worship to the full potential of humankind to be realized in the future (O'Connor 1991). Lunacharskii was a distinctive example, in that he himself was at the same time the leader of "Proletarian Culture." The equally important imprint from the past was Lunacharskii's messianism, whereby he believed that revolutionary Russia was to build "a messianic kingdom on the earth" (Duncan 2000: 54–55). Other leading Bolsheviks saw the affinity between socialism and religious universalism as well, including Felix Dzerzhinskii, who sought a universalism to transcend ethnic tensions in his own identity, and Alexander Shliapnikov, who came from an Old-Believer family inspired by the religious rebellions against the tsarist state (Allen 2015).

A materialist-revolutionary view of "Russia"

Evading an essentialist and culturalist conception of "Russian," the Bolsheviks' notion of a multinational Russia carried organizational, physical, and material connotations. Aleksei Rykov, the first chairman of the Soviet Supreme National Economy Committee, was an ethnic Russian. At school he had read historian Dmitrii Ilovaiskii's textbook, and he refuted Ilovaiskii's monarchist interpretation in legitimizing multinational integration (Shlestov 1990: 51). Accordingly, Rykov's understanding of Russia was a revolutionary one that evaded any essentialist limitation, holding that each nationality should be equally respected for its language, culture, and economic interests. This stand persisted into the years after the takeover of 1917. In debating with the opponents of federation, Rykov emphasized that unification had to be confined to the economic dimension, and even in the economic dimension, a hyper-centralized control should be merely expedient and temporary (Shlestov 1990: 136). He urged regional leaders to survey the geographical and economic information within their jurisdiction, so that the ultra-centralized War Communist Model would be more compatible with the special conditions of a region. This put enormous pressure on bureaucrats, as such survey work required a number of professionals who were simply unavailable in the Soviet Russia of that period (Shlestov 1990: 144).

Nikolai Bukharin, the Bolshevik's leading theoretician, defended a multinational Russia by negating nationalism—including Russian nationalism—entirely, which led to his disagreement with Lenin (Cohen 1980: 61). Bukharin condemned tsarist Russia as an imprisoner of weak nations, in which, he believed, the sole common denominator—the Russian language—was no more than an abusive language to facilitate class exploitation. This stemmed from his early obsession with the Russian radical writer Pisarev, who depicted Russia as evil soil unable to grow a healthy culture (Cohen 1980: 10–11). Bukharin thought the different parts of the former Russian empire should stay together because these regions relied on each other for resources. (Bukharin and Preobrazhensky 1966 [1922]: 195). They should hold together for this reason, not because they were one nation. Bukharin viewed the idea that they were of one Russian nation as mistaken. He thought national enmities were outdated, the vestiges of intertribal

Reconciliation with traditional "Russia" and "China"   91

hostility, and that the bourgeoisie lied to convince its own proletariat that the latter's enemies are not to be found among fellow countrymen but among the people of other lands (Bukharin and Preobrazhensky 1966 [1922]: 196). He argued that the working class would speedily realize that the bourgeoisie sought independence for the sake of their own right to flay the proletariat (Bukharin and Preobrazhensky 1966 [1922]: 199).

Mikhail Kalinin, "head of the Soviet village," developed a more material concept of a Soviet multinational Russia. Like most Russian Bolsheviks, he had no early positive experiences associated with his Russian identity. His deeply held concept of Russian integration surfaced only after the revolutionary takeover of 1917 (IMTsK 1975: 9–12). Appointed as the principal leader of the 1920 electrification of the national economy, Kalinin, together with Krzhizhanovskii, Bubnov, and Aleksandrov, directed the planning of the first round of economic regionalization. This project, in its 1922 edition, divided the former tsarist Russian territory into twenty-two zones, encompassing the non-Russian areas such as the Western borders, the Caucasus, Ukraine, Kuznetsky-Altai, Western Kazakhstan, and Central Asia. This work, as Soviet economic geographers later put it, was an agenda-setting work of building a unified socialist economy through engineering interdependency among regions (Baranskii 1965: 65–66). In April 1919, a concept of mutual integration had appeared in Kalinin's speech, arguing that Soviet Russia had to acquire rich resources ("oil, wool, cotton, and bread") from Don, Turkestan, Baku, and Siberia (IMTsK 1960: 49). According to Kalinin, the integration of multiple Russian nations didn't need special legitimization after a socialist revolution had been completed, as they had mutually depended on each other over the previous millennium. They "used to be free … until Russia transited into serfdom" (IMTsK 1960: 255).

Unlike Kalinin, who traveled within the Russia proper, Sergei Kirov, the party head in Leningrad who was assassinated in 1934, spent a significant part of his pre-1917 years at the imperial periphery, in the Caucasus, where he wrote columns for a local liberal newspaper and mingled with socialists (Kirilina 2001: 25–26). As an ethnic Russian originally from Viatka, he was not moved to patriotic fervor by his reading about international conflicts (Kirilina 2001: 18–19). Rather, it was his incitement of agitations in factories across Northern Caucasus that led him to see this region as indivisible from Russia. After the February Revolution, Kirov declared a Republic of Derska, but he soon retreated northward to Astrakhan, where the 11th Army, under his command, was to guard the mouth of the Volga into the Caspian Sea. For the remainder of the Civil War, he actively worked on guaranteeing the oil transportation from Baku to Astrakhan to fuel the Soviet forces at the southern front. This led him to be in charge of the guerrilla uprisings in Georgia and Azerbaijan, both of which in were annexed to Soviet Russia in 1920

92   *Revolution in China and Russia*

under the title of Transcaucasian Federation (Morozov 1949: 5–7, 11–12). In August 1920, in a letter to Lenin, Kirov claimed that "local Muslims and Armenians counted on the Soviet state to solve the problems that had tortured them" (OGIZ 1944: 11).

Revolutionary de-Russification would have a far-reaching and recurrent historical impact as a core element of the October legacy. Though under Stalin's reign the Soviet ideology retreated, in the sense of bringing back certain Russian elements—cultural symbolic, linguistic Russification, and massive promotion of Russian cadres—the Soviet framework had never been shaken to the point of homogenization into a Russian nation state (Rees 1998: 101–2). After Stalin's death, Soviet rulers invoked Lenin's internationalism for their agenda. It was based on the slogan of "return to Lenin" that Khrushchev implemented his programs of "Soviet civic nation state," the anti-church campaign, reconciliation with the West, and regionalization (Brudny 1998: 42–43; Kurganov 1961). The Brezhnevian power division with local governors and Gorbachev's glasnost started with making the federalist structure work again.

How a de-Russified revolutionary cultural politics worked between 1917 and 1927

Many Bolshevik ideologues were educated in cultural milieus that were radically opposed to Russian nationalism, viewing it as the origin of the nation's misery to which revolutionaries and modernizers should never return. This aversion stemmed from a variety of sources. One was the longstanding debate regarding the origin and character of Russian culture. Many Bolsheviks, like "Westerners" of the early 1800s, despised Russian native culture as a combination of Byzantine and Mongolian legacies that prevented integration into modern Western civilization. This concern was manifested in the Bolsheviks' struggle in Siberia and the Far East to which they were exiled and deported. To maintain their "European" and "proletarian" mindset, they made every effort to remain separate from the local "oriental," "Asian," "agrarian" cultures: not learning local languages, not marrying local women, and even not engaging in agricultural labor. This attitude was also manifested in the early stages of World War I, when certain future Bolsheviks, such as Georgy Chicherin, asserted a war-supporting position that autocratic states, including the fatherland, should be defeated by progressive states like Britain and France (Debo 1966: 652–63).

Alienation also came from ethnic politics. A certain cadre of those who were considered to be non-Russians, especially Poles and Jews, had a sense of "rootlessness": born into one ethnicity, socialized in a second language, and possibly

Reconciliation with traditional "Russia" and "China" 93

educated in a third country. To these people, Russian nationalism, either official or societal, was first and foremost a program of exclusion, discrimination, and oppression, whereas their own nations either seemed too weak to withstand Russia's dominance or alien to their own sense of identity. For these people, the futurist face of Marxism, with its reason-based universalism, was intellectually and politically more attractive. In this regard, a representative case was Karl Radek, a German-speaking Jew born in Lemberg (now L'viv) in what was then the Austro-Hungarian Empire. Radek socialized with Poles, traveled across Western European countries, and devoted himself to the Russian revolutionary movement (Lerner 1970; Radek, Cummings and Brown 1966 [1935]).

In other occasions, indifference was a result of unfamiliarity. Common to the background of most of the Bolshevik leaders was the long experience of overseas exile. This had the effect of alienating these individuals from Russian society and people. Unlike most CCP elites, who stayed in the USSR for no longer than two years, many Bolshevik leaders, such as Lenin, Zinov'ev, Kollontai, Bukharin, and Bogdanov, left Russia in their early years and stayed in Europe for over a decade. Immersed in overseas dissident readings, engaging in partisan polemics, and struggling for subsistence, they did not find it easy to closely follow the cultural trends occurring inside of their homeland. To these people, their intellectual and linguistic comparative advantage vis-à-vis their rivals resided in their familiarity with Marxist classics rather than native mobilizational symbols.

While personal development took shape during the years prior to revolution, one major concern—to distinguish the Bolsheviks from counterrevolutionaries—came from the revolution itself. This was evident in the debate on "Proletarian Culture," which formally started in 1922, but which had arguably surfaced in 1920 (Biggart 1987). The concern was that, because many reactionaries were cultural conservatives or had built their political opposition on the restoration of bourgeois legacies, they could use culture as a weapon after they had been politically and militarily defeated. Accordingly, it was necessary for the Soviet state to create a "proletarian culture" to counterbalance the foes of revolution (Calverton 1929). This concern led to a blossoming of cultural experiments throughout the 1920s, including Lunacharkii's "God-building" project to forge a socialist religion and new Soviet citizen (O'Connor 1991); Trotsky's librarian-soldier program (Baker and Hurych 1991); and Krupskaya's insistence on all-round human development (Read 2006).

In such a context, in waging mass mobilization, ideologues would first consult their orthodox Marxist "toolkit"—the insufficiency of this toolkit would surface only as mobilization extended from a narrow worker-intellectual group out to the ocean of workers and peasants. Other than a

94   *Revolution in China and Russia*

minority of "Proletarian culturists" who had no interest in politics or minimal knowledge of Russian folk culture (Lunacharskii 1968: 236–38), few leading Bolsheviks denounced the old Russian cultural legacy uncritically. For Lunacharskii, for example, socialist culture was based on the past but forward-looking, which led to his future-oriented project of building God. According to Lunacharskii, capitalist society failed to meet humans' psychological needs, which had allowed religion to survive the industrial revolution. Socialism would solve this problem by offering a god—the fulfillment of human potential. This project underwent intense criticism after Lenin's death, and Lunacharskii was accused of confusing the masses when the Soviet state attempted to suppress religion (O'Connor 1991).

For Trotsky, communist education placed priority on training the technical staff that were sorely needed—diplomats, military commanders, and economic planners—and on imparting a socialist outlook to non-Russian nations (Trotsky 2020 [1973]: 144–45, 153–55). In terms of human development, he highlighted economic reason, which taught individuals to organize production in a rational way. He also suggested that an educated socialist should be able to analyze dialectical connections between areas rather than self-limit and be biased to a single narrow one, as bourgeois specialists had done (Trotsky 2020 [1973]: 183–86). As part of his attack on "Proletarian culture school," Trotsky did mention that worker correspondents should study the linguistic habits and psychology of readers. However, in this regard he put emphasis on technical improvement, such as using maps, avoiding jargon, and instilling a socialist outlook by reporting social events (Trotsky 2020 [1973]: 163–66, 233–34). He opposed the annihilation of the past, but stopped short of reintegrating folklore, tsars, and generals.

Likewise, Krupskaya's "communist ethics" project drew little on the past. In her project of 1918 on socialist education, she argued that cultivation should go against the bourgeois principle of downplaying absolute obedience, competition, the notion of private property, and strife among students—according to Krupskaya, this would be a way to prevent militarist combat among proletarian nations (Krupskaya 1957). After the Civil War, her ideal of cultural construction switched to advocate a personality cult of Lenin, which started the institutionalized practice of personifying socialist ideology in the Soviet mass education system. Recollecting Lenin's personal life, Krupskaya elaborated a list of features as the standard virtues that every socialist citizen was supposed to possess: passion with attachment to working class, aesthetic taste in reading radical Russian writers (Chernyshevskii, Shchedrin, Belinskii, Dubroliubov, Pisarev, Nekrasov), socializing with international socialists, and collectively fighting bourgeois democracy (Krupskaya 2011: 45–46). Krupskaya was also opposed to sheer utilitarianism, the so-called "productionism." Rather, she insisted in the overall

Reconciliation with traditional "Russia" and "China" 95

development of the human being, to eliminate the gap between mental and physical labor (Read 2006: 252). Like Trotsky, she opposed a radical break with the past, but never went to the extreme of Stalin's "revolutionary patriotism."

It cannot be denied that many Bolshevik ideologues were nationalists mentally, in the sense that they continued to consider Russia a distinct national entity playing a role in the World Revolution. Yet even these people in the 1920s had not moved so far as to advocate for a full recovery of traditional cultural symbols. At this stage, national socialists had more urgent affairs to deal with. During the Civil War, the red patriotic element was downplayed in the propaganda in favor of an emphasis on the spread of communism outside of Russia by exerting influence among foreign socialist and syndicalist groups (Westergard-Thorpe 2016). Individuals like Stalin were boosting "socialism in one country," but this doctrine was largely a program of economic autarchy and political contraction against the idea of world revolution (Ree 1998).

Nor did involvement in ethnopolitics lead the Soviet state to immediately recover old traditions. Prior to their seizure of power, the Bolsheviks had limited concern for the nationality question. The concept "internationalism" became a regularly used term by the Bolsheviks only after the takeover in November 1917. This term remained an ambiguous one, in that "nation" referred to national minorities as well as to national states (Borisova 2016). Though overt, it first and foremost applied to more substantial political affairs, such as permitting self-determination, obtaining national independence, demarcating national borders, and economic decolonization (Stalin 2013, 4: 296–97, 351–60, 398–401, 5: 90–97, 47–50).

During the Civil War, when the Bolsheviks were coming to occupy state and national powers of resource distribution, there were repeated attempts to forge a highly centralized indoctrination machine. Yet, such efforts could be best evaluated as formal, if not superficial. The Bolsheviks' unpreparedness for Civil War in 1918 impeded the desired administrative centralization of cultural production, with priority given to military and economic nationalization. This period saw the foundations of many bureaucratic institutions set up to monitor political education, film, print, and publishing, including the Political Department of the Red Army (PUR), the filmmaking subsection of the Extramural Educational Ministry (January 1918), Gosizdat (May 1918), the State Central Publishing House (early 1919), and the Central Book Committee (Tsentrokniga) (Kenez 1985: 58, 96–99; Kenez 2001: 31). Limited by extreme material hardship, these institutions could barely meet their goals of approaching the masses, and they had to rely on propagandists improvising and taking individual initiative. Despite having completed several rounds of nationalization, they had not yet established

96 *Revolution in China and Russia*

a strong policy of censorship or of directing the content of cultural products. Cultural production either broke down entirely or was downgraded to rather simple forms. Many institutions that proved stable and efficient came into being after the Civil War, such as Goskino (1922), Sovkino (1925), Krasnaya Pechat' (1922–1928), and Agitprop within the Central Committee (1928).

In terms of institutional coherence, the young Soviet state had not yet worked out a unified standard of aesthetics for creating working-class arts (Bonnell 1997: 26). Within the Bolshevik effort to create a communist cultural hegemony, a fight broke out between the school of "Proletarian culture" and centralizers on whether a proletarian ideology should be instilled by a central body or grow spontaneously from social cells. This debate persisted among the Red Army's Political Department, Lunacharskii's Commissariat of Enlightenment, and Krupskaya's Department of Extramural Education (Kenez 1985: 58). Even within the cultural radicals, what "proletarian culture" meant remained disputed—the dominator excluded religion and low habits (Fitzpatrick 1992: 22–23), but such a minimum did not suffice in creating a clear and coherent standard to guide cultural production and censorship.

Such a lack of coherent ideology even applied to the cornerstone of Leninism—the cult of Lenin. Though "Leninism" was becoming a useful shorthand for the Bolshevik program during the Civil War, what "Leninism" meant, precisely, remained unclear. It was not until April 1920 on the celebration of Lenin's fiftieth birthday that leading Bolsheviks started writing articles to discuss this nomenclature. Meanwhile, Lenin accepted a low level of publicity, partly because of his own apathy, partly because the Bolsheviks did not yet have an agency to centralize propaganda and agitation, and partly because of the resistance from the young idealists against the domination of the highest body over the working class (Tumarkin 1983: 79–96). The massive commemoration—Lenin Corner, Lenin evenings, little Leninists—started only after the death of Lenin in 1924. Yet even this process took time. As Krupskaya warned, to deliver Leninism to the countryside, agitators must keep peasant needs and limitations in mind. It took time to vulgarize Lenin into songs, tales, legends, poems, jingles, and riddles, to collect his correspondence with ordinary people, and to indigenize him into local literature (Tumarkin 1983: 217–19). It was around the early 1930s that Lenin's impact reached the non-Russian periphery.

The Bolsheviks faced other difficulties in forging a machine of cultural production during the Civil War. One was the shortage of qualified cultural workers. Having long been a tiny party conducting propaganda among the intelligentsia and urban workers, the Bolsheviks lacked agitators who were familiar with the masses' reading habits and psychology, especially when

Reconciliation with traditional "Russia" and "China"   97

faced with a large number of peasants. This problem surfaced in the Civil War but only gained attention after it, when special resources were allocated to "reader study" in journalists' unions, the Central State Publishing House, and newspapers (Lenoe 1998: 20–21). Even worse, the war-caused devastation drove many cultural elites to flee the Bolshevik-controlled regions, which further reduced the technical possibility of training proletarian cultural workers (Kenez 2001: 31).

The campaign "Closer to the People" started only after the Civil War, with the aim of popularizing propaganda and agitation. The tactics included making the layout, appearance, and thematic organization friendly to the "laboring masses," as well as removing "obscure and bureaucratic" language. Most importantly, a plan was put in place for a slow-moving project to create a "Soviet working-class intelligentsia" and to create a new style of common speech, in opposition to the conviction of educated intellectuals that only official events and "serious" literature were naturally privileged (Lenoe 1998: 41–42).

Material hardship was another difficulty. It was the Bolsheviks' long-standing plan to use film for propaganda and political education. Yet, the severe shortage of equipment (Russia was unable to mass-produce until the end of the 1920s) and raw materials restrained the Bolsheviks' ambition. Without the materials the Bolsheviks were unable to train enough skillful projectionists and scriptwriters. During the Civil War the propaganda machine could only produce extremely simple newsreels "agitki" (Kenez 2001: 33–34). To overcome the shortage of both equipment and personnel, through the 1920s the Red Army ran hundreds of hours of courses to train projectionists. Before "cinefication" became a reality, film remained the entertainment of a small circle of intelligentsia rather than a propaganda instrument (Kenez 2001: 73–77). It is also remarkable that all prestigious Soviet masters of cinema—Pudovkin, Eisenstein, Vertov, Dovzhenko—generated their expertise, formulated their artistic principles, and shot their first masterpieces after the revolution in the 1920s, though some found the opportunity to shape their skills by shooting revolutionary newsreels (Marshall 1983: 24–25, 66–69, 99, 228–29).

Certain core patterns that would come to dominate future Soviet propaganda, such as "mass journalism," also took shape after the revolution of 1917, though not without resistance. During the NEP, Sergei Ingulov's "healthy criticism" was influential among journalistic circles. Reminiscent of Gramsci's "Cultural hegemony," this stream argued for diversity under communist rule, which meant that newspapers should retain the autonomy to criticize the communist party (Lenoe 1998: 9). This movement was superseded as the intra-party struggle reached a clear resolution. From 1926 on, the practice of "creating news" emerged but remained contained by the old-school professionalism that focused on the "dark side": stories about fires, accidents, crimes, trials, and society scandals. It was after 1928 that "mass journalism," in which reporters were not passive journalists but rather agitators, began displacing the old alternative. They went to the fields and factories to organize events such as labor competitions, and reported those events in a militant and martial tone (Lenoe 1998: 71).

The effort of forging a "red cultural worker" was most evident within the military, that is, the "commissar system." Yet, their work could hardly be identified with indoctrination, let alone called nationalist. During the Civil War, the Bolsheviks trained thousands of political directors and dispatched them to the commands of armies, divisions, brigades, and regiments. These political directors were given the mission of instilling a "proletarian" political consciousness in the Red Army, in order to achieve three goals: consolidate discipline, engender loyalty, and improve combatant performance. However, in reality, this plan was offset by many factors: the shortage of educated staff familiar with Marxism and the Bolshevik program; the low level of literacy; the lack of books, newspapers, pamphlets, and paper; the mismatch between a high-speed cavalry-based operation and the slow-moving indoctrination.

With these difficulties, the actual duties of political directors concentrated on three functions, they amounted to something closer to overt supervision and coercion than to moderate indoctrination. First, they restored and defended the old military bureaucracy to ensure that peasant soldiers obeyed their "bourgeois and landlord" officers. The latter's authorities had been destroyed amid the anarchist and defeatist zeal in the first stage of revolutionary takeover. In achieving this goal, commissars used the power of coercion, supporting old military experts as they exerted harsh punishment. Second, commissars monitored commanders, most of whom had graduated from tsarist military schools and switched to the Soviet regime. Here obedience stemmed from the timidity of the old officers, who feared that resistance would be framed as disloyalty and then incur trouble to their families. The third function was engaging in combat. Though in comparison with the CCP, the Bolsheviks had far less interest in inventing an art of asymmetric war to blend conventional military elements and political elements, and many commissars, over the course of the Civil War, learned to be military commanders. Behind such merging was the Bolsheviks' conviction that overlapping personnel better secured political loyalty than indoctrination.

Commissars became full-time political educators only after the end of the Civil War, when the Bolshevik state believed that most commanders had been proved politically reliable and the intra-military counterrevolutionary plots, if any, could be easily detected by secret police and informants (Smilga 1920: 21–24). In terms of nationalism, there were agitations for red patriotism during the Civil War, to cater for the Russo-centric sentiment among the old officers, bourgeoisie, and intelligentsia (Novikova 2019; Sablin 2017). Such agitations depicted the Whites as the agents of the Entente. Yet they were expedient.

In general, the massive transformation of Soviet artists and masses into red cultural workers who were well-disciplined by a hyper-centralized propagandist machine would occur in the late 1920s and the 1930s. Such a transformation, though gaining momentum from geopolitical pressure, as well as from radical economic changes, could not be achieved immediately because they faced resistance from multiple sources. First, leftist and progressive cultural professionals of prerevolutionary Russia, even willing to follow the Party's line, had an enormous psychological barrier to going fully against their early aesthetics. This, for example, manifested in the historical plays composed to celebrate past Russian rulers—even though progressive artists had made the concessions to avoid fully negative evaluations of these historical figures, they were still accused by censors of insufficiency (Perrie 2006).

Second, the "Soviet" cultural professionals were in the process of being shaped. The process was time-consuming for musicians and writers as it had been for the above-mentioned cinema directors too. Leading composers— Shostakovich, Prokofiev, Khachaturian, Knipper, and Dzerzhinsky— completed their professional education in the 1920s after the Civil War, when Russia's musical creativity remained in close contact with the contemporary West. Despite the varied closeness in their training to formalism and the avant-garde, it was not until the disciplinary movement in the 1930s that these composers began to transiti into a traditional and folk style identified by the state as "Soviet patriotism" and "socialist realism" (Abraham 1970: 25–26, 42, 44–45, 52). Among writers, pre-revolutionary literati had been exploring the concept of "new man" and "Soviet men." However, even for Gorky and Esenin, their writings of the early 1920s depicting "little people" would not meet the standard of the 1930s (Bykov 2013: 17–19, 58–59). Many future Soviet writers, such as Babel, Fedin, Kataev, Leonov, Makarenko, Panferov, Sholokhov, and Shpanov started their writing careers during the Civil War, but mostly as journalists, reporters, and short-story writers (Bykov 2013: 84–88, 92–93, 157, 193–94).

Third, the lack of institutionalized communication between political leaders, censor officers, and cultural professionals produced inertia, tensions, and confusion—again, this problem persisted until a hyper-centralized system of cultural production fully took shape. Toward the end of the 1920s, such a lack of connection largely stemmed from the political marginalization of crucial figures such as Lunacharskii (Bykov 2013: 35–40) and Krupskaya, which meant a transfer of power from scholarly party elites to Stalinist cultural bureaucrats.

The fourth and the most important barrier was mass illiteracy and under-education, which limited not only the size of the audience but also the number of propagandists. Certain undergirding of cultural devices—the standard Russian language, for example—would not become available among poorly educated workers until the early 1930s, which limited the widespread use of modern technology such as radio broadcasting as an instrument for propaganda (Lovell 2012). Within the army, where illiteracy liquidation was most fast-moving, the campaign did not affect the army until the second half of 1919. The first successful textbook, which came out in the same year, was by D. Iu. El'kina, an ex-SR who joined the Bolsheviks in 1919 (Kenez 1985: 78–79); in November 1920 the country had 12,067 *likpunkts* teaching 278,637 students (Kenez 1985: 82–83).

A revolutionary Russian nation?

One possibility of infusing nation and revolution without resorting to a dark past was to invent a revolutionary tradition for the nation. This is by no means easy. On the one hand, perpetrators of a coup can hardly fabricate their ties with the entire nation in an absence of memories and cultural materials. On the other hand, a great revolution that had been sustained for a century and which penetrated most social strata is hardly separable from the formation of a nation, as in France. Inventing a tradition also poses a high demand on technical support, which only well-established regimes can afford. Radical groups in constant exile and imprisonment are unable to organize experts in writing a satisfying history. Therefore, the longer the time and larger the scale of mobilization a revolution has needed, the more advantaged revolutionaries are in undertaking this approach.

The Bolsheviks had been creating the image of a revolutionary Russia long before 1917. As Lenin emphasized in 1918, communism was not to be built from hollowness; communists could only inherit the revolutionary and progressive parts of Russian historical legacies (Lenin 1956: 15–16). Lenin's and other Bolsheviks' self-boasting citation of "revolutionary democrats" of the nineteenth century, as well as the effort of collecting literature on historical rebellions, all indicated that the Bolsheviks recognized a distinct "Russian revolutionary tradition." However, such a scattered narrative hardly counts as an institutionalized effort to invent a tradition. There were few textbooks or historical pamphlets that specially reflected the position of the Bolsheviks—even for Lenin himself, reading Rozhkov's textbook, which Lenin disliked, was the only option, as no other historians were writing about the Russian history of revolution. Such an intellectually barren land, however, was related with the organizational character of the Bolsheviks.

Reconciliation with traditional "Russia" and "China"   101

In the years prior to 1917, not only did the young Bolsheviks not have their own party historians, but general interest in Russian history was low among the radical intellectuals. Within the Russian socialist movement few activists were professional historians, or had they received historical training. People did write about Russian history in a Marxian tone, but most accounts were written in an ad hoc manner (Mazour 1975). Few of these pieces and excerpts counted as serious monographies or books. An example of this type of style include abstract formulas, written to discuss the philosophy of history, to illustrate such concepts as class, feudalism, state, materialism, and the law of social evolution. These pieces usually came from Bolshevik propagandists; examples include Sergei Kirov's *Great Explorer* (1911), Stepan Shaumian's *Evolutionism and Revolutionism in Social Science* (1905), and Stalin's *Anarchism or Socialism?* (1907) (all reproduced in Illeritskii and Kudriavtsev 1961: 399–400).

The second category of writings tackled more specific historical periods and subjects, such as Russian feudalism, peasant rebellions, the Emancipation of 1861, the development of Russian capitalism, and the making of the working class. These works, mostly in the format of small essays, column series, or pamphlets, expressed had concern with the formation of the Russian nation but they did not make such concerns explicit. Some denied the existence of a unified Russia in order to highlight social division. For example, M. C. Ol'minskii's 160-page-long pamphlet, *State, Bureaucracy, and Absolutism in History of Russia*, challenged the "All-people tsarist state" as a political lie. The Bolsheviks later criticised the author for taking such a stance, and for underestimating the close tie between tsar and landlord class (Illeritskii and Kudriavtsev 1961: 401–2). Conversely, Lenin's historical narratives, affected by Nikolai Fedoseev's analysis of the Emancipation (Illeritskii and Kudriavtsev 1961: 353–54), conveyed a more explicit nationalist tone in arguing that medieval Russia underwent a stage of feudalism like most Western European societies, whereas the divided peasant rebellions were now united by the development of capitalism, thereby giving Russia the great opportunity of formenting modern revolution (Illeritskii and Kudriavtsev 1961: 376–84). The work that went furthest, if its single-page length is not seen as showing a lack of seriousness, was V. V. Voronskii's *The Emergence of Russian Working Class*, which mentioned that Russia's development, as well as the atrocities of Ivan III and Ivan IV, were driven by the responses to foreign aggression (Illeritskii and Kudriavtsev 1961: 403).

A third stream of writings, probing Russian history in a scholarly and Marxist way, bore resemblances to that of the future "revolutionary literati." Yet there were two distinctions: the authors were aloof from, if not hostile to, the Bolshevik movement; and bearing internationalist orientation, the literature presented the Russian nation in a negative tone. Mikhail Pokrovskii, later the founder of the Soviet Marxist historiography, was briefly with the Bolsheviks between 1905 and 1907 (Illeritskii and Kudriavtsev 1961: 471–72). In terms of content, Pokrovskii, as his Ukrainian critics pointed out in the 1920s, depicted Russian history in a negative, if not nihilist way. His narrative was based on vehement opposition to Russian chauvinism, while at the same time it portrayed minimal positive depictions of non-Russian nations (Amacher 2018). Georgi Plekhanov, founder of Russian Marxist historiography, characterized imperial Russia as a stagnant deadlock, too fixed to conceive an alternative. According to Plekhanov, the starting point of Russian history had been wrong—entering "orientalism," the society simply lost the capacity for continuous endogenous change. Based on such pessimism, Plekhanov concluded that Russia could only be rescued by external forces. Plekhanov's thesis affected another outsider of the Bolshevik movement, Leo Trotsky, who persisted in his internationalist opposition to Stalin's "Socialism in one country" until the end of his life (Baron 1974).

Unlike Pokrovskii, who used the terminology of the German statist school, Nikolai Rozhkov was more like a Marxist historical sociologist who had little interest in glorifying Russia's past. Striving to "seek general rules to understand the complexity of society," his conclusion was similar to that drawn by Plekhanov and Trotsky, that Russia was centuries behind Europe. Rozhkov briefly sat in the central committee of the Russian Social Democratic Labor Party, but he quit the political movement after the 1905 Revolution. After that, his personal relationship with Lenin deteriorated. Lenin hated his *Russian History in Comparative Interpretation* and exiled him to Pskov in 1922. It was only because few people could teach Russian history from a Marxist perspective that he evaded repression and was called back to teach at Moscow State University (González 2017: 16–22, 250–51, 274–76).

When the October Revolution came in 1917, the Bolsheviks barely had a history. In a fourth-grade textbook by Andrei Vasil'evich Shestakov, the Bolsheviks' involvement in the pre-1917 revolutionary struggle looks minimal, even with the author's exaggerations. Before 1905, the sole and most important event was the rise of Lenin, who, after organizing the Union of Liberation, was arrested and exiled abroad. Lenin's major role, in Shestakov's account, was to insist in a "historically correct direction." In Shestakov's telling, the Bolsheviks almost missed the 1905 Revolution, except for advocating for and participating in the Moscow Uprising by a few members (Shestakov 1955: 165–66). He largely skipped the years between 1906 and 1914, with only a brief section given to the strike of 1912 in Lensky Forest, when the Bolsheviks were meeting in Prague to expel Mensheviks from the SD (Shestakov 1955: 174–75). Shestakov depicted the unrest during World War I and mentioned that the Bolsheviks penetrated the military to agitate soldiers. In his narrative, it was only after the downfall of

Reconciliation with traditional "Russia" and "China"   103

the tsar that the Bolsheviks rapidly increased in number, to around twenty thousand (Shestakov 1955: 185–94). Compared to Shestakov's textbook, Stalin's *Short Course* gives a better explanation of why the Soviet regime did not use the Bolsheviks' pre-1917 history to invent a revolutionary Russia. There was no incentive for Stalin to underplay the Bolsheviks' significance in the years before 1917, but even so, there was too little to boast of. Most of this classic's treatment of the Bolsheviks before 1917 was devoted to trivial polemics, to demonstrate that Lenin was always correct, not in mobilizing the masses, but rather in believing that revolution would come. Any mention of actual confrontations with the tsarist state had to be vague and brief, out of a concern that these unrests were either spontaneous or often mixed with other factions and parties, who were condemned by the Bolsheviks as "traitors," "revisionists," "opportunists," and "Trotskyists" (CCCPSU 1939).

The Bolsheviks began to intertwine two threads in the history of the Civil War when they had been in power. In fighting the Whites, who were allegedly backed by the Allies, the Bolsheviks framed the revolution as the defense of Russia, which was a popular sentiment among the masses, officers, and intellectuals. Though the official discourse denounced any wars between nations as imperialistic and bourgeois, the language of red patriotism prevailed among the Red Army and supporters of the Soviet regime, with various interpretations. The war with Poland in 1920 was a direct confrontation, which aroused the culmination of Russian nationalism. Nevertheless, there was one more necessary step in upgrading this history to the status of a tradition—that is, the development of body a historical literature—and this step was never taken. In this period, the absence of officially recognized historical books was offset by the journalistic writings from the Bolsheviks' sympathizers in the West, among whom the most famous were John Reed's *Ten Days that Shook the World* and Morgan Price's *My Reminiscences of the Russian Revolution* (Warth 1967: 250). Praised by Lenin, John Reed's *Ten Days* was allowed to circulate as a quasi-official historical textbook on the October Revolution until Trotsky lost power.

The first official Soviet research institution to study the Bolshevik revolution, "the Commission for the Collection and Study of Materials on the History of the October Revolution and the History of the Russian Communist Party" (Istpart), was founded in 1920 and started to dominate the study of Bolshevik history from 1928. Throughout the early 1920s researchers studying revolutionary history were pulled in multiple directions by the Kremlin's infighting, and research was ultimately brought to a standstill. The downfall of Trotsky and his alleged allies caused delays and cancellations of many projects, including a general survey on Bolshevik elites, known as Granat Encyclopedia, and a multi-volume *History of the October*

Revolution (McNeal 1958: 270). In this period, the lack of an official historical textbook continued. Several memoirs and short courses authored by witnesses were published in the middle 1920s, including Alexander Shliapnikov's *Seventeenth Year* and Sergei Piontkovskii's *October 1927*. These volumes, including Trotsky's later three-volume *History of the Russian Revolution*, were all about the power seizure in 1917 rather than the entire Civil War. And their circulation was soon limited, as their authors fell into political disgrace (McNeal 1958: 271).

A centralized process of engineering a revolutionary history was inaugurated in 1931, marked by the foundation of the Secretariat of General Editing the History of the Civil War at the initiative of Maxim Gorky. This institution's editorial board included the most powerful patrons of Stalin's inner circles, which was sufficient to resist unwanted interference. This project began a stable process of engineering a tradition, albeit one with heavy omissions and distortions. As the Soviet state became established, the work of telling the story of the October Revolution came to be fused with Russian national pride. The October Revolution not only placed Russia among the advanced nations of a world in the march to socialism, as claimed in the revolutionary years, but also rescued Russia from economic collapse and partition by threatening powers. When the second volume of *Istoriia grazhdanskoi voiny v SSSR* (*The History of the Civil War in the Soviet Union*) was published in 1943, the Civil War had been re-framed as a national war in defense of Russia. In addition to the Civil War, Stalin's revolution from above was also regarded as an invented tradition. The grandiose industrialization, the conquest of the Kulaks, the mega-projects across union republics, and the defeat of the Nazis and Japanese all became national traditions to celebrate in a Russo-centric Soviet fatherland (Shestakov 1955: 235–60). In Anna Pankratova's tenth-grade textbook, which was the least prone to the High Stalinist Russo-centrism, the Soviet industrialization of the 1930s was contrasted with that of Western countries as a unique approach that ‚not only reversed the regular sequence of development, but also achieved a miracle-level faster speed (Pankratova 1952: 313–15). The economic development was depicted as a diffusion from the Russian core to national peripheries, which, for the first time, integrated Belorussia, Central Asia, and Eastern peoples into a unified modern economic space. When it came to the bond among multiple Soviet nations, Stalin was eulogized as "the political symbol of the unity of the Soviet People" (Pankratova 1952: 344). The Soviet–German War (1941–1945) was celebrated as the Soviet Union's greatest contribution to liberating people from fascism (Pankratova 1952: 367).

The vacuum of nationalism continued during the years of the Civil War. Though the Bolsheviks had seized power in Moscow and Petrograd, they could barely claim the monopoly of Russia's national sovereignty, given that

Reconciliation with traditional "Russia" and "China"   105

vast territories remained in control of the Whites. The Bolsheviks were preoccupied more with repressing counterrevolutionaries than developing a socialist historical science. Historical research almost ceased, due to the loss of personnel, the closure of training institutions, and the destruction of archives and libraries. Over the tough years of 1919–21, around 20 percent of prerevolutionary historians were shot, whereas the rest lived in extreme material hardship, and this led to malnutrition, exile, and deportation (Dubrovskii 2017: 88–90; Shteppa 1962: 16–17). As part of the revolutionary break with the past, in many places the conventional history-philology departments (историко-филологический факультет) were abolished and reorganized into social science faculties (факультеты общественных наук). The newly established Communist Academy did not include a department of historical studies. Most institutions were closed throughout the 1920s. Former professionals involved in historical-related work were concentrated in a few institutions, as the Bolsheviks were interested in archives and ethnographic studies, such as GAIMK (State Academy of History of Material Culture) and RANION (Institute of Russian Association of Science-Research Institutes of Social Sciences) (Dubrovskii 2017: 90–91).

The 1920s saw the rise of red patriotism and a hesitation to resist nationalism. In general, historical research and training, and the source and precondition of a socialist nationalist historiography was being recovered. Research became feasible after the conclusion of the brutal Civil War, with the massive expropriation of private and church archival and librarian collections. However, technical factors continued to slow the process. College semesters were regularized, but courses were simplified to allow fast-track students to displace "bourgeois experts." Old-school historians were called back from prisons and exile, but they were overloaded by "work for society" obligations (Shteppa 1962: 5–11). There was a general shortage of usable historical textbooks, except for Pokrovskii's outline of Russian history published in 1923. Materials were so scarce that historical teaching became a preaching of Marxist theoretical models and formulas (Shteppa 1962: 39–40).

In terms of ideological orientation, the 1920s at best counted as a transitional decade characterized by red patriotism; the return of Russian nationalism was absent. Though the war against Poland of 1920 was won and the German Revolution of 1923 failed, internationalism and anti-traditionalism remained dominant. When historical research was recovered, priority was given to revolutionary studies. 1923 saw the beginning of this switch with the creation of two journals—*The Russian Past* (Русское прошлое) and *Annals* (Анналы). Research articles in these journals covered Russian and foreign revolutionaries, as well as the adaption of relations of production. Research on serf uprisings continued to depict medieval

Russia as evil soil with disrespect for individuals (Shteppa 1962: 26–29). Meanwhile, the official historiography—the Pokrovskii school—was evolving into a new generation. They simultaneously fought old historians and pre-revolutionary Marxists. Against the former, they continued the Pokrovskian position of highlighting class and criticizing Russian chauvinism. Against the latter, they claimed they were developing a new method to base Marxist historiography upon scientific analysis (Dubrovskii 2018: 145–49).

The 1920s produced the first generation of Soviet historians. However, in terms of academic genealogy, training background, and ideological orientation, many of these historians were at odds with the ideological switch to Russian nationalism. A biographical survey of those from the "Pokrovskii school," who were purged in the 1930s, shows that these people, being participants of the Civil War, were selected from the Red Army, factories, and propagandist-cadres. They completed college education in historical subjects between 1922 and 1929. Most of them specialized in four areas: history of Russian and world revolutions, Russia's economic development of the nineteenth and twentieth centuries, factories and workers, and Leninism. Some of them, such as E. Ia. Gazganov and A. I. Lomakin, became the editors of Lenin's full collection (Artizov 1994). With a few exceptions such as E. N. Kusheva, these "red professors" rarely touched history prior to the eighteenth century, which was in the absolute control of old-school historians (Dubrovskii 2018: 177).

After the 1920s: Moving into a socialist Russia
after the Revolution of 1917

Before the revolutions in Russia and China, historians had been developing historical narratives that had an integrationist perspective, with the purpose of explaining or tracing how non-majority ethnic groups had "joined" the nation, thereby making it multi-ethnic. Russia had published many versions of school textbooks. They commonly highlighted five discourses. One was biological and territorial, arguing that the "Slavic peoples" had shared common land, language, and primitive religion from the birth of the Russian state in the ninth century. This narrative defined "Rus" in a broad way, indicating that the descendent peoples of the ancient Rus had spread to a vast territory not confined to the present domain of tsarist Russia. Such a narrative suggested an irredentist effort that targeted Poles and other Western Slavic peoples. A second narrative, not surprisingly, highlighted Christianity, which pointed to "little Russia," the duchies of Kiev Rus, as a tunnel to transmit Greek Orthodoxy from the Byzantine Empire to the entire Slavic world (Platonov 1917: 28–32). The third narrative emphasized common "others" of peoples on the Russian land, ranging from the Swedish, the German Teutonic Orders, the Golden Horde rulers, and later Turkish, British, and French rivals (Platonov 1917: 60–61). Depicting leaders and operations in a heroic way, historians depicted Russia as a protector of peripheral peoples. The fourth narrative was a celebration of modernity, which eulogized Russia as a missionary who brought European civilization to the eastern borderland. Lastly, "the curse of the conqueror" was used as well, pointing to Mongolians-Tartars, Poles-Lithuanians, and Nordic invaders from the North. These five narratives, bearing unspoken targets, were applied by textbook authors of contrasting ideological orientations.

The Bolsheviks continued to require their "revolutionary literati" to draft a socialist nationalism as late as the 1930s, after a long process of institutional centralization, training, displacing, and disciplining. The "revolutionary literati" came from two groups. The first was the young Soviet historians, the red professors, who were sensitive and flexible enough to adapt to the official shift to Russian nationalism; these included I. I. Mints (local history of the Civil War), M. V. Nechkina (Russian aristocratic revolutionary movement), A. M. Pankratova (revolutionary Russian factories), and A. V. Shestakov (agricultural history from 1861 to 1917). Not specializing in nationality questions or pre-modern histories, these young scholars did not directly engage in writing. Rather, they played the administrative role of organizing and coordinating specialists or assumed relatively basic work, such as authoring elementary school textbooks.

It is noteworthy that these scholars were a minority. The majority of "red professors" failed to make the shift. Some were assigned to the mission but failed to produce satisfying outcomes, which led to repression. One example was N. N. Vanag, who specialized in the Russian economy of the nineteenth and twentieth centuries and became a leading historian. Unable to work out a narrative that connected the Russian nation to other imperial nations, he was arrested in 1934. Similar experiences were shared by S. M. Dubrovskii (history of agricultural economy), G. S. Zaidel (history of the Second International), and A. L. Sindrov (economic history of World War I). Others with more relevant expertise, such as M. M. Tsvibak (in Central Asian economic history), failed by overdoing their attacks on old-school historians, who proved more qualified in writing a nationalist history of Russia.

"Revolutionary literati" also came from among disciplined old-school historians. Ironically, these figures were more directly involved than the young "red professors"—they were the actual writers rather than coordinators. This was largely due to their expertise. Unlike "red professors" who worked on most recent events, old-school historians specialized in pre-modern Russian history, which was vital to the creation of an all-time-spanning

Russo-centric patriotic narrative. What also mattered was method. Less disciplined by abstract Marxist theories, old-school scholars were better at writing about individuals, stories, and details, which better matched Stalin's desire for historical research and teaching that provided vivid and concrete patriotic models to educate Soviet citizens.

But the turn to "revolutionary literati" was not easy for the old-school historians. They bore the "original sin" of being "bourgeois intellectuals." During the Civil War some had served in the White military or could not specify their activities in the White-controlled zones, and they suffered wave after wave of repression. Nor was their intellectual transformation to Bolshevism smooth—they needed to accommodate their analyses to the official Marxist framework. Boris Grekov was one example. A specialist in the historic relations among Slavic peoples, he served in the Vrangel' military and thus suffered repression in the late 1920s as a "foe of the people." The brutal torture finally forced him to compromise. In 1940 he published a book that imposed the Marxist theory of development on Kiev Rus (Dubrovskii 2017: 492–93).

The study of medieval Russia became a breakthrough means of evading the complicated issue of multi-ethnicity. In a historical monograph published during the period of High Stalinism, the author wisely concluded his writing with the end of the reign of Ivan III, on the grounds that hitherto, Rus's unification had been completed and the sole-national period had ended (Mavrodin 1951: 258). Evading Russia's dirty multinational history in a cunning way, this book, with an epic-like writing style, offered a story of how the medieval Russians endeavored to learn from advanced civilizations and throw off the control by formidable enemies. In this book, Russians were depicted as victims, sufferers, rescuers, firm defenders of a nation, and most importantly, forerunners of oppressed nations and national liberators. The others who had bullied Russia were defined as the Swedish, Golden Horde, Lithuanian-Poles, Moldavians, and Germans. Many citations from Chernyshevsky and Belinsky were surprising in that they differed from how these figures had been invoked by Lenin and early Bolsheviks (Mavrodin 1951: 9–11).

There was a consequence of the belated reversion. Taking shape after the foundation of the Soviet Union, Soviet patriotism was restrained by internationalist, institutional, and ideological frameworks. Recent literature has argued that Stalin's "Retreat" carried multiple facets, which used the Russian language to promote the Soviet culture, which itself was multinational and cosmopolitan in nature (Clark 2011).

Stalinist Russia revived many "feudal pasts," but the Soviet projection of identity in the 1930s and 1940s was far more than a past-based nostalgia. The Stalinist "Soviet identity" was a mixture of Russia's past, Soviet

Reconciliation with traditional "Russia" and "China" 109

achievement, and an ambitious vision of a promised communist future. This narrative is clearly illustrated in school textbooks for pupils. An example is the geography textbook by Nikolai Mikhailov, which won the 1948 Stalin Prize. This textbook, titled, "On the Map of the Motherland," actually spent only a few pages on the physical conditions of Soviet territory. Most of the remaining chapters were devoted to depicting a dynamic momentum that had heroically transformed the pre-revolutionary landscape since Stalin's new deal. An epic of conquering nature under communism, rather than historical and physical legacies of the past, was central. From this perspective, with emphasis on socioeconomic process, a multi-ethnic narrative was developed by highlighting how nations, Russian as well as non-Russian, gained unprecedented improvement and were integrated into a unified economic space. A Soviet patriotism was asserted to contrast the present with the prerevolutionary period, when foreign capitals robbed Russia's natural resources in a way never benefiting the people (Mikhailov 1956: 74–81), while a future was envisioned that "Russian melodies drift over Moldavian land; Slavic sailors patrol Baltic borders; Armenians eat fish from the Gulf of Finland, Azerbaijanis are fed by bread transported from Volga, and Volga workers are fueled by coal from Kazakhstan" (Mikhailov 1956: 289).

In the post-Stalinist era, the geography textbook was used to rescue the retelling of the Russian past without invoking Stalin's open restoration of the old legacies. The patriotic educational pamphlet, *Russian Travelers*, published in 1956, traced the geographical discovery of the Russian space from the fourteenth century to the early Soviet era. This pamphlet continued the Stalinist Russo-centric narrative that described a process of expansion from the Moscow core to the Eastern periphery, but it reframed the expansion as an endeavor coordinated by Russians, non-Russians, and even foreigners. The earliest generation of Siberian explorers, "Zemleprokhoditsy," were a group comprising Russians, Baltics, and Poles, who worked together in competition with contemporary British and Dutch geographers (Severin 1956: 15–19). The pamphlet did not conceal the fact that leading Russian sailors, like Vasilii Golovnin and Mikhail Lazarev, received early training in cooperation with Britain and Sweden (Severin 1956: 107–16), and it highlighted competition with the West. Russian explorers completed the circumnavigation as early as 1806; Russians were the earliest explorers of the northwestern coast of America, the Arctic, the Sea of Okhotsk, and Inner Asia; research by Russian geographers and sailors was recognized by Western colleagues and notes were translated into French, English, German, and Dutch (Severin 1956: 84, 100). Long voyages by Russians were also celebrated as heroic actions to break the isolation of Eastern societies, like India, Japan, and China. The journey to the Great Wall of China by Nikolai Przheval'skii, as well as the fight between Russian sailors' and Japanese feudal rulers, was imbued with

110   *Revolution in China and Russia*

a symbolic meaning of awakening the sleepy East, bringing it to the rhythm of the modern world (Severin 1956: 159).

China's cultural crisis of the 1910s

Comparing Russia with China seems asymmetrical. Unlike Russia, which started state-building as late as the ninth century (largely by borrowing elements from adjacent giant powers), the Chinese had been in an enclosed space for a period with an incomparably long duration. Not as messianic as the Russian intellectuals and state, the Chinese, at least on the eve of the rise of the CCP, were not in a position to expand their revolutionary thinking to include the rest of the world—on the contrary, from the late nineteenth century, the country was facing the perennial threat of being invaded and partitioned from outside. It was also apparent that China had a clear identity, based on a common written script, and that this elite identity drove the nationalist revolution of 1911 that terminated the alien Manchurian Qing Dynasty (Wimmer 2018). Originating in Han proper, the Chinese revolution also did not face the same ethnopolitics as the Russian radicals. Minorities were far away at peripheries beyond the reach of the revolution, and the Han-minority conflicts had been overshadowed by China's suffering at the hands of imperialist powers (Liu 2004b). In the CCP's official historiography, the decade after the end of the Qing era was reconstructed ex-post facto as a nationalist narrative, according to which the revolutionaries had been nationalists ("patriots" in the CCP's terminology), from the first moment of their radicalization, in defending China from the intrusion of imperialism (Zhou 2018).

Yet, as China was a late developer its historical pride should not be overstated. In fact, like Russia and other "backward" empires, China suffered a deep sense of cultural inferiority vis-à-vis the West. This sense was originally marginal, but after a century of defeats and humiliating concessions it became real. The concept of "China" was severely questioned in the aftermath of the end of the Qing, especially for revolutionaries who sought rapid and overall social change, leading them to view Chinese traditional cultural structure as an obstruction. As in Russia's Westerner–Slavophile debate, a collective disappointment with the political revolution of 1911 quickly grew into skepticism and a negation of traditional Chinese culture in favor of the Western one. In this "New Cultural Movement," as in Russia's Cultural Revolution and Kemal's modernization project of de-Islamization, China was understood as an ancient but stagnant civilization had lost the race with the West in the past. Chinese culture was criticized for suppressing individual sovereignty, which limited the people's capacity

Reconciliation with traditional "Russia" and "China" 111

to sustain the republic created by the 1911 Revolution. An endeavor for cultural reconstruction thus defined this period, the decade prior to the rise of the CCP.

Certainly, the cultural revolution of the 1910s was diverse and far more complicated than a simple "China–West" dichotomy. Both conservatives who supported an untouched preservation of the past and radicals who asserted a full negation in favor of rootless cosmopolitanism were in the minority. Anarchists who advocated for an abolition of national culture echoed the contemporary fin de siècle trend, wanting neither nationalist aggression aimed at the conquest of other peoples, nor an imposition of any hegemonic ethics from inside. Most people, however, adopting various approaches, sought to reconstruct a Chinese culture compatible with the contemporary world template. In most cases, their critique of the Chinese tradition was selective or strategic. Old drama and operas, for example, were not abandoned entirely, but rather reinvented, amalgamated with elements learned from Europe (Liu and Li 2016: 26, 86–87). The old literary and historical classics were scrutinized with a modern social scientific approach, to dissect the "ghost hidden under the obscure words" (Liu and Li 2016). Traditional folklores were reinterpreted with a critical and reflective perspective, which initiated the style of "new wine in old bottles" (Liu and Li 2016: 91–93).

The early CCP's critique of and indifference to old Chineseness

The CCP's protracted revolution infused Russia's two stages of mass mobilizations into one. The opening period, like the Bolshevik revolution, was radically critical of the Chinese past. It is not difficult to find radical words in early CCP members' writing, such as "the traditional opera is toxic for youths" (PDRO 1979: 24–27); "only Western-trainees are qualified to study Chinese history" (SCBC 2000); and "filial piety should be replaced by equal love between parents and children" (Shen 1990: 353–54). This certainly had to do with the CCP's leadership. Early CCP leaders such as Li Dazhao, Chen Duxiu, and Qu Qiubai were mostly urban-based students and professors, who shared a vague boundary with contemporary anti-traditionalist intellectual currents. They were heavily influenced by the anarchists, who sought to get rid of restrictions of state, family, and traditional morality. Though the majority of this foundational generation had perished by 1927, their legacy was far-reaching, restraining the CCP from embracing a traditionally defined China: throughout the revolution the CCP never altered its anti-Confucian position, and they continued to label the KMT's cultural conservatism as reactionary.

The formative literary stage for the CCP was not concerned with the nation's past, and it took a decade to start a historical turn in which a new concept of Chinese nation was developed from a Marxist perspective. The early stage was one of preparation, having little to do with substantial historical writing, when most future literati were learning the concepts of Marxism. It persisted from the late 1910s to the turn of the 1930s, an era in which Marxism was studied in translation and introductions and textbooks were written. Most writers who left records during this period were full-time revolutionaries, public commentators, and literary critics. Many had college degrees and faculty positions, but in economy, sociology, modern literature, and journalism rather than in history. Some had experience of studying in Japan. Such a landscape was not surprising. At the turn of the 1920s, as the later CCP leaders Zhou Enlai and Zhang Wentian recollected, the domain of historical studies remained in the firm control of the old literati, who were positioned to explain Chinese history from a racist, if not dynastic perspective. In this situation, training in "modern" disciplines, such as economy and sociology, provided more access to the opportunity of writing an explanation-seeking socioeconomic history.

The CCP's history-related writings of this period covered a wide range of topics outside Chinese history: biographies of foreign communist heroes, history of feminism, philosophy of history, "social evolution," and translated volumes such as Karl Kautsky's *Class Struggle* and Herman Gorter's *Introduction of Historical Materialism* (Gui 1992: 20–22, 31, 85–89). As for Chinese history, books of this period adopted an analytical style that modern sociologists would categorize as "comparative historical." These writings used China as one brief case, in comparison with others such as ancient Egypt, Greece-Rome, Germany, Babylonia, and Russia to interpret Marx's idea of social evolution (Gui 1992: 26–27, 31, 38–39, 45–47, 54–55). These articles, pamphlets, and books were written for the purpose of teaching, propaganda, and self-studies. In terms of ontology, the authors strove to displace "non-Marxist" philosophies of history, such as psychological, racist, biological, and moral ones. They also rejected descriptive narratives of social life, but rather sought the unity and laws behind history.

Few historical writings of this period probed China in any historical depth. For example, the CCP's two co-founders, Li Dazhao and Chen Duxiu, both professors at leading universities, rarely touched empirical research. Li made the well-known critique that China's old historiography was "a familial history of emperors, dukes, generals, and bureaucrats," advocating that historians must seek explanations for events at the level of socio-economic relations rather than reducing macro-level social changes to cases of individual morality (Zhang 2009: 347–51). However, notwithstanding a few ad hoc interpretations of contemporary archeological findings in his textbook, Li

Reconciliation with traditional "Russia" and "China"   113

never wrote a monograph of his own on Chinese history (Gui 1992: 18–19). Similarly, though Chen argued that history was not a study of historical materials but a science of social change, his reputation was based on his advocation of replacing scholarly Chinese with vernacular rather than any substantial historical studies (Gui and Yuan 2010: 733–38).

Because history was used less for itself than to illustrate Marxism, books and pamphlets published in this period bore titles that were not explicitly historical. Qu Qiubai's *Introduction of Social Science* (Shehui kexue gailun), for example, was organized in a way that was similar to a Durkheimian-style sociological monograph. By selecting evidence from multiple historical societies, the author demonstrated that social thought, customs, and morality varied across time, depending on social forces, rather than remaining absolute (Gui 1992: 45–47). Other pamphlets of this time carried similarly abstract titles such as "A History of Social Evolution" (Shehui Jinhua shi) or "An Outline of Social Change" (shehui Jinhua shigang) by Cai Hesen, Deng Chumin, Ma Zhemin, and Yang Pao'an (Gui 1992: 22–23, 41–43).

This period was also characterized by a low level of organizational centralization and coordination, which was vital to the systematic shift of historical scholarship in a country such as China with its well-established historiographical tradition. Up to the end of the 1920s the CCP had remained a tiny revolutionary movement possessing neither a state of its own nor a clear core of leadership. This limited the Party's capacity to produce and control literati. Throughout the 1920s organizations like League of Left-wing Writers or the Yan'an Institute of Marxist–Leninist Studies did not exist. Not unlike the Bolsheviks at the turn of the 1920s, the CCP exerted its influence mainly through personal connections, friendship, and ideological attraction (ILCSSA 2010: 10). Because, as yet, there had been no disciplinary campaign like Yan'an Rectification, there was no consensus to serve as a guideline for historical writing. It was thus not surprising that during this period many writers maintained a loose relationship with the CCP, joining the Party only briefly, as Li Da did, or retaining a position of outside sympathizer, as did Deng Chumin and Ma Zhemin.

The CCP's pressure to engage more in traditional cultural symbols predated Japan's invasion of the Northeast in 1931, and the confrontation with imperialist powers in coastal cities had shown that a Leninist anti-imperial narration did not suffice when sustaining revolutionary mobilization. Peasants and workers, mostly illiterate, were unable to imagine China and its relationship with the world, which made anti-imperialist propaganda pointless.[1] Certain grievances could be clearly associated with the impact of imperialism, such as the displacement of rural artifacts by imported goods as well as the racist discrimination against Chinese sailors,[2] but for the rest, the more relevant frames were domestic-centered and technical: the reluctance of bureaucrats

114 *Revolution in China and Russia*

and politicians to grant welfare to workers, the lack of agricultural equipment, the spread of counterfeit money.[3] Mobilization at the level of grassroots agitation pressed for a discourse shift.

The reconciliation with tradition did not mean that the revolution had ended. Rather, pursuing a goal of destroying the old world, the revolution itself could never achieve a full retreat to the past. There was thus a perennial tension, throughout the Chinese Revolution, between the need to invoke the past in the interest of mobilization, and the revolutionary desire to destroy and negate the past. When it came to individuals, the structural tension was evident in several aspects: the anarchist vigilance, central to early revolutionary zeal, against the imposition of a new moral order that would limit the sovereignty of both the masses and the individual, the cultural workers' resistance to the folklore-oriented turn in favor of an international, cosmopolitan, and Soviet artistic style, and, finally, the fight against the KMT's and reactionaries' efforts to restore Confucian hegemony. The following sections will elaborate how the CCP coped with such a challenging mission.

Reconciliation as revolutionary mobilization expanded and deepened

As the revolution transformed from an intellectual-centered, urban-based movement into a rural mass mobilization, the reconciliation with traditional culture started. This transition involved a process of learning as well as a course of personnel replacement. On the one hand, invoking traditional language and symbols was an efficient—though not the only—way to speak to the broad masses. Many CCP elites came to conclude that they should no longer look down upon the peasants, but rather admire them as heroes with the virtues of a strong work ethic, determinacy, and selflessness (Yun Daiying: 1925, August 25). On the other hand, the transition from a limited mobilizational scale to a broad one entailed a radical shift in the composition of the mobilizers. As an increasing number of rural workers were mobilized, revolutionaries from an elite urban background, or those who may have studied abroad became a minority, and the international and cosmopolitan frame that the latter had developed from exposure to the Soviet Union and the West was gradually displaced. As for the timing of the transition, this expansion of mobilization can be pinpointed to the second half of the 1920s, when the CCP's organization grew rapidly and the revolutionary center transferred from urban to rural. It is thus misleading to reduce the reconciliation with the past to a response to Japan's invasion of Northeast China. Though Japan's threat was looming after 1928, the intrusion was far away and not adjacent to the CCP's central zones. Nationalism remained an abstract notion imported from the West, and it was irrelevant to most of the people the CCP needed to mobilize. Anti-Japanese slogans did enter the CCP's official discourse from the turn of the 1930s, but it was the change of the revolutionary course rather than geopolitics that shaped the reconciliation with the past.

The reconciliation unfolded first and foremost in a folk approach, the easiest way to achieve an affinity with a revolutionary agenda. The folk approach also required the least intellectual capacity and it encountered relatively less obstruction than an overall ideological reconstruction. This is the most revolutionary way of accusing the old culture of being "elitist" and claiming to replace it with a culture of the masses. Turning against the claims of "peasant backwardness" that was present in the early 1920s, the CCP allowed peasant cultural icons into its discourse, as a strategy to circulate revolutionary thought. Ballads were rewritten as revolutionary songs ("new wine in old bottles"), in sharp contrast with the Soviet-imported alien symbols. From the late 1930s nativism intensified and further displaced preexisting alien Soviet culture. Writers who had been accustomed to reading foreign operas and literature were sent to learn the peasant language (EBPHA 1988: 11–12). New operas and dramas were composed to inspire as well as to teach lessons from historical rebellions and transnational wars, such as the Late Ming resisters, Li Zicheng, Taiping Tianguo, and the Opium War (EBPHA 1988: 52, 69, 81). Classical operas like *Jiang Xiang he* were performed widely to preach the idea that military commanders and commissars should cooperate with each other rather than fighting among themselves (Huang 2016: 142).

The turn of the 1930s exemplified a mixture, or more precisely, a stratification. At the top level of the revolution, the preexisting internationalist and Soviet-style ideational regime was exposing its shortcomings. The Soviet trainees belonged to the May Fourth generation but were distinct from these in that their anti-traditionalism carried a pro-Soviet character, but only in its internationalist definition. These people had been trained in the Soviet Union of the 1920s, long before Stalin's full "Retreat" to Russo-centric patriotism started. In terms of propaganda and arts, what they mainly learned in the Soviet Union came from the "proletarian culture" generated during the Russian Civil War. Upon these elites' insistence, Soviet Russian symbols permeated CCP institutional titles, banners, slogans, and posters, which defeated any attempt to invoke nationalism. Having trained in the Soviet Union or attended school in China's central cities, cultural internationalists were the best-educated individuals among the guerrilla zone population. Many of them could speak one or two foreign languages, mostly Russian and Japanese. They were also competent enough with general propaganda work, such as authoring pamphlets, writing newspaper articles, and giving lectures. However, their limitations were as salient as their advantages.

Their central concern was to break with the past, which, in a sense, means interpreting native traditions as a negative source of resistance to revolutionary change. This concern was manifested in a commitment to introducing foreign culture to conquer and transform local resistance. The dramas, operas, and "bulletin dramas" covered the topics such as the liberation of Black American slaves, the fates of worker-soldiers in World War I, and Soviet soldiers in the Russian Civil War (EBPHA 1986 1: 5, 44, 93–95, 104, 147). When creating revolutionary songs, these internationalists preferred to use foreign melodies—Soviet, Japanese, Britain, French—to native ones. For example, the "Song of Worker-Peasant Revolution" used the melody of the "Song of Imperial Japanese Navy," while "National Revolution" put new lyrics to the French ballad, "York Brothers" (EBPHA 1986 2, 652–59).

Yet the internationalists fell short in their outreach in terms of both number and quality. First and foremost, this group was tiny vis-à-vis the size of population of the guerrilla zone. Solely by their own efforts, internationalists could reach only a small fraction of the local population. Nor did they have sufficient cultural capability to transform their dry theoretical knowledge and ideological position into propaganda digestible for the nearly illiterate masses. They were neither professionals nor full-time members of cultural institutions. Some had basic training in the arts, such as drama directing and wood painting (EBPHA 1986 1: 269–70), but most of them learned the skills of propaganda through auto-didactic groups and crash courses—for example, Li Bozhao, the most senior leading artist, was trained in explosives and bayonetting in Russia but received basic instructions in dancing and drama direction (Yan 2017: 466–67). The inadequacy of their skills was reflected in the brevity and crudeness of the artistic works they created, as the CCP leaders themselves later conceded (GPD 2001 9: 61). In many cases, their works were less art than naked propaganda. In terms of the division of labor, these cultural internationalists mostly occupied formal roles in military and civilian affairs. In addition to propaganda and artistic performance, they needed to participate in battlefield medical service, mass mobilization, and real fighting. For example, Qian Zhuangfei, the author of and leading actor in several famous dramas, was most famous as a legendary intelligence officer of the Red Army. Qu Qiubai, the most erudite scholar in the guerrilla zone, was the general secretary of the CCP. As a result, these figures were not only busy with irrelevant affairs but also suffered huge casualties as regular guerrilla partisans and urban conspirators (EBPHA 1986 1: 35).

It was this shortage of cultural internationalists that created the pressure for a shift toward reconciliation with traditional cultural elements. The initial step, however, at the turn of the 1930s, was by no means an overall intellectually formulated national narration to replace the Soviet internationalist system of cultural icons. Instead of celebrating the nation's virtues and history, traditional symbols were merely mobilized at a superficial level to circulate the idea of class struggle. They were also invoked as a device of political agitation and military teaching, since they constituted the mobilizers' deep cultural mentality and came as the most expedient script. Most red cultural workers of this period were recruited from among peasants, elementary school students, rural teachers, and even profit-seeking folk troupes. Typically, these people, lacking the capability of composing or even of creating lyrics to an existing melody, simply mobilized existing native symbols and formats to propagate revolutionary ideas. For example, they re-texted an old Beijing opera to demonize the KMT leader Jiang Jieshi and mocked at the humiliating Sino–Japanese Tanggu Agreement. Similarly, the anti-Japanese nationalist opera, *Wangguo Hen*, was based on an old drama program (EBPHA 1986 1: 162–71, 175). Unlike the sometimes-highbrow internationalists, they felt no need to keep native culture at arm's length and thus were not ashamed of mobilizing traditional symbols.

The displacement in personnel was a significant boost for the reconciliation. Commanders who grew up in domestic contexts felt more comfortable invoking China's past. Originating from the May Fourth Movement, though, they eventually developed a subtle approach to not only showcasing their impressive knowledge of China's past but also to demonstrating their ability to maneuver the great legacies to the advantage of revolution, progress, and national revival. Criticizing reactionaries' use of traditional icons, such as Guan Yu and Zuo Zongtang, the CCP commanders emphasized that the values resting in these icons—martial spirit, wisdom, and patriotic courage—could play a positive role in the revolution. As Liu Bocheng said, the military arts of the Spring–Autumn and Warring States were outdated, suited only to a society of low productivity unable to sustain massive intense war. This remark alluded negatively to the KMT's and the fascists' contemporary uncritical worship of conservative military ethics (Huang 2016: 77). Legends and cases from the past were often invoked to justify the necessity of radical switches that the revolutionary rank-and-file found difficult to accept. For example, mobilizing military men for economic production was justified by the ancient Chinese army's farming operations at the front of Inner Asia (Huang 2016: 125). Historical lessons were cited for strategic utility as well. Chen Yi, a major citer of classics, invoked the palace intrigues of the Song and Ming Dynasties to warn that the CCP forces had to be careful, in fighting the KMT, not to convey the impression that the communists were engaging the "party struggle," which had a negative connotation in Chinese historiography (Huang 2016: 119). Chen also liked citing Chinese classics on leisure as well as offering patronage to heritage preservation, to create the image that the CCP was open to inherit all great national legacies (Huang 2016: 95, 142, 204).

It must be noted that the reconciliation with the past was restrained and limited, constantly in tension with the revolutionary zeal to break with a reactionary past. Though familiar with native symbols, red cultural workers had been reported to have a weaker revolutionary consciousness. In many cases, old folk dramas were performed without any adaptation, which was condemned as downgrading political education to sexual entertainment, as Luo Ronghuan criticized (EBPHA 1986 1: 158). Not understanding the ideological content of revolutionary propaganda, they often poured "new wine" into inappropriate "old bottles." For example, sentimental melodies were adopted to express revolutionary enthusiasm or celebrate agricultural labor (Yan 2017: 54). Such mistakes, in fortunate cases, could be corrected by commissars, but the commissars themselves were mostly poorly educated. It was also difficult to estimate the effect of mass illiteracy—to overcome this problem, people with different levels of literacy were combined into teams so that they could teach each other (EBPHA 1986 1: 24–25).

The influx of petty intellectuals into guerrilla zones, though important for the CCP's shift to a more sophisticated nationalism, also obstructed the folklore-level reconciliation. Depressed, unemployed, dropping out of schools in urban regions, these petty intellectuals (mostly students and elementary school teachers) found themselves attempting to realize their ambitions in rural areas where they were decidedly unappreciated. Obsessed with showcasing their expertise, however, they produced products the CCP did not want to see. In better cases, they were a more refined version of the cultural internationalists of the late 1920s, imposing foreign forms and works that made the peasant-soldiers feel alien. For example, in Yan'an students insisted on performing foreign dramas like *Thunderstorms* and *The Forty First*, which only a tiny elite fraction of the audience could appreciate. The group was thus nicknamed the "Royal Troupe" (EBPHA 1988 1: 426). In worse cases, though, poorly trained petty intellectuals produced numerous coarse works of their own that were not solid by any aesthetic standard: native, Soviet, Japanese, or Western. According to a survey by the leading writer Zhao Shuli and philosopher Yang Xianzhe, the record of journal submissions in 1942 showed that "cultural workers" were enthusiastic in writing hollow poetry, often in imitation of foreign fashions to their understanding. In most poetic works—abstract, short, obscure—readers could hardly see the relevance to the ongoing war; people were also eager to write about the subjects beyond their experiences and observations, which led them to absurd fabrications (Xu and Li 1983: 37–40).

Despite such resistance, the CCP pressed to engage traditional culture as mass mobilization deepened, which led to an overall rectification of intellectuals in the 1940s. Under a persistent and coordinated campaign, the cultural workers were eventually channeled in to a stream that was centered on exploring the past to serve the revolution, which paved the way for the creation of complex historical artistic works. As the communist party's disciplinary power significantly strengthened over the first decade of revolutionary civil war, its control of cultural production became firm. The guerrilla school systems, though technically under the control of senior cultural elites, accepted Mao's general line that they should train agitators and cultural workers at speed in order to serve the communist party's agenda, rather than adhere to the "slow-and-good" standards of the bourgeois experts. The CCP forced collective work coordinated by a political center, in contrast to individuals' free creation (EBPHA 1988 2: 17–18). By 1945, the rule had been set that students coming from the cities had to live in villages to learn the peasant language and local arts (EBPHA 1988 2: 12–13). CCP leaders dictated that cultural workers should devote themselves to formats welcome to the peasant-soldiers. For example, Western drama, which was popular among intellectuals and students, should give way to traditional Beijing operas, even those with programs drawn from classics (EBPHA 1988 1: 223, 335, 349–51).

Being more confident in their cultural capability, toward the end of the long revolution the CCP leaders claimed that cultural workers should create new classics rather than relying solely on old ones—they had to realize that old classics were not always adaptable to new ideological contents. This period saw the creation of neo-classical operas and dramas based on historical figures, such as *Wen Tianxiang, Su Wu, Xi Taihou, Tianguochunqiu* (EBPHA 1988 1: 52, 188, 435). Elite Marxist historians, like Fan Wenlan, offered comments on the adaptations, such as the historical drama, *Taiping Heaven Kingdom* (EBPHA 1988 1: 69). This period, together with the next stage—the Civil War (1946–49)—also laid the foundation for the CCP's future cultural and artistic development. There were personnel development programs. Working teams were sent out to find talented children. Incorporated into the CCP system at a young age and gaining their expertise there, these people would have fewer tensions with the communist party than "bourgeois experts" did (EBPHA 1988 2: 2–3; 4: 13–14). Many artists who would lead the crafting of socialist neo-classicalism after 1949, such as Xie Tieli, completed their early training in this way (EBPHA 1989 1: 358). In terms of material accumulation, cultural workers, under the CCP's coordination, collected rich folklore—songs, ballads, and local dramas, for example—in Northeastern China. These materials contributed greatly to the full blossoming of socialist neo-classicalism after 1949 (EBPHA 1989 2: 663).

Retelling China's past at an intellectual level

Reconstruction at the grassroots level in absorbing folk culture only portrays a partial picture. The CCP's turn to China's past to invent a tradition, which required a higher intellectual capacity in nation building, started at the turn of the 1930s. This process was more challenging in comparison with instrumentally and strategically invoking traditional symbols and icons. It had to offer general guidelines on how to make use of the nation's past without letting that past corrupt the ongoing revolution. As the mobilization expanded, the CCP increasingly faced pressure to convince its supporters and allies that it was not an ignorant barbarian seeking to break everything from China's past. This concern had to do with the outbreak of the Sino–Japanese War, but it was also associated with a broader process of modern revolutionary penetration into every aspect and layer of society. It is analogous to Gellner's thesis on homogenization—to revolutionize the entire social system, revolutionaries could not confine their supporters to one or two classes, but rather had to mobilize the majority. Inventing a nation, therefore, was one way of creating such a revolutionary homogeneity.

The central thesis of the CCP's nation-inventing endeavor was the combination of an anti-Hegelian thrust and a Leninist one, in refuting any characterization imposed from outside of the party, either by the KMT, the Japanese, or the "New Culture Movement" of the 1910s led by elite intelligentsia. Claiming that the legitimate subjectivity of defining China rested exclusively in the "Chinese people," who were in constant historical change, the CCP granted itself the power to decide how to interpret and manipulate "tradition" and "revolution." This placed historians and history scholars at the center of the nation-inventing project. Although at the end of the 1910s the leftists loathed the construction of Chinese history, seeing it as a total mistake and stopping themselves from probing it, from the late 1920s onward, an exploration of re-discovering China gained momentum. By fitting China's past into Stalin's five-phrase formula, Marxist historians, like Guo Moruo, Wu Yuzhang, Jian Bozan, Fan Wenlan, and Hou Wailu, strove to demonstrate that China was a West-like "normal" system, which was able to move upward from a primitive to advanced stage without relying on external intervention (Gui 1992: 38–39, 54–55).

The decade from the late 1920s to the late 1930s saw the formation of the CCP's revolutionary Chinese historiography. The leading communist historians—Fan Wenlan, Guo Moruo, Jian Bozan, He Ganzhi, Hou Wailu, Lv Zhenyu, and Wu Ze—had completed their professional training and started engaging in the substantial effort of fitting Chinese history into a Marxist framework. These people shared similar backgrounds and trajectories. They were all born in the 1890s, mostly from decent families, and held bachelor's degrees or above, which was rare in China of the 1920s. They had been in contact with the CCP when they were at college, though few of them officially joined the Party. Such ties strengthened in the 1930s, even though many of them were teaching at universities in KMT-controlled areas. Following the CCP's instructions, these historians engaged in debates with non-communist historians, through which they developed a Marxist narrative.

The intellectual process of inventing a historical Chinese nation was an arduous course of knowledge absorption. For example, to probe whether or not China had experienced a stage of "slave society" in the remote past, historians had to use archeological evidence, which was neither ample nor as easily accessible as it is in the current era of digitalization. Only professionals with special training in reading skills after years of learning and exploration were capable of deciphering these materials. Both Guo Moruo's, *A Study of China's Ancient History* (Zhongguo gudaishi yanjiu) and Lv Zhenyu's *Chinese Society of the Yin and Zhou Eras* (Yinzhou shidai zhongguo shehui) were based on oracle bone scripts and inscriptions (Gui 1992: 181, 210–11). Using textual sources was not easy either. To carve out an alternative to the old dynasty- and elite-centric historiography, a Marxist historian was expected to make use of materials that were not easily found in China's traditional biography-style anals, such as those exploring socioeconomic conditions, technology, and ordinary people's everyday life. Finding and using these materials was not easy and it took time (Jian 1962: 49–59). Marxist historians who used myths and legends as materials, like Hou Wailu and Wu Ze, carefully examined the materials because they were competing with the influential rivals in the "Gushibian School" who questioned the authenticity of ancient Chinese written records.

The invention of a historical Chinese nation gained momentum also through organization. Once qualified individual scholars were available, there was access to a large group of experts who could be recruited to work on a single large project—it was also amid such coordination that individual scholars became qualified. Such collective collaboration was not easy: it not only required an established or semi-established state to collect resources, but it also had to be preconditioned by successful organizational centralization. Centralized research institutions did not come into being until the late 1930s, when the CCP had established a stable and secure guerrilla base in Yan'an (Gui 1992: 272). The CCP's literati finally took shape in the 1940s. Huge projects—multiple volumes of Chinese history from a Marxist perspective, specialist as well as general—were published at the turn of the 1950s. As popular textbooks for elementary and middle schools came into being, historical teaching became institutionalized in the CCP-controlled regions. The work of the literati also started affecting the CCP's ideology and leadership, as the description of Chinese history in the speeches of Mao and other leaders became crystallized. Nevertheless, this was not the completion. Projects based on extensive collection of materials, like Bai Shouyi's research, would need to wait for another decade, and would appear in the 1950s and 1960s when the CCP fully controlled China's social and intellectual resources (Wang 2020 Vol. 2: 685).

Mao's intellectual biography exemplifies the CCP's reconciliation with the past. Mao was different from contemporary CCP leaders in that he didn't carry out overseas study and he lack foreign language ability, which eventually led him to be labeled as a "native" leader obsessed with Chinese classics. In fact, Mao's early years were distinctive in his enthusiasm for knowledge from the outside world. His reading in the early 1920s, thanks to Changsha's and Beijing's atmosphere, encompassed a wide range of subjects, from Washington's and Napoleon's biographies, Kant, and Darwin, to even fin de siècle writers like Bergeson and Schopenhauer. His intellectual switch occurred in the second half of the 1920s, when the revolution's mobilizational scale extended to rural areas and a broader combination of social groups. His citations covered classics, mainly *The Water Margin* and *Romances of Three Kingdoms*, with which he drew an analogy with the CCP's mountainous guerrilla war, but he warned that such an analogy was dangerous as it conflated old-style war with modern revolution. Throughout the long revolution, Mao's citation of Chinese history was dense, but not confined to "progressive" works. For Mao, all experiences and lessons, either from ancient emperors, generals, or from rebellions leaders and common people, could offer insight into the revolutionary state-building, war-waging, and mass mobilization. Mao was particularly interested in the psychology that was concealed underneath traditional cultural legacies. According to Fu Sinian, a historical philologist who visited Yan'an in 1946, in a private conversation Mao showed deep knowledge of contemporary folk literature, much of which the communist party would officially denounce as regressive.

With Mao's support, from the turn of the 1940s on, specialists in ancient philosophy began to explore the "revolutionary and democratic values" in traditional Chinese thought, a process similar to Stalin's socialist neo-classicalism of the 1930s (Huang 2014: 86; Ye 2016: 136; Zhu 2000: 297). As Marxist philosopher and educator Kuang Yaming recalled in a private conversation, Mao suggested that the CCP should keep a restrained and flexible attitude to Confucian legacies, not to vehemently denounce Confucius but rather to organize scholars to carry out "quiet and comprehensive research" on this ancient thinker (Huang 2014: 48). Later, Chen Boda began to write on the revolutionary values of Confucius, Mencius, Laozi, Mozi, and Xunzi. Xunzi, for example, was celebrated as a simple materialist who advocated that all should participate in labor regardless of social background and that

Reconciliation with traditional "Russia" and "China"   123

technical knowledge about agricultural production ought to be part of the curriculum (Huang 2014: 86). Based on Chen's and other scholars' research, in 1944 Mao argued that Confucius was a great thinker and his teaching philosophy was helpful to the Chinese Revolution. Mao openly claimed that revolutionaries should take in Confucius' emphasis of not discriminating against students who came from humble social backgrounds; but he criticized Confucius' devaluation of manual labor in education (Huang 2014: 74–75).

In debating with the KMT and other "reactionary" scholars, the CCP eventually found a fit spot to infuse China's past into the revolutionary track. The general guideline was to deny any claim of cultural essentialism in defining the "Chinese Nation" or "Chinese culture," and to insist that China's national cultural characters could only be defined by the people historically. Using the words of Ai Siqi, a philosopher and Mao's writing assistant, as a Marxist party, the CCP thought there could be no ethical or moral standards that applied to every society in history (Huang 2014: 60). This guideline sounded hollow but had a clear target, the KMT's effort of restoration of Confucianism as Chinese Nation's cornerstone. This guideline was also based on CCP literati's long research on old classics. In parallel with Chen Boda, Fan Wenlan, for example, conducted extensive critical research on the *Six Classics*, concluding that these pieces were not absolute law, but rather ideological products manufactured by "feudal rulers" to tame the people (Huang 2014: 50). Mao joined this critique, saying that traditional Daoist thought entailed dialectic elements but lacked emphasis on struggle and momentum (Huang 2014: 58–59). This period saw a break with the May Fourth Tradition, claiming that critique of the past should continue but a revolution had to engage the nation's existing tradition, history, and culture.

The relationship between the discourse shift and the expansion of revolutionary mobilization was also manifested in outliers, the Chinese Trotskyists. Chinese Trotskyists, originating among the Chinese students in Soviet Russia of the 1920s, inherited the Plekhanovan view that in backward societies the system was interlocked in a vicious cycle, and only external forces would be able to smash it. They became a tiny faction after the Trotsky–Stalin split and the CCP–KMT break. Adhering to the Trotskyist ideal that revolution had to be made solely by the working class, they were active only in urban areas. Trotskyists criticized the CCP's rural war for granting leadership to the backward peasantry and cutting the alliance between workers and peasants. During World War II, they also advocated what appeared to be an unrealistic transnational uprising to overthrow Soviet bureaucracy, Chinese reactionaries, and imperialist powers altogether.[4] Not surprisingly, the mobilizational scale of Trotskyists was limited, and most of their energy

124   *Revolution in China and Russia*

was devoted to polemics and programming. Many activists spent their time not at front of mass mobilization, but rather in prisons writing memoirs and pamphlets. All these were reminiscent of the Bolsheviks before 1917. Such a limited scale of social engagement allowed for the preservation of the most utopian ideological program, which did not yield to pressure to adapt the language of mobilization. Trotskyists' language persistently followed a theoretical tone of anti-imperialism and class struggle, involving no concession to peasant icons, folk arts, or historical figures.

The greater opportunity to invent a CCP China

The ambition to write a new national history for China was plagued by distractions. Not possessing a state machinery of its own, the CCP of the 1920s devoted tremendous resources to ideological indoctrination, through giving talks to officers, building up friendship with the KMT generals, and making speeches to soldiers and the general masses. Most of the work was conducted by the best educated CCP elites, the future revolutionary literati. However, these activities hardly promoted the development of nationalistic historiography. Propaganda was about the present rather than the remote past, explaining China's class structure, the atrocity and economic exploitation of "imperialism," the land problem, and the Comintern. The historical topics it touched on were mostly China's recent resistance and struggles—the Taiping and Boxer Rebellions (Gui 1992: 85–89). In general, propaganda was aimed at showing that the communists possessed a more intellectually well articulated program, in order to displace the KMT from the United Front.

Another source of distraction came from the CCP's work on its own recent history, partly as a way to draw lessons and partly as a platform of intra-Party power struggle. By the end of the 1930s, a series of major setbacks had occurred—such as the February 7th Massacre and the April 12th Massacre—which required reflection and which spurred the need for scapegoats. The literati were involved in producing pamphlets on these themes, such as Cai Hesen's *History of the Party's Opportunism* (Dang de jihuizhuyi shi), Deng Zhongxia's *Brief History of China's Labor Movement* (Zhongguo zhigong yundong jianshi), Peng Pai's *Peasant Movement in Haifeng* (Haifeng nongmin yundong), the collective-authored *The Massacre of February 7th* (Erqi da tusha de jingguo), and later, Hua Gang's *History of Great Revolution* (Da geming shi) (Gui 1992: 58–60, 67–68, 76–77, 252).

The CCP was more advantaged in inventing a revolutionary tradition. The 1920s and the 1930s, of course, were too early to write a CCP history. A few pamphlets and lecture notes were published during this period, such as Cai Hesen' *The History of Our Party's Opportunism*, Qu Qiubai's *A Concise History of the Chinese Communist Party*, and Li Lisan's *A Report on Our Party*. Some of these works were not associated with history, but rather, were reports for the Soviet Union on China's leftist movement, including Qu Qiubai's *Socialism in China* and Zhang Tailei's report on the Comintern's Third Congress (Zhou 2014: 63–64). Some others were written in retrospect, to reflect on the first CCP–KMT united front, in order to draw lessons from the recent past. These works highlighted criticisms of leaders and thus carried a style of ideological polemics that was not that different from the Bolsheviks' *Short Course*. But even in this period, the CCP had a people's history—the mass movement intent on abolishing unequal treaties with the "imperialist powers," the Northern Expedition, and the local Soviet regime, as well as engaging in rural guerrilla war. It was the mobilization of a nation, not merely the intra-CCP power struggle.

From the late 1930s onward, given that the CCP regime had stabilized in the Northwest, there was an institutionalized effort to collect materials about CCP's history. In Yan'an, under Mao's supervision, three collections were published, including telegraphs, written decisions, documents, and dictations gathered over the previous twenty years: *Before the Party's Sixth Congress*, *Since the Party's Sixth Congress*, and *Two Routes*. Based on these collections of raw materials, official textbooks, and pamphlets, with the mass audience in mind, they celebrated the CCP's endeavors in achieving mass mobilization and anti-imperialist heroism (Wang 2021: 69–73). From this period on, the CCP, having learned from its early mistakes of classism, was open to compromise and cooperation with social forces other than peasants and workers. The textbooks published in this period greatly criticized the "Closed-door Policy" in the party's history, emphasizing that the revolution ought to be the cause of the entire nation, not only that of one or two classes.

CCP's history began to be taught at border regions' schools on a regular basis, the notes of which were published as books upon the foundation of the PRC: Hu Qiaomu's *the Thirty Years of the Chinese Communist Party*, He Ganzhi's *The History of Modern Chinese Revolution*, and Hu Hua's *The History of China's New Democratic Revolution*. To be in accordance with the CCP's "democratic united front" in 1949, these textbooks covered the party's history in such a way that they celebrated its broad mass foundation. They all presented the revolution as a process of mobilizing "middle groups" rather than merely peasants and workers. "Middle groups," referred to a vague constellation of groups covering a wide political spectrum, which excluded only the hardest KMT core. "When our party dealt with middle groups inappropriately, we made mistakes and our cause suffered frustrations" (Hu 2008 [1951]: 82–83). "We have three lessons on dealing with the bourgeoise: a correct political route to unite with them; proletariat must win their support; we must respect the interests of the bourgeoise" (He 1984 3: 647–48).

The effort of narrating a revolutionary China extended to pre-CCP and even pre-modern Chinese history. The 1950 edition of the school history textbook, which was based on the local lecture notes of the CCP's North China Commission of Education, was mainly a history of peasant uprisings and dynastic changes, with little information on the economy, social life, or the technology of ancient China (Shi, Zhang and Wu 2015: 169). Such a tendency, interrupted by the experiment of educational decentralization in the "Great Leap Forward" and the "Cultural Revolution," returned in the late 1970s after Mao's death. Ancient history was taught as "a history of class struggle," with all other subjects—science, ethnic relations, and economics—removed. The political history was so dense that even many insignificant peasant uprisings were introduced, and, inevitably, it conveyed a sense of repetition and redundancy (Shi, Zhang and Wu 2015: 239).

By 1949 CCP's reconciliation with the past was more advanced than that of the Bolsheviks in 1917, but it was incomplete. There were no unified school textbooks nationwide to teach China's past in a way that was consistent with the CCP's revolutionary agenda. Whereas school education provided basic writing training, it was no preparation for the work of creating a new post-revolution culture. Based on detailed depictions of peasants' and soldiers' lives, authors needed to develop a clear model of "new men." Achieving this model required familiarity with modern literary theories, as well as with critical perspectives. Techniques mattered too. The skill of well-structured writing, based on close reading and imitation of modern novels and dramas, could hardly be taught by crash courses or derived from non-theory-oriented field observation. This largely explains why the old generations of revolutionary literati were often criticized for their lack of modern literary knowledge, and described as "unable to catch up with the momentum of revolution" (Li 1993: 81–96).

Moving to define a historical Chinese nation

China's intellectual exploration of articulating a unified foundation of a multi-ethnic China started in the late 1920s, two decades after the fall of the Qing Empire. When depicting the common denominator of ethnic groups, the most striking departure by Chinese scholars from pre-1917 Russian historiography lay in the emphasis on mutual interaction between the periphery and core, that is, a negation of a unidirectional annexation from the core to the periphery. The Chinese scholarship of this period was imbued with several tendencies, not without mutual conflicts. A narrowly defined Han-centric nation came to be discarded by most historians after the 1920s. Rewriting the historical Chinese nation as a deeply amalgamated multi-ethnic community was intended to demonstrate that the current feeble Chinese had once possessed a tradition of martial spirit and they were able to revive it, through the nomad-minorities who were less corrupted by the agrarian civilization. The multi-ethnicity-oriented reconstruction also reflected the politics of irridentism. Tracing contemporary minorities' biological lineages up to the nomad empires in the North or pirate fleets in the South, Chinese historians were developing a narrative that minorities had absorbed Chinese civilization and then migrated out to spread its elements to the outer world. When it comes to the concrete forms of "interethnic amalgamation" (minzu ronghe), historians' disagreement centered on how violent it was. Whereas some highlighted war, forced assimilation, and ethnic cleansing, others emphasized peaceful coexistence, economic interdependence, division of labor, and mutual learning in culture, costume, and the arts.

The blunt style of expansionism reflected the tsarist empire's geopolitical aggression, which did not hide its ambition, but rather openly claimed that the Russian state was a product of fighting and conquest in the name of religious universalism, modernity, and Europeanization. Confident and comfortable with an expansionist stance, the Russian Empire believed it could maneuver the rising nationalism to its advantage. Cast into historiography, this stance yielded research that had little need to articulate the peaceful coexistence of nations, but rather tended to frame "nationality" in an "objective" way, to highlight the elements most visible—language, religion, and territory. This style was inherited by Soviet Russia, which viewed nationalism as an ally and device to be used in its mission of creating a world revolution.

By contrast, Chinese historiography of the 1920s and 1930s stemmed from the timid mentality of a weak nation that had suffered foreign invasion and partition for nearly a century. Almost unable to reach any periphery by strength, the state as well as the intellectuals had no means but to claim an affiliation of peripheral ethnic minorities to China in order to defend the precarious borders. Such claims were actually useless, as they did not translate into any military forces to contain intruders, but there was no other card the Chinese could play to demonstrate their patriotism. In articulating such affiliation, historians and political elites invoked everything possible, objective as well as subjective, with the hope of convincing the people that the peripheral minorities had been part of China, and that their potential secessionism backed by foreign imperialists was historically ungrounded.

128 *Revolution in China and Russia*

Summary and conclusion

To transform an empire into a nation state, nation-builders must have pride in the nation's culture. Without such pride, nation-builders would avoid the "one nation" approach, resorting to a federation, union, internationalism, or other alternatives to underplay "one nation." For revolutionaries, feeling proud of a nation's past is challenging because revolution aims to break the old legacies. However, no revolutions are able to dis-embed themselves from their historical legacies and cultural context, no matter how anti-traditionalist they claim to be. Revolution-makers must also recognize that there is no unbreakable boundary between the nation's past and the revolutionary future. A sophisticated interpretation of the past can justify the revolution and provide it with instrumental support for mobilization and elite incorporation. A clumsy incorporation of the past can confuse and de-legitimize a revolutionary movement. Thus, the manipulation of the interpretation of the past imposes a high demand on the cognition and ability of revolutionaries. Whereas insecure but radical revolutionaries like the Bolsheviks of 1922 turned to a blunt rejection, revolutionaries more experienced with traditional culture, like the CCP after the 1930s, eventually developed a subtle infusion. The differences between the two revolutionary groups were not inborn, but stemmed from the process of making a revolution.

Each empire had a "core nation," which the revolutionaries sought to reframe to make a "one-nation" socialist state. One factor that led the two revolutions to different attitudes toward the traditional culture of the former "core nation" was the scale and depth of mobilization. A brief mobilization confined within industrial and intellectual populations did not demand a radical shift of revolutionary discourse to embrace the past. These were the conditions of the Bolshevik revolution. The Bolsheviks' direct negation of old Russian culture made sense, in that the openness toward traditional cultural icons and the glorification of the nation's past was a complicated project both ideologically and intellectually, which required technical support and which could arouse backlash from the inside. The Bolsheviks' radical critique of traditional Russianness during the revolution of 1917 reflected the double mentality of ideological confidence and insecurity. However, when the mobilization expanded to the entire society, the discourse designed for a narrow circle had to be altered. Whereas the Bolsheviks ultimately started this shift at the end of the 1920s, one decade after the revolutionary takeover, the CCP began this course in the late 1920s, two decades before the national victory of the revolution. The mechanism remained unchanged: when the revolution was transitioning from a worker-and-intellectual-based one to a rural and social one, covering all of society, the future-oriented elite revolutionary discourse had to absorb elements from the past and from folk culture.

This chapter complicates two pieces of knowledge in the preexisting literature. First, the "Great Retreat," the return from futurist ideology to embrace a core nation's past, cannot be reduced solely to geopolitical pressure from outside. Many scholars interpret the revival of traditional cultural icons as a strategic response to the rise of fascism around the Soviet Union and Japan's intrusion into China. Instead, the "Great Retreat" was an inevitable outcome of successful revolutions. A successful revolution, whether or not it encountered foreign intervention, had to build power upon the entire society rather than upon one or two classes. To ensure that the regime functioned, the revolutionaries had to extend the mobilization to the majority of the population, encompassing peasants, intellectuals, technocrats, and even traditional elites. Such an expansion was by no means a physical juxtaposition of multiple social elements, but it often involved brutal purges and forced transformation. However, a shift in discourse and framing was necessary so that they could speak in a way that would facilitate communication with the population and this would significantly ease mobilization by reducing the cost and resistance. No matter how Leninists exaggerated the leadership of the proletariat, their revolution had to become a multiple-class united front and a revolutionary nation. They thus needed a revolutionized nationalism to homogenize the social system. In China, this shift started when the KMT–CCP Civil War began, and in the Soviet Union, it started under Stalin.

Moreover, the "Great Retreat" was not a simple restoration of the past, though some Trotskyists argued that it was. When invoking a nation's past, revolutionaries always wanted to transform it to facilitate the revolution. However, the extent to which they could achieve this depended on the revolutionary course. Rather than "blunt rejection," there was "blunt take-in," whereby the traditional and revolutionary discourses were joined without change. When the switch from rejection to take-in occurred at an early stage of the revolution, the revolutionaries, lacking clear programs and technical experts, had to incorporate the past bluntly. This occurred during Stalin's restoration of the 1930s, which relied on old-school historians and, almost unchanged, incorporated the old cultural icons into the Soviet pantheon. By contrast, the "Great Retreat" occurred during the Chinese revolution slowly, when the CCP had generated a tradition of its own. When the switch occurred, the CCP elites were better prepared than the Bolsheviks of the late 1920s in terms of support from red specialists, familiar with the taste of allies, and the experience of peasant mentality.

The difference between the Bolsheviks and the CCP speaks to temporality. The two revolutions shared similar components, like the Great Retreat's affinity to traditional culture and the reconciliation with the nation's past. Still, these components entered the revolutionary course at different sequences, timing, and pace. Broadly categorized, the Bolsheviks and the CCP recovered national tradition to varying stages of their revolution. Still, in the Soviet Union, it occurred after the takeover of national power, while in the CCP it happened long before that. Moreover, in the Soviet Union, the reconciliation with Russia's past came almost immediately after the blunt rejection was renounced, and moved very fast, completed within a few years under Stalinism, long before the outbreak of the Soviet–German War. To create a rapid and easy reception by the masses, the Soviets anchored their reinterpretations of Russian traditions mainly in visual dimensions, such as drama, opera, biography of tsarist elites, painting, and sculpture. By contrast, in the CCP revolution, the retreat to absorb traditional culture into revolutionary discourse was an incremental course that endured for three decades. The CCP's absorption was also more comprehensive and covert. Connecting the revolution with contemporary rural languages and arts was only one aspect. Mao and his literati had an ambition of reinventing China's ancient philosophical and political thoughts.

Notes

1 Yun Daiying, August 25, 1925, www.marxists.org/chinese/yundaiying/mia-chinese-ydy-19250822.htm.
2 Deng Zhongxia, January 5, November, 1924, www.marxists.org/chinese/dengzhongxia/marxist.org-chinese-gong-192411a.htm.
3 Deng Zhongxia, December 29, 1920, www.marxists.org/chinese/dengzhongxia/marxist.org-chinese-gong-19201219.htm; Yun Daiying, December 25, 1925, www.marxists.org/chinese/yundaiying/mia-chinese-ydy-19251229.htm; Luo Yinong: August 25, 1926, www.marxists.org/chinese/luoyinong/mia-chinese-luoyinong-19260825.htm.
4 www.marxists.org/chinese/fourth-international/china/mia-chinese-fi-19510915.htm.

4

Revolution, nationalism, and multi-ethnic integration

The decline and collapse of the empire created opportunities for anti-imperialist revolutionaries, but the nation-building work after the empire tested them. Those who didn't stand the test lost their power. A burning question was how to integrate the multiple nations and ethnic groups into a single polity. Former empires that retained control of their entire territory took different routes to this goal. At one extreme was maintaining a loose enough federation so that all constituent nations enjoyed almost full sovereignty. This occurred in the British Commonwealth, the French Union, and the initial days of the Soviet Union (only in the constitutions). The other extreme was rejecting diversity and forcing the nation into a homogenous whole. Very few polities achieved this. The Portuguese military government refused decolonization in favor of a Greater Portuguese nation, but they failed. The Nazi and the Japanese empires of World War II counted as successful cases, but they were short-lived. Most sustainable routes of reorganizing empires into nation states were found between these extremes.

As defenders of imperial domains and supporters of nationalist movements, the Bolshevik and the CCP revolutionaries rejected loose confederation and homogeneous one-nation. They moved into an intermediate track characterized by nation-based centralized control. Such a route stemmed from the double faceted nature of communist ideology. Communism welcomed nationalism as a weapon to undermine world imperialism, but it did not want it to be a contender for unified world communism. This chapter makes a further argument. Beyond the ideological root, power relations in the process of revolution played a significant role in shaping communist revolutionaries' perception of borderlands. As victims of world imperialism (Russia's status was more complicated), Russia and China had good reason to manipulate nationalism to undermine their enemies abroad. Yet, as latecomers to modernization, they lacked the areas of superiority that guaranteed success in controlling nationalism. More likely, foes such as Britain, Germany, and Japan manipulated nationalism against them. The revolutionaries gradually sensed this threat as their revolutions moved from central areas

134   *Revolution in China and Russia*

(certain types of) nationalism were bound to arouse the sentiment of aggression (Kedourie 1993; Kohn 1944; Tagore 2001), and the idea that conflict in general could cultivate a sense of in-group solidarity (Sumner 1906). Numerous classic studies have been completed on how war and conflicts forged nations. Territorial nationalization created a fixed border within which nation-building proceeded (Tilly 1985). Mass education and military conscription are necessary to instill a sense of nationhood (Weber 1976). The improvement of combat efficiency, through geopolitical competition, places more pressure on polities to adopt nationalism (Posen 1993). To transform conflict into a process of national-solidarity cultivation, war-makers must maintain robustness to achieve centrifugal ideologization and cumulative bureaucratization (Malešević 2010: 188–91). The effect of war and conflict in transforming empires into nation states is central in explaining why there were so many different paths of transition.

Warfare as a double-edged sword in nation-building

Wars may have complicated effects on nation-making. This book focuses on two intertwined uncertainties. First, warfare could work to merge a multinational empire into one nation, or dissolve one empire into multiple nations. Whereas war had the effect of fostering solidarity, it also aroused fear. The fear of killing drove collaborative movement and secessionism among ethnic groups in the borderlands. Related to this was the center's anxiety about possible secessionism. Such a concern could lead to a fierce effort of integration, to ensure that ethnic minorities did not become a "fifth column," switching to the side of the enemy. Gaining momentum from both state and non-state forces, wartime vigilance often escalated to violent xenophobia and even to ethnic cleansing, which made war a centrifugal factor rather than a glue. In a moderate scenario, the fear of secessionism led to the center's precautionary concession, not precautionary repression. To pacify potential separatists, the center could further loosen and level the existing imperial structure, to transform the imperial polity toward an alliance of multiple brother nations. Therefore, for sober rulers, war was never a guarantee for nation-building—the old regimes that rushed into the gamble of playing nationalist cards were mostly likely to lose the war. It was a question of balancing and calculating how far it could go to use international war as an opportunity to foster homogenization and integration.

Numerous cases can be found of war exacerbating preexisting ethnic division (Hutchinson 2017: 97–98). The incorporation of Mennonites during the two world wars in North America moved along multiple paths.

Revolution, nationalism, and multi-ethnic integration   135

While the first exclusion and then inclusion of Mennonites in the United States indicates an extended ethnic definition of American national identity, the consistent harassment and exclusion against Mennonites in Canada suggests that the timing of entry and the structure of allies affected the impact of war on transethnic nation-building (Neufeldt 2009). Other cases were even more mixed, like tsarist Russia during World War I, where wartime xenophobia translated into exclusive campaigns against non-Russians (Lohr 2003), while at the same time Russians and Armenians were allied in the ethnic cleansing of Muslims in Central Asia (Buttino 2014). Pressed by a generally deepening geopolitical crisis, the Ottoman and Qing empires tightened their control over borders, to replace indirect rule with direct rule, which stimulated the separatist movement (Hechter 2000). In retrospect, war is often commemorated as having transcended ethnic cleavage, for example, as Yugoslavia and post-Soviet states show (Brunstedt 2011; Haug 2012), but the participants in the war did not think in this way. Again, at least, caution and calculation displaced a simplistic proposal to use war to integrate the nation.

The second uncertainty, from a class perspective, was that an international war could solidify a country as well as tear it apart. In the former case, war played a role in overcoming preexisting class cleavage, which had a cooling effect on the revolutionary impulse in European socialism during World War I (Nation 1989). The war created opportunities for internal division, civil war, and even revolution. The incumbent regime could be undermined during the war and thus lose its capacity for repressing revolution, as Skocpol argues (1979), or it could suffer a significant weakening of legitimacy, which constrained its flexibility in coping with domestic rivalries, as occurred to the post-1871 French state (Hutchinson 2017: 80–81; Ousby 2002). As with Skocpol's thesis, contenders, more strategically, had the option of offering up the old regime in the first instance, stepping back themselves to preserve their forces. Engaging in a real fight, revolutionaries could also obtain symbolic power, legitimacy, physical strength, combat skills, and eventually become capable of challenging the incumbent state.

How to deal with international war and civil war had been a perplexing question for communist revolutionaries. On the one hand, the engulfing of communism by nationalism was overwhelming. Since the 1880s, leading European powers had been advancing nation-building, which day by day eroded the transnational class identity that had undergirded the workers movement during Marx's and Bakunin's time (Anderson 2002). Humanitarian intellectuals bearing romantic cosmopolitan ideals were being displaced by "technical utilitarian socialists" who viewed national governance as more realistic (Weber 1964: 298–302). Throughout the 1870s and 1880s, the social basis of class universalism was diminished by mass national education, conscription, and tariff protectionism (Joll 1956; Stuart 2006: 175–76; Weber 1976). In 1914, all these changes led to the collapse of the European internationalist antiwar movement—in Lenin's words, "The Bankruptcy of the Second International." On the other hand, nationalism appeared as a fosterer of revolution. As Skocpol (1979) states, interstate war led to the state collapse of the old regimes in France, Russia, and China, which created political openings for revolutionary takeover. According to Lieven, the move of the major powers into suicidal wars were a complicated combination of geopolitics, but one of these factors was the authoritarian regimes' desperate sensate of crisis in their confrontation of the rise of anti-imperial nationalism (Lieven 2015). Lieven and Skocpol suggested that revolutionaries were able to manipulate nationalism to their advantage, rather than inevitably succumb to it, as the European socialists did in World War I.

Communists, as nation-builders and revolutionaries, considered the subtle relationship between international war and civil war. As nation-builders, they had to deal with the empire's legacies: the peripheral ethnic riots and secessionist nationalism. Such centrifugal movement could be both helpful and harmful to the revolutionary cause. Secessionist movements indiscriminately attacked every enemy who declined their quests, be they foreign colonizers, invaders, old regimes, or local bandits. Such indiscriminate attack had a distracting effect, undermining the foes of communist revolutionaries and easing communists' expansion and triumph. By the same logic, however, the communists themselves—given their class and their hyper-centralizing ideology that denied the significance of national identity—could themselves become the target of secessionism. In these circumstances, secessionism brought about unwanted outcomes, including the loss of territory, population, and tax income, as well as being a security threat from the rear. This double-edged aspect of secessionism thus put communist revolutionaries into a position of constant calculation of whether and how to choose between the two approaches: to integrate empire into one revolutionary nation, or to level it into an alliance of multiple revolutionary nations.

Communists also faced threats from outside. Very few communist revolutions were free of foreign intervention. External enemies intruded sometimes to conquer a society, and sometimes merely for the purpose of putting down a communist movement. In either situation, communists faced the choice of whether or not to self-frame as "defenders of the fatherland." This was not an easy decision as communists were supposed to always prioritize class struggle and not to engage in any conflicts that might be suspiciously similar to old imperialist war. No matter how communists maneuvered this course, dealing with international war had an impact on their transformation of imperial legacies. While foreign invaders had an interest in maneuvering peripheral nationalism against communist revolution, the actual

Revolution, nationalism, and multi-ethnic integration 137

engagement varied across regions and over time. Such variation impelled communist revolutionaries to carefully formulate and adjust their strategies. When a communist regime was insecure in handling ethnopolitics within its jurisdiction, it was very difficult to provide substantive support for devastating secessionism. In contrast, when a communist regime was a long distance from real ethnopolitics or sensed it as technically unlikely to collide with external powers, a rhetorical support for self-determination consistent with the Marxist notion of transnational proletarian solidarity could be preserved.

The Bolsheviks preserved the internationalist ideology and ideological restraint from the idea of a greater Russian nation. This stance was derived from multiple factors. Out of a complicated diplomatic negotiation, external foes, German-Austrian allies as well as the Entente, abandoned the idea of intruding into and occupying Russia by themselves. As for the lost territories where de facto states had been declared, the Bolsheviks, who were not close enough to touch them, supported their quest for national independence to further block external powers outside of the former Russian Empire. This settlement enabled the Bolsheviks to pinpoint the Whites, who were locked within a now enclosed space, as their major target. This pushed forward the frame of anti-chauvinism, rather than a Russified defensive patriotism. In the Bolshevik Revolution, despite the presence of foreign invasion and intervention, the logic of civil war overwhelmed the logic of international war. On the Soviet domain, the Bolsheviks' hyper-centralized mobilizational style and war arts sufficed to maintain control. The young state was not in a weak position in creating a narrative a of multinational Russia and in exhorting non-Russians to remain.

Russian Bolsheviks' limited sense of the imperial periphery

Except for a vague notion of a multinational Russia, the Bolsheviks' knowledge and experiences of the Russian Empire's periphery were limited and superficial before the revolutionary takeover of 1917. Under tsarist autocracy, Russia had generated an intellectual trend and political belief that this country could not be anything other than a multinational entity. Nationalism, despised as an imported invention fabricated by the Jewish, was rejected as unsuited for Russia. Rather, what the Russian great thinkers were obsessed with was the universal messianic idea for liberation and incessant incorporation of peoples (Sakwa 2006: 418–19). There was a recurrent thread in Russian political thought, transcending ideological disagreements, that Russia should encompass multiple peoples and nations to build the most ever complete civilization of human beings. In commenting on the debate between the Jewish and British model, Peter Struve, labeled by Lenin as the leading "legal Marxist," suggested that Russia should follow the British approach to incorporating and adapting to whatever cultural elements it encountered in expansion, rather than stubbornly adhering to an essentialist definition of tradition promoted by the Jewish (Struve 2000: 95–97).

The notion of a multinational Russia was taught at school. Prerevolutionary history textbooks for elementary schools, despite their concealed ideological stances and technical differences in periodization, depicted Russia as a multinational entity, the formation of which had been ongoing for centuries. The school textbooks compiled between the late 1890s and World War I mostly used dukes and tsars to set up chapters and they introduced each ruler's achievement in incorporating territories. The verbs used did not conceal or evade the character of annexation, but rather made it explicit—"fall" (*padenie*) of Poland, conquest (*pokorenie*) of Siberia, Khiva, and the Caucasus, "joining" (*prisoedinenie*) of Ukraine. Certain areas, such as Galicia and Lithuania, were compiled into the chapter title of "Northwestern Russia." By depicting historical wars, these textbooks also implied that other regions, such as the Balkans, Baltic states, and the Cossack Hetmanate, had been in intense interaction with Russia, directly or indirectly, for centuries (Davydkin and Seleznev 1911; Gorbov 1914; Presnianov 1915; Sipovskii 1884; Turtsevich 1913).

Literature—at least Bolshevik-approved literature—helped to rejuvinate the notion of a multinational Russia. It is debatable among literary scholars to what extent the classical authors—Pushkin, Gogol, Tolstoy—embraced Russian imperialism. Scholars suggest that these authors, though deeply engaging with peripheral themes in their writings, retained a critical stance toward official colonialist policies (Layton 1995). Others argue that their writings fulfilled a complicated function of romanticizing governmental expansionism, in addition to portraying Russia as an entity equivalent to the West (Thompson 2000), where peripheries, like Ukraine, were represented as wildland awaiting to be civilized (Shkandrij 2001). More recently it is also argued that writers such as Gogol strove to explore the periphery of Russia in creating a new genre, style, and language to mediate between his subversive Ukrainian cultural identity with a broad identification with Russian patriotism (Bojanowska 2007).

In comparison with historical textbooks and classical literature, the emerging discipline of ethnography was more attentive and offered a deeper knowledge of the empire's non-Russian periphery. Prior to the revolution of 1917, most peripheral nationalities lacked visibility at the most accessible level of historical and literary discourse. They did, however, have very limited influence that was confined to small groups of elite archeologists, ethnographers, and philologists, who were titled as "Orientalists"

Revolution, nationalism, and multi-ethnic integration 139

or "Eurasians." Toward the turn of the twentieth century, scholars of ethnic backgrounds from the Southern and Eastern peripheries of the tsarist empire had completed their training and started using European scholarship methods to study their home ethnic groups. The research of this period was academically provocative and politically subversive, with the ambition to demonstrate that the peripheral nationalities were even more advanced than the Russian center and should be awakened. But although their works had some circulation, they hardly challenged the dominant image of the peripheries (Tolz 2011: 120–29).

The Bolsheviks, generally undereducated radicals who had left school early, inherited the notion of a multinational integration of Russia mainly through school textbooks and the reading of outdated literature; contemporary elite scholarship of Eurasianism and Orientalism had the least influence on them. The Bolsheviks and other socialist parties offered contemporary authors' pamphlets and books in their libraries and training schools. The "Russian Highest School of Social Science" at Paris, for example, had an extensive curriculum, which included several general historical books— *Research on Russian Literature* by P. Boborykin, *Oprichina under Ivan the Terrible* by K. Valishevkii, *The Origin of Contemporary Russia*, and *History of Russia in the Sixteenth Century*.[1] The socialist democratic school within Russia had a more special focus in Russian history, covering rebellious movements in historical Russia and its peripheries. On January 28 1904, the Social Democratic Party circulated a call for literature in order to establish a library associated with the Central Committee. The letter said it would be interested in all types of movements, as long as they could contribute insight and inspiration to socialist subjects—such as, the Old-Believers, ethnic riots at the peripheries, anarchists, Slavism, student protests, and others.[2]

Rarely did the Bolsheviks' citations of classical literature invoke issues regarding nationality or imperial integration; and ethnographic scholarship was outside their range. The Bolsheviks' knowledge of the periphery came mainly from their revolutionary activities. The superficial presence in the empire's periphery, in many cases, reinforced rather than weakened their preexisting notion that these parts were indivisible from Russia. Travel across the tsarist empire, especially to its periphery, cultivated the Bolsheviks' concept of a multinational Russia, albeit very superficially. Most leading Bolsheviks had experience of living and working at national capitals and regional centers. This allowed them to recognize the empire's ethnic diversity and peripheries. Exile and deportation played a central role. In his diary, the famous commissar Iakov Sverdlov recorded his life in Siberia in great detail. Due to the deprivation of funds and subsidies, exiles struggled with extreme material hardship, which forced them to engage with local environments to some degree, by learning about agricultural labor. This dictated a

140   *Revolution in China and Russia*

transethnic cooperation both among exiles and with local people. Sverdlov also detailed that political prisoners were more willing to maintain their cultural distinction than general criminals were. Hostile to the Asian and rural settings, they usually refused to study local languages or marry local women, but rather kept reading German and French literature. The presumption was that once a chance was available, they would escape back to European Russia immediately (Sverdlov 1957: 33–34, 37–38, 47–48).

Some Russian Bolsheviks had long been living in the peripheries, but in highly Russified institutions isolated from local contexts, such as military bases and prisons. Emel'ian Iaroslavskii, a founder of the Bolshevik soldier movement, was born in Chita. Iaroslavskii's father was a Russian deported from Ukraine due to his rejection of military conscription, and his mother had grown up in Transbaikal (Fateev and Korolev 1988: 15–16). After his father's death, Iaroslavskii moved to Nerchinsk, a town closer to China's border, where he met with non-Russians as well as political exiles sent from the Western Russia (Fateev and Korolev 1988: 16–17, 66–70). Having joined the socialist movement and been conscripted, he went to Finland to receive military training, a skill he thought necessary for fighting against the para-military organizations of the Russian rightists. This, as well as later revolutionary activities, led to his imprisonment and exile, mostly conducted in Far East, until the February Revolution (Fateev and Korolev 1988: 43–44). Iaroslavskii was also passionate in building local museums of natural history, which, he argued, would help peripheral people understand the "richness of their fatherland" (Fateev and Korolev 1988: 57–64).

It was usual for early Bolsheviks physically to reside at the peripheries, but to be politically socialized by the atmosphere of the imperial core, which embodied tsarist Russia's tight integration as a modern empire. Mikhail Frunze, the Red Army's supreme leader after the Civil War, grew up at the Russian central Asian city of Bishkek, ethnically a Moldovan and Russian hybrid. Residing with his parents at a Russian settlement, his education was mainly Russian—the two-volume Russian history, the Slavonic Church, and excerpts from fashionable French novels printed in magazines (Ladimirov 1985: 13–14). At the higher grades of elementary school, his teachers came from Russia proper, and he and other students had a great fuller exposure to contemporary Russian culture, such as Gogol's drama (Ladimirov 1985: 14–15). After the death of his father, he moved first to Almaty, the political center of Russia's political radius to Turkestan, and then to St. Petersburg, where he received a university education and joined the socialist movement. Meanwhile, Frunze retained his Central Asian characteristics—he spoke fluent Kirgiz, which enabled him to make travel plans back to Central Asia to pursue academic research. His botanical research reached a professional level—he collected more than 700 types of plants, of which about 300 were previously

Revolution, nationalism, and multi-ethnic integration 141

unknown (Ladimirov 1985: 26). His later revolutionary experiences show how the notion of an integrated Russia and the identification with a non-Russian Asian frontier combined in Frunze's political thinking. Supporting Lenin's 1920 idea of "national armies," Frunze emphasized the necessity of keeping national armed formations at the borders of Bryant, Turkestan, and Tatarstan. He suggested that these units, unlike most units, should not be transferred in order to avoid losing their knowledge of local topography and population (Bezugol'nyi 2016: 71–73).

Unlike Kalinin who traveled within Russia proper, Sergei Kirov, the head of Leningrad assassinated in 1934, spent a significant part of his pre-1917 years at the imperial periphery, in the Caucasus, where he wrote columns for a local liberal newspaper and socialized with socialists (Kirilina 2001: 25–26). Being an ethnic Russian originally from Viatka, he didn't develop a patriotic sense from his reading of international conflicts (Kirilina 2001: 18–19). Rather, it was his provocation of agitations across factories in the Northern Caucasus that led him to see this region as indivisible from Russia. After the February Revolution, Kirov declared a Republic of Derska, but soon retreated north-ward to Astrakhan, where the 11th Army, in his command, was to guard the mouth of the Volga into the Caspian Sea. For the remainder of the Civil War, he actively worked on guaranteeing the transport of oil from Baku to Astrakhan to fuel the Soviet forces at the southern front. This led him to be in charge of the guerrilla uprisings in Georgia and Azerbaijan, both of which were annexed into the Soviet Russia in 1920 under the name Transcaucasian Federation (Morozov 1949: 5–7, 11–12). In August 1920, in a letter to Lenin, Kirov claimed that "local Muslims and Armenians counted on the Soviet state to solve the problems that had tortured them" (OGIZ 1944: 11).

In general, unlike in China where the peripheries were largely closed to and isolated from Han Chinese, migrating to work at the peripheries was common in tsarist Russia. The distance of travel was not necessar-ily long, but it was distant enough to send the person into a culturally and linguistically entirely different region. This situation arose in part from the fact that Russia's industrial centers, under the tsarist regime, were located not far from borders and, in many cases, at the peripheries. Whereas Mikhail Tomskii, a St. Petersburger, traveled to Tallinn, where he witnessed the 1905 Revolution (Gorelov 2000: 6–7), Viktor Nogin, a Muscovite, was forced to live in Poltava after his arrest for radical activi-ties (Podgornyi 1966: 5–6). The empire's multinationality was also in evidence at central locations where different people gathered and passed through. For Viacheslav Molotov, his radicalization stemmed from the location of his family at Nolinsk, a town to the north of Kazan, a loca-tion associated with exiles. It was a Ukrainian Social Democrat, who lived with Molotov and who was acquainted with his elder sister, who introduced him to the revolutionary movement (Nikonov 2005: 24–25). Yet such travel was superficial, and cannot be simply converted into a statistical proportion; it did not alter, but rather reinforced the notion of multinational integration, which the Bolsheviks had learned from textbooks and literature. Though boosting national self-determination, the Bolsheviks, like their conservative, liberal, and non-Bolshevik socialist foes, by no means expected to lose the vast domain of the former tsarist empire. According to Lenin, in post-revolutionary Russia no nation would be given privilege, but the entire area of Russia should stay together. Each nation's culture and language should be respected, but individuals would freely choose the language that maximized their benefits and convenience, which was to make the universal use of the Russian language voluntary rather than coerced (Lenin 1971: 8–11).

Russian nationalism as the major target of revolution

Russian nationalism existed before the revolution of 1917, but it was confined to a technical level, not involving serious thinking on how to build up a post-monarchist space. After the defeat by Japan in 1905, state Russian nationalism gained momentum—impressed by the combat bravery of Japanese soldiers, the military establishment started routinizing "patriotic education," which instilled soldiers with the Orthodox religion and a dedication to monarchy, hailed historical war heroes as examples, and gave them a set of ethics for everyday deeds.[3] However, in parallel, the opening up of the Duma system and the decree on religious freedom boosted the public expression of non-Russian nationalism and thus led, through conflict, to various versions of non-state Russian nationalism (Kappeler 2001: 341–48). This response immediately confronted the incipient project of creating Russian nationalism with the difficult question of how to deal with Russia's multinationality. Russian nationalism receded between 1914 and 1917, dissolving into misinformation about and the demonization of Germans, rather than positively integrating native symbols and thoughts in order to shape a coherent national doctrine that united all ethnic groups into one combatant political entity (Brandenberger 2002).

The interval of 1917 was chaotic and perplexing, as Russian nationalism began to make the transformation from a technical device to a political doctrine. At the moment of the tsar's abrupt downfall, there was no consensus as to where the domain of the new Russia should end and how the new territory should be organized. The rightists, who had lost their legitimacy with the fall of the monarchy, preferred a racist approach and soon disappeared. The new establishment—ministers of the Provisional

Revolution, nationalism, and multi-ethnic integration 143

Government—claimed an adherence to a republican, multinational, and indivisible Russia, which was inscribed in the title of the new polity: Republic of Russia (Rossiiskaia Respublika). However, except for insistence in the continuation of war, which reduced a multinational Russia to a confrontation with a significant other, this state did little to formulate a common civic frame (Rosenberg 1974: 18–19). After the February Revolution, the Orthodox Church launched a campaign named renovationism, which released the clergy's longstanding quest to remove the state from religious affairs. Such a resistant stance against the incorporation of religion into the counterrevolutionary cause was welcomed by the Bolsheviks, though both sides soon recognized that proletarian and religious values were incompatible (Roslof 2002: 15–19). Among officers, the disappointment with the tsar that had accumulated during the three years of war led to widespread support for the replacement of the monarchy by a republican system. Yet, lacking clear civic thought with regard to replacing the dynastic universalism, White nationalism first had an apolitical tone and then, in its confrontation with non-Russians, lapsed into military dictatorship and Russian chauvinism, defying the quests of non-Russians (Karpenko 1992: 29, 80–82; Mawdsley 1987: 197–99).

Within the spectrum of the progressive parties, the political forces to the right tended to preserve and cultivate the notion of a multi-ethnic Russia to succeed the Romanov empire, while the forces to the left tended to deconstruct such a concept and dissolve it into an anarchist community or an outward-looking revolutionary movement to spill over beyond Russian borders. Monarchist liberals, "Octoberists," were political nationalists with a clearest idea of Russian nation. They called for the construction of an inclusive Russian nation based on a combination of monarchy with representatives of the people. The direct connection between monarchy and the people, the cornerstone of the new community, would be able to eliminate distinctions caused by bureaucratic apparatus, class, and ethnicity, to shape a unified Russian nation. Insisting on "a unified and indivisible Russian nation regardless of differences in ethnicity and belief," Octoberists in their program of 1906 opposed ideas of unionizing Russia or transforming Russia into a union of multiple states (Pavlov and Shelokhaev 1996: 59–60). In criticizing some cosmopolitan Kadets of 1905, they insisted that the notion of "Russian" (both Rossiiskii and Russkii) should never be removed (GARF 2000: 62–68). Octoberists also suggested that Orthodox education should be reformed to nationalize the empire, with the Slavonic Church replaced by Russian-language teaching (GARF 2000: 280–81).

Based on their experiences of local self-governance, the Kadets, who were middle liberals, proposed a Russified federal republican state.

Promising that local people would retain rights to develop their own special cultures and languages, liberals insisted that the state should be a national community, in the sense that Russian would be the working language of the central apparatus, army, and navy (Pavlov and Shelokhaev 1996: 53–54). Beyond this, liberals optimistically leaned on the universal mindset—toward zemstvo-style self-governance. They envisaged that, except for the few most basic cultural specialties to reckon with, zemstvo-based civility would be "broad and flexible enough" to overcome the diversity among ethnic groups (Pavlov and Shelokhaev 1996: 27–37). The civic proposal was also viewed as a transitional stage, as well as a strategy to avoid revolution. In a critique of Gorki's celebration of vulgar toilors, Nikolai Berdiaev argued that a mature "all-national culture" equivalent to Western European ones had not yet taken shape in barbarian Russia; such a national culture could only be cultivated gradually rather than created by revolution (Pavlov and Shelokhaev 1996: 103). The Russian historian Sergei Andreevich Kotliarevskii argued that the slogan of "indivisible Russia" had to be softened—giving Poles, Transcaucasians, and Ukrainians autonomy would deflect the idea of revolution (Pavlov and Shelokhaev 1996: 113–15).

In comparison, leftist parties were more ambivalent and divided on the idea of constructing an overarching Russian nation, favoring a more decentralized structure. Like liberals, leftists thought of universal political principles as primary in shaping new men—the right-wing Mensheviks actively sought to incorporate as many broad elements as possible in order to consolidate a post-imperial democracy. Yet, unlike liberals, leftists were far less devoted to retaining a community that was congruent with the territory of the tsarist empire. Their voice was often raised in a call to dilute Russianness rather than accentuate it. In this regard, the Trudniki (Labor Popular-Socialist Party) rested closest to an all-Russian nationalist organization. Trudniki claimed a break with the conspiratorial tradition of the Russian socialists, self-identifying as a legal party in pursuit of the broadest alliance of laboring people. Its program was one of class mediation, not excluding or representing any single social group (Sypchenko and Morozov 2003: 64–65, 79–89). Reducing the nationality question to everyday welfare, Trudniki did not raise out its position until the Revolution of 1917, from which point on, it came into conflict with the Bolsheviks. Trudniki denounced the pro-Bolshevik communists in Ukraine for the latter's revolutionary separatism, insisting that the Republic of Russia should hold together in its advancement to democracy (Sypchenko and Morozov 2003: 386–87). Inviting Entente powers to intervene in the Russian Civil War, Trudniki warned that Russia was not the Hapsburg Empire and a policy of Balkanization should not apply (Sypchenko and Morozov 2003: 412–13).

Revolution, nationalism, and multi-ethnic integration   145

The Menshevik faction was more complicated. Its right wing sought the role of mediator, opposing the exclusion of the financial Kadets from Russian democracy on the grounds that their inclusion was vital to an inclusive Russian nation (Galili and Nenarokov 1996: 314–19). The middle and internationalist wings, however, showed a different face. The old Menshevik Iurii Martov expressed such a complexity on the eve of the Bolshevik takeover in October. Martov argued for the necessity of expanding the local autonomy of national minorities as a check on the "Russian" center, which appeared to be moving to a counterrevolutionary stance. Meanwhile, he insisted that the revolution had to be carried out by a unified political and economic front, with no peripheries or regions left isolated (Galili and Nenarokov 1996: 383). Another leading Menshevik, R. A. Abramovich, expressed a similar position that a unified revolution would protect the rights to native language and culture, but each group should fight against the nationalism and chauvinism of their own nation. National liberation should not become a fight of nationalism (Galili and Nenarokov 1996: 229–30). Leftist Mensheviks were doubtful of the liberals' vague stance on the nationality question, believing that the masses needed more than liberals sought, which could only be provided by a political revolution. The Jewish Menshevik Lydia Dan denied the possibility that Jews could be liberated simply through assimilation into a framework of liberal monarchy (Haimson 1987: 75).

The Socialist Revolutionaries (SR) agreed, in principle, to reorganize tsarist Russia into a federation, but they hardly held a clear position on whether this new community should be a Russian national one. The SR viewed the February Revolution as inefficient. In terms of building a new community, they had exclusive criterion for membership, only considering "toilers" as the constituents (White 2011: 14, 36–38). The left-wing SR held a position close to that of the Bolsheviks, who believed ethnopolitics could be exploited for a deepening revolution. Placing priority on supporting local spontaneous uprisings against every form of counterrevolutionary, they were thus denounced by defensist revolutionaries as the foes of a "federal socialist Russia" who were to cause the loss of Ukraine, the Caucasus, and Siberia (Leont'ev, Liuhudzaev and Rublev 2015: 145–46). A more consistent thread of the SR was its anarchist vision of a stateless world, where workers and peasants self-governed around factories and communes (Astrakhan 1973). They celebrated a "world federation of soviet socialist republics," and even brought back the old populist program of "commune self-governance" (Leont'ev, Liuhudzaev and Rublev 2015: 158–59). This stance went against both the liberals' integrationist as well as the Bolshevik's centralist visions of reorganizing the former Russian Empire

Bolsheviks: International war as a second priority

A vague conception of a multi-ethnic nation could be clarified by a war(s) with a significant other(s), as occurred to many multicultural and multi-ethnic nation states, like Canada, Finland, Ireland, and the United States. Yet, it was at this moment that the Bolsheviks demonstrated their location at the leftist end of the political spectrum of 1917. Whereas Socialist Revolutionaries, Mensheviks, and Trudniks were more or less captivated by defensive nationalism, the Bolsheviks, especially Lenin, were of a mind to counter popular pressure, continuing to adhere to revolution as the top priority, and not to allow for any distraction. The Bolsheviks did not entirely abandon the discourse of defensive nationalism, but rather manipulated it to the advantage of power seizure and consolidation. There was a difference across the official frame, conversation, and strategy in practice. The Bolsheviks' tactics also differed from those of the White generals, who prioritized the ongoing international war and insisted in keeping the Russian Empire's territory intact. This contradiction, which revealed the absence of a unified "structure," led to the two sides addressing the notion of the Russian nation in opposite ways: as something to destroy or as something to preserve. Contriving to conclude the international war immediately and not to get it restarted, the Bolsheviks managed to preserve the internationalist character of its ideology.

To justify the revolution, the Bolsheviks had tended to depict Russia as a large and weak power in decay, lapsing into a crisis of survival. For example, Stalin claimed that, for the century following the War of 1812, Romanov Russia had been in decline vis-à-vis newly arising rivalries—Germany, Japan, and the United States. "The setback in Crimea and the Far East deprived Russia of its military status of 'European gendarme' and placed Russia in a precarious position similar to the Austro-Hungarian Empire, the Ottoman Empire, or even China" (IMEL 1947 5: 62). In the economic area, Lenin's pamphlet, *Imperialism, the Highest Stage of Capitalism*, expressed the concern that Russia, for its slow-moving pace in industry and manufacture, counted only as the second-tier of the six imperialist powers (Lenin 1948). This Bolshevik discourse before 1917 was consistent with the general political concern of that period. The anxiety was widespread among most political forces that Russia was becoming a semi-colony of the West, as its industry and finance were penetrated by foreign capitals. The prewar decade saw a rapid increase of the proportion of enterprises controlled by non-Russians—Germans, French, Poles, and transnational Jews, which aroused concerns among nationalists and liberals (Lohr 2003). Such a national crisis was perceived by most political parties, regardless of their ideological orientations. Warning that Japanese and US enterprises were rapidly displacing

Russian ones, Octoberists, the right-leaning centralists, suggested that free ports should be closed. These people also pointed out that Russia's navy-building had fallen behind that of neighboring powers (GARF 2000: 45, 74–75). Octoberists were concerned that Russia was losing influence in the Balkan region, as many small nations were achieving autonomy under the intervention of Germany and Austria (Semyonov and Smith 2017). Even the moderate financial technocrat Sergei Vitte, the prime minister who opposed military expansion and geopolitical adventurism, conceded that Russia had to invest in education and speed up transportation development in order to catch up with Western powers (Vitte 1960).

As the revolution started, however, the deep cleavage of Russia's national crisis surfaced. The old military establishment, based on their firsthand experiences at the front as well as their narrow focus on war, continued to fear that Russia was rapidly falling from the status of declining power to that of becoming a precarious prey, a situation similar to what was happening in India, Turkey, and China. The had grounds for such anxiety. Failing to force the Provisional Government to conclude a uniliteral peace treaty, the German General Staff—on the eve of the Bolshevik takeover—planned a total offense to destroy Petrograd (Novikova 2018: 40). From the other camp, fearing Russia's switch to Germany's side, in October 1917 the French General staff drew up a plan to partition Russia: the Baltic region would remain occupied by Germany; a confederation of Ukraine and Poland would be established under the supervision of Austro-Hungary; Finland and Eastern Siberia would respectively belong to Sweden and Japan; the Don, Kuban, and Northern Caucasian Cossacks were to establish independent republics of their own; the remaining territory of Russia would be integrated into a Moscow republic joint controled by the Allies (Kononova 2018: 105). Such a situation provoked intense nationalist backlash among the personnel who worked for the former establishments—diplomats, officers, and intellectuals (2018: 256–59).

The Bolsheviks' discourse, which diverged from the nationalist position, eased the path for the Soviet regime to sign the humiliating Brest–Litovsk Peace. The Bolsheviks' justification was threefold: Soviet Russia had exhausted its capacity to continue the war; the war, by its nature an imperialist one, had nothing to do with the interests of the laboring masses; and Soviet Russia could survive by navigating between two antagonistic relationships—between Britain and Germany, and between America and Japan (Degras 1951: 35–36, 44–45, 78–79). This decision led to mounting pressure—from the Entente powers, from the nationalist-minded middle class, from officers, from German uprisers, and from socialists who looked for an imminent world revolution. But Lenin's position was not without grounds. It is true that the Russian Civil War was never "civil," in that multiple foreign powers were involved (Smele 2015). Yet, what mattered was that the Bolsheviks believed that the external interventions could be maintained at a superficial level. Though the Entente had sent detachments to safeguard Russia's ports and railways, the Soviet regime intentionally evaded direct confrontations with Entente forces—it was only in exceptional circumstances, such as those in Estonia, that British and American forces exchanged fire with the Bolsheviks (Moffat 2015: 246). In a tacit response, the Entente interventions prioritized safeguarding strategic hubs and transportation lines, rather than striking at the Bolsheviks (Somin 1996: 35–41). The Bolsheviks' strategy proved correct, capturing the cleavages underneath the seemingly inevitable structure of antagonism. The war-devasted railways were so incomplete that interventional militaries were forced to stay at a few coastal spots where they landed (Willett 2003: 203). Additionally, inconsistency and poor coordination were at work in undermining the Entente's willingness to engage. The Canadian government quit the intervention at first, deeming the Kolchak government as an even worse military dictatorship, and this started a domino process (Richard 2013: 64–65). Japan and the US competed with each other in Eastern Siberia and both refused to move into the west to Baikal Lake (Moffat 2015: 259–60).

Aware of the low likelihood of direct confrontation with the Entente, the Bolsheviks held to the priority of advancing revolution and civil war by manipulating popular nationalist sentiment. The intelligence arm, Cheka, was assigned the task of creating an impression among the populace that Russia was encircled by Western powers and that domestic counterrevolutionary plots had international support from foreign enemies. To this end, individual Western diplomats and journalists who had been involved in activities that could be branded anti-Soviet were targeted as conspirators (Andrew and Mitrokhin 2001: 25–27). In a speech in 1920, Dzerzhinskii claimed that the SR rebellion against the Brest Peace had involved diplomats from the Entente, and that the White generals served as their agents. He even cited evidence that the Mensheviks were business collaborators with the Entente (IMLpTsK 1967: 265–66, 284–85, 289–90). In real combat, the Bolsheviks exploited nationalist sentiment to put legitimate pressure on the Whites by accusing the latter of receiving foreign aid. For example, Kliment Voroshilov, Stalin's minister of defense in the 1930s, played the patriotic card by negotiating with the White headman, Momentov. When Voroshilov's workers-based partisan detachment was besieged by the White's Cossack calvary, he held a meeting to negotiate with general Momentov, warning that they should stop receiving weapons from the Germans (Akshinskii 1976: 64–65).

The Bolsheviks' evasion and manipulation of Russian defensive nationalism was not an inevitable outcome of the structural cleavage, but rather hinged on their special foundation of legitimacy, organizational integration, and informational capacity. The combination of these agent-level factors

Revolution, nationalism, and multi-ethnic integration   149

allowed the Bolsheviks to attain the strategic flexibility and cost-assuming ability that their domestic rivals did not possess. In this regard, the counterrevolutionaries were a counter group. Some Whites, like Petr Krasnov, viewed German aid as essential to repelling the Bolsheviks, but they by no means wanted to serve as a watchdog for foreign powers. Such a stance put them into a self-defeating crisis, since the White movement claimed a monopoly on patriotism and safeguarding Russia. In fact, Krasnov faced enormous pressure from the populace as well as from the Entente, and lost financial support because of his approach to the Germans (Venkov 2000: 118–42). Similarly, Petr Vrangel, another White leader, initially resisted approaching Britain and France, preferring to develop a collaboration with the Germans through the Ukrainian Skoropatskii state, on the grounds that Russia had been freed from its obligations to the Entente (Venkov 2000: 280). Nikolai Iudenich, determined to defend a Russia of the pre-1918 domain, refused to grant autonomy to Finland and Estonia, which not only brought him into tension with the British government, but also removed the possibility of establishing a stable anti-Bolshevik government (Venkov 2000: 406–7). The old military's patriotic legitimacy limited the flexibility in handling the situation around the end of World War I.

Ethnopolitics in the Bolshevik Revolution

One major factor that enabled the Bolsheviks to continue their internationalist discourse was the increasingly secured control over minorities, which precluded the rise of political separatism. Unlike the CCP Civil War of the 1930s, where local partisan warfare dominated and had the high cost of drawing manpower from local populations, the Bolsheviks of 1918 mainly relied on a highly centralized Red Army, which was capable of moving fast from one front to another. This separation from the local population was to the Bolsheviks' advantage in controlling the multi-ethnic troops under their proletarian banner. In the theater of Ukraine, there had been tension between the provincial revolutionary committee (heavily populated by Ukrainian nationalists) and the local branch of the Republican Revolutionary Military Commission, but centralization was advanced after the arrival of Vladimir Antonov-Ovseenko. As the full-power representative from Moscow appointed by Lenin, Antonov-Ovseenko was backed by forces brought in from Petrograd, including the Latvian Shooting Regiment and the Baltic Fleet Sailors, as well as infantry troops consisting of workers from the Nikolai Putilov Factory at Petrograd, all of whom were elite forces who had participated in the October power seizure (Rakitin 1975: 205–12). Based on this force, Antonov-Ovseenko moved on to build up an armored division and Black Cossack calvary, whose supplies and weapons were all transported from Moscow by railway, not from local nationalists. It was backed by such a force that Antonov-Ovseenko was able to deprive the local Rada of its power and transfer all power to the Cheka, while at the same time exerting symbolic soft policies toward former tsarist governors (Rakitin 1975: 201–2). He continued to frame Ukraine as an internationalist theater where proletarians from Russia, Ukraine, and Latvia, as well as Hungary, Czechoslovakia, and China jointly fought against German imperialists and the Whites (Rakitin 1975: 217).

With logistic supplies centralized, the Bolsheviks had a reduced fear of separatism from within, even though some forces heavily drew manpower from local populations. In marching to Siberia and Central Asia, Valerian Kuibyshev, general commissar of the Red Army, established the 24th Steel Shooting Division based on Samara factory workers. As Kuibyshev claimed, this division was Lenin's army, with "all fighters concerned with Lenin's health and fighting for Lenin's security" (Dubinskii-Mukhadze 1971: 127–33). With a strong emphasis on centralization and discipline, Kuibyshev chaired the enaction of the Red Army's code of political work, which was to be the foundation of the indoctrination of the Soviet armed forces. With Lenin's approval, upon entering Turkestan he created a Turkestan section of the RKP to unite local revolutionary groups (Pokrovskii 1963: 42–43). Kuibyshev resolutely declined the proposal of establishing armed forces of each nationality, asserting that "separate national formations" were unable to safeguard the Soviet fatherland. It was under his command that Muslim forces were in close coordination with the rest of the entire Eastern front, exerting no national autonomy. As the program of the 24th Samara Steel Division stated: "No nationalities have their own scripts ... we have only one face, the proletarian face ... even if Chinese comrades joined us, we transform them into Samara khodi" (Samara 1921: 9). Meanwhile, Kuibyshev was opposed to Islamophobia, insisting that the Red Army had to immediately conscript Central Asian soldiers and allocated them with weapons and uniforms. He maintained that making the Soviet armed forces "the homeland of all nationalities" was the sole means of precluding bourgeois nationalism (Dubinskii-Mukhadze 1971: 165–66).

Many legendary Soviet units in the Civil War were multi-ethnic by composition and retained a certain locality during the initial period, but they lapsed into close restraint by Moscow. To start with the ones established by Antonov-Ovseenko, the 9th Red Putilovskii Cossack Calvary Regiment comprised Siberians, including Siberian Russians, Chuvashi, and Votiaki. No longer local, this troop was transferred to Poland, joining the offense on Warsaw in 1920. After the Soviet–Polish pact, it entered Ukraine to fight Ukrainian nationalists (Grenaderov-Tenishchev, Semchuk and Popov

Revolution, nationalism, and multi-ethnic integration 151

1930: 12). The 24th Samara Steel Division started as a battalion of the old tsarist army. The battalion, headed by an Armenian officer, survived the brutal battle with the Austro-Hungarian Czechoslovakian forces. As part of the old military bureaucracy, this unit had a weak sense of locality from the start, and any such locality was further weakened with its transfer to the Eastern front and first supplemented by Samara workers to expand into a division and then joined by Muslim battalions (Samara 1921: 12–13). The 44th Rifle Regiment was initially commanded by Polish partisan Kviatek, Warsaw railway worker and veteran of the 1905 Revolution, and commissar Peter Nemtsev. After the Brest peace, Kviatek was transferred to Moscow for a short training course and then placed into cooperation with the red commander Nikolai Shchors. The reestablished unit was sent to Ukraine to fight local nationalists. After defeat by the German counter-guerrilla operations, they retreated back to Russia and thus underwent another round of composition shift (Zhitomir 1928: 10–11). CCP-style local partisan groups did exist, but they did not play a major role, except by being incorporated into a centralized command and transferred into a nationwide war circulation. The Chongarskaia 6th Calvary Division, based at Kuban steppe, for example, was a local group during its foundational period. This weakness led to its withdrawal from combat and assumption of responsibility for grain allocation in support for the Red Army nearby. Not having a institutionalized connection with the Red Army, the partisans could obtain a small number of weapons from Voroshilov's forces. It was only after the separation from their homeland that such troops were given real combat opportunities (GG 1924: 5–6).

With major supplies under secure control, the Bolsheviks created the impression that it was not Russia, but rather non-Russian nations that were fighting for self-liberation vis-à-vis foreign intruders and counterrevolutionaries. Anti-imperialist and revolutionary nationalism was created by the Soviet state, and to survive and thrive it had to stay dependent on Soviet forces. This strategy was clearly manifested in Andrei Bubnov's activities in Ukraine. At the breakout of the Civil War, Andrei Bubnov, a Russian old Bolshevik, was dispatched to Ukraine, the "South of the Country." Entering the multiparty institution, the "Commissariat of Insurgency," as the Bolshevik representative, Bubnov started the Bolsheviks' control over the Ukrainian nationalist movement—he and other Bolshevik agents were backed by Soviet regular forces deployed close to the Russo-Ukrainian borders. To secure logistic support and organizational control, Bubnov established numerous training centers alongside the Ukrainian borders, which periodically sent pro-Bolshevik activists back to Ukraine. Thus, he contrived to transform the partisan groups and Soviet apparatus scattered across Ukraine into a unified "insurgency force," which appeared to be fighting against reactionary Ukrainians, Germano-Austrian forces, and the

152   *Revolution in China and Russia*

collaborative Skoropadskii regime to liberate the motherland—it was these forces upon which the Red Army's 44th, 45th, and 60th divisions were to be founded. Successfully transferring the "Commissariat of Insurgency" to Moscow, Bubnov deprived other parties—the SRs, Mensheviks, and leftist Ukrainians—of influence, and made Ukrainian nationalism a fully Moscow-controlled enterprise (Rodin 1988: 34–49). Meanwhile, Bubnov moved on to further tighten the control on the Ukrainian forces. A special commission on accounting and redistribution was established to centralize the railway system. The leader of the 12th Army was court martialed—accused of using wagons without the Center's consent. All the Ukraine-based armed forces were reorganized and modeled on the Soviet Russian Red Army, creating commissar systems (Rodin 1988: 58–59).

A similar strategy was used in the Caucasus, where after the tsar's downfall, Azerbaijan, Armenia, and Georgia declared independent non-Soviet republics while Terek and Stavropol had become autonomous Soviet republics. Moscow manipulated the concept of "laborers' national liberation from imperialists and bourgeois nationalist government" to squeeze non-Bolshevik forces out of this region. Under the leadership of Grigorii Ordzhonikidze, the Civil War in the Northern Caucasus soon became a course of centralization after its inauguration. In a chaos of armed conflicts and economic crush, Ordzhonikidze established a commission of emergency, which eventually took back power from local Soviet insurrectionist groups, most of which were unable to regularly attend the congress of Caucasian Soviets. This Commission of Emergency later dictated that the autonomous Kuban autonomous oblast', Black-Sea Province, Stavropol Soviet Republic, and Terskaia Soviet Republic be merged into the RSFSR, in the name of uniting all forces to jointly fight counterrevolutionaries. But the appearance of autonomy was intentionally maintained for the sake of propaganda—at Ordzhonikidze's insistence, the city Tsaritsyn was allowed to be formally independent of the administrative region it was de facto affiliated with. Later on, reinforced by the Latvian division transferred from North Russia by railway, a special strike corps was established as the core of the Southern front in fighting the Denikin Whites, and Ordzhonikidze was appointed as chairman of the Revolutionary-Military Commission (Kirillov and Sverdlov 1962: 107–18).

After the Northern Caucasus had been conquered, Ordzhonikidze played the same trick in the Southern Caucasus. In all three countries, the Bolsheviks, making use of the chaos caused by the devastation of war, supported local partisans to organize pro-Moscow armed rebellions. Once insurrections suffered setbacks, the Soviet forces entered these territories, in the name of stopping counterrevolutionary massacre (Kirillov and Sverdlov 1962: 125–45). Moscow's control over the Southern Caucasus

Revolution, nationalism, and multi-ethnic integration 153

was secured in several ways. Diplomatic agreement had been achieved between Soviet Russia and Kemalist Turkey to block this intermediate belt from any third force (Kurban 2017)—it was after the withdrawal of British troops in autumn 1919 that Ordzhonikidze began to plan Russia's invasion. The Moscow-supported insurrections and strikes were organized with the clear purpose of centralizing control over the facilities of strategic importance, so as to deprive local nationalists of power. For example, under Ordzhonikidze's command, the crew of the Transcaucasian railway and Batum port struck to fight "the fake national government colonized by the British," while at the same time all insurrectional groups remained under the tight control of representatives from Moscow, to make sure that the offense was confined to the Georgian non-Bolshevik government, and not extended to the Entente, the Germans, or the Turkish, so as "not to be dragged into the war plot" (Kirillov and Sverdlov 1986: 99–101, 131–39). The format of "nation state" was preserved conditionally—as Stalin commented, the three Southern Caucasian republics differed from Belarus and Ukraine in that they had established independent national government before returning to Soviet Russia, and thus a Transcaucasian federation ought to be imposed on the three republics to ensure control (Gasanly 2013: 528).

Denouncing Russian nationalism was the passive face of the coin. The Russian Civil War was a crash process that compressed multiple stages, simultaneously encompassing empire restoration, world revolution, and elimination of domestic counterrevolutionaries. To maximize its power, the Bolshevik regime attempted to maintain a subtle flexibility between encouraging national self-determination and advancing a social-transformative agenda, by developing an official discourse of proletarian solidarity. Sergei Gusev, the Red Army's commissar and guerrilla specialist, pointed out that both Reds and Whites were absorbing multi-ethnic soldiers in huge numbers, a situation in which poor coordination could lead to destabilization (Gusev 1925: 55–56). Hence, both sides competed to ride the wave of spontaneously erupting nationalism while not allowing that nationalism to distract from the core political agenda. The Bolshevik way was to downplay ethnicity and nationality, which were replaced by a wide array of other concerns. Some highlighted civic values, such as a unified proletarian class, democracy, international friendship, and the elimination of exploitation, whereas others emphasized technical issues like iron discipline and standardization. When it came to specific terms, a geographical connotation was implied, such as "Russia's working class," "Russia's laborers," and "Samara's class brothers."

As military control became secured, the Bolsheviks' conceptualization of nation and nation state was arbitrary, not fully confirming ethnic boundaries but rather often prioritizing geopolitical issues. The Soviet–Polish border was a sensitive case in this regard. By ethnic standards, the status of Belarus was in question. Ivar Smilga denied Belarus's cultural distinction, arguing that the Belarussian language was merely a dialect of Russian (Lubachko 1972: 110–12). Nor was political loyalty a problem. Summoned by Mikhail Sverdlov, Belorussian communists had confirmed their obedience to Moscow, not intending to create a separate Belarussian nation state (Lubachko 1972: 13–14). However, influenced by Moscow's setback in the Soviet–Polish War of 1920, Gavriil Miasnikov, an Armenian Bolshevik who participated in the leftist opposition for freedom, insisted that Belarus should merge with Lithuania to become a separate nation state (Lubachko 1972: 90–101). His argument was echoed by Vilhelm Knorin, a Latvian Bolshevik, on the grounds that a seemingly independent and natural nation state under the control of Soviet Russia would help maintain Russia's access to the European market (Lubachko 1972: 50). However, later on, Georgi Chicherin maintained that Lithuania ought to be secured as a nation state, as a buffer to counter the influences from Poland. This position gained approval and thus led to the foundation of a Belorussian Soviet Socialist Republic (Airapetov 2020: 41). Following the same logic, Georgi Chicherin insisted that Moscow immediately conclude a peace pact with the Estonian government while, at the same time, negotiating to remove economic blockage, as a strategy to estrange Estonia from Britain and France, two powers it had counted on. When a Soviet-controlled nationalism was unfeasible, an anti-imperialist nationalism was a second best option (Zarnitskii and Sergeev 1966: 118–20).

The Bolsheviks' creation of the Soviet Republic of Karelia embodied the pattern of controlled nationalism as well. In the Karelian case, the format of nation state was imposed, and opponents were removed. Right before World War I the Finnish territory was under tight control by tsarist Russia: Helsinki was the major base of the Baltic Fleet, and the city Viipuri was the headquarters of the 42nd Army (Smith 1955: 483), which rendered a constant threat that Russians could attack back to seize these facilities. After the February Revolution, the Bolsheviks' penetration quickly expanded—the Whites' intrusion into Karelia during the Finnish Civil War provided an excuse for the Bolsheviks to support the Finnish Reds in this area, which inaugurated a long course of intervention. The Entente's forces had been concentrated around Severodvinsk and Murmansk, but did not move further northward. The creation of the Karelian Commune (KTK) was a step forward—to relieve the KTK's financial dilemma, Lenin made the decision that Moscow would purchase grain with gold at a price higher than the international one and aided the construction of a hydro-electronic power plant in the Kondopozhskii krai, which strengthened the Bolsheviks' economic control (Egorov 2011: 35–55). Within the Karelia region, Bolshevik

Revolution, nationalism, and multi-ethnic integration   155

control was initially limited, in a fragile coalition with leftist SRs, but as power went to the local Cheka branch and the newly established Red Army formations from the other side of the border, local partisans' leverage vis-à-vis Moscow decreased (Wright 2012: 304–5). It was on such a foundation that the Bolsheviks began to debate whether and how to transform the Karelian Commune into a Soviet national republic. The proposal that finally triumphed was "Finnization," which was to make Karelia a center of Finnish language and culture, as well as a region mainly populated by Finnish, as Georgi Chicherin pointed out (Kilin 2012: 26). But this proposal was fiercely protested by Karelian Reds, who insisted that Russian dominance should not be impeded. The leaders of the opposition were immediately removed and exiled to Siberia (Kilin 2012: 21–25). The Karelian case again shows the importance of agency: though Russification had a deep foundation among the populace as well as within the leftist parties, the leaders' calculation could go against its popularity. The Soviet national model of indigenization was not a compromise, but rather a strategic offense.

To deal with complicated geopolitics, the Bolsheviks even considered creating a second Soviet non-national polity. This idea was attempted in creating the Far Eastern Republic (DVR), a buffer state founded in 1920 and dismantled in 1922. The title of this state was not a universal one like "Soviet," but a regional and territorial one, with no ethnic connotation. In the formation of this republic, Moscow supported Buryat-Mongolian, Korean, and Chinese nationalism in this region, to counterbalance the Japanese and the Japanese-supported Whites led by Semenov. This republic came into being amid an emerging consensus between Moscow, Tokyo, and Washington, that as long as Moscow refrained from Sovietizing this region, the US and Japan would not maintain a full occupation (Sablin 2020: 189–98). As leftist SRs and Mensheviks refused to participate, the power fell into the hand of the Bolsheviks, headed by Alexander Krasnoshchekov as president, which further confirmed Soviet Russia's status in this region. While within the Bolshevik leadership multiple conceptions of the DVR coexisted, Krasnoshchekov insisted that the republic had to be in direct leadership by Moscow, rather than under the RKP(b)'s Siberian bureau. Retaining autonomy in economic affairs, Krasnoshchekov proposed to build this buffer state into an demonstration of revolutionary internationalism supporting the cultural development and liberation of the Russian, Chinese, Buryat-Mongolian, Korean, and Japanese populations (Sablin 2020: 272–74). It was through the DVR that many leading CCP elites first entered Soviet Russia.

Secured control was also evident in the way in which the Bolsheviks sensed the danger of a separatist tendency growing out of a nationalist movement it had cultivated. They used harsh repression in a straightforward way to reassert the principle of centralization vis-à-vis "national communists." At the PKP conferences, the Volga-Tartar communist Mirsaid Sultan-Galiev faced several fatal accusations: organizing national sections within the communist party and building alliances with conspiratorial forces outside of the party—a provocative challenge to the Leninist principle of banning factionalism; colluding with British and French imperialists to penetrate Soviet Central Asia; conspiring with bourgeois Islamic nationalists in Turkey and Persia to establish pan-Islamic organization overseas; and striving to build a pan-Islamic and pan-Turkic republic within Soviet Russia (Sultanbekova 1992: 22–37). With the Basmachi rebellion crushed by the Soviet regular forces, the Bolsheviks, having secured control over Central Asia, asserted that "our periphery doesn't lack revolutionaries, but rather lacks partisanship (partinost') ... we must immediately send reliable and experienced political workers to the periphery to establish party organizations among semi-proletariat and artisans, to prevent progressive intellectuals from becoming Islamic nationalists" (Sultanbekova 1992: 42–45). Likewise, later in Ukraine and Azerbaijan, repression targeted national communists Nikolai Skrypnik and Nariman Narimanov, warning that these republics were under the control of Moscow and the Union center had no need to compromise.

When it comes to open and official language, the Bolsheviks used the term "nationalism"—Russian and non-Russian alike—in a negative manner, to demonize its domestic rivalries as well as secure a centralized control over the forces of its own. The term nationalism was associated with aggression, ethnic cleansing, antisemitism, exploitation, and collaboration with imperialists from outside. When Semen Budennyi, one of the first five Soviet marshals, was accused of poor discipline and banditry, he defended his troops by attributing anti-Semitic atrocities to Ukrainian nationalists and the White Russian general Vrangel' (Sokolob 2007: 161–63, 171–73). Likewise, the failed offensive against Poland, initially framed as a march to bridge revolutionary Russia to Germany, was attributed to the evil Polish nationalism. According to Karl Radek, the extent of nationalist intoxication of the Polish working class had been significantly underestimated, and it would freeze the revolutionary movement for the time being (McCann 1984: 481–83). In the Southern Caucasus, the Armenian Dashnaktutiun state was accused by the Bolsheviks of being aggressive nationalists, who provoked a war with Turkey and incurred massive slaughter of civilians (Kirillov and Sverdlov 1962: 141). Peripheral nationalists were also denounced as accomplices to the Entente plot—it was reported that in Chechenia and Terskaia Cossack land, local residents blocked Cheka staff, which made this region a fragile border penetrable for British spies (Gatagova, Kosheleva and Pogovaia 2005:

61–62). Baltic and Ukrainian nationalists were accused of being economic agents who collaborated with Germany to destroy Soviet Russia's trade, while the Russian White nationalists concentrated in London were "British spies," according to Viacheslav Menzhinskii, chair of OGPU, who were penetrating the Soviet Union through a "Russo-Asian Company" to arrange wreckers in the program of electrification (Smirnov 1985: 156–59). In light of the view of peripheral nationalism as the fifth column of imperialists, under Menzhinskii's leadership all border control of imports and exports was transferred from the People's Commissariat of Foreign Trade to a Cheka's special branch affiliated with the RKP's central committee (Smirnov 1985: 180).

Reflections on the Soviet model during and after the revolution

As already noted, the tendency towards Russification never disappeared in the flood of revolution: both the Bolsheviks and the population they were mobilizing were dedicated to the idea of reorganizing the former empire into a Russian socialist national state, or Russian federation, which was less at odds with the former administrative structure with which they had been familiar. It was the priority of revolution over international war that drove the Bolsheviks to manipulate nationalism as a revolutionary weapon rather than a slogan to re-Russify the socialist empire. Nevertheless, reflections on the pattern of Soviet internationalism had started even when the revolution was still ongoing. The feeling that a revolutionary internationalism could not be used to organize an established state was growing, as the Bolsheviks accumulated firsthand experiences of the nationality question. While using vilification of "the other" as a frame within which to invent and unify multiple nations, the Soviet state had to keep the entire society at a restless state of revolutionary struggle. Since the failures of the uprisings in Germany, Hungary, and Romania, such expectations seemed decreasingly realistic. Certainly, in a sense, the Soviet Union in the post-revolutionary decades had been locked onto such a track, but it is also true that once the new state became settled, keeping an all-out revolution constantly going was increasingly difficult. A return to a settled identity-construction became attractive.

The concern with centrifugalism was not groundless, and it grew as the revolution expanded geographically. The program of maneuvering nationalism was not as well controlled as the Bolsheviks had initially anticipated. Once national consciousness was awakened and encouraged, it could grow in directions the Moscow Center didn't want to see. Even though control through coercion and economic dependency still functioned, the social and political cost remained huge. In Soviet Azerbaijan, for example, Nariman Narimanov, a former nationalist, pursued a monopoly in dealing with the oil revenue produced by Baku mining. Narimanov also pursued an autonomous role in Soviet diplomacy. Echoing Lloyd George's advocation for the incorporation of the Southern Caucasus into a Turkey-centered economic zone, Narimanov insisted in maintaining a direct business relation with the West, bypassing Moscow. This position was both in accordance and at odds with Moscow's intention that Soviet republics, including the Transcaucasian Federation, should attend the Genoa Conference as if they were independent states. Such a tendency towards autonomy annoyed Maxim Litvinov, who insisted on a unified, Russia-controlled stance (Gasanly 2013: 549–51). Narimanov also coordinated Azerbaijan's interference with the foundation of the Soviet Republic of Iran, which created the image that Persian communists were receiving support not solely from Russia but also from a newly liberated former Islamic nation (Chaqueri 1995: 233). With a similar momentum, Ukraine requested that the Soviet republic should possess an embassy alongside that of Soviet Russia in countries where the Ukrainian population was concentrated (Gatagova, Kosheleva, and Pogovaia 2005: 66). Unlike in Azerbaijan, Ukrainian nationalism had an important leader in ethnic Russian-Bulgarian Christian Rakovskii, who chaired the Ukrainian Economic Council by July 1923. In dealing with famine and massive unemployment, Rakovskii aimed to establish business relations with Britain, Germany, and France, independent of Moscow's supervision, which created a way to trade Ukraine's raw materials with the West in exchange for agricultural machinery, technological expertise, and trust credits. Economic nationalism was also manifested in a direct contact with American relief organizations and an open refusal to transfer Ukraine's grain to feed Russia (Conte 1989: 155–70).

The unleashing of peripheral nationalism in the name of the revolution led to a backlash from Russians—the sensation of being sacrificed and betrayed had been prevailing before the Soviet Union was officially declared—and this was another factor that the Bolsheviks had to reckon with. Many debates arose when the borders of newly proposed Soviet nation states were demarcated—Georgi Chicherin, for example, was opposed to the incorporation of counties inhabited by ethnic Russians into the Karelian Republic, on the grounds that Russians had made a great sacrifice and ought not to be further offended (Kilin 2012: 26). In Caucasian areas, such as Dagestan and Chechenia, Russian agents complained that local non-Russian cadres lacked skills, and that Russians had to complete all the work for non-Russians. Russian agents thus requested respect equivalent to their contribution, not wanting to see slogans such as "Russians, please leave our republic, and we can govern it by ourselves" (Gatagova, Kosheleva and

Revolution, nationalism, and multi-ethnic integration   159

Pogovaia 2005: 43–44). The same sentiment prevailed at Russo-Mongolian borders, where Russian agents, in opposition to the Oirat-Mongolian autonomy, complained that Russian power ought to be expanded, given that the Oirat Mongolians didn't have the capacity to safeguard their borders against the Whites (Gatagova, Kosheleva and Pogovaia 2005: 51–53).

Support for a Russified structure came not only from ethnic Russians, but also from Russified non-Russians who had a real need to diminish skepticism of their political loyalty to Russians, as the Belarussian, Eastern Ukrainian, and Southern Caucasian Bolsheviks demonstrated. One basic consideration behind the "One-Russia" plan was simplicity and convenience. Based on his experiences in the Balkans, Rakovskii felt that the ills brought about by nationalism could be prevented by simply preserving the old one-Russia structure without creating new nation states within it. It was from such a logic of avoiding redundance that Rakovskii, in the aftermath of the February Revolution, sided with Grigorii Piatakov in support of abolishing all small republics in Ukraine (Conte 1989: 144). In defending Baku from British intervention, Stepan Shaumian, the Armenian Bolshevik, viewed all native Armenian nationalists as British and Turkish spies. In a desperate blockage through which no weapons or grain could be delivered from Moscow, Shaumian maintained the hardline position against the moderate SRs and Mensheviks in fighting the British, on the grounds that Baku's oil and transportation line was vital to safeguard Russia. This led to his murder (Dubinskii-Mukhadze 1968: 249–54). The language of countering Russian chauvinism was a vigilant response to such hovering nationalism—as Rakovskii debated in drafting the Soviet constitution of 1923, power should be devolved as much as possible from the union secretariat to national republics in that the Russian population and bureaucracy were overwhelmingly stronger (Conte 1989: 179).

The other side of the coin of Russians' arising discontent, and a major lesson from the ongoing revolution, was the fact that nationality was not an objective concept, but rather was subject to invention, reinvention, and manipulation, indicating that a revolutionized approach of Russification would not be as hard-going as the pre-revolutionary approach. The Bolsheviks' Leninist principle of centralization, the Marxist economic determinism indicative of Russians' special status as an advanced proletarian cultural cluster, the revolutionary reinvention of the Russian historical tradition, as well as the formidable machinery of coercion formed over the Civil War, were all workable factors to soften and sustain Russification, to reorganize the former empire into a Russian national federation. Josef Stalin embodied all of these, and his revolutionary career involved a complicated attitude toward Russia and Russification. Originally a Georgian, Stalin learned Russian as a second language, speaking it with an accent. His early poetry expressed a nostalgia for the Georgian land (Stalin 2013: 17–29) and antipathy to Russian teachers' discrimination against Georgian students (Montefiore 2007: 46). Nevertheless, over the course of the revolution Stalin became a supporter of Russification, in the sense of using the Russian language as a common communication device and in the concept of a multi-ethnic Russian nation as an overarching framework of the new socialist state. In May 1918, in a letter of report, Stalin was accused of refusing, against the Bolshevik majority, to put the question of founding a Tartar-Bashkir republic on the agenda (Gatagova, Kosheleva and Pogovaia 2005: 17). Stalin's debate with Lenin on whether the socialist state should be a "union" or a "Russia" is well known. In a letter to Lenin at the end of 1922, Stalin insisted in rescinding the formal independence and integrating non-national republics into autonomous regions of a Soviet Russian federal republic. He warned that powers devolved during the Civil War to national republics should be taken back immediately—that they had been breeding grounds for de facto independence. Stalin gave as an example the fact that in Georgia the republic leadership developed a bilateral economic relationship with Turkey allowing the Turkish lira to legally circulate (Gatagova, Kosheleva and Pogovaia 2005: 78–79). Stalin's navigation between Georgia and Russia suggests that ethnicity and cultural identity did not necessarily translate into one's political stance.

Stalin preferred the old tsarist structure to the adventurist approach of reorganizing the empire into an internationalist union of independent nation states. In the position of commissar of nationality affairs, Stalin argued that the federation of national republics was a poor imitation of the Austro-Hungarian Empire, an outdated model which had proved bankrupted since World War I (Gatagova, Kosheleva and Pogovaia 2005: 39). Well-known for his proposal for building a Great Russian national federation to cover all non-Russians, Stalin was also the first person who suggested that nationality could be defined subjectively. The four components of nation elaborated in his Marxism and Nationality Question—common territory, common market, common language, and common psychology—were all arbitrary and vague, serving the purpose of disqualifying certain groups being nations. Around the end of the Civil War, Stalin had been warning that the republics in Transcaucasia were issuing independent national money and developing diplomacy with Turkey bypassing Moscow. He dismissed the necessity of pleasing Ukrainian linguistic indigenization, arguing that after land revolution peasants had had no interests in seeking independence (Gatagova, Kosheleva and Pogovaia 2005: 76–77). Though Stalin finally conceded to Lenin in not insisting in his Great Russian program, his thought of using Russian language and icon as the Soviet Union's universal foundation survived and persisted.

Revolution, nationalism, and multi-ethnic integration 161

Stalin's preference for a Greater Russian unity involved a perspective of economic determinism, which considered the absolute obedience of the peripheries to the center to be essential to sustaining the revolution. In October 1920, Stalin made a speech in defense of his proposal for a Russified and centralized structure. According to Stalin, the periphery and core were mutually dependent. Central Russia needed raw materials, fuels, and grain products to self-support; without aid from the more advanced Central Russia, peripheries would fall into the yoke of imperialism. This was the source of the Entente's plan to block Central Russian economically, cutting off its contacts with the peripheries (Gatagova, Kosheleva and Pogovaia 2005: 39). Stalin's one-Russia plan was also evident in a belief in Russia's overall superiority in providing management, industrial technology, and military protection to peripheries (IMEL 1947 4: 296–97, 345–46, 351–55, 408–10; 5: 90–92). In March 1921, he wrote to Lenin regarding the plan for electrification, advocating against the federalist approach that the Soviet republics should have a single unified economic plan (IMEL 1947 5: 51). He argued that a plan of economic recovery should respect the historically formed regional division of labor, while defense should be based on a unified federation, given that the resources had been so scarce and the Entente was employing a policy of divide and rule (IMEL 1947 5: 147–50).

Certainly, it would be misleading to overstate Stalin's persistence in Russification, as observers who imagined the Soviet project as a sheer conspiracy to conceal Russian dominance did. Stalin's reign continued the mixed legacies left over by the revolutionary years. The Soviet state continued to develop a transnational identity based on a jointly made revolution and war. "Partisanshchina" had been a negative term in the Bolshevik's ideological dictionary—referring to the dark side of the Civil War: Whites, bandits, deserters, and poorly disciplined Red combat units. Yet, under Stalin's reign the idea was rehabilitated. Identifying "good partisans," based on Red heroes of the Civil War like Vasilii Chapaev, officials glorified the guerrilla fighters in the war against Napoleon and the peasant rebellions against tsardom (Cornish 2014: 5–6). In a pamphlet published in 1947 to celebrate the 300th anniversary of the foundation of Simbirsk, the peasant rebellion led by Stepan Razin was glorified as interethnic solidarity across Chuvash, Cossacks, Mordvins, and Mari peoples fighting against tsarist rule. It was emphasized that the revolutionary partisans bore a deep attachment to the Russian homeland, hating foreigners—the German mercenaries serving in the tsarist army (Karzhavin 1947: 19, 31–32).

The management of the Soviet–German War was complicated. Apart from shaping an image of transnational solidarity in fighting fascism, it was used as a step to explore an ethnicity-dissolving Soviet identity, which carried a connotation of nation state. The guerrilla resistance boosted a Soviet identity as well as a national one, mutually embedding the two. The common experiences of suffering under Nazi atrocity, with the deportation of certain conventionally alien populations, forged a national identity that transcended previous ethnic cleavages (Amar 2015). This galvanized Stalin's postwar response of using the Soviet–German War as a device to reinforce Russian identity, though such an effort was in parallel with other considerations. The anti-cosmopolitan movement in the aftermath of the war was punitive in character in an effort to warn local nationalists, especially in the areas that stayed under Nazi occupation. Estonia and Georgia were respectively selected as models of bad nationalism (Zubkova 2004: 145–46). Revolution never ended. Coup, uprising, war, and conflict in general were always invoked as the common denominator of multiple nationalities.

The CCP's early geographical imagination of the revolution

The CCP revolution resembled its Bolshevik predecessor with regard to the nationality question in many ways. There was a collective perplexity about where the post-imperial border should end and how to reorganize the former imperial periphery. How to justify a new multi-ethnic community remained an intellectual and political challenge. As in the Bolshevik revolution, minorities were viewed as potential allies to counterbalance the domestic and international foes of revolution, though they were not fully trusted and there was anxiety around ensuring that they did not become foes of the revolution. Although China was ethnically more homogeneous in a numerical sense, the CCP's attachment to the periphery was far weaker than that of the Bolsheviks. Meanwhile, there was a tendency to see the revolution as taking place in a unified geographical space—and to view peripheral minorities as a fence around the revolution in inland China.

Despite the similarities, the two revolutions were marked by sharp differences. The CCP's relationship with the periphery involved more uncertainty, in that the revolution's reach was geographically limited. Moving back and forth between the concepts of a narrowly defined inland China and a multi-ethnic China, the CCP elites appeared to lack the Bolsheviks' clear understanding of the ways in which a particular section of the former empire was strategically vital to a particular stage of revolution. Moreover, in comparison with the Bolshevik regime, which had secured control over the periphery by the end of the Civil War, the CCP was fighting on a weak side of the protracted contestation, with limited and fragile influences on many minority groups, who had more direct exposure to the KMT, Japanese, and Soviets. The CCP revolution was more mixed. The protracted guerrilla war was a revolutionary subversion, as well as a means of establishment.

Revolution, nationalism, and multi-ethnic integration   163

The CCP had come to sense that multi-ethnic solidarity under its jurisdiction could not rely solely on fighting a common foe—be it national or class enemies—but rather had to be embedded in some peaceful cultural identity similar to banal nationalism.

The first years of the post-imperial period were perplexing. Though the late Qing state had made some attempts at merging Qing and China, such as naming Qing citizens as "Chinese" in its citizenship law (Huang 2017: 49) and compiling geographical textbooks that encompassed Mongolia and Tibet (Zhao 2006: 16–18), the work of legitimization remained centered on the dynastic cornerstone—this was how the loyalist Yang Du articulated the necessity of preserving a constitutional monarchy (Huang 2017: 91). Thus, after the Revolution of 1911, it was necessary to invent a non-monarchial framework to legitimize the idea that Han proper and non-Han peripheries should continue as one China. There were many proposals. The Beiyang solution was moderate, enshrined in the five-color national flag, symbolic of five major ethnic groups—Han, Manchurian, Mongolian, Hui, Tibetan. Such a design openly acknowledged perplexity: the multiple peoples had a common past but the commonality needed to be redefined, and how to best redefine the commonality remained an open question. Diverging from the humility of the Beiyang solution, Sun Yat-sen's was more assimilationist, based on his conception of the model of the United States. According to Sun, "China" remained open to all peoples; no matter who or how many joined, they had to be assimilated into Han culture (Liu 2017: 20–21). Alongside this assimilationist route, non-Han peripheries were depicted as the "fences" and "gates" of China, which had been suffering the encroachment by imperialist powers (Esherick 2006). Related to this was an approach to nation-building through the creation of an "other"—a common denominator to connect multiple nations within the Qing territory and even throughout East Asia, blurring the boundaries between nationalism, regionalism, and imperialism (Zhang 2014). Efforts were also made by leading scholars to find or fabricate historical traditions—non-Confucian and non-dynastical—underlying the nationalities of the former Qing domain, such as historical heroes, a feudal system sponsored by local strongmen, and Buddhism (Zarrow 2012: chap. 6).

The most senior cohort of the CCP was made up of those who participated in the Revolution of 1911 and its extension of the 1910s—the expeditions of 1913 and 1915 against General Yuan Shikai and the expedition of 1917 against the restoration of the Qing Dynasty. Unlike the Bolsheviks who had participated in the Russo–Japanese War and World War I, most senior CCP elites were young enough to have missed the First Sino–Japanese War and the Russo–Japanese War, and grew up in the long peace between 1901 and 1931. These CCP elites gained their perception of the former imperial periphery from news of China's defeats. The memoirs of these elitists have two common features. They deplored the geopolitical crises since the First Sino–Japanese War, which was unconsciously a collective framing of the Qing's losses of Taiwanese, Korean, Vietnamese, and Xinjiang peripheries to "China's national humiliation." In this sense, they had differed fundamentally from the early anti-Qing KMT of the 1890s who envisaged a Han China. On the other hand, these CCP elites also deemed the notion of multinational China as thin and tenuous, which meant they were affected by fashionable internationalism, oscillating back and forth between the periphery's self-determination and the defense of a multi-ethnic China extending from Xinjiang to Korea.

Though not explicit, early CCP members conceived China as almost congruent with the domain of the Qing Empire and they viewed it as a heroic ambition to recover the lost territories; but a Bolshevik-style technical and material perspective was absent. This conception did survive until the late stage of the CCP revolution. Wu Yuzhang, a former KMT-participant in the 1911 Revolution and later a senior CCP leader of education, clearly remembered the psychological impact of China's defeat by Japan in 1894, which made China's Manchuria territory of contest between Russia, Japan, Britain, France, and Germany (Li 1978: 4–7). Later, in 1903, when studying in Japan, Wu participated in the "Movement of Resisting Russia," which was a protest against Russia's occupation of Manchuria during the Boxer Rebellion (Li 1978: 19–21). As seen in Wu's memoir, most protest was based on an emotional lament of the losses of territory, despite the protestors never having been to the borderlands. In this regard, Lin Boqu was an exception. For Lin Boqu, the CCP's vice chair of the NPC after 1949, identification of Manchuria as an integral part of China translated into radical operations. Returning from his study in Japan, Lin traveled to Jilin, with the assigned mission of agitation in the Qing's Manchurian homeland. In Jilin he joined the local Qing government as an officer for education. In a report, he wrote that this region, bearing rich natural resources but located in between Russia and Russia, needed the development of education to maintain its precarious status (Lin 1984).

In the perception of early communists, the southern Qing periphery was an integral part of China too. As Mao Zedong recollected in the 1940s, at elementary school he was emotionally impacted by a pamphlet on the "partition of China," from which he learned that "China lost Annam and Burma," and this made him a Chinese nationalist (Mao 2002: 15). Xie Juezai, a jurist and later a leader of the CCP's judicial system, wrote in his diary of 1920 that the local people in Taiwan wanted to remain as part of China's fence and to transform the island to a republic so that it would not be annexed by Japan (Xie 1984: 81). Qu Qiubai, the CCP General Secretary,

Revolution, nationalism, and multi-ethnic integration

was a sincere Tolstoian in 1919. With the Russian populist movement as a model, he argued that citizen education should be spread to China's peripheries, including "Mongolia, Xinjiang, and Tibet" (Y. Zhou 1992: 116). Behind this notion of an expanded multinational China lay a belief, as Li Dazhao argued, that the peoples on the former Qing domain had generated certain irreversible blending, which could function as the foundation of a new Chinese nation (Huang 2017: 125). The CCP's conception of a multinational China persisted into the Sino–Japanese War. In a textbook on the united front policy of the University of Resistance (Kang ri jun zheng da xue), authored by Kai Feng (Kai 1938: 11–13), China's "national humiliation" was narrated as a continuous process of losing its peripheral fences, from Taiwan, Ryukyu, and Annam, to Burma, Ili, Macau, and Sikkim. In 1939, the first edition of Mao's *Chinese Communist Party and Chinese Revolution* continued the statement that China lost Burma, Bhudan, Ryukyu, Nepal, Vietnam, Korea, Hong Kong, and Macau to imperialist powers, though Mao's later versions omitted these names (Liu 2017: 24).

Nevertheless, the CCP's perception of a post-imperial multi-ethnic China was far from stable and consistent. Beyond affinity with the Qing-created concept of China, the CCP elites, when returning to the nationalism that had justified the idea that all former imperial members should continue to stick together, were not as confident as they emotionally protested against Japan and Britain. Nationalism was criticized by the CCP elites as redundant, with incoherent patriotic slogans that were not based on institutionalized ideological indoctrination (PDRO 2000 1: 19–26). Nationalism was often invoked at social events to lament China's humiliation, and the display of heroic sentiment was mocked by Deng Xiaoping, for example, as "bar-and-ball patriotism" (Yang 1998: 42–43). In terms of content, Chinese nationalism looked like a coarse improvisation that attempted to incorporate all "good values;" hence, it fell into superficiality and incoherence (Xu 1987 1: 33–35). For the CCP elites who completed their education in the 1920s, like Chen Yun, Gao Gang, Bo Yibo, and Wang Jiaxiang, post-imperial nationalism, at the level of everyday life, offered little to the youths who were seeking meaning, discipline, diligence, and austerity (Bo 2008: 32–40; Dai and Zhao 2011: 8–10; PDRO 2005, 1: 33–34; PDRO 2012, l: 1, 11–13; Qiang and Li 1990: 1–5; Sitao 2010: 1–4).

It was this dissatisfaction that exposed the CCP's other face when they were dealing with the post-imperial dilemma: internationalism and self-determination. Affected by the federalist trend, as well as misreading the Bolshevik Revolution, early CCP leaders called for a confederal solution to address the legitimate gap between the Qing Empire and a modern multinational China. Li Dazhao commented in 1923 that there was no reason to connect self-determination with the disintegration of China. Once peoples in the peripheries were fully liberated as both nations and individuals, they would not be willing to separate out (CDUF 1991: 55–57). Yun Daiying articulated a similar thought, based on his observation of the Soviet experiences. Rebutting the critique that federalism would lead to the disintegration of China, Yun asked how many peoples had founded independent states of their own after the Soviet Russia encouraged self-determination (CDUF 1991: 78). Yun also criticized the early KMT proposal of recovering the Ming dynasty domain as an empty idea, which could only lead to the meaningless grieving for a defunct dynasty. As Yun said, without suggesting any feasible solution to China's nationality problems, a narrow Han nationalism would inevitably lead to a mafia state (Yun 1927). Xiao Chunv, in an emotional defense of the CCP's Mongolia project against rightist nationalists, claimed that, as long as the Manchurian emperor could be driven away, no periphery counted as an "inseparable part of China" (CDUF 1991: 65). As the CCP's general secretary, Chen Duxiu, made explicit, the CCP had nothing to do with the partition of China—the Party's priority goal was to eradicate warlord dictatorship, after which all nationalities could come back to constitute a liberal Chinese confederation (CDUF 1991: 73).

Not possessing a state of their own, early CCP elites also saw separatism and self-determination as tools to subvert the reactionary government in Han-inhabited provinces—the pre-1922 CCP invoked "provincial independence" as a proposal to counter the plan of "military unification" by Beiyang states. As Wu Yuzhang recalled, during the May Fourth Movement, students were traveling in southern provinces to counter the militant unification plan of the Beijing government. Students claimed that the idea of federalist self-governance corresponded to Soviet internationalism and should be combined with socialist education and protests (IHCAS 1959: 14–16). Mao, in 1920, was an enthusiastic supporter of self-governance in Hunan province. In several newspaper essays, Mao claimed that a unified and cumbersome China should be replaced by a constellation of independent republics. For his home province, he advocated for a "Republic of Hunan" to be built into a model of early modernization vis-à-vis the rest of China. Mao appreciated this proposal, not only because it counted a counteraction against the Hunan governor Zhang Jingyao, but also because separatism was heading in the direction of the world trend toward separatism and de-imperialization. Mao cited Russia, Czechoslovakia, Ireland, and Korea (Wang 1968: 50–52).

Chen Duxiu, who bore an anarchist tendency and after 1927 became a leader of an anarchist faction, exemplifies the most important facets of the CCP's separatist preference at the opening period of the revolution. Chen's thoughts regarding nationalism was multifaceted and they varied over time. It seems that Chen did not reject a cultural nation as long as it was enlightened, but he refuted statist nationalism that served a small group of rulers.

Revolution, nationalism, and multi-ethnic integration 167

He deemed it necessary to nationalize China, in the sense of universalizing a unified national language and teaching individuals to participate in national politics. This, as Chen said, would avoid leaving politics and defense to the emperor and dictators (Chen 1993 2: 53–54, 55–56). Chen in general supported a federal structure to reorganize China, but he limited its relevance to Mongolia, Tibet, Hui Xinjiang, and Qinghai, the areas he named as "China's past colonies" (Chen 1993 2: 579–80). With regard to the peripheries, Chen warned that the US, Britain, and Japan were repeating their activities in Turkey, Persia, and Sakhalin, penetrating Xinjiang for its oil and coal resources (Chen 1993 2: 612–13). Meanwhile, he supported the self-governance of Outer Mongolia, arguing that Chinese warlords had no respect for self-governance and would sponsor the reactionary ruling strata to repress revolutionary movement from below (Chen 1993 2: 699). By equating federalism with warlordism, Chen implied that province-based federalism had to be preconditioned by democratic governance from below (Chen 1993 2: 379–82, 577–78). This stance extended to Chen's comments on Tagore's cosmopolitanism—Chen argued that a nationless cosmopolitanism had to be based on the material and scientific civilization had evenly benefited small and weak nations so that these small nations could be secure in international politics (Chen 1993, 2: 655–57, 664–66, 703–4).

An early figure who invoked ethnic mobilization to counter Han establishment was Xuan Xiafu, a renown propagandist who conducted coalition-building work within the KMT. From October 1925 Xuan was sent to the KMT forces in Gansu, a multi-ethnic province at the northwestern periphery where the CCP had no state presence. After his arrival, Xuan found that there were conflicts between Tibetans and the local governor. Linguistically talented, Xuan learned the Tibetan language and became able to freely communicate with Tibetan monks, local leaders, and the general populace. Under his coordination, an association of Tibetan Culture and then an alliance of Tibetans across Tibet, Qinghai, and Gansu were founded. Faced with such a pressure group, the KMT inspector made concessions, agreeing to punish the local governor for his alleged brutal behavior against Tibetans. With this successful campaign, Xuan Xiafu impressed a clan leader, who later sponsored the creation of schools to teach Tibetan children in their mother tongue (Fang 2004: 9–12).

During the Civil War of 1927–37, the CCP had minimal concern about siding with the KMT, which led it to promote a maximized version of internationalism. During the Long March, the CCP's central leader, Zhang Guotao, led the campaign to create a first Tibetan state, in 1936. As an early trainee studying in the Soviet Union, Zhang had attended the Congress of Far Eastern Laboring Nations in 1922, which was a rare experience among his contemporary socialists. Though Zhang was annoyed by the Russians, lack of enthusiasm for liberating small nations, he gained a clear sense of a transnational united front against imperialist powers (Zhang 1991, 1: 205–9). During the Civil War, Zhang led an independent guerrilla base, through which he gained rich experience in state-building. Toward the end of the Long March, when Zhang's forces passed the west of Sichuan, Zhang recognized that a powerful secessionist movement by local Tibetans would significantly distract the KMT and its affiliated indigenous rulers, to the benefit of the communists. Zhang considered the Red Army's internationalism to be more sincere than the Dalai Lama's plan for a Greater Tibet, which was backed by the British, and the Han warlord regime's assimilationist program respected the autonomy of minorities. Hence his claim that the Red Army would make every effort to help Tibetans until they achieved independence (Sheng 1985: 428–30).

Zhang Guotao's actions show how, as the KMT's military pressure peaked, the CCP's power-seeking internationalism accordingly crossed what had been a red line, asserting that autonomy movements had to occur within the limitation of "single Chinese Nation." This policy had been rather close to the Bolshevik policy of 1922. In June 1932 the CCP's Sichuan Committee issued the resolution to support the Yi people and Tibetans in establishing states in parallel with the Chinese. In 1934 the Eastern Qian Committee claimed it would concede the Miao's and Yi's rights to separate from China as long as they would fight the KMT warlords (CDUF 1991: 243). In 1936 Mao Zedong and Zhou Enlai dictated that the Red Army should help the Inner Mongolians establish independent states, to build up a buffer zone on the norther front (CDUF 1991: 368). Liu Shaoqi, in October 1937, gave a speech in defense of minorities' full self-determination, in that the CCP had to present itself as a more generous liberator as the Japanese was manipulating self-determination to neutralize and divide the Chinese resistant movement (CDUF 1991:568). In a nutshell, as long as the separatist movement did not impose a stable threat to the CCP establishment, it was encouraged.

The formation of guerrilla state during the revolutionary war

The perplexity and oscillation of the CCP in the 1920s and 1930s stemmed from multiple factors: the general intellectual uncertainty about nation-building in the aftermath of the Qing collapse, the CCP's lack of first-hand experiences of the peripheral areas, and, most importantly, the tiny scale of revolutionary mobilization geographically and ethnically. Early CCP support for peripheral self-determination certainly involved political naivety, but also made sense strategically. When CCP activities were concentrated in a few provinces in South and East China, the party had no

Revolution, nationalism, and multi-ethnic integration   169

radius to the northern and western borders of the former empire. Any chaos and revolts in these areas could only hurt the enemy of revolution—the Beiyang warlords, the KMT, and the British and Japanese imperialists. Nor had the CCP yet established any stable state. As a tiny party parasitic to the KMT state machinery in Guangdong, the CCP had little involvement in real state running, among either the Han or minority populations. Minorities' riots, which had been as salient as the Han Green riots in the 1920s, were not yet a threat to the tiny CCP organizations, which mostly crowded in large cities.

Such a state of separation began to change as the CCP's Civil War with the KMT commenced, heralding a massive transfer of revolutionary stronghold from central cities to rural areas in Jiangxi, Hunan, Hubei, and Fujian. With guerrilla warfare expanded, the CCP developed organizationally from tiny groups of worker mobilizers to runners of real states. Though the initial expectation was to immediately take back large cities in an October-like victory, it soon became clear that the revolution had to settle down in the mountainous countryside for the long term. It was in this process of settling down that the CCP began to engage with multiple ethnicities—mainly the Tujia, Miao, Yao, and Zhuang in the central guerrilla base areas, as well in Inner Mongolian and Hui in the border areas the CCP's activities reached. In areas firmly under the jurisdiction on the CCP, minorities were the subject of revolutionary discipline, conscription, taxation, as the Han population was. In areas outside CCP control, the CCP supported minority revolts against local states as this made trouble for the CCP's enemies. In the Long March of the middle 1930s, for example, the CCP created multiple autonomous minority regimes in the Hui and Tibetan areas, in the name of supporting peripheral self-determination (Fang and Cai 2000: 605–6). Having created these states, the CCP and Red Army continued to move forward, and thus would never face the backfire of separatism and political autonomy. Such trouble, if any, would be left over to local enemies of the CCP and the KMT in chasing.

Non-Han minorities started entering the CCP guerrilla state in the late 1920s. Like the Hans, they were subjected to revolutionary discipline and integration, though few members of minorities reached a high echelon until the middle 1940s.[4] Within the CCP's jurisdictions, there were no slogans to support self-determination or autonomy. Their ethnic distinction was recognized, but only at a cultural level, and it was often invoked to justify the claim that the counterrevolutionaries' evil rule had reached such a wide range of populations that a revolution to overthrow it was necessary. Within the CCP leadership, the least distinct non-Han groups were Hanized minorities. They mostly came from the regions where the CCP movement originated—Hunan, Jiangxi, Hubei, and Fujian, which were the most multi-ethnic regions in Central China, inhabited by Miao, Dong, Bai, Tujia, and Hakka. Despite their non-Han ancestries and registered ethnicities, these future communists were not that different from their peer Han colleagues in their revolutionary path. This was not only because of their intense interaction with Hans but also because of their educational background and revolutionary trajectories. Most of them completed their education after the late 1910s and participated in radical movements in the 1920s, when a notion of multi-ethnic China had stabilized and accordingly led them to identify with a Han-dominated Chinese nation.

The memoirs and autobiographies of these Hanized CCP elites contained little reference to ethnic issues, beyond mention of the geographical environments where they grew up. Rather, they commonly highlight that ethnic features made no difference in shaping a Chinese revolutionary. Su Yu, the CCP's most prestigious colonel general, an ethnic Dong, started his elementary education in Hunan rural area, in 1913. Educated at a private school, he studied Chinese Confucian classics, many pieces of which, as he recalled in his war memoir, he could still recite by heart in later years. After leaving his home village, Su studied at a province-sponsored teacher-training school, where he became acquainted with students from other regions and eventually became involved into CCP-led radical activities. Though not understanding communist ideology, Su agreed with the anti-warlord program and viewed the unification of China as necessary (Su 2005: 5–6, 10–11). Another member of a minority, Teng Daiyuan, the PRC's first minister of railway transportation, shared a common trajectory with Su. Born an ethnic Miao, Teng originally came from the same province as Su. Attending elementary school after the May Fourth movement of 1919, he and Su met each other at the same teacher-training school (Tan 2010: 222). Teng received a Western-style education, which covered English language, gender equality, free marriage, and liberal democracy (Tan 2010: 219–20). In an economic essay written in 1925, Teng had accepted the version of Chinese nationalism that sought a China free of imperialist theft of natural resources and cultural control of education (Tan 2010: 217–18).

Most Hanized-minority communists came from the province of Hunan. In addition to Su and Teng, there was Liao Hansheng, the CCP's first military commissar, in 1949, and later the dean of the Nanjing Military Academy. Liao originally came from a Tujia family in rural Hunan. Born in 1911, the year of the anti-Manchurian revolution, Liao was named by his father "Hansheng," which literarily means the rebirth of a Han China. Liao's family had been peasant-scholars for several generations, receiving old-style Confucian education (Liao 1993: 1–2). A sympathizer of the anti-Qing nationalist revolution, Liao's father joined He Long's national army. Partly

Revolution, nationalism, and multi-ethnic integration 171

because of familial relations, He Long sponsored the elementary level education of Liao and two of his brothers, and later sponsored a province teacher-training school at Changde, where Liao received regular modern Chinese education and became involved in the CCP movement (Liao 1993: 6–8). Liao had no confusion about his identity, nor did he question a Han-dominated China. Two decades later in 1949, he would command the CCP army in conquering the Hui warlords in northwestern China. Jiang Hua, an ethnic Yao, also came from Hunan province—as the CCP's supreme Jurist, he is best remembered as the chair of the show trial of Mao's wife in 1981. Jiang's home county was a settlement for the Yao for centuries. The Yao, as Jiang recalled in his memoir, had their own national language, but most were able to speak Mandarin. Despite its serfdom system, Yao customs were less bound by Han Confucian etiquette, such as foot-binding and rigorous gender segregation, which meant they resembled the tenets notion of socialism (Jiang 1993: 3). Jiang was born 1907 into a Yao peasant family. Entering a village private school in 1917, he completed public elementary education in 1925, where he engaged with the anti-imperialist and unificatory nationalist movement (Jiang 1993: 7–8). Afterward, Jiang entered Hengyang Normal Middle School, where he would meet his CCP guides (Jiang 1993: 17–18).

Another province that yielded important CCP generals was Guangxi, a region adjacent to Vietnam and populated by the Zhuang. Close to Yunnan, the KMT's base in fighting the Northern warlords, and Guangdong, the center of the first KMT–CCP united front, this province exported many cadres to the CCP military leadership. Like the minorities in Jiangxi and Hunan, these ethnic Zhuang and Yao cadres were subject to unified guerrilla states, not allowed and even unwilling to pursue an autonomous polity. Their ethnicity was invoked only to celebrate the wideness of the CCP's revolutionary mobilization. A martyr to the cause was the legendary Zhuang commander Wei Baqun, who was murdered in 1931. Wei started his military career in the 1910s at the Army Academy (Jiangwutang). After the break between the CCP and KMT, Wei Baqun became a local partisan leader. His policy resembled "indigenization," purposefully promoting ethnic Zhuang cadres and adhering to the notion of equal land redistribution among Han, Yao, and Zhuang peasants. The guerilla mobilization he organized also had an ethnic focus, attacking ethnic-Han landlords. Nevertheless, Wei Baqun was under the close control of the CCP guerrillas—upon request he gave most of his manpower to the CCP's 7th Army (Fang and Cai 2000: 558–60). One of Wei Baqun's long-enduring admirers was Wei Guoqing, the CCP's Guangxi governor during the Cultural Revolution, who came from a Zhuang family in Guangxi. With a few years of Chinese Confucian education, Wei's father was a leader of local peasant committee. Born in 1913, Wei received a basic education in the Chinese classics, both at a public school and under his father's private tutelage (CCPHRO 2007 6: 333–34). He joined the peasant riots, following his father during the Northern Expedition, and he later joined the CCP uprising led by Wei Baqun, Deng Xiaoping, and Zhang Yunyi in Guangxi (Ya 2017: 69–70). In a nutshell, ethnic distinction was recognized, and ethnicity-associated clan and kinship factors functioned in easing mobilization, but as long as the CCP was in local power, these factors were not permitted to be separatist in character. In these belts of inner frontiers, the CCP's "One China" was based on substantial control.

Minority cadres from the Northeast were too closely integrated into the CCP guerrilla state to consider any national separatism. The most senior CCP Manchurian elite, Guan Xiangying, came from a peasant family in Liaoning. Though his genealogy was traced back to the Gualgiya clan, long before his generation, the family name had been Hanized and changed to Guan. Guan was sent to a public elementary school in 1918, where he immersed himself in the Chinese classics that romanticized civil wars and green rebellions (Wang 1986: 6–7). After graduation, Guan migrated to Dalian, a cosmopolitan metropole where the Russian and Japanese presences were most concentrated. It was during his study at a business special school and later work at a newspaper agency that Guan encountered conflicts with colonial authorities, which led him to adopting an anti-Japanese Chinese identity (Wang 1986: 9–10). Wan Yi, the CCP's leader of military scientific research, was also an ethnic Manchurian. Wan was born in 1907 in Jinzhou, a formal Japanese colony, in a Manchurian–Han mixed family. Wan's father was a Hanized peasant who had a solid Chinese identity and was fond of Chinese classical romances, while Wan's mother was a Han woman. According to Wan's memoir, such Manchurian–Han marriages remained limited in the late-Qing period. His parents were able to break this taboo mainly because Wan's father had been in military service for years (Wan 1998: 1). Wan entered a public elementary school, to find that every subject was taught in Japanese. His father then made the decision to withdraw him (Wan 1998: 3–4). Migrating to the province of Fengtian, the jurisdiction of Chinese warlord Zhang Zuolin, Wan joined a local state branch, and later the Chinese military, where he continued to learn Chinese from educated colleagues (Wan 1998: 5–6). In the cases of both Guan Xiangying and Wan Yi, ethnopolitics mattered little.

The CCP as the weak side of the revolutionary contest

Not all multi-ethnic regions were under the CCP's secure control. Many frontiers were located at the border areas between the CCP's jurisdiction

Revolution, nationalism, and multi-ethnic integration   173

and the enemies such as local warlords, the KMT, and the Japanese. In these areas, the CCP could exert influences but the power balance was subtle and unstable. They addressed this insecurity with a two-pronged approach. On the one hand, the CCP, unable to secure control, instead employed a "One-China" discourse to exhort peripheral minorities not to engage in separatism—the CCP was aware that such separatism was mostly supported by the Japanese and the Soviets. In this case, a weak position in the power contestation was made up for through discourse and emotion. The CCP worried that continuing internationalist support for national self-determination would further push peripheral minorities into the camp of the Japanese and Soviets. On the other hand, in its articulation of a "One-China" framework, the CCP was flexible, and did not seek coherence. The official discourse, in practice, oscillated between highlighting ethnic distinction in an ambiguous ways that were suggestive of nation and the concept of a multi-ethnic Chinese nation, depending on the power dynamics among triangular and even rectangular players.

The CCP's activities among Mongolians, Huis, and Northeastern minorities exemplify this approach. The CCP's discourse in Inner Mongolia demonstrated a strong correlation with the strength of the state presence in this region. Before the end of the Long March, in 1936, the CCP had never formed stable guerrilla states in the Northwest. The party's activists in the Inner Mongolian borders, including Li Dazhao, Zhao Shiyan, and Deng Zhongxia, carried out agitations among local peasants and soldiers, as well as exhorting Mongolian students at the Beijing Mongolian–Tibetan Middle School, but no real state was created (NZD 1983: 23). Balancing support for national self-determination and the call for One China, the CCP's discourse was mixed, with multiple frames juxtaposed with each other. Radicalism under the KMT–CCP united front was moderate, restrained within the KMT's insistence on a multi-ethnic China, so long as it satisfied the One-China criteria. The CCP presented its stance as opposing Great Mongolianism, a security concern from Moscow as well, which even aroused local suspicion of the CCP's tendency towards economic Hanization (Xie and Qian 1988: 26). At this stage the CCP did not have an established state to build or defend. Most activists served in the army led by General Feng Yuxiang, which was recognized by the CCP and the Soviet Union as an ally of the KMT from the Northwest. Feng's National Citizen Army combined Feng's private forces and recruited groups, including local Mongolian militia, defeated KMT troops, and local military forces from the Northeast. The CCP activists—Chen Geng, Ke Qingshi, Xuan Xiafu, Zhao Zuolin, and others—shared common backgrounds: returning from special training camps in the Soviet Union or squeezed out of urban areas by the KMT's terror, they were students or teachers who possessed the skills of propaganda and agitation valued by Feng Yuxiang in integrating a heterogeneous force (Ren 2016: 76–93).

After the KMT–CCP split, in 1927, the CCP further lost its state presence in Inner Mongolia and its ideological orientation for national self-determination became unleashed. Activists in Inner Mongolia, Kuibi and Li Yuzhi, organized an unsuccessful coup, and later a tiny state in Alashan was created by the CCP but it lasted only a few months (Fang and Cai 2000: 523). Such a "nothing to lose" status impelled the CCP to move toward agitation for national self-determination by any means destructive to the CCP's enemy. In 1934, at the height of the CCP–KMT Civil War, the CCP leftists created a Worker-Peasant-Soldier Alliance, calling for the founding of an independent Inner Mongolian Republic in exclusion of all KMT reactionaries. As the CCP's program stated, this republic would be Mongolian-speaking and would carry out diplomacy friendly with the Soviet Union and People's Republic of Mongolia. It is noteworthy that such a call for self-determination was claimed to be a countermeasure against Japan's support for Mongolian separatism (Xie and Qian 1988: 161, 319), which was reminiscent of the Bolsheviks' strategy of creating buffer states in the Russian Civil War. As the CCP's major guerrilla base moved from Central China to Shann'xi, however, the slogan of Mongolian–Han solidarity to fight imperialism and domestic class enemies once again became dominant (NZD 1983: 38). Meanwhile, the CCP's official recognition of the Mongolian nationality never disappeared. In Yan'an, a memorial hall for Genghis Khan as well as a Mosque were established, together with associations for promoting Mongolian and Hui national culture. Mao formally endorsed these institutions, calling for Inner Mongolians to restore the glory of Genghis Khan in fighting against the Japanese (NZD 1983: 81). Yet Japan's surrender did not secure the border for the CCP. Following the Bolshevik's strategy in the Civil War, the Soviet Forces founded a small national state, the Republic of North Rehe, in Chifeng, with CCP cadres blocked out. Conversely, local nationalists began to pursue an independent revolutionary movement, beginning to contact the People's Republic of Mongolia (CDUF 1991: 995). Through intervention by the Soviet Union, the CCP finally contrived to harness the Inner Mongolians' effort in creating an autonomous republic, confining autonomy to a regional level within the One-China framework (CDUF 1991: 1011). Nevertheless, the CCP's weak status remained unchanged.

The CCP's weak status at the Inner-Mongolian border area was clear across multiple dimensions. One was personnel. Unlike the ethnic non-Hans in central provinces, the CCP's Inner-Mongolian cadres carried a more salient transnational character. These people retained their distinct ethnic identities and languages throughout the CCP revolution. In the course of power seizure, they sought to secure an equal status for their home nationalities

Revolution, nationalism, and multi-ethnic integration 175

by drafting a concept of a multinational China. Among these individuals, the highest-ranked was Ulanhu (Wu Lanfu). He was not only the CCP's governor of Inner Mongolia and a major designer of the PRC's nationality model, but also achieved the rank of vice state chairman in the 1980s. The childhood part of his memoir includes narratives of intense ethnic conflicts between Mongolians and Hans, either the warlord state, inhabitants, or bandits. While denouncing ethnic persecution and exploitation, Ulanhu expressed sincere admiration for his Han neighbors' organizational solidarity in defense against bandits (Wu 1989: 6–7). Ulanhu's elementary education was completed at Tumochuan, a longstanding public school where students received bilingual training on modern subjects. Through many alumni of this school who studied in Beijing, Ulanhu gained connections, which would later send him to Beijing Mongolian–Tibetan Middle School, the CCP's stronghold (Wu 1989: 23–25). During the KMT–CCP Civil War of the 1930s, Ulanhu had been active in Western Inner Mongolia, tasked with preventing the local Prince De (Demchugdongrub) from collaborating with the Japanese. After Prince De had joined the Japanese colonial institutions, Ulanhu turned to conduct agitational work within the local Mongolian calvary security division and successfully transformed the latter into a pro-CCP force. After a setback against the Japanese, Ulanhu contrived to channel this troop southward to Yan'an. After a reconstruction and supplement, this troop returned to the steppe as a mobile force to safeguard the CCP state's northern front (Wu 1989: 193–209).

Ulanhu's trajectory was similar to that of two of his close associates, Kui Bi and Ji Taiya. The former was the other Mongolian sitting in the CCP's Eighth Central Committee, whereas the latter was the CCP's ambassador to Mongolia. Like Ulanhu, both Inner Mongolians attended the Tumote Elementary School and Beijing Mongolian–Tibetan Middle School. They were different, however, in that their revolutionary paths had a longer geographical separation with the CCP one. After brief training in Moscow, Kui Bi and Ji Taiya worked in Outer Mongolia for years. The former returned to China after the breakout of the Sino–Japanese War, to organize guerrilla war in Inner Mongolia, securing a buffer on the steppe between Yan'an and the Japanese. The latter stayed in Outer Mongolia from 1938 to 1946 as a leading propagator to report the CCP's performance in the War (Fu 2014: 291–94). In general, the Ulanhu-led Inner Mongolian communist group retained a resistant request for autonomy even after the CCP had officially abandoned the confederal program, which would persist until the ultimate foundation of the PRC (Gong 2002: 49–51).

The CCP's ethnic-Han cadres did not have a strong hand over the Inner Mongolian border—their strategy was not so much one of coercion as a subtle combination of exhortation, exchange, and informal ties. This was embodied by a key figure, Gao Gang, who founded the Shan'ganning border area in the early 1930s and who eventually became one of the CCP's top leaders, governor in Northeast, and the general manager of the CCP's logistic supply during the Civil War and the Korean War. Resulting from a frustration with the intra-party power struggle, Gao spent years at the Inner Mongolian border with the task of creating a calvary regiment. While in post, Gao developed strategies to build an alliance with Mongolian heads and local KMT officials, wherein he formulated the principles of "political equality plus economic aid," which was to be the cornerstone of the CCP's nationality policy for the ensuing years. After returning to Yan'an, Gao assumed the top position as the Calvary Commander of the Shan'ganning border area, the equivalent of the leader of the capital garrison; but he retained his post as the chair of the Commission on Mongolian Affairs, later to be renamed as the Commission on Ethnic Minority Affairs. Throughout the Sino–Japanese War, Gao and his subordinates continued to mobilize and expand networks with Inner Mongolians, to secure the CCP's horse-supplying and united front on the steppe (Dai and Zhao 2011: 74–79).

The CCP's weakness lay in the fact that even though a guerrilla state was spread out deeply into the steppe, it had no secure control equivalent to the Bolsheviks' rule on the non-Russian periphery. To make up for the limitation of military power, the CCP cultivated a vague "One-China" discourse with the hope that Inner Mongolians, who were not under the CCP's full control, would not respond to the Japanese support for separatism. Such subtlety was manifested in a sustained effort to secure a steppe guerrilla state created by Li Jingquan and Yao Zhe, two senior CCP generals, in Daqingshan Mountain. According to CCP historians, this would have been a connection of strategic importance between the CCP's central area and Soviet Outer Mongolia to prevent the Japanese's penetration into Inner Asia (Qi 2019). As early as 1938, when the Japanese military was still trapped in intense campaigns in East China, Mao had judged that the Japanese would annihilate the KMT main forces and encroach westward to block the CCP's guerrilla center. This led Mao to make the preemptive move in building a buffer at the Shan'xi-Inner-Mongolian border (Yang 2020). As the KMT regimes escaped, Li and Yao's troops quickly occupied the mountainous and rural areas. Yet, they quickly recognized that they would continue to be the weak force vis-à-vis all other groups for a long term. To deal with the efficiency of the Japanese calvary, the infantry-based troops had to be transformed. Facing a shortage of horses, Li and Yao turned to local nomads and monks, princes, and security officers to find horses (Su 2006). They invited Mongolian nomads to teach equine skills as well as collect equipment for cavalry building (Huang 1962). In comparison with the KMT forces on the same territory, the CCP had to engage local nomads, not only because

Revolution, nationalism, and multi-ethnic integration 177

they lacked the motorized vehicles that the KMT had, but also because they sought to maintain an intelligence network independent of the one consisting of old bureaucrats (Li and Li 2018).

A similar region to Inner Mongolia was the Hui Northwest, which was under control of the Ma warlord family, covering the provinces of Gansu, Ningxia, and Qinghai. This region was adjacent to the Yan'an area and thus vital to the CCP's security. As Li Weihan recalled, during the Sino–Japanese War, the CCP was wary that Japan would plot for the creation of an Islamic Hui nation state encompassing Qinghai, Ningxia, Gansu, as well as part of Xinjiang, Tibet, and Inner Mongolia, which would pose a severe threat to the CCP's headquarters from the west. It was out of such concern that Li Weihan and Jia Tuofu, two leaders of the CCP's Northwestern Commission, chaired an extensive ethnographic survey among the Chinese Muslims across Northwestern provinces, from which they derived the conclusion decisive to the PRC's nationality model that support for self-determination and national liberation had to be cautious (NZD 1983: 78–81). Li Weihan and Jia Tuofu coauthored a short pamphlet, *Outline of the Huihui Nationality Question*, which exerted in a moderate and flexible tone that Hui Islam was a nation not just a clan, as the KMT had asserted, but they were part of the Chinese nation and had a closer historical tie with Han Chinese than the Japanese (W. Zhou 1992: 63–64). In Yan'an, a special institution called the "Academy on Nationalities" was founded in 1941 under Li's and Jia's leadership to provide ethnic minorities with leadership training and to establish a department of nationality studies. This institution made a priority of recruiting youths from Inner Mongolia, the largest proportion of whom were ethnic Mongolians. As part of its training program, there was a regular cadre exchange between Yan'an and the Daqingshan guerrilla base, sometimes functioning as a strategic retreat to evade the thrust of the Japanese, and sometimes as a means to replenish and train (Ma 2020). Later, in 1944, this training school moved northward to the Inner Mongolian border areas, with the purpose of achieving full engagement with the ethnic minority population. Apart from technical training, such as military command, a focus of the teaching was the history of Chinese revolution, to couch the story of the CCP's struggle in a multi-ethnic context. The graduates of this institution were sent back to the Inner Mongolian areas occupied by the Japanese and the KMT or detached to operational forces to facilitate the CCP military's move on the steppe (Wu and Wang 2020). The CCP's leading experts on nationality mostly came from this institution, including Li Weihan and Jia Tuofu, who carried out heavy survey work on the conditions of the local Inner Mongolian and Hui population.

Li Weihan's biography exemplified the ways in which the CCP's internationalist ideology translated to its proposal for a Chinese multinational

178   *Revolution in China and Russia*

state in competition with the KMT's program of assimilationist nationalism. As a senior communist who had been active since the late 1910s, Li had extensive connections, and he therefore sat on the CCP's fourth, fifth, and sixth central committees. His long service led eventually to a role as a specialist on the united front. As the CCP expanded into former northwestern imperial frontiers, his work in this role extended to the mobilization of the minorities to fight against the CCP's Han enemies. According to Li's periodization, the CCP's serious engagement with the nationality question started in Yan'an, during the Sino–Japanese War. As the department director of the United Front, Li made continuous efforts to shape minorities into nationalities that were independent in every way, but unable to found independent states. Under the direction of Li, together with Jia Lifu, minorities in Yan'an founded separate associations, educational institutions, and even military units (Li 1986: 452–66).

Apart from the routine work of nation-inventing, Li Weihan and Jia Tuofu also gained knowledge of Northwestern minorities by observing the minorities' fight against the KMT. In April 1940, Li outlined a situation that required discretion—while the Japanese were encouraging Hui Muslims to separate from China's anti-Japanese movement, the KMT aggressively sought to assimilate this group, denying its ethnicity. Li noted that the CCP needed to propagate internationalism, in opposition to the KMT's assimilation efforts, but must not go so far as to give the misleading impression that it was allowing secession (Li 2016: 558–59). Three months later, in a report regarding the affairs of Inner Mongolians, Li claimed that the CCP had to develop an internationalism to achieve Mongolian–Han equality within the Chinese nation, which was distinct from both Japan's oppressive colonialism and the KMT's assimilationism (Li 2016: 577–79). In supporting a spontaneous Hui insurrectional force in Haigu county, Li and Jia recognized that remaining ambiguous and subtle was the best solution to the nationality question, in that the Muslim uprisings countered the local KMT corps who asserted assimilationist Han-Chinese nationalism, which relieved the CCP's pressure (W. Zhou 1992: 64–65).

The CCP's state-building was least developed in the Northeast, where Japan had established full colonial rule in 1931. The Japanese rule was so penetrative that no local resistance movement could sustain any stable guerrilla zones, and, as a consequence, none of the CCP's officially identified nineteen anti-Japanese guerrilla base zones was in the Manchukuo territory. Lacking weapons and grain, the Northeastern Anti-Japanese Alliance, the leading armed resistance organization in this region, had to hide in forests to evade the fierce anti-guerrilla exterminations (Fan 2012). Most of the spontaneously formed local organizations of resistance had perished by 1932. From 1933 small armed groups were reestablished under the self-designated Northeastern People's Revolutionary Army. The CCP's connection with these divisions was vague—though a few division- and regiment-level officers claimed to be CCP members, among the insurrection forces in Manchuria there was not a unified CCP military organization recognized by the Party center in Jiangxi. Even such a thin connection was soon broken. In 1940, unable to endure the extreme shortage of logistic support, most of the surviving anti-Japanese forces— probably only about 600—crossed the border into the Soviet Union, where they would be eventually transformed into the intelligence detachments of the Soviet Far Eastern Military (Fang and Cai 2000: 635–40). Between 1940 and 1944, the CCP guerrillas made several intrusions into Manchuria to restore base zones, from the Hebei border and the Soviet Union, but they all failed (Neimenggu diqu dangwei dangshi yanjiushi 2011: 144–48). After the Soviet–Japanese Pact of April 1941—an attempt by Moscow to evade confrontation with Tokyo that would continue until the August Storm in summer 1945—Chinese resistance forces were not allowed to return to China. During this period, the Chinese forces were trained by the Soviets in driving, parachuting, wireless communication, and skiing, skills that would support them for intelligence-gathering in tiny groups. From the breakout of the Soviet–German War, these forces switched to a model of labor-army, due to the decreased grain supply by the Soviet side (Li 2013).

Isolated from the CCP center for over a decade, the Manchurian communists exerted a discourse quite different from the inland, which still carried connotations from the old Comintern days: a call for a united front of small nations in the Far East against imperialism, encompassing Koreans, Mongolians, Taiwanese, and indigenous hunting tribes. The slogan "Safeguard the Soviet Union" continued after the Sino-Soviet War of 1929, which, as CCP cadres reflected afterwards, ignored the psychology and needs of local Chinese people, alienating the mass from supporting the CCP organizations (Liu 2020). As the Sino–Japanese War expanded, the CCP's discourse in Manchuria remained more international, transnational, and multinational in its tone than rigid multi-ethnic Chinese nationalism. The special circumstance in the Northeast—that it was officially under the rule of the Japanese puppet-state Manchukuo—even offered a counterfactual insight into what discourse the CCP would have adopted if the revolution had started under the Manchurian-Qing imperial state as the Bolshevik Revolution had done under the tsarist regime. Wang Minggui, a veteran commander of the Northeastern People's Revolutionary Army, recalled that, when hiding in the mountains, they made an alliance with Oroken hunters, the hunters pledging that "all Koreans, Hans, and Orokens jointly fight the Manchukuo" (NZD 1983: 121). Zhou Baozhong, the secretary of the

CCP's Manchurian Committee as of 1932, supported Koreans to establish an independent Korean national army, though he highlighted the political leadership by the CCP. According to Zhou, the solidarity between Chinese and Koreans was vital to thwarting the plot of divide and rule by the Japanese imperialists. Zhou also required Koreans to master the Chinese language as a necessary skill for fighting in China, while at the same time he insisted that the Koreans should maintain their own language (Jin 2019). It is also noteworthy that Zhou was an ethnic Bai from Yunnan province. His early education, during the transition from the Qing to the Republic, was entirely a Chinese classical one, first Confucian texts and then green-style romances (Zhao 2015: 5, 8). In 1917, Zhou Baozhong joined the Yunnan provincial army in the northern expedition, in the course of which the political atmosphere familiarized him with Sun Yat-sen's program of Chinese nationalism (Zhao 2015: 9–12).

The internationality of the Northeast was also found among Koreans. After the Revolution of 1911, Koreans were not recognized as any of constituent nationality of China, but rather viewed as a migrant people. Struggling to live in between the Russians, Japanese, and Chinese, they diverged into multiple political forces—Chinese communists, Soviets, Korean nationalists, and Japanese collaborators. Zhu Dehai, the CCP's future state governor in Yanbian, the highest-ranked Korean within the Party prior to 1956, had a trajectory that overlapped with the first three streams. Having little to do with China, Zhu was born in Russia's Far East, with Korean ancestry. Escaping from post-1905 war-caused banditry, Zhu's family moved back to Korea, where Zhu completed his elementary education under close instruction of the Korean national communist Jin Guangzhen (Cui 2012: 3–4). Zhu's early radical path was thus closely associated with the Korean Communist Party, until the latter was disbanded in 1930. After that, in keeping with the Comintern's "one country, one party" rule, Zhu, like other Korean communists active in China, switched his organizational affiliation to the CCP and was sent to Moscow Eastern Toilor University for revolutionary training (Cui 2012: 4–5). Zhu could barely speak Chinese, and he was soon transferred from the CCP class to the Korean communist class. After graduation, Zhu was sent to Yan'an, where he was in charge of managing Korean communist emigrants. During this period, Zhu still retained his distinct Korean identity, viewing his mission as preparing for a return to his homeland to forment a Korean anti-Japanese communist revolution free of foreign intervention. This thought persisted until 1945, when the Soviet Union invaded Korea. From then on, Zhu changed his stance to transform Koreans in China into a Korean nationality as part of the Chinese nation (Cui 2012: 9–14).

Revolution, nationalism, and multi-ethnic integration 181

Internationalism: the periphery beyond the CCP's reach

Apart from the Northeast and Hainan Island, there was a third or outer circle of the former Chinese empire, a frontier where the CCP was unable to maintain any presence. This included the South-Sea islands, Xinjiang, Tibet, and Taiwan. With revolutionary activities at the southern periphery, Hainan Island was another case that challenged the One-China idea. Hainan was a multi-ethnic region mixing the Han, Miao, and Li peoples. As in the Northeast, CCP partisans had established a mountain-based quasi-guerrilla force on this island in the years after 1927, in an effort to sustain a transportation line to secure manpower and resource exchanges with the Chinese diaspora in Southeast Asia, but the base could not be stabilized. Nor was Hainan adjacent to any of the CCP's major guerilla local centers (Wu 2020). During the Pacific War, Hainan Island became an international transborder area with different parts controlled by the CCP, the KMT, and the Japanese. As early as the 1936, when the KMT–CCP Civil War was still ongoing, the CCP center had suggested that local partisans absorb multi-ethnic and diaspora populations to found a guerrilla state, as a base to integrate the revolutionary activities in Greater South East Asia. The same order was made in 1940, when it was stated that CCP forces should build guerrilla states in minority-populated areas under the name of the National Resistance, since cities and plain areas had been occupied by the KMT and the Japanese. It also suggested suspending the radical land and cultural revolutions that had been destroying temples and other religious sites (Zhonggong hainanqu dangwei dangshi bangongshi 1988: 17–19).

Yet, the local CCP continued to carry out a state-breaking strategy not unlike that of the civil-war years. The Hainan partisan leader, Feng Baiju, was originally from this island, but he had been educated in Nanjing and Shanghai, where he fully participated in the anti-Japanese nationalist movement of the 1920s. In terms of identity, like most of his CCP contemporaries, Feng had no problem with the notion of a republican multi-ethnic China (Zhonggong hainanqu dangwei dangshi bangongshi 1988: 327–43). Returning to Hainan after the CCP–KMT split, Feng actively executed the CCP center's line to build up a local guerrilla state, by carrying out a united front policy among ethnic minorities, but with limited success. According to Feng's own reflections, the slowness of his progress had much to do with Hainan's geographical isolation far from the national revolutionary center, which impeded the acquisition of manpower, information, and experience (Zhonggong hainanqu dangwei dangshi bangongshi 1988: 342–43). The effort of building a guerrilla state in the western part of the island, among the Miao and Li populations, was not sustainable, since there was a significant linguistic barrier between partisans and inhabitants. The partisan forces made three strategic moves but failed to establish a stable base, as the CCP had done in other regions of the country (Li 2019). Hence, to relieve military pressure, CCP partisans continued to agitate minority uprisings, since any of them would disrupt the KMT controlled areas (Yan 2015).

Xinjiang is a unique case, which shows how the CCP's state expansion transformed initial support for internationalism to a One-China frame over the long revolution. The CCP's presence was weakest in Xinjiang, a region isolated geographically and blocked from the CCP by the Ma family in Qinghai. Under the rule of Sheng Shicai, Xinjiang had been heavily penetrated by the Soviet Union. With Xinjiang's local departments of police, military, and finance staffed with Soviet advisors, Moscow maintained strict oversight, tasked with blocking any influences from outside, including that from the CCP. The CCP's presence in Xinjiang hardly counted as a state. Since 1936, a tiny liaison team had been stationed in Dihua, the members of which, approximately 400, came from the CCP Red Army that entered Xinjiang. As Soviet advisors decreased due to domestic terror, these individuals eventually entered local regime branches, by Sheng Shicai's invitation. Apart from giving political lectures and providing financial advice, these CCP military devoted most of their time to technical training on special skills such as the telegraph operations, driving, veterinary medicine, and intelligence-gathering (Cai 2005: 195–220). Such a regime was not sustainable for long. From 1939 onward, Sheng switched to an anti-Soviet position. Viewed as Moscow's agents, many CCP elites were arrested or assassinated, including Mao's brother Mao Zemin and the co-founder of the CCP, Chen Tanqiu (Cai 2005: 225–30). In consequence, in the years between 1939 and 1946, Xinjiang remained fully isolated from the CCP. It would not be until early 1946 before the CCP would recover its contact with Xinjiang local communist Abdukirim Abbasof and in the summer 1949 the first CCP missionary Deng Liqun entered Xinjiang.

It was in the context of this isolation that the "Three-District Revolution" took place, in 1944, when the result of the Soviet–German War had become clear. Supported by Moscow, local Xinjiang nationalists declared an Eastern Turkestan Islamic Republic in the three districts along the Sino-Soviet border (Yining, Tacheng, and Ashan). With little information on the events, the CCP center in Yan'an, threatened by the KMT's military encirclement, voiced their support from afar, claiming the revolt to be a heroic revenge against Han chauvinism (Liu 2004a). However, as information accumulated, the CCP's attitude became mixed. Eventually figuring out the independence-seeking intention of the rebels, through Dong Biwu's contact with Abbasof in Nanjing, Mao openly conveyed the stance that the uprisers should stay within the framework of a unified China—to do otherwise would be a

Revolution, nationalism, and multi-ethnic integration   183

dangerous mistake to be exploited by British-American imperialism (Du and Du 2009). Meanwhile, located far away from the western end of the Sino-Soviet border that it could not influence, the CCP continued to face the strategic temptation that "nationalism does not hurt." There was the opinion as well that as long as the republic was distracting the KMT forces, the CCP should support its secessionist appeal, helping insurrectionists make a Xinjiang nation state. It was this confusion that propelled the CCP to send off Deng Liqun as an information gatherer and letterman (Wang and Qi 2004).

Certainly, the CCP's successful de-nationalization of Xinjiang and Inner Mongolia was supported by the Soviet Union. As the Cold War escalated, Stalin switched from making buffer states in Asia to the more practical goal of squeezing out US-British influences immediately, as Soviet Russia had done with Kemalist Turkey in the Southern Caucasus in the early 1920s. Nonetheless, the CCP's original aim of making a multi-ethnic China shaped the dynamic as well—it was because of Liu Shaoqi's secret visit to Moscow, as well as the intense requests from Yan'an, that Stalin considered the incorporation of the Xinjiang and Inner Mongolian nationalists into the CCP movement. Having handled a state regime for over two decades of armed struggle, the CCP had a better knowledge of the complexity of ethnopolitics than it had had in the early 1920s. It was better informed of when and where secessionism could be a trouble or a benefit. And in this they had the advantage over the Bolsheviks in 1921.

Beyond Xinjiang, the CCP's presence was minimal in Outer Mongolia, Taiwan, the South China-Sea islands, Vietnam, and Korea, all of which were located at the vague border belt of the former Qing Empire. The CCP's discourse referring to these regions continued to be internationalist, supportive of national liberation and self-determination, as a costless counter-frame against the Japanese and the KMT. Such a propagandist campaign against KMT assimilationism and Japanese Asian racism was well articulated in the CCP literati's war polemics. Chen Boda, one of Mao's most renown secretaries and a leading agitator of the Cultural Revolution (1966–76), played an active role in refuting Jiang's definition of Chinese nationalism. Identifying all minorities as different religious groups of a longstanding Chinese nation, Jiang claimed that historical China had experienced no international wars except for Ming China's war with Japan. Making a rebuttal to this, Chen argued that the CCP had considered the wars between the Han and minorities as wars between nations. The CCP also celebrated the military figures who fought in these wars as national heroes (CDUF 1991: 96). This, Chen argued, clearly indicated that Japan's invasion could not account for the CCP's discourse shift. On the contrary, it was the CCP's state presence that best explained the communists' decisions about when to exhort internationalism and when to mute it.

184   *Revolution in China and Russia*

Unlike that of the Bolsheviks, the CCP's internationalist discourse was manifested in the composition of its international staff—there were no equivalents to Georgii Chicherin, Maxim Litvinov, Mikhail Borodin, Alexandra Kollontai, and Leonid Krasnov. Almost none of the CCP's first generation of diplomats had served as professional revolutionaries overseas—these people were "international" only in comparison with their parochial colleagues who had never left guerrilla bases or seen foreigners. Most selected members had experienced at least one of the following in their revolutionary career: enrollment in Huangpu Military Academy during the first KMT–CCP cooperation, study in the Soviet Union, cooperation with the United States Observation Army Group in Yan'an (1944–1947), service in the CCP's news agency in Hong Kong, Chongqing, Wuhan, and other capital cities, and participation in the peace negotiations with the KMT at the end of the Sino–Japanese War (Fu and Li 1995). Such a standard of selection guaranteed that most "international persons" had been incorporated—as Zhou Enlai said in 1950, the CCP started its exposure to international society quite late, only during the Sino–Japanese War, which meant it had rather limited foreign experiences (Yun 1996: 8).

In comparison with the Bolshevik diplomats of 1918, the CCP diplomats had far less exposure to foreign societies. Very few of these individuals had long-term experience of living abroad, let alone having made close connections with Western socialists, as the Bolsheviks had. Most CCP ambassadors never had traveled outside of China prior to their appointments, nor did they speak any foreign language. Exceptions were few and, by the national takeover in 1949, the CCP's overseas network of the 1920s and 1930s had dwindled to nothing. Chen Shuliang, ambassador to Romania, had studied in Japan for master's degree in economics between 1935 and 1936. He was selected mainly because of his experience with the Beiping Military Mediation Group. Huan Xiang, director of the Europe–Africa Section at the Ministry of Foreign Affairs, returned from Britain in the early 1930s and was then self-employed as an independent journalist until the closure of his newspaper by the KMT in 1948. Before joining the CCP in 1948, he had served as the KMT general Gu Zhutong's translator and news officer (Ruan 2019). Wang Renshu, ambassador to Indonesia, had been a leftist writer and journalist, having devoted the years from 1941 to 1948 to teaching, writing, and activism in Southeast Asia (RCCCPH 1980– 21: 268). He authored a pamphlet in 1948 that analyzed the Indonesian anti-colonial movement from a Marxist perspective (Wang 1948).

Other people with foreign experiences and linguistic skills, interestingly, were mostly assigned to the domestic sections of the Foreign Service. Li Kenong, the CCP's head of intelligence and director of "Central Social Department," was appointed deputy Minister (Xu and Zhu 2003). Dong

Yueqian, a graduate in English literature from Beijing University in 1937, was appointed as chief of staff of the executive office. Dong had served as translator at the CCP's negotiation with the KMT in Beiping (Zhao 2003: 421). Ke Bainian, one of the CCP's major translators of Marxist classics, served as the chair of Yan'an's Office of International Studies. Graduating from a US-sponsored missionary university, Ke was renowned as an expert on the US for his popular question-and-answer pamphlet (Ke 1948), though he had never traveled to the US. Qiao Guanhua, director of news section and China's future ambassador to the UN, attained a doctoral degree in Germany in the 1930s. During the Civil War, Qiao was in charge of the CCP's news agency in Hong Kong, where he published numerous columns on international relations (Qiao 2000). Gong Peng, Qiao's wife, was born in Japan. She was selected for foreign service mainly because of her major in English language as well as their experience as a translator for Mao Zedong and Zhou Enlai during the Sino–Japanese War.

Still a revolution: Similarity with the Bolsheviks

The KMT's nationality policies underwent a transition from a pre-1911 advocation of Ming-Han China to a post-1930 support for Chinese assimilation nationalism, which, as the target of the CCP revolution, help shaped the non-assimilationist stance of the CCP's nationalism. After 1911, the KMT immediately switched to support for the retention of the former Qing territory based on a Han-centric assimilation. Through the United Front of the 1920s, Sun Yat-sen had made it explicit that he would not accept Soviet Russia's interference into Xinjiang and Outer Mongolia in return for Moscow's aid. To prepare for war with Japan, the KMT, at the same time they were fighting warlords and communists, strengthened their incorporation of the de facto separated peripheries. In the early 1930s, a discussion regarding Xinjiang's strategic significance arose within the KMT, which identified Xinjiang as the periphery least penetrated by imperialist powers and vital to Sino-West transportation (Huang 2004: 11; Wang 2001: 235). In terms of the cultural stance, the KMT's nationalism moved from Great-Hanism to the melting-pot "New Chinese Nation" program. This doctrine was raised by Jiang Jieshi in his *China's Destiny*, but it was articulated most clearly in a textbook used in the Mongolian–Tibetan Special School. The author argued that all nationalities in China, whether Han or non-Han, counted not as nations but rather merely as religious groups (zongzu). These groups had been a common nation since the Qin–Han unification and they shared biological features. Their present linguistic and cultural differences

186   *Revolution in China and Russia*

were reducible to geographical barriers. The newly invented Chinese nation would absorb advantages of all groups to overcome each's barbarian elements (Cao 1939: 87–89).

As the Sino–Japanese War loomed and expanded, the KMT nationalists and statist intellectuals started to carry a militarist-assimilationist attitude, and an essentialist definition of the Chinese culture emerged. Challenging Sun Yat-sen's relative avoidance of minority issues, the KMT officials promoted the argument that the remote peripheries had been separable parts of China since the very ancient period (Leibold 2007). In 1933 the KMT state accepted scholar Shao Yuanchong's claim that the Yan and Huang Emperors were the common ancestors of various nations in China (Leibold 2007: 121–22). It then followed that archeological research began to demonstrate that southern nationalities shared common biological roots with Hans, as a counter-response to Japan's agitation of national self-determination in China's Southwest (Leibold 2007: 135–42). The Warring State school (Zhan guo ce pai), a loose group of writers, officials, and historians, suggested a return to the mystified martial spirit of Spring–Autumn and Warring State period, China's Axis Age, to overcome the problems such as de-masculinization, insufficient combat bravery, disorganization, and weak national consciousness (Cao and Guo 2013).

Conclusion

Within a given imperial ethnic structure, the ways of transforming empires into nation state(s) were multiple. The role of agency thus cannot be denied. Two contradicting considerations shaped the revolutionaries' stance in ethnopolitics: to undermine counterrevolutionaries by supporting national self-determination and to retain the former empire's domain, making it a base to advance the revolution. Communist ideology viewed the nation state as a bourgeois precondition to socialism. This orientation led communists to boost an internationalist solution. Because counterrevolutionaries usually supported a strong assimilationist or imperialist solution, communists fought them by focusing their internationalist ideology on supporting the national self-determination of ethnic minorities. But the support for self-determination was not unconditional. Communists, as a group socialized within old imperial political norms, deemed the natural disintegration of the former imperial domain unacceptable. There was no reason that revolution, a pursuit of bringing about happiness, should expand as far as possible to reach all people. Such expansion should overcome not only class lines but also ethnic boundaries. The revolutionaries did not want an outcome in which all nations separated from the empire to escape the revolution. The

Revolution, nationalism, and multi-ethnic integration   187

revolutionaries sought to reorganize the former empire in a progressive way whereby multiple regions, ethnic groups, and nationalities could live more equally, especially in the cultural and linguistic dimensions.

The crucial difference between the Bolsheviks and the Chinese communists lay in how they dealt with the status of the major ethnic group of the former empires. The Bolsheviks downgraded Russia into one of the fifteen republics underneath the internationalist Soviet Union and made it clear that the Russian republic was not a republic of Russians. The Chinese communists upgraded China to be an overarching political roof that encompassed former borderlands. Under the "Chinese Nation" roof, every ethnic group, Han or non-Han, was a member. The difference in ethnic structures played a role in shaping this divergence. The numerical superiority of ethnic Hans vis-à-vis minorities was overwhelming, but the Russians were a weak majority. But ethnic structure alone cannot explain every outcome. One ethnic composition could lead to multiple modes of the nation state. Diversity may force a backstep to tolerance and pluralism. It may also provoke a strong assimilationist stance, as occurred in both Russia and China among non-communists: the Whites sought an indivisible and homogenous Russia, and the KMT of the 1940s asserted an assimilationist approach to Hanize minorities. Ethnic homogeneity could also trigger generous affirmative actions. When major ethnic groups felt secure about their control, they could build up various autonomous entities, real or in name, to display their generosity. This was what the Bolsheviks did at the end of the Civil War. The CCP's intimation of the Soviet model also reflected Han security since the Hans were the absolute majority.

To understand why the two communist parties made such different choices, we need to see who these people and their rivals were when setting up the models of nation states. The Bolsheviks supported the continuation of a multinational Russia, but they generally lacked a framework for legitimizing such an entity. This doesn't mean that such frameworks were absent in Russia in the 1910s; but the Bolsheviks, because of their atheist, anti-monarchist, and anti-militarist stances, could not accommodate themselves to these frameworks. In the Bolshevik's mind, a Greater Russian framework was too closely tied with the tsarist state and thus could not be advocated for openly. Though many Bolsheviks felt unwilling to continue a Greater-Russian framework, their foes had been too weak at the end of the Civil War. The White movement had been defeated, and separatists at the former empire's borderlands, lacking resources and international support, were unlikely to pose any real threat to the Soviet state. This situation gave the Bolsheviks great leeway to fulfill their ideological commitment to make a Soviet state that celebrated, accepted, and created nations. The Bolsheviks believed that they had sufficient forces to control the nations they celebrated, accepted, and created.

Very differently, when the CCP came into being, the post-imperial transition had moved to a stable phase, where a progressive notion of a multinational China had been invented and circulated among the elite and mass discourse. Not thinking of China as reactionary, the CCP were inspired by this concept. They viewed retrieving the former Qing's borderlands as patriotism, though the specific forms of retrieval could be flexible. Unlike the Bolsheviks, the CCP was the weak side in competition for borderlands. When manipulating minorities' self-determination, the CCP had no upper hand in relation to their major rivals, the Japanese and later the Soviets. They thus feared that support for national self-determination would cause real separatism, which would lead to the annexation of China's borderlands by Japan and Russia. Certainly, the CCP's three-decades-long revolution was complicated and multifaceted. The CCP's support for self-determination varied over time and across areas. Many factors shaped the variations. The CCP played up self-determination in the regions it could not reach, such as the western borders of Xinjiang. It played down this discourse within its jurisdictions, worrying that real separatist movements would undermine the revolutionary regimes. The CCP also reckoned with the attitudes of Han elites, but only when it was in close alliance with the latter. Displaying an internationalist loyalty in the face of Moscow was equally important, though Maoists often wanted to deflect Moscow' attention.

A crucial difference between the two communist parties lay in their familiarities with borderlands and ethnopolitics. The Bolsheviks were familiar with Russia's non-Russian borderlands. For the Bolsheviks, there was a vital intersection between ethnicity and region. Russian Bolsheviks commonly stayed in non-Russian areas (Ukraine, Baltic, Belarus, the Southern Caucasus, and Central Asia), and non-Russian Bolsheviks (Ukrainians, Germans, Polish, Jews, Latvians) stayed in Russian areas. In comparison, the CCP's familiarity with China's borderlands was much weaker. Except for a few ethnic non-Hans, very few CCP leaders spent significant periods of their lives in the borderlands. Most CCP leaders came from Han areas, either large cities or towns of regional centers. This difference has many implications. First, though tsarist Russia was demographically more multiethnic than imperial China, in terms of interethnic interaction and fusion, the Bolsheviks had more intense experiences than the CCP. This discrepancy stemmed from the two empires' different legacies in geography-based ethnic segregation and the Comintern's ethnic Balkanization of China's communist movement. Second and most importantly, the CCP's unfamiliarity and long-term isolation from borderland minorities led them to fear real separatism. With the sole exception of Ulanhu, the CCP had no equivalents to Ordzhonikidze, Dzerzhinskii, Shkrypnik, Kapsukas, Frunze, and others who were able to play the role of "fifth column" among borderland

Revolution, nationalism, and multi-ethnic integration 189

minorities. Most of the CCP's emissaries and correspondents in the borderlands were ethnic Hans, and these people stayed there only briefly. As the CCP was not yet geographically adjacent to the minorities, they could propagate a discourse of self-determination. But once they confronted real borderland nationalism, the CCP cadres were not confident in steering these movements and thus switched back to the language of "One China."

Notes

1 Stanford, Hoover Institution Archive, *Nicolaevsky Collection*, Box 78, Folder 11.
2 Stanford, Hoover Institution Archive, *Nicolaevsky Collection*, Box 669, Folder 08.
3 See *Voennyi sborkni*, August 1914, 139.
4 One exception was Deng Enming, an ethnic Shui, who attended the CCP's first congress as a formal delegate. He was murdered in 1931.

Conclusion: Two revolutions in communist and world history

This book makes two contributions. First, while most literature regards China's national model as an imitation of the Soviet federation, this book highlights the differences between the two polities, pointing out that the People's Republic of China, despite its framing of minorities as sub-nations, is closer to the ideal type of modern nation state, unlike the Soviet Union, which is an open union accepting of new nation states and institutionally lacking an overarching national core. Second, by tracing the differences between the two back to the two great revolutions, this book engages the scholarship on nationalism. It argues that the ethnic composition of the population, geopolitical conflicts, and external interference shapes a society's national model with multiple results. The revolutionary course, particularly the role of leading elites, navigated a path to the final historical product. The two revolutions represented two distinctive paths to reorganizing empires into nation states: transforming the empire into a union of nation states and transforming the empire into one multi-ethnic nation state.

A central theme running through this book is negotiation between a society's contextual conditions and the nation-state models it seeks to adopt. This book also argues that this negotiation is shaped by the course of the revolution. In theory, nations, even within the Western world, could be organized in multiple ways. When this theory is put into practice by imposing it on the geo-political world outside the West, it resulted in a struggle between the Western template and the local conditions upon which that template was being imposed. Underneath the appearance of the nation state as a dominant world format, evasion, resistance, and manipulation prevailed. Such interaction further diversified the forms of nation states and complicated the ways in which a nation was drafted in the non-Western world. Faced with the world pressure of becoming nations, and fearing exclusion from the global stage, the elites of city-states, tribes, and dynastical states had to change. However, such adaptation was limited and often practical. Most elites undertook to frame their nations to their advantage, partly because what "nation" looked like in the West remained unclear, and partly because

Western colonialism lacked the absolute power to replicate the format of a nation state in an entirely Western way. In such a proliferation, Russia's and China's roles were outstanding. As traditional dynastic empires, they both resisted the notion of nation states. They suffered defeats, but their vast sizes and geographical locations prevented partitions. Neither were any Western powers able to transform them entirely. Through revolutions, Russia and China ultimately switched to embrace the idea of the nation. As occurred elsewhere, their understandings of the nation significantly deviated both from the West and from each other.

Russia and China in the world history of great revolutions

The Russian and Chinese revolutions were of world-historical significance. They took place in the first half of the twentieth century, which made these two revolutions different from the revolutions before and after them. The Russian and the Chinese revolutions faced three historical particularities. First, by the early twentieth century, the global empires had reached the limits of expansion and were beginning to contain each other as well as suppress the latecomers. There were limited opportunities for newcomers to create new global empires that were comparable to the Dutch, Portuguese, Spanish, French, and British. This shrinking of opportunity for expansion led to the two world wars and the collapse of direct colonialism. Therefore, to create a new sphere of influence, latecomers had to develop new frames and strategies. Second, formal empires and direct colonialism were undergoing their final stage. The previously marginal norms of democracy, republic, popular sovereignty, Enlightenment, and secularization became grounded and obtained global dominance in the twentieth century, especially after World War II. The old devices that had legitimated formal empires, such as monarchy, religion, and irrationalism, were losing their power. As democratization and mass mobilization diffused, this shift of landscape meant that political rule, be it national or transnational, had to develop a new position in relation to a society's past. Third, nationalism as an operative ideology and principle obtained legitimacy, and the nation state became a dominant political template. This change was not only costly for the survival of traditional empires, but also disturbed the nationalist movements themselves, arousing more autonomous/self-determinist quests from the inside. The imperial defenders, the nationalist contenders, and the minority leaders within nationalist movements all bore more self-conscious norms of nationalism than their counterparts in the nineteenth century or earlier.

The revolts of the Netherlands and the British "Glorious Revolution," in the sixteenth and seventeenth centuries knew little of modern nationalism.

The Dutch revolutionaries (if this term was correct for them, given that the War lasted for eighty years) were in a patrimonial company-state that bore neither notions of popular sovereignty nor secular nationality nor contiguous territories (Adams 1994). The revolts constituted a war against religious persecution by the Spanish Empire, and bore a heavy medieval character—no national standing army but a multinational and multilingual composition of mercenaries and volunteers, truces, and recurrences hinging on dynastic alliances, and collective voting by the oligarchs. It was religious disagreement rather than national identities that drove the "revolution" (Lem 2018: 3–14). The Glorious Revolution had a conservative character as well. The fight originated in religious affairs. Though the loyalists had used Scotland as a rebellious base and spot to incur foreign interventions, people did not recognize the necessity of creating a separate English national identity (Kumar 2000). Since the monarchy survived the Glorious Revolution, the tension between meddling constitutionalism and the nation's past was not as acute as it would be in the French and Russian Revolutions. Both the Dutch and the British empires faced a vast globe: the Spanish and the Portuguese had only conquered a part of the world, whereas the Dutch and the British, through the strategic flexibility and low cost provided by their company-state models, were able to quickly displace the old empires (Phillips and Sharman 2020).

The American and the French Revolutionaries were more self-conscious about nationality. Yet, since they were the first revolutionaries to deal with this issue, they still had larger leeway to evade, postpone, and dismiss the nationality-affiliated questions. After the Independence of 1776, the American revolutionaries had been beset by the absence of a secular American identity that was well-rooted in mass memories, and led to a prophecy that a particular major disagreement would tear apart the fragile federation in the future (Berens 1978). This anxiety translated into a restlessness that fostered the ensuing centuries of expansion, first into the South and the West and then into Latin America, the Pan-Atlantic world, the Pacific, and Asia (Gould and Onuf 2005; Ziesche 2006). In setting the boundaries for community members, the American Revolution also preserved slavery, tacitly consented on the eradication of the indigenous people and a White supremacist immigration regime, which made "Americanness" fall far from the ideal type of nation (Gerstle 2001). In the period before the widespread of national consciousness, these behaviors incurred moral castigation; but they faced fewer barriers than they would in the post-1945 world. The French revolutionaries of 1789 were arguably the inventors of the modern nation: citizenship, Enlightenment, popular sovereignty, and secularism (Bell 2002). One advantage was that most of the world at the moments of 1776 and 1789 did not yet know what nationalism was—even

Conclusion 193

within France, the norm of the French citizen became grounded much later, after almost a century of infrastructure-building and public education had displaced the Catholic church and village-based community identities (Weber 1976). This situation encouraged some French rulers, from Napoleon Bonaparte to the interwar mandate system and then the Fourth Republic, to consider integrating the entire Europe and former French possessions into one single nation (Cooper 2014; Pedersen 2015). Some of these projects failed with the disintegration of the French empire (Chafer 2002). The British, French, and American revolutionaries alike had encountered the tensions between territorial state and ideological universalism, between Enlightenment and conservatism, and between ethnopolitics and support for nationalist movement. All relieved and evaded these dilemmas by reaching out to create global empires.

The Iranian Revolution of 1979, which took place after the Russian and the Chinese Revolutions, marked a new epoch in world revolutions. The Iranian Revolution took place when the transition from empires to nation states was almost completed (except for the Soviet space where a next wave of nation-building would occur in the 1990s following the fall of communism), while at the same time the world entered a new form of imperial rule, whereby great empires exerted influences through nationalism. The Khomeini regime faced historical conditions that the previous modern revolutions had not met. First, unlike in the seventeenth and eighteenth centuries, the world of the late 1970s was in the control of a few global empires. These empires, primarily the US and the Soviet, exerted influence in indirect ways, through military alliance, economic integration, and developmentalism. There was a radical power transfer from the old empires (the German, Japanese, British, French, Dutch, Spanish, Portuguese, and Belgian) to the new ones (the US, the Soviet, as well as the Chinese). Nevertheless, even this radical power shift was drawing to its completion. The Iranian revolutionaries would have encountered significant difficulties had they attempted to release the tension of nation-building through imperial expansion (Menasheri 1990). Second, the world ideological landscape was undergoing a shift, moving away from Enlightenment and reverting to religious conservatism. The universal ideologies that had been based on rationality and Enlightenment were encountering discredit and crisis. This crisis came to the socialist bloc in the 1970s and would transfer to the liberal bloc after the collapse of the Soviet Union. Such an ideological shift meant that to maintain influences outside of national borders a state had to find new ideologies alternative to communism and liberalism. This created a new dynamic in the conventional dilemma in which nationalists had sought a balance between inventing a new tradition and countering the nation's "backward and reactionary" past. And this explains the rise of religious fundamentalism that

194   *Revolution in China and Russia*

followed and was inspired by the Iranian Revolution (Esposito 1990). Third, by the time of the Iranian Revolution, the nation state had become the only legitimate political model—the Pahlavi Dynasty overthrown in the revolution was probably the last polity that carried "empire" in its formal title. Meanwhile, not only had nationalism been accepted as a major principle of territorial rule, the demarcation had been almost completed when the Portuguese Empire finished its decolonization. From this moment on, revising existing national borders and sovereignties would be illegitimate and incur sanctions, even though ethnopolitics were displacing class warfare.

Two extended models: Yugoslavia and Cuba

The Soviet and the Chinese models represented two distinctive ways of reorganizing empires into nation states through communist revolutions: transforming the former empire into a union of socialist nation states and transforming the empire into one socialist nation state where the multiethnicity was institutionalized. Yugoslavia and Cuba represented two other outcomes. In these two cases, the principle by which communism engaged nationalism remained similar to that in the Soviet and Chinese models, but the outcomes were more varied. The Socialist Federal Republic of Yugoslavia (SFRY), in form, was a national federation. Its federal structure resembled the Soviet Union's, consisting of six national republics and two autonomous units. However, the federation was organized under the master framework of "Yugoslavian Nation" (Bunce 1999). Whereas "Soviet" was a class-based, ideological concept not carrying ethnic or geographical connotations, "Yugoslavia" was a serious state-led nation-building project, cultivated to transcend the republic-based nationalities of Serbia, Croatia, Slovenia, Montenegro, Bosnia-Herzegovina, and Macedonia. Because the effort of building a homogenous nation carried a strong Serbia-centric tendency, the breakup of Yugoslavia brought about Civil War, which constituted a sharp contrast to the relatively peaceful dissolution of the Soviet Union (Vujačić 2015). In this sense, Yugoslavia even differed from Czechoslovak Socialist Republic, where the federal structure was a simple juxtaposition of two separate nations. It lies between the Soviet Union and China, more national than the Soviet Union but more federal than China.

Cuba represented a path more comparable to China. By form the Republic of Cuba was a unitary nation state. It asserted an anti-imperialist nationalism and strove to be a model for the world revolutions among non-White populations. Yet, unlike People's Republic of China, the Castro regime fostered a nationalist discourse that denied any racial and ethnic divisiveness, which meant that it was not an "affirmative action empire." Once in power,

Conclusion

195

the Castro regime simply claimed that race had ceased to be a politically relevant category (Clealand 2017: 1621–22). This differed from China in general, where the CCP celebrates the "Chinese Nation" while at the same time institutionalizing non-Han ethnic groups as "nations" with their "autonomous" state apparatus. Nevertheless, the difference should not be viewed as statically categorical. The CCP system varied over time and at some points its distance from Cuba was smaller. The CCP state wanted to highlight a unified and homogenous Chinese nation, which, during Mao's "Great Leap Forward" and "Cultural Revolution," led to state-led actions to undermine the autonomous system, eliminating the distinctiveness of non-Han minorities. Thus if the Soviet Union–Yugoslavia–China–Cuba comparison can be understood as a spectrum, with internationalist federation at one end and homogenous unitary nation state at the other, Yugoslavia lies between the USSR and China, and China lies between Yugoslavia and Cuba.

Yugoslavia and Cuba deserve separate analysis also for methodological reasons. They were more homegrown than other communist regimes, involving substantive revolutionary processes and struggling with heavy ethnopolitics. These two regimes were homegrown in the sense that they were not "installed" by foreign militaries. The Yugoslavian communists, like the Chinese, maintained guerrilla states throughout World War II. Though benefiting from the Soviet offense on the Nazi forces in achieving the final stage of war, they liberated the Yugoslav territories mostly on their own. Nor did Yugoslavia become a puppet-satellite of Moscow. The Tito–Stalin split came early enough, in 1948, even before some Eastern European states came under the yoke of Sovietization. Yugoslavia's autonomy in social and diplomatic policies was so salient that the USSR and China attacked it as a challenger and traitor. Cuba's homegrown character was more salient. When the revolution broke out, the Soviet Union, in the aftermath of Stalin's death, had not yet extended its hands to the Western hemisphere. When Fidel Castro seized power in 1958, he had not even self-claimed as a Marxist–Leninist (Pettinà 2011: 325–26). In a sense, it was the Cuban Revolution that opened the window for Moscow to interfere into American affairs through a substantive military presence—before Castro's victory, the Soviet Union had only achieved very small-scale and superficial infiltration in a few Latin American countries, the most salient of which was in Guatemala (Pettinà 2011: 324).

These two revolutionary regimes involved substantive mobilizations. In terms of the processes of power seizure, they both underwent tough armed struggles: Tito's guerrilla warfare was more similar to the CCP's rural experiences, whereas Castro's quick conquest of the Cuban island from Havana and defense against the US invasion better resembled the Bolsheviks' Civil War. In both cases, the roads to state power were mobilizational. These two regimes came into being in the classical period of communist revolutions, Yugoslavia in the middle 1940s and Cuba in the late 1950s. Both regimes existed for a long period (Yugoslavia from 1945 to 1992, and Cuba, still in existence, since 1958). This experience allowed them to undergo a substantial period of socialist state-building and nation-building, which entailed deep social mobilization as well. The length of survival also allowed for rich variations and adjustments in their respective nationality models. Almost in every way, the Yugoslavian and the Cuban revolutions were different from the world's next wave of revolts that came in the late 1970s and 1980s, represented by the Iranian Revolution and the collapse of the Soviet Union, which George Lawson terms "negotiated revolutions" (Lawson 2005).

Moreover, the revolutions in Yugoslavia and Cuba also embodied how the Soviet model could vary in a broader geographical and social context. In comparison with the Soviet Union and China, both Yugoslavia and Cuba were small countries, one located at the hinterland of Europe and the other in Central America. Yugoslavia sheds light on the intersection of the German-Austrian circle with the Middle East and Muslim world, whereas the Cuban Revolution was distinctive in its impact on Black American nationalism and on the non-White world. These two polities also differed from Russia and China in the depth of their historical traditions. The notion of "Yugoslavia" ("Southern Slavs") had been growing since the mid-nineteenth century in the fight against the Hapsburg Dynasty, but had remained a largely undeveloped concept drafted by politically marginal intellectuals (Jelavich 2003: 95–110). Cuba's history before Spanish colonialism was less national than other Latin American countries and put the nation-building work in Cuba at a disadvantage (Hennessy 1963: 346). These two cases thus in general embodied the three of the theses of this book—their nationality models, though distinctive, were created through the three relationships in their respective communist revolutions: (1) the inter-revolution relationship, (2) the revolution–society relationship, and (3) the revolution–counterrevolution relationship. The following explains why their nationality models, like those Russia and China, cannot be simply reduced to structural factors.

First, while communists tended to be cosmopolitan or imperial-minded, the ones who seized state power early would force the latecomers to be national and local. Both Yugoslavia and Cuba actively exported their national models abroad, to compete with Moscow and Beijing (Yugoslavia aimed at the Balkan–Danube area and the Non-Alignment Movement, whereas Cuba aimed at Latin America, Africa, and the Black Third World). At the Bandung Conference, Yugoslavia initiated a discussion about whether the non-Russian republics and Eastern European nations differed from the colonial societies. With the answer "no," Belgrade hinted that Yugoslavia

Conclusion 197

was offering a genuine model for national liberation and decentralized social-ism (Niebuhr 2018: 114). Yet, Yugoslavia and Cuba, like the CCP, came to be contained by Moscow and Beijing, and thus had to become more "national" than they had envisioned. Believing that they had created and tested a model of manipulating anti-fascist war, Tito was eager to build up a small third International to exert control over the Albanian, Greek, and Bulgarian resist-ance movements, which led to his bolder postwar proposal of founding a Yugoslav–Bulgarian Balkan socialist federation (Banac 2017: 577–78). Yet such ambition aroused the vigilant attention of Moscow. While discreetly maintaining his relationship with Moscow, Tito suspended his support for Greek guerilla partisans. In the early postwar years he moved on to univer-salize the route of manipulating the postwar electoral system, at first with Moscow's consent. But he ultimately went too far, and this led to Yugoslavia's break with the Soviet Union (Swain 1992: 659–60).

The Non-Aligned Movement faced a similar barrier. Emerging at the turn of the 1960s, this movement embodied Yugoslavia's global ambition of offering a social model for developing nations and creating a path to avoid the US–Soviet confrontation. This proposal was attractive at its onset, as the Algerian Civil War, the Berlin crisis, Nuclear proliferation, and the Sino-Indian War raised fear that newly born nation states were at the precarious edge of world war and intervention by empires (Lüthi 2016). By leading this movement, Yugoslavia also gained the US's recognition as "a Mediterranean power" and extended its influences into Africa (Lampe 2013: 106). However, as the Non-Aligned Movement expanded, it faced pressure from both the US and the Soviet sides. Celebrating the Non-Aligned Movement as a significant force against world imperialism, Brezhnev assigned Cuba to be its president-state, which skewed the movement to engage the Cold War in Africa. The weapons trade with Iraq, Syria, and Iran that fueled the warfare in the Middle East further discredited Yugoslavia as a leader of this movement (Lampe 2013: 106–12). As most members found the logic that they had to engage in the Cold War to maintain neutrality self-defeating, the movement lost momentum, pushing Yugoslavia back to its Balkan and national outlook.

Cuba engaged a similar process of reaching out to create a global revo-lutionary empire. Castro's and Guevara's ambitions were not confined to the island of Cuba. To secure real independence and ideologically a broader liberation of non-White nations, Castro made bold attempts, by extensively supporting revolutionary movements in Latin America and Africa, includ-ing Guinea-Bissau, Angola, The Horn of Africa, Guatemala, Nicaragua, Dominica, Venezuela, and Chile. The Cuban regime formulated an ideo-logical alternative to Maoism and the Soviet Union's economic determin-ism. Cuba emphasized self-reliance, insurrection to ignite revolution, and an affinity with Blackness (Duncan 1976: 161–63). The aim was to gain leverage vis-à-vis both Washington and Moscow. Some of these adventures conformed to Havana's relationship with Moscow, whereas others led to tension. Castro's intervention in the guerrilla movements in Latin America irritated the Soviet Union, when the latter was seeking for normalization of diplomacy and trade with the established governments of this region (Harmer 2013). Cuba's revolutionary export also irritated Beijing, which was also cultivating nationalism in Latin America and Africa in competition with Moscow. Ultimately unable to afford the pressure from Moscow, in the late 1960s Castro softened his stance and reverted to following the Soviet model (Gleijeses 2017a: 373–76). Cuba's intervention in the Angola Civil War went against the Soviet Union, but once it was underway, Moscow supported it with both transportation and weapons. Cuba's actions in Ethiopia, on the other hand, were well coordinated with the Soviet Union (Gleijeses 2017b: 103–8). In return, the Soviet Union limited its intervention in the Americas, reaching a tacit consensus that this space should be left to Cuba. From the mid-1980s on, as the Soviet Union reduced its presence in the Third World, Cuba found it increasingly difficult to sustain revolutionary projects overseas. This pressured Havana to return to its national tradition of revolution, decreasing the legitimate reliance on a global ideology.

Second, in-depth revolutionary mobilization impelled communists to invent a tradition that would legitimize and assert revolutionary values through celebrating a national past. In Yugoslavia and Cuba, the preconditions were more complicated, as they both lacked a long pre-revolutionary history compared to that of Russia and China. Such thin soil delayed and complicated their efforts at cultivating tradition. The Tito-led communists seized national power in a protracted guerrilla war and engaged in in-depth transethnic mobilization. This prompted the Yugoslavian state to invent a historical tradition that celebrate the "Yugoslav" peoples' fight against alien occupiers. As early as in 1948, Tito, in his report to the Communist Party of Yugoslavia's Fifth Congress, had set the tone for the developing Yugoslavian historiography: the unification of multiple Yugoslavian peoples was progressive, though the interwar dictatorship failed to represent it; most centrifugal ethnic hostility could be attributed to the Serbian chauvinists, their Entente sponsors, and the domestic non-Serbian bourgeoisie who preferred national oppression to mass mobilization from the bottom (Banac 1992: 1085–86). Under this guideline, professional historians were struggling between two coexisting understandings of Yugoslavia—that of a new homogenous nation dissolving all existing ethnic segregations, and a sheer geographic concept physically combining separate histories of constituent nations (Brunnbauer 2011: 363–64). Nevertheless, archeological work and historical research inventing the nationalities of each republic

Conclusion 199

went undisrupted, which served as a device for political mobilization more stable than the "Yugoslavian history."

In contrast, Castro completed the power seizure in quick uprisings conducted by small guerrilla groups. Thus, there was no massive social mobilization comparable to that of Russia and China. At the time of the overthrow of the Batista regime, Castro had not yet even declared himself to be a communist. The state-led tradition-inventing came late, after the regime began systematically transforming society. The first step was to draw a continuity between the Revolution of 1959 with other revolts and uprisings in history—against Spain and the United States (Duncan 1976: 164). Immediately after the uprising of July in 1959, Castro founded the Instituto Cubano del Arte e Industria Cinematográficos (ICAIC), a monitoring and supportive institution to promote revolutionary cultural production. Yet, apart from passive censorship, the role of this institution remained undefined and disputed for a long while, revealing that Cuba's "communist revolution" was not as penetrative as in Russia and China. There was an official call for active responses to exigencies of particular historical moments, but intellectuals resisted the official discourse, and there was no Zhdanov-style discipline (Gordy 2015: 66–68; Manuel 1987: 173–75). It was later, after Castro's speech "Words to the Intellectuals" (Palabras a los intelectuales), that Soviet-style cultural control became more institutionalized. However, as the tendency to carve out a national path different from the Soviet and the Chinese continued, debates continued about the role of intellectuals in the revolution—essentially, the extent of closeness between the state and the cultural professionals. Particularly, a subject of extended debate was whether, and if so how, the revolutionary literati could make use of the cultural past (Gordy 2015: 74). Partly because of this uncertainty and hesitation, Cuba's turn at glorifying its national past took place only in the late 1980s, some time later than in the other communist states. The ideological switch celebrated transculturation as Cuba's core identity, transferring the historical legitimacy of the communist party from Marxism-Leninism to the War of independence (González 2016). In general, Cuba's cultural control was not as Stalinist as that Russia or China. Such practices as borrowing pop music from the United States continued, and the official propaganda preferred to draw on preexisting legacies rather than inventing new traditions (Manuel 1987).

Finally, communists tended to moderate their slogan of "self-determination" when they faced strong enemies, fearing that "self-determination" could be manipulated to generate real separatism. Both Tito and Castro faced formidable foreign threats when they seized power. This situation favored the CCP's strategy of keeping minorities' rights of "self-determination" vague, rather than the Bolsheviks' strategy of decomposing any master frame of nation. According to Tito, a new Yugoslavia should include not only Serbia, Croatia, and Slovenia, as per the 1918 version. Rather, Macedonia, Montenegro, Bosnia, and Vojvodina had to be separated out from Serbia as equal entities (Tito 1984: 48–50). However, like the Chinese communists, Tito did not negate the fruit of 1918, arguing that the various peoples of Yugoslavia should hold together rather than break apart, which Italian and German fascists were agitating for (Tito 1984: 44). Throughout the war Tito suspended the intellectually complicated question of "what Yugoslavia is," instead relying on identifying fascism as the common foe of the various Yugoslavian peoples, with all wartime ethnic cleansing attributed to fascists and their collaborators (Pesic 1996: 8–9). The Yugoslav communists highlighted "centralization" until its relationship with the USSR normalized. It was after the Yugoslav–Soviet reconciliation that Tito began to emphasize the power of national republics and maneuvered nationality issues to gain the support of neighboring states.

Following the Soviet model, Yugoslavia maneuvered its internal nationality questions to foster its agenda abroad, attempting to melt its complicated ethnopolitics into a global new international order that legitimized Yugoslavia as a model for oppressed nations. This practice started during World War II. Toward the end of the war, Tito, backed by the encroaching Soviet army, sought out territories held by Italy and Austria (Trieste and Istria respectively), claiming that these lands were populated by ethnic Croatians and Slovenians who suffered from fascist persecution. The same claim extended to Albania, where, after Italy's defeat, Tito had worked with Enver Hoxha to prepare a pan-Yugoslavian federation. Yet as the Soviet Union withdrew support, Tito stepped back from playing the nationalist card and returned to an emphasis on federal authority, especially relying on the military, security, and diplomacy to block Moscow's penetration (Niebuhr 2018: 27–49). However, as relations with the Soviet Union improved after Stalin's death, Belgrade, feeling geopolitically secure and less threatened by internal separatism, continued to maneuver ethnopolitics against its neighbors. For example, it weaponized the problem of ethnic Macedonians against Bulgaria (Yugoslavia insisted that Macedonians were a nationality; Bulgaria denied this identity). It also framed the Kosovo issue to accuse Albania of interference (Belgrade blamed Tirana for carrying out direct diplomacy with Kosovo, bypassing the Yugoslav federal government) (Jiang 1981: 170–71). The intrusion into Austria never ceased as well. Securing an entry into the former Hapsburg economic circle was a priority for Tito, and the problems of Croatians and Slovenians were a weapon to achieve this goal (Niebuhr 2018: 44).

Cuba, a tiny polity constantly under immediate threat from the United States, officially denied racial and ethnic divisiveness, in case such divisiveness

Conclusion 201

could be manipulated by the external enemies. This partly explains why Cuba, a multi-ethnic society, did not move on to a Soviet-style federal system that weaponized race and ethnicity. A core value that the communists inherited from pre-communist nationalism was the notion of "racial harmony" and "mixed nation." The nationalists aspired to make a unified Cuban nation to transcend race. Such an emphasis on racial harmony was used to turn the discussion away from race, and to discourage Black activism (Clealand 2017: 53–56). Unlike the Bolsheviks, the Chinese, and the Yugoslavians, who boosted self-determination and developed national recognition, Cuban communists adopted melting-pot style nationalism. Invoking communist ideology, they invented the notion of "erasing race"—downplaying the significance of race by removing social inequality and oppression. In practice, this policy, as in the prerevolutionary regime, was manifested in institutional silence—few Black people were incorporated into the government, nor did the legislative branch pass any formal laws against discrimination (Clealand 2017: 75). In the Cuban revolution, communism was entirely an instrument added to overcome racial heterogeneity to cultivate a political nation.

For linguistic and space reasons, my discussion on Yugoslavia and Cuba is based on secondary sources written in English. Nevertheless, the relationships and mechanisms I have traced across the Soviet and Chinese cases are valid. In shaping nationality models, the revolutionary process sometimes worked in opposition to structural factors such as ethnic composition and geopolitical pressure. And the precise ways in which this process unfolded—factors such as intra- and inter-party disagreements, conflicts, and purges—was dependent upon the revolutionaries of various groups and periods. For example, Tito declined the greater Serbian proposal, which stemmed from the 1918 kingdom of Yugoslavia and remained popular among the communist military and the security service. Rather, he chose a path that legitimatized the federal authority through a discourse of class solidarity, while at the same time tentatively cultivating a concept of Yugoslavian nation. This choice cannot be reduced to the structure of Yugoslavia's nationalities—"Russia" as an imperial notion carried a stronger tradition and memory of statehood than "Yugoslavia" did, but the Bolsheviks moved forward to build a de-ethnicized federation. Because of Tito's personal power, the "Yugoslavia" option translated into Yugoslavia's institutions and systems, but it was not free of resistance. There was internal disagreement first from Croatian communists during World War II and then from Alexandar Rankovic, who was deposed in 1966 with the accusation of "Greater Serbianism." Even Tito himself was changed and adapted as necessary. The extent of centralization degraded over time, as the external security environment improved—"the 1950s was the only decade when there was serious talk of meddling the separate cultures of the South Slavs into a unified Yugoslav culture." Before

the promulgation of the 1974 Constitution, Tito purged the liberal nationalists in every republic, to ensure that the devolution of sovereignty would not
arouse a Croatian or Slovenian "Spring" (Haug 2012: 285–86).

Similarly, Castro's denial of the political relevance of ethnic and racial
attributes was not the sole path that had existed in Cuban history. Before
Castro's revolution, Cuba lacked a unified, clearly defined national identity.
There was a tradition of trans-racial mobilization left over by the uprisings between 1868 and 1898, but the interpretations of these revolts were
diverse. There were competing interpretations of Jose Marti's thought, for
example, ranging from the aim of joining the United States and the British
Atlantic commonwealth, to that of maintaining a non-mobilizational conservative regime in defense of slavery (Fuente 1999: 51–52).

Besides Yugoslavia and Cuba, a special case that deserves comparison
is communist Albania. Communists came to power through a revolution
that took the form of a long guerrilla war against Italians and domestic
nationalists. The revolution was homegrown. Though Enver Hoxha was
initially sponsored by Tito as a proxy to penetrate Italy and a member of a
future Yugoslavian federation, his regime shortly attained autonomy in the
wake of the Soviet–Yugoslav split. Political mobilization persisted from the
1940s to the end of the communist regime in 1992. Despite the conceptual
thinness of the "Albanian nation," created by the Allies as a state to block
Serbia after the fall of the Ottomans (Guy 2012), the Hoxha regime com-
mitted vast resources gathering historical materials to support the concept,
mainly by highlighting the historical fighters against the Ottoman Empire
(Idrizi 2020: 68–69; Iskenderov 2008: 38–40) and framing the modern
Albanian nation as a heroic defender of the European civilization against
the Ottomans (Brunnbauer 2011: 363). In terms of the intensity with which
intellectuals were disciplined and education systems were reformed, Hoxha's
campaign was comparable to Mao's "Cultural Revolution" (Blumi 1999).

Albania was diplomatically isolated. The ties with Tito's Yugoslavia were
close, but tensions accumulated as Tito pressured Hoxha to eliminate non-
communist forces from the anti-fascist united front (Rieber 2017: 50–51). In
power, the Hoxha regime first broke with Yugoslavia after the latter's excom-
munication by Moscow, then split with the Soviet Union, feeling threatened by
Khrushchev's de-Stalinization, and finally, it was alienated from China after
Mao's death. In terms of geopolitical insecurity, Albania's level of precarity
was close to Cuba, and even worse. The only longtime friend of Tirana, the
People's Republic of China, was far away, unable to offer immediate military
aid in the event of external invasion. In this situation, the Albanian regime
was rhetorically aggressive but behaviorally discreet. Albania's uniqueness
also lay in its introversion. There was no global mission comparable to that
of Tito's and Castro's. Though the Albania homeland was densely covered by

Conclusion   203

fortresses and shelters, no Albanian military was deployed abroad. In terms of nationality policies, Enver Hoxha exerted a program of brutal assimilation and ethnic cleansing, to melt the Catholic Ghegs and the Orthodox Tosks into one homogeneous Albanian nation (Blumi 1997: 385–88; Fischer 1999: 189–91). This approach was distinctive, with no nationwide equivalent in the Soviet Union, China, Yugoslavia, or Cuba. The only nationalist card Tirana played was in Kosovo, which was populated by ethnic Albanians; but this strategy differed from the Yugoslavian and Soviet practice of multinationalization as an ethnopolitical and geopolitical weapon.

Implications of the nation-building of world communism

The three relations within/between revolutions revealed in this book contain general implications. Beyond the Soviet Union and China, these mechanisms were at work in shaping the nationality models in other communist states as well. However, this book cannot analyze all these cases. There are many factors that rule out such an all-encompassing comparative analysis. One is exogenous roots. In comparison with the Soviet Union and China, many communist regimes were installed by external actors (Moscow, Beijing, Belgrade, Hanoi, etc.) and thus lacked originality (though the Russian and the Chinese revolutions involved significant external influences as well). Their formative processes mixed external forces and indigenous factors, which renders comparative analysis difficult. Moreover, relying on foreign military intervention, some of these regimes, such as Somalia, Ethiopia, Afghanistan, Angola, Mozambique, and Sechele were too short-lived for historical analysis. This also applies to Vietnam, Laos, and Cambodia, where the revolutionary courses persisted but the nation-building unfolded in a global context of post-communist transformation. In still other situations, the formative processes of these nationality models were incomplete and my theoretical thesis is thus difficult to test. Some communist regimes, such as most Eastern European countries, Mongolia, and Afghanistan, were not created by revolutions at all, but rather by military occupation. The communist organizations in these cases lacked crucial elements of revolution, such as overseas network-building, social mobilization, and the independent fight against counterrevolution. Some cases lacked salient processes of nation-building and interethnic integration. The ruling elites invested little in inventing a tradition out of or creating a transethnic concept of nation.

The formation of the North Korean communist state involved Soviet and Chinese factors and only attained autonomy as the Moscow–Beijing alliance broke up. The indigenous partisan movement persisted but remained weak,

204 *Revolution in China and Russia*

given Japan's overwhelming military strength until 1945, and the Kim Il-sung regime was "installed" by the Soviet military (Armstrong 2017: 443). The communist movement in North Korea also involved limited ethnopolitics. Though a homogeneous Korean nation was a myth (Campell 2015), the ethnic heterogeneity in Korea was far less salient than it was in Indochina and in Eastern Europe. One indicator is that most political fights during the twentieth century occurred between competing camps of Koreans—between the Shanghai exile government and the homegrown resistance movement or between the Yan'an faction and the Soviet faction (Lankov 2011: 3–4; Shen 2015). These competing factions claimed to be genuine Korean patriots and revolutionaries, rather than representatives of different ethnic groups. In Korea, the communist movement was not an instrument to overcome regionalism and ethnic cleavages. Marxist–Leninist ideology faded under the Kim family, which rendered pointless any Soviet- or CCP-style of struggle to recreate a nation. From 1955 onward, as the split between China and the Soviet Union became final, Marxism eventually became displaced in North Korea by "Juche" thought. In the late 1970s, the internationalist discourse was dropped from the official ideology, and replaced by the language of blood, race, and common history of a greater Korean nation (Lee and Bairner 2009: 393). Later on, the uniqueness claim further deviated into a discourse of legitimizing dynastic succession and the Suryong system (Chung 2013). These factors disqualify North Korea as a suitable case for analyzing how communist revolutions dealt with multi-ethnicity.

The Indochinese revolution was homegrown, which partly explains the regimes' survival amid the collective collapse of communist regimes in Eastern Europe. The revolution across Vietnam, Laos, and Cambodia involved several protracted guerrilla wars that intertwined international and peninsula-internal conflicts (Vietnamese–Japanese, Vietnamese–French, Sino-US, Vietnamese–US, Vietnamese–Cambodian, Vietnamese–Lao, Vietnamese–Sino, Lao–US, and Vietnamese–Thai), which persisted from 1945 to 1979. At its initial stage, the movement as an entity was supported by Moscow and Beijing, but it attained increasing autonomy in the Sino-Soviet split as well as the Chinese–Soviet–US competition during the Vietnamese War (Brown and Zasloff 1977: 114–15). The regimes in Vietnam, Laos, and Cambodia each faced ethnopolitical issues. The leadership had a heterogeneous ethnic composition and extensive transnational experience within the French and Japanese colonial empires (Vu 2016: 277–81). The heavy ethnopolitics also brought about a revolutionary ambition to build a pan-Indochinese federal state rather than to foster separate national liberations (Singh 2015: 627). The revolution also saw brutal ethnic cleansings, which occurred against Chams, Miao, Chinese, and other minorities (Deac 1997: 265–68; Goscha 2012: 93–94). However, the Indochinese revolutions lacked the classical

Conclusion 205

communist components and was closer to general Third World movements of decolonization. Completing wars of unification in the middle 1970s, these communist regimes shortly entered new reconfiguration of power. Vietnam invaded Cambodia and eradicated the Khmer Rouge in 1978 and then entered a conflict with China in 1979, which would last for another ten years. These regimes became institutionalized during the time when global Soviet socialism was drawing to a close. The Pol Pot regime survived for only four years and had no persistent tradition-inventing work. Vietnam carried out history writing and archeological work early in the 1950s but suffered disruptions by the ensuing wars. The systematic work of inventing tradition occurred as late as the late 1970s (Cherry 2009: 105–6). Communists in Laos soon found that they were unable to impose Marxism-Leninism and hence reverted to Buddhism, after a brief attack on monks and temples (Ladwig 2017: 282–83). Their nationality models took shape in the global post-communist transformation and should be analyzed in a different context.

In Europe, the map was monolithic: most communist regimes were created not by bottom-up revolutions but by the Soviet Union's military occupation. There were few protracted civil wars sustained by well-organized guerrilla states comparable to the ones that occurred in East Asia. Except for Yugoslavia and Albania, Eastern European communist regimes were all installed by the Soviet armed forces in the aftermath of World War II, though the specific paths varied. East Germany simply came under Soviet occupation upon the defeat of the Nazis. It remained as a garrison zone until 1949, when Moscow, after quitting the Allied Control Council, created a nation state, and declared it a socialist regime. The socialist states in Romania and Bulgaria retained some homegrown elements. Communists seized power through anti-fascist uprisings as the Soviet army entered their territories, and then, backed by the Soviet Union, squeezed out the non-communist elements from the government. These semi-indigenous historical roots enabled these two regimes to incrementally attain some independence after Stalin's death. In Poland, Hungary, and Czechoslovakia, the Soviet Union annihilated Nazi forces but felt uncertain on whether to move on with Sovietization. The Soviet Union first created multi-party coalitional governments led by local communists, and then, as US–Soviet relations deteriorated, forced non-communists to step aside. The substantial period of multi-party rule partly indicated another historical likelihood and explains why in these three countries massive anti-Soviet protests would take place, respectively in 1956 and 1968.

Other socialist states, despite their historical roots distinct from the Soviet and the Chinese paths, still embodied the revolution-nationalism mechanisms discussed here. First, imposing the model of nation state upon a non-Western society was challenging, even more challenging in Eastern Europe, Latin America, and Africa than in Russia and China. Retaining an empire or a universal order was a way to overcome the complicated ethnic politics and weak statehood. Thus, many national communists sought to create federal polities that resembled the Soviet Union and China, such as greater Balkan federation, greater Romania, great Hungary, greater Korea, Indochinese federation, and greater Mongolia (Mevius 2005: 114–16; Radchenko 2009; Tismaneanu 2003: 51–53). This collective ambition stemmed not only from the geopolitical agenda but also from the backgrounds of the communist elites themselves, many of whom had transnational-multi-ethnic backgrounds and lacked a clear national consciousness. However, their imperial-cosmopolitan ambition was contained by Moscow and Beijing, and redirected to the maintenance of "nation states" (Sandag 2000: 154; Tudev 1982: 146; Zhelitski 1997). Even so, they still wanted to play the role of little leaders who oversaw other socialist states and revolutionary movements. Such competing imperial ambitions often led to frictions within the socialist camp. East Germany, Czechoslovakia, and North Korea played such an active role in reinforcing the civil wars in Africa and Central America (Cooper and Fogarty 1985: 56).

Second, despite the absence of a Bolshevik/CCP-style civil war, most communist regimes sought social transformations within a short period, which involved the processes equivalent to intense revolutionary mobilizations. The urgent demands of mobilizing a mass of population impelled these regimes to ease their communications with the societies by moving beyond Marxist–Leninist language and invoking national traditions. At the level of agency, as more homegrown elites entered communist parties, displacing and diminishing the "internationalists," the cadre groups as an entity would find using national symbols to be more comfortable. Therefore, over the long term, all communist regimes attained a backward-looking perspective, increasing their exploration of the nation's past, though their willingness and ability to integrate national tradition with Marxism varied (Boia 2001: 191; Ch'oe 1981; Kořalka 1992: 1027–28; Kunicki 2012; Mevius 2005: 251–55; Todorova 1992: 1107–8; Trencse'nyi 2010: 142–43). Many communist regimes carried out such work discreetly as well. Technically, re-narrating national traditions in service of a socialist mobilization was challenging, leading to the extensive state-organized work of recreating the tradition. The caution also came from the fear of irritating superpowers and being accused of "bourgeois nationalism," especially for the regimes that struggled between two antagonistic neighbors. In Romania and North Korea, for example, fear of suspicion retarded the tradition-inventing work for a considerable time (Granville 2009: 367–68, 372–73; Lee and Bairner 2009: 392; Petrescu 2009: 528–29).

Conclusion 207

Third, as nation-builders, most communist regimes faced the tension between creating a unified and homogenous nation and supporting ethnic minorities' self-determination. Except for the Soviet Union, all socialist regimes took shape in semi-colonial or "oppressed" societies, thereby forging a unified and functional nation state itself was evidence of the success of socialist revolutions. And, based on Marxist–Leninist ideology, a culturally homogeneous and politically centralized nation state was the pre-condition of socialism. Centralization and unification were also a test of power and served as a showcase of the exercise of power for these regimes to the aim of deterring and disciplining the population and rivals (Dragostinova 2016: 118; Fleming 2010: 63–64; Gigova 2016: 204–6; Korkut 2006; Lendvai 1969: 236–44; Mark 2006). This explains the enormous ethnic cleansings, forced migration, and coerced assimilation under communist regimes. Meanwhile, these regimes had to consider self-determination, partly because they lacked the power to dismiss all minorities' quests, partly because they saw an opportunity in maneuvering ethnopolitics to leverage greater power in terms of territorial gain and political influences. The ruling elites' knowledge played a significant role in calculating the balance of national unification and self-determination, and, in the long term, they tended to become more skillful in manipulating self-determination as domestic power became consolidated and the experiences of rule accumulated.

Generalizability for twentieth-century world nation-building

The mechanisms by which the communist revolutions shaped nationality models in Russia and China worked universally for nation-building in the twentieth-century, which combined the principle of nationalism with secular ideologies. The triple-element scenario emphasized here is significant—nationalism, secular ideologies, and the (broadly defined) twentieth century (including cases in the late nineteenth and the early twenty-first centuries). By origin, "nation state" was a political model imposed by and diffused from the West. This model manifests in the quests for the congruence between a homogeneous culture and a unified political citizenship. In a general atmosphere where Enlightenment-affiliated ideologies (liberalism, socialism, rationalism, developmentalism, etc.) triumphed and competed with each other, a significant proportion of nation-building projects around the world combined the principle of nationalism with secular ideologies. In the twentieth-century, meanwhile, the "revolutionary" element became attached to nation-building. Forging a nation state out of a multi-ethnic society was necessary and had to be completed within a short period. This was challenging, but popular if not mandatory. Many newly declared nation states came into being in a few significant decades: the 1920s, 1940s, 1960s, and the 1990s. Many nationalist revolutionaries, to their disillusion, did not attain the resources for nation-building they had anticipated, such as electrified industries, transportation, dams, and public health and education. Nevertheless, nationalism was the sole alternative available for them, and they had to adopt European dress, even if their societies had possessed a local tradition of statehood (Drayton 2022: 364). In the sense of completing a systematic transformation within a short period, the massive waves of nation-building in the twentieth century were all "revolutionary."

As an operative ideology, nationalism functions when it merges with an ideology or thought that provides a blueprint for how a society should be organized (Haugaard 2002; Malešević 2011). A secular ideology, be it liberalism or socialism or Enlightened world religions, tends to envisage a universal order and cosmopolitan citizenry. Such a transcendent ideology also bore two practical considerations: to overcome the complicated ethnopolitics in building a nation state (if ethnicity could be downplayed to a minimum, then the internal divisiveness of national liberation could be minimized), and to contrive alliance with other oppressed nations (these nations shared grievance toward the same imperial enemies, and commonalities left over by the same colonial rule that could facilitate mobilization) (Aboitiz 2022). Thus, it is understandable that the nationalist carriers of secular ideologies often bore ambitions beyond territorial borders. Their initial ambition was not to create a nation state, but rather a regional federation or a world community. With leaders thinking on the scale of such aspects as region, race, continent, and hemisphere, the nationalists of the twentieth century had advocated for Wilsonism, Pan-Africanism, Pan-Asianism, and the developmentalist "New International Economic Order" (Getachew 2019). This was especially the case for the first generation of nation-builders, where the general level of nationhood was thin, and the traditional political wisdom reckoned more with power struggles, factions, and imperial competition than with national issues such as border demarcation, identity building, and ethnic homogenization. Yet the preexisting hegemonic forces that held power in the world order would contain these universalist-minded nation-builders within national borders. This applied equally to the relationships between socialist superpowers and their followers, and the powerful states and their followers in the liberal-democratic world.

Apart from the guiding ideology, nation-building needs participants and mobilizers. When such manpower comes from an elite group who oppose an all-society and cross-strata mobilization, this elite group may endorse a project that is alien to the masses. Yet the broader the social strata from which the participants come, the more a nation-building project must mobilize the languages, symbols, and icons from the society's past. An all-encompassing

Conclusion 209

mobilization of existing cultural items is crucial for a nationalist movement that embraces secular ideology rather than using religion as a tool of revolt. In the deeply religious society of both pre- and post-1979 Iran, for example, the Pahlavi dynasty relied on non-religious historical materials and memories, downplaying Islamic legacies. Whereas in Khomeini's revolution, the non-Islamic tradition came in turn to be neglected and suppressed (Bari 1986). Inventing tradition aroused frictions with the internationalist frameworks the nation-builders claimed. For example, when the Japanese Empire upheld the "Manchukuo" (1932–1945) with popular values from Chinese classical literature and the Confucian values of motherhood, it risked awakening resistance against the Japanese-led "Greater East Asian Co-Prosperity Sphere" (Duara 2003). Difficulties also came from the process of navigating between a secular ideology (which usually carries a counter-tradition character) and the traditional values that have a wide appeal among the masses, which yielded a dilemma termed "vertical integration" that was missed in the view of "imagined community" (Cooper 2022: 346). As already discussed, the challenge of such reinventing had impeded many communist regimes. Making such a twist was especially challenging when nation-builders needed to complete this process quickly. In this regard, many short-lived governments that collapsed in the face of coups or foreign invasions were less successful than the communist regimes discussed here. At least most communist regimes in Eastern Europe and East Asia had persisted over four decades and such a length allowed for explorations.

Lastly, nation-state builders must address the multi-ethnicity question in the context of continued external threats. Both the Russian and the Chinese revolutions were typical in that they mixed "civil" wars with international conflicts. The twentieth century was a period when the global empires had learned to exert their influences through maneuvering nationalism. Commonly, internal divisiveness was associated with interference from abroad or could incur big-power confrontation through a continuous escalation. It has been long argued that modern empires originated out of the need to create a secure external environment for the formation of the core nation (Conrad 2022: 327). External threat could compel state-builders to suppress divisiveness or outward aggression. In the former case, the insecurity posed by external threats may lead to centralization, forced assimilation, and even ethnic cleansing. This partly explains why nationalist movements are omnipresent but the declarations of nation states came in "waves" rather than in sporadic continuum. Once a nation state gained international recognition, it turned inward, using the legitimacy granted by the world system of nation states, to suppress internal minorities that campaigned for autonomy/independence (Beissinger 2002; Walker 2022). In another situation, external threats could impel the nationalists to foster irredentism and territorial

210 *Revolution in China and Russia*

annexation, and even to adopt imperial behaviors. As long as the internal ethnic grievances posed no direct threats to the nation-builders themselves (this tricky situation occurred when these nation-builders were not yet in power, or only occupied a part of the national territories, and had nothing to lose by agitating resistance), they were a potential danger to international and domestic enemies. Therefore, it is not uncommon that weak and small nations, in their effort to overthrow oppressors, advocated for pan-ethnic cooperation—as in the Polish nationalists' call for penetration into the Middle East, inspired by the Russo–Japanese War (Puchalski 2017). Which approach to adopt depends on the status of nation-builders: their distance from the national power, their geographical location, their familiarity with ethnic affairs, and perceptions of the external rivalries' relative strength.

Revolutionary legacies in contemporary Russia and China

Revolution never ends. Historical legacies become diminished over the long term, but their shadow lingers. The Soviet model created by the Bolshevik Revolution underwent significant changes after Lenin's death. Initially, it entered a serious march toward institutionalization, termed "indigenization," in which national republics were encouraged to develop their own cultures and they began to gain real power independent of the union center. Under Stalin's reign, indigenization came to a halt, even reverting to re-Russification in many places, giving way to collectivization, industrialization, terror, and war preparation. It was as late as in the years of Khrushchev that a process of re-federalization came into being, in the name of restoring the tradition of the October Revolution. This switch galvanized the awakening of national consciousness among non-Russians, which, together with the disproportionately faster growth of Asian and Muslim population vis-à-vis Slavs, became a burning concern to the Brezhnevian officials. To counterweigh arising nationalist sentiment, the Soviet state of the 1970s invoked the revolutionary legacies again, with the aim of "internationalizing" every national republic into small Soviet Unions. Gorbachev's Glasnost and Democratization bore imprints of the revolution as well. The belief that erupting nationalism from the bottom would aid reformers to undermine the conservative bureaucrats was a continuation of Lenin's project of maneuvering nationalism to both foster revolution and preserve empire. And revolutionary thinking crept into Putin's regime. Whereas Ukrainians celebrated a separate national tradition, many Russians, having inherited a Soviet mindset, continued to view Ukraine as a fake concept fabricated by Russia. Such sentiment was popular, leading Putin and his inner circles to believe that the invasion of Ukraine would reinforce his legitimacy.

Conclusion   211

Though revolution had ended, as Trotsky had said in the 1920s, over the past century a revolutionary ghost of internationalization has never fully left Russia's stage of nation-building.

The imprint of revolution on China's nation-building is far more straightforward than it is on Russia's. The "One-China" framework survived multiple waves of ethnic classification and anti-Han campaigns, establishing the institutional foundations for assimilationist and quasi-assimilationist changes after 1949. Over the recent decade, the national model created in the revolution has incurred intense criticism. Critics argued that Beijing had moved too far in cultivating non-Hans' economic and cultural privileges, which turned the Chinese Nation into a mosaic on the verge of disintegration. However, these critics neglect the fact that, from the middle-1950s on, the CCP has been oscillating between ideals of "one nation" and "multi-ethnicity." In parallel with cultivating multiple "minzu," China's nation-building has also been a recurrent effort to homogenize the entire nation. The first tide of such effort came in the "Great Leap Forward," in the name of "equalizing economic foundations of all ethnic groups," which broke the CCP's promise not to unleash a socialist transformation in minority areas as it did in Han zones. The second, during Mao's "Cultural Revolution," was more brutal, with some minority autonomous regions arbitrarily abolished. The 1980s saw a wave of retreat and reversion, with many minority elites rehabilitated, a project as part of the CCP's self-negation of Maoism. It was in the 1980s that the PRC finally completed its ethnic classification, identifying fifty-six "minzu" as members of the Chinese Nation. The panic after the collapse of the Soviet Union, however, triggered a new wave of highlighting the idea of the "One Single Nation." Unlike Mao's border policy, this process was complicated by China's marketization, which aroused a new round of centrifugalism from the borderlands. Riots and violence recurred under Hu Jintao's administration. Under Xi Jinping, homogenization again attained momentum. This round appears more comprehensive and determined than previous ones, as well as more connected with the CCP revolution. As part of a broader project highlighting the Chinese character of the CCP revolution, an extensive program of state-sponsored archeological excavations cultivated the idea of an essential "Chinese civilization," to demonstrate that the historical formation of multiple ethnic groups was identical with the formation of a unified Chinese Nation. Such a project would have encountered more obstructions, if it had not been impossible, under a Soviet-style internationalist system. The legacies of revolutions still work.

History cannot be hypothesized, but this book suggests that China's nation state model could have been molded differently. As this book argues, by the end of 1949, the CCP was far more receptive to a Chinese nation state than the Bolsheviks of 1922 had been to a Russian one. In any case,

Moscow's influences and local unique ethnic composition could still lead to the foundation of autonomous regions in Xinjiang, Tibet, and part of Inner Mongolia. Yet, if the logic of the revolution persisted, the CCP of 1949 would not be motivated to carry out ethnic classification and set up autonomous units in the borderlands of China. In other words, the People's Republic of China would have been far closer to model a nation state than it looks today. Changes came from the post-1949 events. The unanticipated Korean War and Mao's "Leaning to one Side" policy led to an uncritical imitation of the Soviet system, including Moscow's nationality policies. Such imitation stemmed from the CCP's lack of experience in national affairs and the motivation to display pro-Soviet friendship, but it succeeded in directing the CCP away from its own revolutionary orthodoxy. Therefore, once Sino-Soviet relations deteriorated, the CCP moved back to its One-China orientation, which was consistent with its indigenous revolutionary path. By the same token, when the CCP critically reflected on their own path, they switched back to Soviet influences. Today, Xi Jinping is determined to bring the revolution back. He highlights the indigenous roots of the CCP revolution and wants to remove foreign vestiges from the nationality system. In this regard, the CCP's revolutionary past would provide a valuable source of historical legitimacy. Revolution has passed, but it never really ends.

Appendix 1

Figures: How the revolutions unfolded

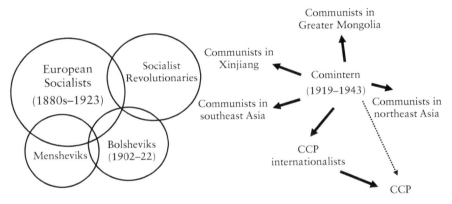

Figure App 1.1 The international overlapping of the two communist revolutions

Note. The left part of Figure App 1.1 shows that up to 1922, the Bolsheviks overlapped heavily with European socialists. Many Bolshevik elites joined Western socialist parties, maintained close cooperation with them, had a profound and lengthy period of residence in Europe, or had a transnational/foreign family background. Such overlapping was not confined to the Bolsheviks, but shared by the Mensheviks, the Socialist Revolutionaries, and other socialist parties. The right part of the figure shows that the CCP's connections with the Bolsheviks were more indirect. Under the Comintern's direction, there were at least five mutually independent communist-leftist movements active in the geographical domain of China, each of which was more or less transnational: Han-inhabited central China, Northeast Asia, Greater Mongolia, Xinjiang, and Southwest Asia. The CCP core leadership had far less overlap with the Comintern than the Bolsheviks before 1922 had with European socialists (as the dotted arrow line shows). And even the limited overlap decreased over the course of the revolution. As

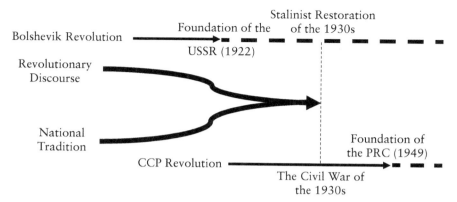

Figure App 1.2 Tradition, nationalism, and revolution

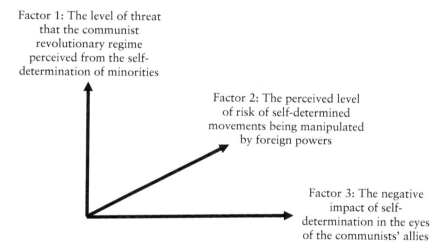

Figure App 1.3 Communists' varied support for borderland self-determination

far as the generation making the PRC is concerned, most CCP elites had never left China or had only briefly traveled outside of China. Within the CCP existed a small number of internationalists. This group maintained more direct contact with the Soviet Union, and were usually pro-Moscow, but they were Chinese by ethnicity and identity. This group was unlike the Bolshevik internationalists who were born into one ethnicity, educated in a second language, and engaged in revolutionary activities in a third country.

Note. Figure App. 1.2 reveals the similarities and dissimilarities of the two revolutions in incorporating national traditions into revolutionary discourses. In both revolutions, at the onset, revolutionaries feared and loathed traditional national cultures, viewing them as backward, ignorant, barbaric, and

Appendices   215

incompatible with revolution. But in the long term, the revolutionary literati eventually developed ways of fusing revolution and traditional national culture in Russia and China alike (the convergence of the two bold arrows). However, the timing of convergence differed. In the Bolshevik Revolution, the intersection came late, a decade after the foundation of the USSR in 1922. In the CCP revolution, the convergence took place long before the foundation of the PRC in 1949. As a result, the Bolsheviks of 1922 created the Soviet state with a strong antipathy against traditional Russian culture, which impeded them from using a frame of socialist Greater Russian nationalism to reorganize the tsarist empire. Differently, the CCP of 1949 viewed "China" more positively. The consensus of the CCP elites of 1949 was not to discard Chinese nationalism but to fuse multi-ethnicity with revolutionary Chinese nationalism.

Note. The three-pronged model of Figure App. 1.3 explains why the attitudes of communist revolutionaries toward the requests of borderland minorities for self-determination varied over time and across areas. When communists supported such requests, they were skewed to the federal way of reorganizing the former empire. But if communists felt self-determination was dangerous, they switched toward the "one greater nation" approach. The first factor affecting the communists was whether a self-determination movement threatened the communist revolutionary regime. Many movements had no such a threat, in that they were geographically far from communists or militarily too weak for communists. But if a movement had such a threat, the communists tended to suppress it. The second factor was whether a self-determinist movement involved the risk of being manipulated by foreign powers. If the risk was high, the communist revolutionaries would withdraw or soften their support for this movement in case foreign powers steered the movement against the communists themselves. The third factor is whether the communists' allies regarded a self-determinist movement as illegal. Communists were not fighting alone. They needed to reckon with the attitudes of their allies, including their perspectives on borderland affairs, which were central to decolonization and nation-building. If these allies opposed a self-determinist movement, equating it with centrifugalism, national traitors, foreign espionage, or reactionary dictatorship, the communists would lower their tone as well, at least making their support for self-determination more covert and ambiguous. Both the Bolsheviks and the CCP kept adjusting their attitudes to borderland self-determination. Each communist party dealt with many movements and geographical sections. In general, the CCP faced more pressure to soften their support for self-determination than the Bolsheviks did. This partly explains why the CCP deviated from the Soviet prototype of nation-building and why the Bolsheviks appeared closer to the Marxist ideal of internationalism. Nevertheless, all three factors were not objective. They were the interpretations of the communist revolutionaries, depending on these people's familiarity with borderlands.

Appendix 2

Tables: Who were the revolutionaries?

Tables App 2.1–2.4 Repression and overseas travel of the Bolsheviks and the CCP

Table App 2.1 Bolsheviks' death dates, in total 104, all central committee members before 1917

Periods	Pre-revolutionary		Post-revolutionary			
Years	1905–07	1907–17	1917–21	1922–33	1934–53	1953–
Number	2	6	12	21	43	12

Table App 2.2 CCP's death dates, in total 76, all central committee members before 1945

Periods	Pre-revolutionary				Post-Rev	
Years	1921–26	1927–34	1934–37	1937–45	1945–50	1951–
Number	2	22	0	1	1	NA

Table App 2.3 Arrests of the leading Bolshevik elites before March 1917

Times of Arrests	Number	Times of Arrests	Number
Never	3	4	8
Once	12	5	7
"More than once"	8	6	10
Twice	21	7	3
Three	16	More > 7	14
		Total: > 322	Total: 94

Appendices

Table App 2.4 The CCP's overseas experiences in comparison with the KMT

	CCPs	KMTs
France and Belgium	9	8
Britain	0	6
United States and Canada	1	19
Germany	1	4
Japan	7	33
Italy	0	1
Turkey	0	1

Note. Tables App 2.1 and 2.2 summarize and compare the two communist parties' experiences of repression. During their revolutions, both communist parties suffered considerable casualties at the top echelons of leadership, but the pattern differed. Before 1917, the repression the Bolsheviks faced was non-lethal. The tsarist government killed very few Bolsheviks. Most Bolshevik deaths during this period came from disease or old age. Consequently, most of the Bolshevik pre-1917 leadership survived into the crucial period of 1917–1922. These people's internationalist understandings of empire-reorganizing molded the founding of the Soviet Union. The mass casualty of the Bolsheviks took place later, during Stalin's purge in the 1930s, but by that time the framework of the Soviet Union had stabilized. By contrast, the CCP suffered significant losses of its top leaders as early as the turn of the 1930s, when the first KMT–CCP united front broke up. The KMT government murdered at least one-fourth of the central committee members, and some others were executed in the ensuing civil war battles and purges. This setback was as destructive as Stalin's terror, but its timing and scale had two consequences that the USSR did not have. First, the CCP's foundational generation was killed, never able to return to the revolution. Those who were killed were more cosmopolitan than the ones who succeeded them in terms of outlook and education. Second, the CCP's impetus to reach out to the international communist movement became significantly diminished, and this further confined the revolution, squeezing it into an enclosed national space, and making the CCP Revolution "national."

Notes to Table App 2.3.

Note 1. Nine cases are missing. The total population is the Bolsheviks' central committee from 1917 to 1923.

Note 2. The table reveals the survival of the pre-1917 Bolsheviks into the post-1917 period from the perspective of the tsarist state. Most Bolsheviks

218 *Revolution in China and Russia*

were arrested more than once, but very few were executed. Rather, they escaped or were released, and then returned to the revolutionary movement. This prevented a Russian-nationalist-minded leadership from dominating the founding of the Soviet Union.

Note. Table App 2.4 compares the CCP's experiences of overseas education with the KMT's. The two parties' experiences in the Soviet Union are not included in this table. This comparison reveals that the CCP leadership was local, not only in contrast with the Bolsheviks but also in comparison with the KMT. Such locality caused the CCP to be more likely to self-identify with nationalism than cosmopolitanism. The CCP elites, in memoirs and diaries, highlighted their experiences of studying abroad, but actually, these people's engagement in their destination societies was superficial. Almost no CCP leader achieved formal degrees abroad. Most attended crash schools that issued diplomas within months or a year, and even so, few obtained such credentials due to drop out and expulsion rates. Regarding destinations, the CCP's overseas education was concentrated in Japan. People who traveled to France and Belgium were all affiliated with the "Work and Study" program (qingong jianxue), sponsored by a few anarchist-minded officials of China's Beiyang government. As the financial support from the Beiyang government ceased, the Chinese students began to make their living through physical labor at factories and they then either returned to China or went to the Soviet Union. By contrast, the KMT's overseas education was more solid. They obtained higher degrees, completed more courses, traveled abroad longer, and studied in a more diverse group of Western countries. Usually, the people who studied in Germany and Japan attained degrees in military studies, and those who studied in the US, Britain, France, and Canada were trained in economics, finance, engineering, and management. Such a comparison suggests that the CCP's preference for nationalism over internationalism had complicated sources. It not only involved China's general cultural distance from the West, but also the backgrounds of these communists.

Tables App 2.5 and 2.6 The educational backgrounds of the two communist parties

Note. Table App 2.5 summarizes and compares the Bolsheviks' and the Russian liberals' educational backgrounds. The samples show the entire central committee members of the Bolsheviks from 1917 to 1923, and the Kadets' central bodies (collected from the Kadets' national conferences). This table suggests that, on average, the Bolsheviks were far less educated

Appendices

Table App 2.5 The Bolsheviks and the Russian Liberals (Kadets), based on central committee members

Highest Levels of Education (%)	Bolsheviks	Kadets
Doctoral degree		2.9
Master's degree		2.9
University (completed)	13.8	52.9
University (uncompleted)	5.3	2.9
Gymnasia (completed)	9.6	1.5
Gymnasia (uncompleted)	1.1	1.5
Vocational school (completed)	22.3	2.9
Vocational school (uncompleted)	3.2	
Primary school	17.0	
Lower	29.8	
Unknown		32.4
Total	94	68

Table App 2.6 The CCP and the KMT, based on central committee members in 1944 and 1945

Education Level	CCP (%)	KMT (%)
PhD	0.0	3.7
Master	0.0	7.3
Bachelor	1.3	34.9
Complete Confucian education	1.3	2.3
Middle school (Gymnasium)	29.9	6.0
Teacher-training school	20.8	3.2
Military-Police school	11.7	27.5
Special Secondary school	14.3	2.3
Primary school	15.6	2.3
Less than three years	5.2	2.3
Unknown	0.0	8.3
Total	77	218*

than the liberals. This discrepancy produces social consequences at the turn of the twentieth century. In that period, Russian nationalism as an intellectual project was being invented among intellectuals. People were seeking a version of Enlightened Russian nationalism that was separatable from

220   *Revolution in China and Russia*

tsardom, despotism, and aggression. In terms of professions, the liberals encompassed writers, literary critics, historians, ethnographers, anthropologists, diplomats, philosophers, and archeologists. They were closer to, and often direct participants in, the ongoing invention of Enlightened Russian nationalism. In contrast, with several exceptions, the Bolsheviks were far from followers of contemporary intellectual fashions. Their fear of Russian nationalism partly stemmed from such unfamiliarity, which led them to believe that it could not be separated from orientalist stereotypes.

Note. Table App 2.6 summarizes and compares the backgrounds of members of the CCP and the KMT. The CCP data is collected from the Seventh Central Committee (1945–1956), which completed the founding of the PRC. The KMT data is collected from the Central Executive Committee of 1944, contemporary to the selected CCP elites. Neither group was well educated. This indicated the similar political origin of the two revolutionary parties. Nevertheless, the contrast remains sharp. Remarkably, few CCP elites completed higher education, but a considerable proportion of the KMT elites obtained bachelor's degrees. Even so, their difference still affected the two parties' attitudes to nation-building. From the 1930s onward, an intellectual trend titled "border school" arose to discuss how the non-Han borderlands should be integrated into the "One-China" nation. As in Russia, the participants of this project were scholars and intellectuals. They carried out archeological and ethnographic surveys at the borderland among non-Han groups. As an ideological hodgepodge, the KMT elites considerably overlapped this intellectual trend. Many anthropologists, philologists, archeologists, and historians were KMT members. This caused the KMT's active and positive echoing of the arising "One-China" discourse. The CCP's political elites had less access to this intellectual orientation, which made them more comfortable using vague narrations such as "the natural fusion of ethnic groups." But the CCP had its literati, and its gap with the KMT was smaller than the Bolsheviks' with the Russian liberals.

Tables App 2.7 and 2.8 The ages of members of the two communist parties

Note. Table App 2.7 summarizes and compares the Bolsheviks' age structure with that of liberals and conservatives. The names of liberals are collected from the Kadets' national conferences, and the names of the conservatives are collected from the Russian rightist parties' national

Appendices

221

Table App 2.7 The Bolsheviks' ages in comparison with the Liberals and Conservatives

Year of Birth (%)	Russian Bolsheviks	Kadets	Russian Rightists
1835–1844			6.1
1845–1854			9.1
1855–1864		31.0	33.3
1865–1874	10.4	51.0	33.3
1875–1884	29.2	17.0	6.1
1885–1894	58.3		6.1
1895–1904	2.1		
Total	48	47	33

Table App 2.8 The CCP's ages in comparison with the KMT

Year of Birth	CCP (%)	KMT (%)
1874 or earlier	0.0	0.04
1875–1884	2.6	12.4
1885–1894	9.1	40.4
1895–1904	50.6	38.6
1905–1914	36.4	6.0
1915 or later	1.3	0.0
Total	77	218

meetings. In terms of generations, these three groups were equivalent to the categories of children, parents, and grandparents. This generational factor affected these groups' attitudes to traditional Russian culture that could be central to the invention of a conservative version of Russian nationalism. The legitimacy of tsarist autocracy underwent a fatal crisis in the Revolution of 1905. After the Winter Palace Massacre and the ensuing repression, the tsar's image as a "little father" collapsed. Yet, when this change occurred, the three groups were at different stages of their life courses. For liberals, the bloody impact was strong, but their belief in the monarchy was entrenched and it would be more difficult to switch to radical republicanism. To this group, a switch to a constitutional monarchy was more acceptable. For conservatives who were already of advanced age at the time, the transformation of mentality would have been even

222   *Revolution in China and Russia*

more difficult. For the Bolsheviks, the massacre and the anti-monarchist wave came at a time when most of them were still forming their political outlooks. This transformed them all into radical revolutionaries. As young urban workers and intellectuals, the Bolsheviks were more anti-religious than the liberals and conservatives were. Commonly under-educated, the pre-1917 Bolsheviks lacked the imagination to invent an Enlightened Russian nationalism. In this condition, their antipathy to autocracy and religion further alienated them from Russian nationalism.

Note. Table App 2.8 summarizes and compares the age structure of the CCP's and the KMT's central-committee members. The comparison shows that the CCP leaders were significantly younger than the KMT leaders. Over one-third of the CCP members were born after 1905, the year in which the Qing court abolished the millennium-long imperial civil service exam. No more than three members of the CCP leadership had direct experiences with this exam and obtained academic titles. The weak ties with Confucian classical education help to explain why the CCP elites were anti-traditionalists in the 1920s and why they insisted on reinventing China's rural culture in the 1940s rather than simply restoring it. The KMT's older age structure explains why their nation-building project embraced fundamentalist Confucianism, though such fundamentalism was mixed with Christianity. It is also notable that over half of the CCP elites were born after Boxer Rebellion, and nearly 90 percent were born after the First Sino–Japanese War of 1894–1895. In the period when these people grew up, China was no more under direct military threat but became increasingly penetrated by imperialist powers through proxy war and economic exploitation.

Tables App 2.9 and 2.10 The two communist parties' exposure to the borderlands

Tables App 2.9 and 2.10 summarize the Bolsheviks' and the CCP's domestic travel experiences, measured by the cities where they completed their final degrees or where they worked the longest. The Bolsheviks were familiar with Russia's non-Russian borderlands, and for them there was a vital intersection between ethnicity and region. It was usual for Russian Bolsheviks to spend extended periods in non-Russian areas (Ukraine, Baltic, Belarus, the Southern Caucasus, and Central Asia), and for non-Russian Bolsheviks (Ukrainians, Germans, Polish, Jews, Latvians) to spend extended periods in Russian areas. By comparison, the CCP's familiarity with China's

Appendices

Table App 2.9 The places where the Bolsheviks studied or worked

Imperial capitals: 38%			
Petersburg	21	Moscow	15
Non-Russian capital cities: 18%			
Tiflis	6	Vilna (Vilnius)	4
Kiev	3	Riga	2
Almaty	2		
Industrial or commercial centers: 29%			
Odessa	3	Ivanovo-Vozneshchenskii	3
Kazan	4	Kharkov	3
Saratov	2	Nizhni Novgorod	2
Samara	2	Rostov	1
Omsk	1	Chita	1
Lugansk	1	Kursk	1
Ufa	1	Orel	1
Simferopol	1	Briansk	1
Foreign cities: 2%			
L'viv	1	Geneva	1
Counties: 13%			
			Total: 94

borderlands was much weaker. Except for a few ethnic non-Hans, very few CCP leaders spent significant periods of their lives in the borderlands. Most CCP leaders came from Han areas, either large cities or towns of regional centers. The distinction has many implications. First, though tsarist Russia was demographically more multi-ethnic than imperial China, in terms of interethnic interaction and fusion, the Bolsheviks had more intense experiences than the CCP. This discrepancy stemmed from the two empires' different legacies in geography-based ethnic segregation and the Comintern's ethnic Balkanization of China's communist movement. Second and most importantly, the CCP's unfamiliarity and long-term isolation from borderland minorities led them to fear real separatism. With the sole exception of Ulanhu, the CCP had no equivalents to Ordzhonikidze, Dzerzhinskii, Shkrypnik, Kapsukas, Frunze, and others who were able to play the role of "fifth column" among borderland minorities. Most of the CCP's emissaries

Revolution in China and Russia

Table App 2.10 The places where the CCP studied or worked

National capitals: 26%			
Beijing	3	Nanjing	3
Shanghai	7	Guangzhou	7
Provincial capitals or equivalents: 45%			
Changsha	1	Xiamen	10
Wuhan	1	Chengdu	6
Taiyuan	1	Xi'an	3
Chongqing	1	Nanchang	3
Tianjin	1	Guiyang	3
Shenyang	1	Dalian	2
Kunming			2
Regional education centers: 8%			
Changde	3	Suide	2
Hengyang	1		
Foreign cities: 3%			
Tokyo	1	Paris	1
Others: 18%			
		Total: 77	

and correspondents in the borderlands were ethnic Hans, and these people stayed there only briefly. When the CCP was not yet geographically adjacent to the minorities, they could propagate a discourse of self-determination. But once they confronted real borderland nationalism, the CCP cadres were not confident in steering these movements and thus switched back to the language of "One China."

Bibliography

Aboitiz, Nicole CuUnjieng. 2022. "Race and Nationalism in Anticolonial Asia." *American Historical Review* 127(1): 355–57.

Abraham, Gerald. 1970. *Eight Soviet Composers*. Westport: Greenwood Press.

Adams, Julia. 1994. "The Familial State: Elite Family Practices and State-Making in the Early Modern Netherlands." *Theory and Society* 23(4): 505–39.

Agursky, Mikhail. 1987. *The Third Rome: National Bolshevism in the USSR*. Boulder: Westview Press.

Airapetov, Oleg. 2020. *Vneshniaia politika sovetskoi rossii i sssr v 1920–1939 godakh i istoki vtoroi mirovoi voiny*. Moscow: Izdatel'stvo rodina.

Akhmedov, Teimur. 1988. *Nariman Narimanov*. Baku: Iazychy.

Akshinskii, V. S. 1976. *Kliment Efremovich Voroshilov biograficheskii ocherk*. Moscow: Izdatel'stvo politicheskoi literatury.

Aleksandrov, Georgii F. (Ed.). 1943. *Istoriia grazhdanskoi voiny v SSSR*, Volume 2, Moscow: Gosudarstvennoe izdatel'stvo 'Istoriia grazhdanskoi voiny'.

Allen, Barbara C. 2015. *Alexander Shlyapnikov, 1885–1937: Life of an Old Bolshevik*. Leiden: Brill.

Amacher, Korine. 2018. "Mikhail N. Pokrovsky and Ukraine: A Normative Marxist between History and Politics." *Ab Imperio* (1): 101–32.

Amar, Tarik Cyril. 2015. *The Paradox of Ukrainian Lviv: A Borderland City between Stalinists, Nazis, and Nationalists*. Ithaca, NY: Cornell University Press.

Anan'ev, G. A. 1982. *Kotovskii*. Moscow: Molodaia gvardiia.

Anderson, Perry. 2002. "Internationalism: A Breviary." *New Left Review* 14: 5–25.

———. 2010. "Two Revolutions." *New Left Review* 61: 59–96.

Andrew, Christopher, and Vasili Mitrokhin. 2001. *The Sword and the Shield the Mitrokhin Archive and the Secret History of the KGB*. New York, NY: Basic Books.

Arjomand, Said Amir. 2019. *Revolution: Structure and Meaning in World History*. Chicago, IL: The University of Chicago Press.

Armstrong, Charles. 2017. "Korean Communism: From Soviet Occupation to Kim Family Regime." In *Cambridge History of Communism*, Vol. 2, edited by Norman Naimark, Silvio Pons, and Sophie Quinn-Judge, 441–66. Cambridge: Cambridge University Press.

Artizov, Andrei Nikolaevich. 1994. "Sud'by istorikov shkoly M. N. Pokrovskogo (seredina 1930-kh godov)." *Voprosy istorii* (7): 34–48.

Astrakhan, Kh. M. 1973. *Bol'sheviki i ikh politicheskie protivniki v 1917 gody*. Leningrad: Lenizdat.

Baibakov, Nikolai N. 2016. *Sobranie sochinenii v 10 tomakh*. Moscow: Nauchno-izdatel'skii tsentr Luch.

Baker, William, and Jitka Hurych. 1991. "Trotsky's Vision of Librarians." *American Libraries* 22(11): 1030–32.

Banac, Ivo. 1992. "Yugoslavia." *The American Historical Review* 97(4): 1084–104.

———. 2017. "Yugoslav Communism and Yugoslav State." In *Cambridge History of Communism*, Vol. 2, edited by Norman Naimark, Silvio Pons, and Sophie Quinn-Judge, 570–96. New York, NY: Cambridge University Press.

Baranskii, Nikolai. 1965. *Ekonomicheskaia geographia v sssr*. Moscow: Prosveshchenie.

Bari, Zohurul. 1986. "Impact of the Iranian Revolution on the Movement of Islamic Revival in the Arab East." *International Studies* 23(3): 239–55.

Baron, Samuel H. 1974. "Plekhanov, Trotsky, and the Development of Soviet Historiography." *Soviet Studies* 26(3): 380–95.

Beissinger, Mark R. 2002. *Nationalist Mobilization and the Collapse of the Soviet State*. Cambridge: Cambridge University Press.

Bell, David A. 2002. *The Cult of the Nation in France: Inventing Nationalism, 1680–1800*. Cambridge, MA: Harvard University Press.

Belogurova, Anna. 2014. "The Chinese International of Nationalities: the Chinese Communist Party, the Comintern, and the foundation of the Malayan National Communist Party, 1923–1939." *Journal of Global History* 9(3): 447–70.

———. 2017. "Networks, Parties, and the 'Oppressed Nations': The Comintern and Chinese Communists Overseas, 1926–1935." *Cross-Currents: East Asian History and Culture Review* 6(2): 558–82.

———. 2019. "Nationalism and Internationalism in Chinese Communist Networks in the Americas." In *Left Transnationalism: The Communist International and the National, Colonial, and Racial Questions*, edited by Oleksa Drachewych and Ian McKay, 387–405. Montreal: McGill-Queen's University Press.

Berens, John F. 1978. *Providence and Patriotism in Early America, 1640–1815*. Charlottesville, VA: University Press of Virginia.

Berger, Stefan, and Alexei Miller (Eds.). 2014. *Nationalizing Empires*. Budapest: Central European University Press.

Bezugol'nyi, Aleksei. 2016. *Istochnik dopolnitel'noi moshchi krasnoi armii: natsional'nyi vopros v voennom stroitel'stve v SSSR 1922–45*. Moscow: ROSSPEN.

Biggart, John. 1987. "Bukharin and the Origins of the 'Proletarian Culture' Debate." *Soviet Studies* 39(2): 1987.

Blumi, Isa. 1997. "The Politics of Culture and Power: the Roots of Hoxha's Postwar State." *East European Quarterly* 31(3): 379–98.

———. 1999. "Hoxha's Class War: The Cultural Revolution and State Reformation, 1961–1971." *East European Quarterly* 99(33): 303–26.

Bo, Yibo. 2008. *Qishi nian fendou yu sikao*. Beijing: Zhonggong dangshi chubanshe.

Boia, Lucian. 2001. *History and Myth in Romanian Consciousness*. Budapest: Central European University Press.

Bojanowska, Edyta M. 2007. *Nikolai Gogol: Between Ukrainian and Russian Nationalism*. Cambridge, MA: Harvard University Press.

Bolobuev, P. V. 1993. *Politicheskie deiateli rossii 1917: biograficheskii slovar'*. Moscow: Nauchnoe izdatel'stvo "bol'shaia rossiiskaia entsiklopediia."

Bonnell, Victoria E. 1997. *Iconography of Power: Soviet Political Posters under Lenin and Stalin*. Berkeley, CA: University of California Press.

Borisova, M. V. 2016. "Analiz formirovaniia diskursa internatsionalizma v srede bol'shevikov v nachale XX veka " *Vestnik Kemerovskogo gosudarstvennogo universiteta* 1(65): 7–10.

Bibliography

Brandenberger, David. 2002. *National Bolshevism: Stalinist Mass Culture and the Formation of Modern Russian National Identity, 1931–1956*. Cambridge, MA: Harvard University Press.

———. 2016. "The Fate of Interwar Soviet Internationalism: A Case Study of the Editing of Stalin's 1938 Short Course on the History of the ACP(b)." *Revolutionary Russia* 29(1): 1–23.

Brown, MacAlister, and Joseph J. Zasloff. 1977. "Laos 1976: Faltering First Steps toward Socialism." *Asian Survey* 17(2): 107–15.

Brubaker, Rogers. 1992. *Citizenship and nationhood in France and Germany*. Cambridge, MA: Harvard University Press.

Brudny, Yitzhak. 1998. *Reinventing Russia: Russian Nationalism and the Soviet State, 1953–1991* Cambridge, MA: Harvard University Press.

Brunnbauer, Ulf. 2011. "Historical Writing in the Balkans." In *The Oxford History of Historical Writing: Historical Writing since 1945*, edited by Axel Schneider, Daniel Woolf, and Ian Hesketh, 353–74. Oxford: Oxford University Press.

Brunstedt, Jonathan. 2011. "Building a Pan-Soviet Past: The Soviet War Cult and the Turn Away from Ethnic Particularism." *The Soviet and Post-Soviet Review* 38: 149–71.

Bukharin, Nikolai. 1924. *O mirvoi revoliutsii, nashe strane, kul'ture, i prochee.* Leningrad: Gosudarstvennoe izdatel'stvo Leningrada.

Bukharin, Nikolai, and Evgenii Preobrazhensky. 1966 [1922]. *The ABC of Communism: A Popular Explanation of the Program of the Communist Party of Russia.* Ann Arbor, MI: The University of Michigan Press.

Bunce, Valerie. 1999. *Subversive Institutions: The Design and the Destruction of Socialism and the State.* Cambridge: Cambridge University Press.

Buttino, Marco. 2014. "Central Asia (1916–20): A Kaleidoscope of Local Revolutions and the Building of the Bolshevik Order." In *The Empire and Nationalism at War*, edited by Eric Lohr, Vera Tolz, Alexander Semyonov, and Mark von Hagen,109–36. Bloomington, IN: Indiana University Press.

Bykov, Dmitrii. 2013. *Sovetskaia literatura: kratkii kurs.* Moscow: Prozaik.

CA [Central Archive of the CCP]. 1989. *Zhonggong zhongyang wenjian xuanji* [Selected Documents of the CCP Central Committee]. Beijing: Zhonggong zhongyang dangxiao chubanshe.

Cai, Jinsong. 2005. *Sheng Shicai waizhuan.* Beijing: Zhonggong dangshi chubanshe.

Calverton, V. F. 1929. "The Sociological Aesthetics of the Bolsheviki." *American Journal of Sociology* 35(3): 383–92.

Campell, Emma. 2015. "The End of Ethnic Nationalism? Changing Conceptions of National Identity and Belonging among Young South Koreans." *Nations and Nationalism* 21(3): 483–502.

Cao, Shuxun. 1939. *Bian jiang jiao yu xin lun.* Nanjing: Zhengzhong shuju.

Cao, Yinglong, and Guo Na (Eds.). 2013. *Minguo sixiang wenji: zhanguoce pai.* Jilin: Changchun chubanshe.

CCCPSU, Central Committee of the Communist Party of the Soviet Union. 1939. *History of the Communist Party of the Soviet Union (Bolsheviks) Short course.* New York, NY: International Publishers.

CCPHRO, Zhonggong dangshi renwu yanjiuhui. 2007. *Zhongguo renmin jiefangjun gaoji jiangling zhuan.* Beijing: Jiefangjun chubanshe.

CDUF, Central Department of United Front. 1991. *Min zu wen ti wen xian hui bian.* Beijing: Zhong yang dang xiao chubanshe.

Ch'oe, Yŏng-ho. 1981. "Reinterpreting Traditional History in North Korea." *The Journal of Asian Studies* 40(3): 503–23.

Chafer, Tony. 2002. *The End of Empire in French West Africa: France's Successful Decolonization?* Oxford: Berg.

Chandler, David P. 1999. *Brother Number One: A Political Biography Of Pol Pot.* New York, NY: Westview Press.

Chaqueri, Cosroe. 1995. *The Soviet Socialist Republic of Iran, 1920–1921: Birth of Trauma.* Pittsburgh, PA: University of Pittsburgh Press.

Chatterjee, Partha. 1986. *Nationalist Thought and the Colonial World: A Derivative Discourse.* Minneapolis, MN: University Of Minnesota Press.

Chen, Duxiu. 1993. *Chen Duxiu zhuzuo xuan.* Shanghai: Shanghai renmin chubanshe.

Chen, Jian. 2010. "Jiang geming yu feizhiminghua xiang lianjie: zhongguo duiwai zhengce zhong wanlonghuayu de xingqi ji lengzhan zhuti de bianzou." In *Lengzhan guojishi yanjiu*, edited by Shen Zhihua and Li Danhui, 1–45. Shanghai: Huadong shifan daxue chubanshe.

Chen, Zhiling, and Yang He. 1986. *A Biography of Wang Ruofei (Wang ruo fei zhuan).* Shanghai: Shang hai ren min chubanshe.

Cherry, Haydon. 2009. "Digging Up the Past: Prehistory and the Weight of the Present in Vietnam." *Journal of Vietnamese Studies* 4(1): 84–144.

Chicherin, Georgi. 1920. *Two Years of Foreign Policies.* New York, NY: The Russian Soviet Government Bureau.

Chung, Young Chul. 2013. "The Suryŏng System as the Center of Juche Institution." In *Origins of North Korea's Juche Colonialism, War, and Development*, edited by Jae-Jung Suh. Lanham, MD: Lexington Books.

Clark, Katerina. 2011. *Moscow, the Fourth Rome: Stalinism, Cosmopolitanism, and the Evolution of Soviet Culture, 1931–1941.* Cambridge, MA: Harvard University Press.

Clealand, Danielle Pilar. 2017. *The Power of Race in Cuba: Racial Ideology and Black Consciousness During the Revolution.* Oxford: Oxford University Press.

Cliff, Tony. 2010. *Lenin: Building the Party, 1893–1914.* London: Bookmarks.

Cohen, Stephen F. 1980. *Bukharin and the Bolshevik Revolution: a Political Biography, 1888–1938.* Oxford: Oxford University Press.

Connor, Walker. 1984. *The National Question in Marxist-Leninist Theory and Strategy.* Princeton, NJ: Princeton University Press.

Conquest, Robert (Ed.). 1986. *The Last Empire: Nationality and the Soviet Future.* Stanford, CA: Hoover Institution Press.

Conrad, Sebastian. 2022. "Empire and Nationalism." *American Historical Review* 127(1): 327–32.

Conte, Francis. 1989. *Christian Rakovski (1873–1941): A Political Biography.* Translated by A. P. M. Bradley. New York, NY: Columbia University Press.

Cooper, Frederick. 2014. *Citizenship between Empire and Nation: Remaking France and French Africa 1945–1960.* Princeton, NJ: Princeton University Press.

———. 2022. "Nationalism and Liberation in an Unequal World." *American Historical Review* 127(1): 346–48.

Cooper, Oran, and Carol Fogarty. 1985. "Soviet Economic and Military Aid to Less Developed Countries, 1954–1978." *Soviet and Eastern European Foreign Trade* 21(1–3): 54–73.

Cornish, Nik. 2014. *Soviet Partisan 1941–1944*: London: Osprey Publishing.

Cui, Guozhe. 2012. *Zhu Dehai pingzhuan.* Translated by Chen Xuehong. Beijing: Yanbian.

Bibliography

Dai, Maolin, and Xiaoguang Zhao. 2011. *Gao Gang zhuan*. Xi'an: Shannxi renmin chubanshe.

Darwin, John. 2013. "Empire and Ethnicity." In *Nationalism and War*, edited by Siniša Malešević and John A. Hall, 147–71. Cambridge: Cambridge University Press.

Davidov, M. 1961. *Aleksandr Dmitrievich Tsiurupa*. Moscow: Izdatel'stvo politicheskoi literatury.

Davydkin, M., and I. Seleznev. 1911. *Kratkaia russkaia istoriia: dlia nachal'nykh uchilishch*. Moscow: Izdanie T-va I. D. Sytina.

DCHTU [Department of CCP History at Tsinghua University] (Ed.). 1979. *Fufa qingong jianxue yundong shiliao* [A Documentary History of the Work-Study Program in France]. Beijing: Beijing chubanshe.

Deac, Wilfred P. 1997. *Road to the Killing Fields: The Cambodian War of 1970–1975*. College Station, TX: Texas A&M University Press.

Deák, István. 1992. "Historiography of the Countries of Eastern Europe: Hungary." *The American Historical Review* 97(4): 1041–63.

Debo, Richard K. 1966. "The Making of a Bolshevik: Georgii Chicherin in England 1914–1918." *Slavic Review* 25(4): 651–62.

Debs, Mira. 2013. "Using Cultural Trauma: Gandhi's Assassination, Partition and Secular Nationalism in Post-Independence India." *Nations and Nationalism* 19(4): 635–53.

Degras, Jane. 1951. *Soviet Documents on Foreign Policy*. London: Oxford University Press.

Dirlik, Alif. 1991. *Anarchism in the Chinese Revolution*. Berkeley, CA: University of California Press.

Dragostinova, Theodora. 2016. "In Search of the Bulgarians: Mapping the Nation through National Classifications." In *Beyond Mosque, Church, and State: Alternative Narratives of the Nation in the Balkans*, edited by Theodora Dragostinova and Yana Hashamova, 105–28. Budapest: Central European University Press.

Drayton, Richard. 2022. "The Poetics of Anticolonial Nationalism." *American Historical Review* 127(1): 361–64.

Du, Han, and Feizhou Du. 2009. "Xinjiang sanqu geming shi yanjiu zhong de jige wenti." *Xi yu yan jiu* (1): 34–44.

Duara, Prasenjit. 1998. "Transnationalism in the Era of Nation-States: China, 1900–1945." *Development and Change* 29: 647–70.

——. 2001. "The Discourse of Civilization and Pan-Asianism." *Journal of World History* 12(1): 99–130.

——. 2003. *Sovereignty and Authenticity: Manchukuo and the East Asian Modern*. Lanham, MD: Rowman and Littlefield.

Dubinskii-Mukhadze, I. 1968. *Shaumian*. Moscow: Molodaia gvardiia.

——. 1971. *Kuibyshev*. Moscow: Molodaia gvardiia.

Dubrovskii, A. M. 2018. *Istoriki v 1930-kh gg. sud'by i vospriiatie zhizni*. Moscow: TSIOGNIS.

Dubrovskii, Alekandr. 2017. *Vlast' i istoricheskaia mysl' v SSSR (1930–1950-e gg.)*. Moscow: ROSSPEN.

DUFYC, Department of United Front of the CCP's Yan'an Committee 2010. *Yan'an shiqi tongyi zhanxian shiliao xuanbian*. Beijing: Huawen chubanshe.

Duncan, Peter J. S. 2000. *Russian Messianism: Third Rome, Revolution, Communism and After*. London: Routledge.

230   Revolution in China and Russia

Duncan, W. Raymond. 1976. "Cuba: National Communism in the Global Settings." *International Journal* 32(1): 156–77.

Durkheim, Émile. 2003. "Review: The History of Russian Civilization by Miliokov." in *Montesquieu and Rousseau*, edited by Émile Durkheim. Shanghai: Shanghai People's Press (Shanghai Renmin Chubanshe).

EBCE [Editing Board for CCP Elites Biographies] (Ed.). 2010. *Zhonggong dangshi renwu zhuan* [Biographies of the CCP Elites]. Beijing: Zhonggong dangshi chubanshe.

EBCES [Editing Board for CCP Elites from Sichuan Biographies] (Ed.). 1984. *Sichuan dangshi renwu zhuan* [Biographies of the CCP Elites from Sichuan]. Chengdu: Sichuansheng shehui kexueyuan chubanshe.

EBPHA, Editing Board of PLA History of Arts: hongjun shiqi. 1986. *Jiefangjun wenyishiliao xuanbian*. Beijing: Jiefangjun chubanshe.

EBPHA, Editing Board of PLA History of Arts: kangrizhanzheng shiqi. 1988. *Jiefangjun wenyishiliao xuanbian*. Beijing: Jiefangjun chubanshe.

EBPHA, Editing Board of PLA History of Arts: jiefangzhanzheng shiqi. 1989. *Jiefangjun wenyishiliao xuanbian*. Beijing: Jiefangjun chubanshe.

Edgar, Adrienne Lynn. 2004. *Tribal Nation: The Making of Soviet Turkmenistan* Princeton, NJ: Princeton University Press.

Egorov, Nikolai. 2011. *Sovetskaia Kareliia istoriia sobytiia liudi dokumenty foto*. Petrozavodsk: Karel'skii nauchnyi tsentr RAN.

Esherick, Joseph W. 2006. "How the Qing Became China." In *Empire to Nation: Historical Perspectives on the Making of the Modern World*, edited by Joseph W. Esherick, Hasan Kayali, and Eric Van Young, 229–59. Lanham, MD: Rowman and Littlefield.

Esposito, John L. (Ed.). 1990. *The Iranian Revolution: Its Global Impact*. Miami, FL: Florida International University Press.

Ezergailis, Andrew. 1976. "The Thirteenth Conference of the Latvian Social-Democrats, 1917: Bolshevik Strategy Victorious." in *Reconsiderations on the Russian Revolution*, edited by Ralph Carter Elwood. Cambridge, MA: Slavica.

Fan, Lijun. 2012. "Zhou Baozhong dui dongbei kangri zhanzheng de gongxian." *Dongbei shidi* (06): 77–81.

Fang, Genfa (Ed.). 2004. *Xuan Xiafu geming lieshi zhuan*. Jiaojiang: Zhonggong jiaojiangqu dangwei yanjiushi.

Fang, Sumei, and Zhichun Cai. 2000. *Zhongguo shaoshu minzu geming shi*. Guilin: Guangxi minzu chubanshe.

Fateev, Petr, and V. Korolev. 1988. *O Emel'iane Iaroslavskom: vospominaniia, ocherki, stat'i*. Moscow: Izdatel'stvo politicheskoi literatury.

Fieldhouse, David Kenneth. 1966. *The Colonial Empires: A Comparative Survey from the Eighteenth Century*. London: Weidenfeld and Nicolson.

Fischer, Bernd J. 1999. *Albania at war, 1939–1945*. West Lafayette, IN: Purdue University Press.

Fitzpatrick, Sheila. 1992. *The Cultural Front: Power and Culture in Revolutionary Russia*. Ithaca, NY: Cornell University Press.

Fleming, Michael. 2010. *Communism, Nationalism and Ethnicity in Poland, 1944–50*. London: Routledge.

Flint, John. 1983. "Planned Decolonization and Its Failure in British Africa." *African Affairs* 82(328): 389–411.

Friedman, Jeremy Scott. 2015. *Shadow Cold War: The Sino-Soviet Competition for the Third World*. Chapel Hill, NC: University of North Carolina Press.

Bibliography

Fu, Hao, and Li Tongcheng. 1995. *Kaiqi guomen: waijiaoguan de fengcai*. Beijing: Huaqiao chubanshe.

Fu, Laiwang. 2014. *Manhua chilechuan*. Huhehaote: Neimenggu renmin chubanshe.

Fuente, Alejandro de la. 1999. "Myths of Racial Democracy: Cuba, 1900–1912." *Latin American Research Review* 34(3): 39–73.

Fyson, George (Ed.). 1995. *Lenin's Final Fight: Speeches and Writings, 1922–23*. New York, NY: Pathfinder.

Galili, Z., and A. Nenarokov. 1996. *Mensheviki v 1917 godu tom 3: ot kornilovskogo miatezha do kontsa dekabria chast' pervaia*. Moscow: ROSSPEN.

GARF, Gosudarstvennyi arkhiv rossisskoi federatsii. 2000. *Partiia soiuz 17 oktiabria: protokoly III sezda, konferentsii i zasedanii TsK, 1905–1915*. Moscow: ROSSPEN.

Gasanly, Dzhamil'. 2013. *Vneshniia politika Azerbaidzhana v gody sovetskoi vdasti 1920–1939*. Moscow: Izdatel'stvo Flinta i Izdatel'stvo Nauka.

Gatagova, L. C., L. P. Kosheleva, and L. A. Pogovaia. 2005. *TsK RKP(b)-VKP(b) i natsional'nyi vopros (1918–1933)*. Moscow: Posspen.

Gati, Charles. 1990. *The Bloc That Failed: Soviet-East European Relations in Transition*. Bloomington, IN: Indiana University Press.

Gerstle, Gary. 2001. *American Crucible: Race and Nation in the Twentieth Century*. Princeton, NJ: Princeton University Press.

Getachew, Adom. 2019. *Worldmaking after Empire: The Rise and Fall of Self-Determination*. Princeton, NJ: Princeton University Press.

GG, Gomel'skii Gubispolkom. 1924. *Chongarskaia 6-ia kavaleriiskaia diviziia istoricheskii sbornik k 6-tiletnemu iubileiu divizii*. Gemel': Izd. Chongarskoi kavdivizii.

Gigova, Irina. 2016. "The Feeble Charm of National(ist) Communism: Intellectuals and Cultural Politics in Zhivkov's Bulgaria." In *Beyond Mosque, Church, and State: Alternative Narratives of the Nation in the Balkans*, edited by Theodora Dragostinova and Yana Hashamova, 151–77. Budapest: Central European University Press.

Gleason, Abbott. 2004. "Panslavism." in *Encyclopedia of Russian History*, edited by James R. Millar. New York, NY: Gale.

Gleijeses, Piero. 2017a. "The Cuban Revolution: The First Decade." In *Cambridge History of Communism*, Vol. 2, edited by Norman Naimark, Silvio Pons, and Sophie Quinn-Judge, 364–87. New York, NY: Cambridge University Press.

———. 2017b. "Marxist-Leninist Regimes in Latin America and Africa." In *Cambridge History of Communism*, Vol. 3, edited by Juliane Fürst, Silvio Pons, and Mark Selden, 95–120. Cambridge: Cambridge University Press.

Go, Julian. 2011. *Patterns of Empire: The British and American Empires, 1688 to the Present*. New York, NY: Cambridge University Press.

Gökay, Bülent. 2006. *Soviet Eastern Policy and Turkey, 1920–1991*. New York, NY: Routledge.

Gong, Yuzhi. 2002. *Dangshi zhaji*. Hangzhou: Zhejiang renmin chubanshe.

González, John. 2017. *An Intellectual Biography of N.A. Rozhkov*. Boston, MA: Brill.

González, Pablo Alonso. 2016. "Transforming Ideology into Heritage: A Return of Nation and Identity in Late Socialist Cuba?" *International Journal of Cultural Studies* 19(2): 139–59.

Goodwin, Jeff. 2001. *No Other Way Out: States and Revolutionary Movements, 1945–1991*. Cambridge: Cambridge University Press.

Gorbov, Nikolai Mikhailovich. 1914. *Russkaia istoriia dlia nachal'nykh shkol*. Moscow: Knigoizd.

Gordy, Katherine A. 2015. *Living Ideology in Cuba: Socialism in Principle and Practice*. Ann Abor, MI: University of Michigan Press.

Gorelov, Ignat Efimovich (Ed.). 1990. *Bol'sheviki: dokumenty po istorii bol'shevizma s 1903 do 1916 god byvshego moskovskogo okhrannogo otdeleniia*. Moscow: Izdatel'stvo politicheskoi literatury.

Gorelov, O. I. 2000. *Tsugtsvang Mikhaila Tomskovo*. Moscow: ROSSPEN.

Goriachev, Iu. V. 2005. *Tsentral'nyi komitet: KPSS, VKP(b), RKP(b), RSDRP(b)*. Moscow: Parad.

Gorodetsky, Gabriel. 2015. *The Maisky Diaries: Red Ambassador to the Court of St James's, 1932–1943*. New Haven, CT: Yale University Press.

Goscha, Christopher E. 2006. "Courting Diplomatic Disaster? The Difficult Integration of Vietnam into the Internationalist Communist Movement (1945–1950)." *Journal of Vietnamese Studies* 2(1–2): 59–103.

———. 2012. *Going Indochinese: Contesting Concepts of Space and Place in French Indochina*. Copenhagen: NIAS Press.

Gould, Eliga H., and Peter S. Onuf (Eds.). 2005. *Empire and Nation: The American Revolution in the Atlantic World*. Baltimore: Johns Hopkins University Press.

GPD, General Political Department. 2001. *Jie fang jun zheng zhi gong zuo li shi zi liao xuan*. Beijing: Jiefangjun chubanshe.

Granat. 1989a. "Deiateli SSSR i revoliutsionovo dvizheniia rossii: entsiklopedia granat." Moscow: Sov. entsiklopedia.

———. 1989b. *Deiateli SSSR i revolyutsionnogo dvizheniia rossii: entsiklopedicheskii slovar*. Moscow: Sovietskaia Entsiklopedia.

Granville, Johanna. 2009. "*Dej*-a-Vu: Early Roots of Romania's Independence." *East European Quarterly* 42(4):365–404.

Grechko, Andrei. 1976. *Sovetskaia voennaia entsiklopediia*. Moscow: Voenizdat.

Grenaderov-Tenishchev, Semchuk, and Popov. 1930. *Istoriia 9-go krasno-putilovskogo chervonnogo kazachestva kavaleriiskogo polka*. Shepetovka: Shepetovskaia gostipografiia.

Gui, Zunyi. 1992. *Makesi zhuyi shixue zai zhongguo*. Jinan: Shandong renmin chubanshe.

Gui, Zunyi, and Yingguang Yuan. 2010. *Zhongguo jindai shixueshi*. Beijing: Renmin chubanshe.

Gusev, Sergei Ivanovich. 1925. *Grazhdanskaia voina i krasnaia armiia: sbornik voenno-teoreticheskikh i voenno-politicheskikh statii (1918–1924)*. Moscow: Gosudarstvennoe izdatel'stvo.

Guy, Nicola. 2012. *The Birth of Albania: Ethnic Nationalism, the Great Powers of World War I, and the Emergence of Albanian Independence*. London: I. B. Tauris.

Haimson, Leopold H. 1987. *The Making of Three Russian Revolutionaries: Voices from the Menshevik Past*. New York, NY: Cambridge University Press.

Hall, John A. 2013. *The Importance of Being Civil: The Struggle for Political Decency*. Princeton, NJ: Princeton University Press.

———. 2017. "Taking Megalomanias Seriously: Rough Notes." *Thesis Eleven* 139(1): 30–45.

Halliday, Fred. 2008. "Revolutionary Internationalism and its Perils." In *Revolution in the Making of the Modern World: Social Identities, Globalization, and Modernity*, edited by John Foran, David Stuart Lane, and Andreja Zivkovic. Milton Park: Routledge.

Hamilton, Richard F. 2000. *Marxism, Revisionism, and Leninism: Explication, Assessment, and Commentary*. Westport, CT: Praeger.

Bibliography

Harmer, Tanya. 2013. "Two, Three, Many Revolutions? Cuba and the Prospects for Revolutionary Change in Latin America." *Journal of Latin American Studies* 45: 61–89.

Harris, George S. 1967. *The Origins of Communism in Turkey*. Stanford, CA: Hoover Institution Press.

Haslam, Jonathan. 1992. *The Soviet Union and the Threat from the East, 1933–41*. Pittsburgh, PA: University of Pittsburgh Press.

Haug, Hilde Katrine. 2012. *Creating a Socialist Yugoslavia: Tito, Communist Leadership and the National Question*. London: I. B. Tauris.

Haugaard, Mark. 2002. "Nationalism and Modernity." In *Making Sense of Collectivity: Ethnicity, Nationalism, and Globalization*, edited by Siniša Maleśević and Mark Haugaard, 122–37. London: Pluto Press.

Haupt, Georges, and Jean Jacques Marie. 1974. *Makers of the Russian Revolution: Biographies of Bolshevik Leaders*. Ithaca, NY: Cornell University Press.

He, Ganzhi. 1984. *He Ganzhi wenji*. Beijing: Beijing chubanshe.

Hechter, Michael. 2000. *Containing Nationalism*. Oxford: Oxford University Press.

Hennessy, C. A. M. 1963. "The Roots of Cuban Nationalism." *International Affairs* 39(3): 345–59.

Hobsbawm, Eric, and Terence Ranger (Eds.). 1983. *The Invention of Tradition*. Cambridge: Cambridge University Press.

Holt, Alix. 1978. *Selected Writings of Alexandra Kollontai*. Westport, CT: Lawrence Hill.

Hroch, Miroslav. 1985. *Social Preconditions of National Revival in Europe: A Comparative Analysis of the Social Composition of Patriotic Groups among the Smaller European Nations*. Cambridge: Cambridge University Press.

Hu, Qiaomu. 2008 [1951]. *Zhongguo gongchandang de sanshinian*. Beijing: Renmin chubanshe.

Hu, Zhiming. 1964. *Hu Zhiming xuanji*. Beijing: Renmin chubanshe.

Huang, Hou. 1962. "Da qingshan shang jian qibing." *Zhongguo minzu* (08): 1–5.

Huang, Jianhua. 2004. *Guomindang zhengfu xinjiang zhengce yanjiu*. Beijing: Minzu chubanshe.

Huang, Liyong. 2016. *Gongheguo yuanshuai du gushu shilu*. Beijing: Renmin chubanshe.

Huang, Wenhuan. 1987. *Huang Wenhuan huiyilu*. Beijing: Jiefangjun chubanshe.

Huang, Xingtao. 2017. *Chong su Zhonghua*. Beijing: Beijing shifan daxue chubanshe.

Huang, Yanmin. 2014. *Huangtu yu hongqi: yan'an shiqi zhongguo gongchandang yu chuantong wenhua yanjiu*. Beijing: Xuexi chubanshe.

Huntington, Samuel P. 1968. *Political Order in Changing Societies*. New Haven, CT: Yale University Press.

Hutchinson, John. 2013. "Cultural Nationalism." In *The Oxford Handbook of the History of Nationalism*, edited by John Breuilly, 76–94. Oxford: Oxford University Press.

———. 2017. *Nationalism and War*. Oxford: Oxford University Press.

Hutchinson, John, and David Aberbach. 1999. "The Artist as Nation-Builder: William Butler Yeats and Chaim Nachman Bialik." *Nations and Nationalism* 5(4): 501–21.

Idrizi, Idrit. 2020. "Between Subordination and Symbiosis: Historians' Relationship with Political Power in Communist Albania." *European History Quarterly* 50(1): 66–87.

IHCAS, Institute of History of Chinese Academy of Science (Ed.). 1959. *Wusi yundong huiyilu*. Beijing: Zhonghua shuju.

ILCSSA, Institute of Literature of Chinese Social Science Academy (Ed.). 2010. *Zuolian huiyilu*. Beijing: Zhishi chanquan chubanshe.

234   *Revolution in China and Russia*

Illeritskii, V. E., and I. A. Kudriavtsev. 1961. *Istoriographiia istorii SSSR*. Moscow: Izdatel'stvo sotsial'no-ekonomicheskoi literatury.

IMEL, Institut marksa-engel'sa-lenina pri TsK VKP(b). 1947. *I. V. Stalin: Sochineniia*. Moscow: OGIS.

IMLpTsK, Institut Marksisma i Leninisma pri TsK KPSS. 1967. *F. E. Dzerzhinskii: izbrannye proizdevenii v dvukh tomakh*. Moscow: Izdatel'stvo politicheskoi literatury.

IMTsK, Institut marksizma-leninizma pri TsK KPSS. 1960. *M. I. Kalinin: Izbrannye proizvedeniia*. Moscow: Gosudarstvennoe izdatel'stvo politicheskoi literatury.

———. 1971. *Vladimir Il'chi Lenin biograficheskaia khronika*. Moscow: Izdatel'stvo politicheskoi literatury.

———. 1975. *Mikhail Kalinin kratkaia biografiia*. Moscow: Gosudarstvennoe izdatel'stvo politicheskoi literatury.

Iskenderov, P. A. 2008. "Enver Khodzha." *Voprosy istorii* 6: 48–64.

Jankowski, James P. 2001. *Nasser's Egypt, Arab Nationalism, and the United Arab Republic*. Boulder, CO: Lynne Rienner.

Janos, Andrew C. 1991. "Social Science, Communism, and the Dynamics of Political Change." *World Politics* 44(1): 81–112.

Jelavich, Charles. 2003. "South Slav Education—Was There Yugoslavism?" In *Yugoslavia and its Historians: Understanding the Balkan Wars of the 1990s*, edited by Norman M. Naimark and Holly Case, 93–115. Stanford, CA: Stanford University Press.

Jian, Bozan (Ed.). 1962. *Lishi wenti luncong (zengdingben)*. Beijing: Renmin chubanshe.

Jiang, Chunze. 1981. *Nan si la fu (Yugoslavia)*. Shanghai: Shanghai cishu chubanshe.

Jiang, Hua. 1993. *Zhuiyi yu sikao Jiang Hua huiyilu*. Hangzhou: Zhejiang renmin chubanshe.

Jiangsu sheng dang'anguan, Jiangsu Provincial Archive. 2014. *Jiangsu sheng danganguan guancang geming lishi baokan ziliao huibian*. Nanjing: Dongnan daxue chubanshe.

Jin, Chenggao. 2019. "Dongbei kangri mingjiang zhou baozhong yu chaoxian minzu geming zhanzheng." *Dong jiang xue kan* 36(4): 50–56.

Joll, James. 1956. *The Second International: 1889–1914*. New York, NY: Praeger.

Jowitt, Ken. 1983. "Soviet Neotraditionalism: The Political Corruption of a Leninist Regime." *Soviet Studies* 35(3): 275–97.

Kai, Feng. 1938. *Kang ri min zu tong yi zhan xian jiao cheng*. Wuhan: Sheng huo shu dian.

Kappeler, Andreas. 2001. *The Russian Empire: A Multiethnic History*. New York, NY: Pearson Education.

Karl, Rebecca E. 1998. "Creating Asia: China in the World at the Beginning of the Twentieth Century." *The American Historical Review* 103(4): 1096–118.

Karpenko, Sergeĭ. 1992. *Beloe delo: izbrannye proizvedeniia v 16 knigakh*. Moscow: Golos.

Karzhavin, D. F. 1947. *Stepan Razin v Simbirske*. Ul'ianovsk: Tipografiia Ul'ianovskogo oblaliagrafupravleniia.

Ke, Bainian. 1948. *Meiguo shouce*. Beiping: Zhongwai chubanshe.

Kedourie, Elie. 1993. *Nationalism*. Oxford: Blackwell.

Keitner, Chimène I. 2007. *The Paradoxes of Nationalism: The French Revolution and Its Meaning for Contemporary Nation Building*. Albany, NY: State University of New York Press.

Bibliography 235

Kenez, Peter. 1985. *The Birth of the Propaganda State: Soviet Methods of Mass Mobilization, 1917–1929*. Cambridge: Cambridge University Press.

———. 2001. *Cinema and Soviet Society from the Revolution to the Death of Stalin*. London: I. B. Tauris.

Khromov, Semen Spiridonovich Хромов, M. I. Vladimirov, S. N. Ikonnikov, G. Z. Ioffe, N. A. Pavlova, and I. V. Sabennikova. 1988. *Valerian Vladimirovich Kuibyshev*. Moscow: Izdatel'stvo politicheskoi literatury.

Kilin, Iu. M. 2012. *Pogranichnaia okraina velikoi derzhavy Sovetskaia Kareliia v 1923–1938 gg*. Petrozavodsk: Izdatel'stvo Petrozavodskogo universiteta.

Kirilina, Anna. 2001. *Neizvestnyi Kirov: mify i real'nost'*. Petersburg: Izdatel'skii dom neva.

Kirillov, V. S., and A. Ia. Sverdlov. 1962. *Grigorii Konstantinovich Ordzhonikidze (Sergo)*. Moscow: Gosudarstvennoe izdatel'stvo politicheskoi literatury.

———. 1986. *Grigorii Konstantinovich Ordzhonikidze (Sergo): Biografiia*. Moscow: Izdatel'stvo politicheskoi literatury.

Kizenko, Nadieszda. 2020. "The Orthodox Church and Religious Life in Imperial Russia." In *The Oxford Handbook of Russian Religious Thought*, edited by Caryl Emerson, George Pattison, and Randall A. Poole, 22–38. Oxford: Oxford University Press.

Kliuchnik, L., and B. Zav'ialov. 1970. *G. I. Petrovskii*. Moscow: Izdatel'stvo politicheskoi literatury.

Kohn, Hans. 1944. *The Idea of Nationalism: A Study in Its Origins and Background*. New York: Macmillan.

Kollontai, Alexandra. 1926 [2011]. *The Autobiography of a Sexually Emancipated Communist Woman*. New York, NY: Prism Key Press.

Kolstø, Pål. 2019. "Is Imperialist Nationalism an Oxymoron?" *Nations and Nationalism* 25(1): 18–44.

Kong, Hanbing. 2010. "The Transplantation and Entrenchment of the Soviet Economic Model in China." In *China Learns from the Soviet Union, 1949–Present*, edited by Thomas P Bernstein and Hua-Yu Li, 153–66. Lanham, MD: Lexington Books.

Kononova, Margarita. 2018. "Mir s Germaniei i politicheskoe soprotivlenie russkikh diplomaticheskikh predstavitelei." In *Bretskii mir: istoriia i geopolitika, 1918–2018*, edited by E. A. Bandareva and E. H. Rudaia, 101–60. Moscow: Veche.

Kořalka, Jiří. 1992. "Czechoslovakia." *The American Historical Review* 97(4): 1026–40.

Korkut, Umut. 2006. "Nationalism versus Internationalism: The Roles of Political and Cultural Elites in Interwar and Communist Romania." *Nationalities Papers* 34(2): 131–55.

Krejčí, Jaroslav. 2000. "Great Revolutions of the 20th Century in a Civilizational Perspective." *Thesis Eleven* 62(1): 71–90.

Krupskaya, Nadezhda. 1957. *Pedagogicheskie sochineniia v desiatki tomakh, 1918–1925*. Moscow: Izdatel'stvo akademii pedagogicheskikh nauk.

———. 2011. *The Selected Works of Nadezhda Krupskaya*. New York, NY: Prism Key Press.

———. 2015 [1933]. *Reminiscences of Lenin*. Northampton: Anarcho-communist institute.

Kumar, Krishan. 2000. "Nation and Empire: English and British National Identity in Comparative Perspective." *Theory and Society* 29(5): 575–608.

———. 2015. "Nationalism and Revolution: Friends or Foes?" *Nations and Nationalism* 21(4): 589–608.

———. 2017a. "The Time of Empire: Temporality and Genealogy in the Development of European Empires." *Thesis Eleven* 139(1): 113–28.

———. 2017b. *Visions of Empire: How Five Imperial Regimes Shaped the World.* Princeton, NJ: Princeton University Press.

Kun, Bela. 1923. "Discipline and Centralised Leadership." *The Communist Review* 3(9–10): digitized by Marxists Internet Archive (2006), www.marxists.org/history/international/comintern/sections/britain/periodicals/communist_review/1923/09-10/dis_and_leader.htm.

———. 1971 [1919]. *Revolutionary Essays (reprinted from Pravda).* London: B. S. P.

Kunicki, Mikołaj Stanisław. 2012. *Between the Brown and the Red: Nationalism, Catholicism, and Communism in Twentieth-Century Poland—The Politics of Bolesław Piasecki.* Athens, OH: Ohio University Press.

Kurban, Vefa. 2017. *Russian–Turkish Relations from the First World War to the Present.* Newcastle: Cambridge Scholars Publishing.

Kurganov, I. A. 1961. *Natsii SSSR i russkii vopros.* Moscow: Komitet za prava i svobodu.

Lachmann, Richard. 2020. *First-class Passengers on a Sinking Ship: Elite Politics and the Decline of Great Powers.* London: Verso.

Ladimirov, M. I. 1985. *O Mikhaile Frunze: vospominaniia, ocherki, stat'i sovremennikov.* Moscow: Izdatel'stvo politicheskoi literatury.

Ladwig, Patrice. 2017. "Contemporary Lao Buddhism: Ruptured Histories." in *The Oxford Handbook of Contemporary Buddhism,* edited by Michael Jerryson. Oxford: Oxford University Press.

Lampe, John R. 2013. "Yugoslavia's Foreign Policy in Balkan Perspective: Tracking between the Superpowers and Non-Alignment." *East Central Europe* 40: 97–113.

Lankov, Andrei. 2011. *The Real North Korea: Life and Politics in the Failed Stalinist Utopia.* Oxford: Oxford University Press.

Lawson, George. 2005. *Negotiated Revolutions: The Czech Republic, South Africa and Chile.* Aldershot: Ashgate.

———. 2019. *Anatomies of Revolution.* Cambridge: Cambridge University Press.

Layton, Susan. 1995. *Russian Literature and Empire Conquest of the Caucasus from Pushkin to Tolstoy.* Cambridge: Cambridge University Press.

Lee, Jung Woo, and Alan Bairner. 2009. "The Difficult Dialogue: Communism, Nationalism, and Political Propaganda in North Korean Sport." *Journal of Sport and Social Issues* 33(4): 390–410.

Leerssen, Joep. 2006. "Nationalism and the Cultivation of Culture." *Nations and Nationalism* 12(4): 559–78.

Leibold, James. 2007. *Reconfiguring Chinese Nationalism: How the Qing Frontier and Its Indigenes Became Chinese.* New York, NY: Palgrave Macmillan.

Lem, Anton van der. 2018. *Revolution in the Netherlands: The Eighty Years War, 1568–1648.* London: Reaktion Books.

Lendvai, Paul. 1969. *Eagles in Cobwebs: Nationalism and Communism in the Balkans.* Garden City: Doubleday.

Lenin, Vladimir. 1948. *Imperialism, the Highest Stage of Capitalism.* London: Lawrence and Wishart.

———. 1956. *Lenin o literature i kul'ture.* Moscow: Iskusstvo.

———. 1971. *Critical Remarks on the National Question: the Right of Nations to Self-Determination.* Moscow: Progress Publishers.

Lenoe, Matthew E. 1998. "Agitation, Propaganda and the 'Stalinization' of the Soviet Press, 1922–1930." *The Carl Beck Papers in Russian & East European Studies* (1305): 1–109.

Bibliography

Leont'ev, Ia. V., M. V. Liuhudzaev, and D. I. Rublev. 2015. *Partiia levykh sotsialistov-revoliutsionerov dokumenty i materialy tom 2, chast' iiul'-oktiabr' 1918.* Moscow: ROSSPEN.

Lerner, Warren. 1970. *Karl Radek: The Last Internationalist.* Stanford, CA: Stanford University Press.

Levenson, Joseph R. 1971. *Revolution and Cosmopolitanism: The Western Stage and the Chinese Stages.* Berkeley, CA: University of California Press.

Levidova, S. M., and E. G. Salita. 1969. *Elena Stasova biograficheskii ocherk.* Leningrad: Lenizdat.

Levine, Marilyn Avra. 1993. *The Found Generation: Chinese Communists in Europe during the Twenties.* Seattle, WA: University of Washington Press.

Li, Hua-Yu. 2006. *Mao and the Economic Stalinization of China, 1948–1953.* Lanham, MD: Rowman and Littlefield.

Li, Kunrui. 2019. "Sanqian zelu kangri zhanzheng shiqi zhonggong qiongya zongdui xuanzhi wenti yanjiu." *Zhonggong dangshi yanjiu* (06): 93–102.

Li, Qiang, and Li Li. 2018. "Guogong liangdang suiyuan kangzhan bijiao yanjiu." *Qianyan* (03): 119–25.

Li, Rong. 2013. "Zhou Baozhong yu dongbei kangri zhanzheng." *Dongbei shidi*: 81–89.

Li, Weihan. 1986. *Huiyi yu yanjiu.* Beijing: Zhonggong dangshi ziliao chubanshe.

———. 2016. *Tong yi zhan xian yu min zu wen ti.* Beijing: Zhong gong dang shi chubanshe.

Li, Xin (Ed.). 1978. *Wu Yuzhang huiyilu.* Beijing: Zhongguo qingnian chubanshe.

Li, Yang. 1993. *Kangzheng suming zhilu: shehuizhuyi xianshizhuyi (1942–1976).* Changchun: shidai wenyi chubanshe.

Liao, Hansheng. 1993. *Liao Hansheng huiyilu.* Beijing: Bayi chubanshe.

Lieven, Dominic. 1999. "Dilemmas of Empire 1850–1918. Power, Territory, Identity." *Journal of Contemporary History* 34(2): 163–200.

———. 2015. *Towards the Flame: Empire, War and the End of Tsarist Russia.* London: Allen Lane.

Lin, Boqu. 1984. *Lin Boqu riji.* Changsha: Hunan renmin chubanshe.

Linkhoeva, Tatiana. 2020. *Revolution Goes East: Imperial Japan and Soviet Communism.* Ithaca, NY: Cornell University Press.

Liu, Weili. 1997. *Liu Renjing.* Shijiazhuang: Hebei renmin chubanshe.

Liu, Wenyuan. 2004a. "Lun Zhongguo gongchandang dui sanqu geming de yingxiang." *Lilun xuekan* (04): 71–76.

Liu, Xiaoyuan. 2004b. *Frontier Passages: Ethnopolitics and the Rise of Chinese Communism, 1921–1945.* Washington, DC: Woodrow Wilson Center Press.

———. 2017. "Zhong guo gong chan dang jiang yu guan de yuan yuan yu fa zhan (1921–1949)." *Er shi yi shi ji* 160(4): 13–34.

Liu, Xinjun. 2020. "Guanyu dongbei kanglian sange zhongda wenti de yanjiu." *Shehui kexue zhanxian* (8): 113–22.

Liu, Yong, and Chunyu Li. 2016. *Xinwenhua yundong yu chuantong wenhua.* Hefei: Anhui daxue chubanshe.

Liu, Zhen. 1990. *Liu zhen huiyilu.* Beijing: Jiefangjun chubanshe.

Lohr, Eric. 2003. "Russian Economic Nationalism during the First World War: Moscow Merchants and Commercial Diasporas." *Nationalities Papers* 31(4): 471–84.

Lord, Ceren. 2017. "Between Islam and the Nation: Nationbuilding, the Ulama and Alevi Identity in Turkey." *Nations and Nationalism* 23(1): 48–67.

Lovell, Stephen. 2012. "Broadcasting Bolshevik: The Radio Voice of Soviet Culture, 1920s–1950s." *Journal of Contemporary History* 48(1): 78–97.

Lubachko, Ivan S. 1972. *Belorussia under Soviet Rule, 1917–1957*. Lexington, KY: University Press of Kentucky.

Lunacharskii, Annatolii. 1968. *Vospominaniia i vpechatleniia*. Moscow: Izdatel'stvo Sovetskaia rossiia.

Lüthi, Lorenz M. 2016. "The Non-Aligned Movement and the Cold War, 1961–1973." *Journal of Cold War Studies* 18(4): 98–147.

Ma, Huili. 2020. "Shilun zhongguo gongchandang dui huizu kangzhan de zuzhi he lingdao." *Hui zu yan jiu* (03): 14–18.

Maiorova, Olga. 2015. "A Revolutionary and Empire: Alexander Herzen and Russian Discourse on Asia." in *Between Europe and Asia: The Origins, Theories, and Legacies of Russian Eurasianism*, edited by Mark Bassin, Sergey Glebov, and Marlene Laruelle. Pittsburgh, PA: University of Pittsburgh Press.

Malešević, Siniša. 2010. *The Sociology of War and Violence*. Cambridge: Cambridge University Press.

———. 2011. "The Chimera of National Identity." *Nations and Nationalism* 17 (2): 272–90.

———. 2017. *The Rise of Organised Brutality: A Historical Sociology of Violence*. Cambridge: Cambridge University Press.

———. 2019. *Grounded Nationalisms: A Sociological Analysis*. Cambridge: Cambridge University Press.

Mann, Michael. 1993. *The Sources of Social Power*. Cambridge: Cambridge University Press.

———. 2012. *The Sources of Social Power: Global Empires and Revolution, 1890—1945*. Cambridge: Cambridge University Press.

Manuel, Peter. 1987. "Marxism, Nationalism and Popular Music in Cuba." *Popular Music* 6(2): 161–78.

Mao, Zedong. 2002. *Mao Zedong zishu*. Taibei: Taiwan shufang.

Mark, James. 2006. "Antifascism, the 1956 Revolution and the Politics of Communist Autobiographies in Hungary 1944–2000." *Europe-Asia Studies* 58(8): 1209–40.

Marshall, Herbert. 1983. *Masters of the Soviet Cinema: Crippled Creative Biographies*. London: Routledge and Kegan Paul.

Martin, Terry. 1998. "The Origins of Soviet Ethnic Cleansing." *The Journal of Modern History* 70(4): 813–61.

Matonin, Evgenii. 2018. *Krasnye*. Moscow: Molodaia gvardiia.

Matsuzato, Kimitaka. 2017. "The Rise and Fall of Ethnoterritorial Federalism: A Comparison of the Soviet Union (Russia), China, and India." *Europe–Asia Studies* 69(7): 1047–69.

Mavrodin, V. V. 1951. *Obrazovanie edinogo russkogo gosudarstva*. Leningrad: Izd. Leningradskogo universiteta.

Mawdsley, Evan. 1987. *The Russian Civil War*. Boston, MA: Allen & Unwin.

Mazour, Anatole G. 1975. *Modern Russian Historiography*. Westport, CT: Greenwood Press.

McCann, James M. 1984. "Beyond the Bug: Soviet Historiography of the Soviet–Polish War of 1920." *Soviet Studies* 36(4): 475–93.

McNeal, Robert H. 1958. "Soviet Historiography on the October Revolution: A Review of Forty Years." *The American Slavic and East European Review* 17(3): 269–81.

Bibliography

Menasheri, David (Ed.). 1990. *The Iranian Revolution and the Muslim World.* Oxford: Westview Press.

Mevius, Martin. 2005. *Agents of Moscow The Hungarian Communist Party and the Origins of Socialist Patriotism 1941–1953.* Oxford: Oxford University Press.

———. 2009. "Reappraising Communism and Nationalism." *Nationalities Papers* 37(4).

Meyer, John W., John Boli, George M. Thomas, and Francisco O. Ramirez. 1997. "World Society and the Nation-State." *American Journal of Sociology* 103(1): 144–81.

Miao, Tijun. 2011. "Zhonggong yida daibiao Chen Gongbo de sida lishi mituan." *Dang sh ibo cai* (3):144–81.

Mikhailov, Nikolai. 1956. *Nad kartoi rodiny.* Moscow: Molodaia gvardiia.

Moffat, Ian C. D. 2015. *The Allied Intervention in Russia, 1918–1920: The Diplomacy of Chaos.* Houndsmills: Palgrave Macmillan.

Mojab, Shabrzad, and Amir Hassanpour. 1996. "The Politics of Nationality and Ethnic Diversity." In *Iran after the Revolution: Crisis of an Islamic State*, edited by Saeed Rahnema and Sohrab Behdad, 229–50. London: I. B. Tauris.

Montefiore, Simon Sebag. 2007. *Young Stalin.* London: Weidenfeld & Nicolson.

Moon, David. 1996. "Peasants into Russian Citizens? A Comparative Perspective." *Revolutionary Russia* 9(1): 43–81.

Moore, Barrington. 1966. *Social Origins of Dictatorship and Democracy: Lord and Peasant in the Making of the Modern World.* Boston, MA: Beacon Press.

Morozov, V. F. 1949. *S. M. Kirov.* Moscow: Izdatel'stvo Pravda.

Mudge, Stephanie L. 2018. *Leftism Reinvented: Western Parties from Socialism to Neoliberalism.* Cambridge, MA: Harvard University Press.

Mullaney, Thomas S. 2011. *Coming to Terms with the Nation Ethnic Classification in Modern China.* Berkeley, CA: University of California Press.

Nation, R. Craig. 1989. *War on War: Lenin, the Zimmerwald Left, and the Origins of Communist Internationalism.* Durham, NC: Duke University Press.

Nedava, Joseph. 1972. *Trotsky and the Jews.* Philadelphia, PA: Jewish Publication Society of America.

Neimenggu diqu dangwei dangshi yanjiushi. 2011. *Zhongguo gongchandang neimenggu diqu jianshi 1919–1949.* Huhehaote: Neimenggu renmin chubanshe.

Neufeldt, Reina C. 2009. "Tolerant Exclusion: Expanding Constricted Narratives of Wartime Ethnic and Civic Nationalism." *Nations and Nationalism* 15(2): 206–26.

Niebuhr, Robert. 2018. *The Search for a Cold War Legitimacy: Foreign Policy and Tito's Yugoslavia.* Leiden: Brill.

Nikonov, Viacheslav. 2005. *Molotov: molodost'.* Moscow: Vagrius.

Novikova, Irina. 2018. "Na puti k brestu: Germanskaia diplomatiia v poiskakh separatnogo mira c Rossiei." In *Bretskii mir. Istoriia i geopolitika. 1918–2018*, edited by E. A. Bondareva and E. H. Rudaia, 6–56. Moscow: Veche.

Novikova, Liudmila G. 2019. "Red Patriots against White Patriots: Contesting Patriotism in the Civil War in North Russia." *Europe-Asia Studies* 71(2): 183–202.

NZD, Neimenggu zizhiqu dang'anguan. 1983. *Neimenggu minzu geming tuanjie shiliao xuanbian.* Huhehaote: Neimenggu zizhiqu dang'anguan.

O'Connor, Timothy Edward. 1988. *Diplomacy and Revolution: G. V. Chicherin and Soviet Foreign Affairs, 1918–1930.* Ames, IA: Iowa State University Press.

———. 1991. "Lunacharskii's Vision of the New Soviet Citizen." *The Historian* 53(3): 443–54.

240 *Revolution in China and Russia*

Ocadchii, Fedor. 2005. *Bessmertnyi komandar turksib*. Almaty: Arys.

OGIZ. 1944. *S. M. Kirov: Izbrannye stat'i i rechi*. Moscow: Gosudarstvennoe i datel'stvo politicheskoi literatury.

Orwell, George. 1946. *Animal Farm*. New York, NY: Harcourt, Brace and Company.

Ousby, Ian. 2002. *The Road to Verdun: World War I's Most Momentous Battle and the Folly of Nationalism*. New York, NY: Doubleday.

Page, Stanley. 1976. "Lenin's April Thesis and the Latvian Peasant-Solidarity." In *Reconsiderations on the Russian Revolution*, edited by Ralph Carter Elwood. Cambridge: Slavica Publishers.

Pankratova, Anna. 1952. *Istoriia SSSR uchebnik dlia 10 klassa srednei shkoly chast' 3*. Moscow: Gosudarstvennoe uchebno-pedagogicheskoe izdatel'stvo.

Pantsov, Alexander. 2002. "Bolshevik Concepts of the Chinese Revolution 1919–1927." In *The Chinese Revolution in the 1920s: Between Triumph and Disaster*, edited by Mechthild Leutner, Roland Felber, Mikhail L. Titarenko, and Alexander M. Grigoriev, 30–43. London: Routledge.

Pavlov, D. I., and V. V. Shelokhaev. 1996. *Rossiiskie liberaly: kadety i oktiabristy*. Moscow: ROSSPEN.

PDRO. 1979. *Wusi qianhou Zhou Enlai tongzhi shiwenxuan*. Tianjin: Tianjin renmin chubanshe.

PDRO (Ed.). 2000. *Chen Yun nianpu*. Beijing: Zhongyang wenxian chubanshe.

———. 2005. *Xi Zhongxun zhuan*. Beijing: Renmin chubanshe Zhongyang wenxian chubanshe.

———. 2012. *Peng Zhen nianpu*. Beijing: Zhongyang wenxian chubanshe.

Pedersen, Susan. 2015. *The Guardians: The League of Nations and the Crisis of Empire*. Oxford: Oxford University Press.

Pelz, William A. 2018. *A People's History of the German Revolution, 1918–1919*. London: Pluto Press.

Perrie, Maureen. 2006. "The Terrible Tsar as Comic Hero: Mikhail Bulgakov's Ivan Vasil'evich." In *Epic Revisionism: Russian History and Literature as Stalinist Propaganda*, edited by Kevin M. F. Platt and David Brandenberger, 143–56. Madison, WI: University of Wisconsin Press.

Pesic, Vesna. 1996. "Serbian Nationalism and the Origins of the Yugoslav Crisis." Peaceworks 8, United States Institute of Peace, Washington DC.

Petrescu, Dragoş. 2009. "Building the Nation, Instrumentalizing Nationalism: Revisiting Romanian National-Communism, 1956–1989." *Nationalities Papers* 37(4): 523–44.

Pettinà, Vanni. 2011. "The shadows of Cold War over Latin America: the US Reaction to Fidel Castro's Nationalism, 1956–59." *Cold War History* 11(3): 317–39.

Phillips, Andrew, and J. C. Sharman. 2020. *Outsourcing Empire: How Company-States Made the Modern World*. Princeton, NJ: Princeton University Press.

Phillips, Hugh D. 1992. *Between the Revolution and the West: a Political Biography of Maxim M. Litvinov*. Boulder, CO: Westview Press.

Piatnitsky, Osip. 1925. *Memoirs of A Bolshevik*. New York, NY: International Publishers.

Pipes, Richard. 1955. "Max Weber and Russia." *World Politics* 7(3): 371–401.

———. 1964. *The Formation of The Soviet Union: Communism and Nationalism, 1917–1923*. Cambridge, MA: Harvard University Press.

Platonov, S. 1917. *Uchebnik russkoi istorii dlia srednei shkoly kurs sestimaticheskii*. Petrograd: Sklad izdanie.

Podgornyi, Igor'. 1966. *V. P. Nogin*. Leningrad: Lenizdat.

Bibliography

Pokrovskii, Mikhail. 1915. *Ocherk istorii russkoi kul'tury*. Moscow: Mir.
———. 1933. *Russkaia istoriia v samom szhatom ocherke*. Moscow: Partiinoe izdatel'stvo.
Pokrovskii, S. N. 1963. *V. V. Kuibyshev v Kazakhstane*. Alma-Ata: Izdatel'stvo akademii nauk kazakhskoi SSR.
Poleshchuk, N. S. 1990. *Nikolai Muralov*. Moscow: Moskovskii rabochii.
Porter, Cathy. 2013. *Alexandra Kollontai: A Biography*. London: Merlin Press.
Posen, Barry R. 1993. "Nationalism, the Mass Army, and Military Power." *International Security* 18(2): 80–124.
Presnianov, A. E. 1915. *Russkaia istoriia kurs mladshchikh klassov* Petrograd: T-vo "V. V. Dumnov, nasl. br. Salaevykh."
Puchalski, Piotr. 2017. "The Polish Mission to Liberia, 1934–1938." *The Historical Journal* 20(60): 1–26.
Qi, Jianmin. 2019. "Cong riben fanggong zoulang jihua kan daqingshan genjudi de zhanlue yiyi " *Zhonggong dangshi yanjiu* (06): 13–26.
Qiang, Xiaochu, and Li Li'an. 1990. *Ma Mingfang zhuanlue*. Xi'an: Shannxi renmin chubanshe.
Qiao, Guanhua. 2000. *Qiao Guanhua wenji*. Changchun: Jilin renmin chubanshe.
Qu, Qiubai. 1985. *Qu Qiubai xuanji*. Beijing: Renmin chubanshe.
Rabow-Edling, Susanna. 2006. *Slavophile Thought and the Politics of Cultural Nationalism*. Albany, NY: State University of New York Press.
Radchenko, Sergey. 2009. "Choibalsan's Great Mongolia Dream." *Inner Asia* 11(2): 231–58.
Radek, Karl. 1923. *Vneshniaia politika sovetskoi rossii*. Petrograd: Gosudarstvennoe izdatel'stvo.
Radek, Karl, A. J. Cummings, and Alec Brown. 1966 [1935]. *Portraits and Pamphlets by Karl Radek*. Freeport, TX: Books for Libraries.
Rakitin, Anton. 1975. *V. A. Anton-Ovseenko*. Leningrad: Lenizdat.
RCCCPH, Research Committee of CCP History (Ed.). 1980–. *Zhonggong dangshi renwuzhuan*. Beijing: Zhongguo renmin daxue chubanshe.
Read, Christopher. 2006. "Krupskaya, Proletkul't and the Origins of Soviet Cultural Policy." *International Journal of Cultural Policy* 12(3): 246–55.
Ree, Erik Van. 1998. "Socialism in One Country: A Reassessment." *Studies in East European Thought* 50(2): 77–117.
Rees, E. A. 1998. "Stalin and Russian Nationalism." In *Russian Nationalism: Past and Present*, edited by Geoffery Hosking and Robert Service, 77–106. London: Palgrave Macmillan.
Ren, Yuehai. 2016. *Chaha'er kangzhan shiliao*. Huhehaote: Neimenggu daxue chubanshe.
Riben gongchandang de sishinian. 1962. Beijing: Renmin.
Richard, Carl J. 2013. *When the United States Invaded Russia*. Lanham, CT: Rowman and Littlefield.
Rieber, Alfred J. 2017. "Anti-Fascist Resistance Movements in Europe and Asia During World War II." In *Cambridge History of Communism*, Vol. 2, edited by Norman Naimark, Silvio Pons, and Sophie Quinn-Judge, 38–62. Cambridge: Cambridge University Press.
Riga, Liliana. 2012. *The Bolsheviks and The Russian Empire*. Cambridge: Cambridge University Press.
RMA (Revolutionary Martyr Association). 1985. *Geming lieshi zhuan*. Beijing: Renmin.
Rodin, A. M. 1988. *A. S. Bubnov Voennaia i politicheskaia deiatel'nost'*. Moscow: Voennoe izdatel'stvo.

Rosenberg, William. 1974. *Liberals in the Russian Revolution: the Constitutional Democratic Party, 1917–1921*. Princeton, NJ: Princeton University Press.

Rosenberg, William G., and Marilyn B. Young. 1982. *Transforming Russia and China: Revolutionary Struggle in the Twentieth Century*. Oxford: Oxford University Press.

Roslof, Edward E. 2002. *Red Priests: Renovationism, Russian Orthodoxy, and Revolution, 1905–1946*. Bloomington, IN: Indiana University Press.

Roszkowski, Wojciech, and Jan Kofman. 2008. *Biographical Dictionary of Central and Eastern Europe in the Twentieth Century*. Armonk, NY: M.E. Sharpe.

Ruan Hong. 2019. *Huang Xiang wangshi*. Beijing: Dangdai zhongguo chubanshe.

Ryskulov, Turar. 1927. *Vosstanie tuzemtsev srednei asii v 1916 gody*. Kzyl-orda: Gosudarstvennoe izdatel'stvo KSSR.

Sablin, Ivan. 2017. "Nationalist Mobilization in the Russian Far East during the Closing Phase of the Civil War." *Vestnik SPbGU, Istoriia* 62(1): 18–25.

———. 2020. *Dal'nevostochnaia respublika ot idei do likvidatsii*. Moscow: Novoe literaturnoe obozrenie.

Said, Edward. 2003. *Orientalism*. New York, NY: Vintage Books.

Saifuding, Azizi. 1993. *Saifuding huiyilu*. Beijing: Huaxia chubanshe.

Sakwa, Richard. 2006. "Nation and Nationalism in Russia." in *The SAGE Handbook of Nations and Nationalism*, edited by Gerard Delanty and Krishan Kumar. London: SAGE.

Samara. 1921. *Tri goda 24 str. zheleznoi Samarskoi divizii iubilenyi sbornik*. Kiev: Izdanie Politicheskogo otdela 24-oi Samarskoi strelkovoi zheleznoi divizii.

Sandag, Shagdaryn. 2000. *Poisoned Arrows: The Stalin–Choibalsan Mongolian Massacres, 1921–1941*. Boulder, CT: Westview Press.

Sanetō, Keishū. 1983. *Zhongguoren liuxue riben shi* [A History of the Chinese Studying in Japan], translated by Tan Ruqian and Lin Qiyan. Beijing: Sanlian shudian.

Sathyamurthy, T. V. 1997. "Indian Nationalism: State of the Debate." *Economic and Political Weekly* 32(14): 715–21.

SCBC. 2000. *A Chronicle of Zhang Wentian (Zhang wen tian nian pu)*. Beijing: Zhong gong dang shi chubanshe.

Scherrer, Jutta. 1999. "The Relationship between the Intelligentsia and Workers: the Case of the Party Schools in Capri and Bologna." in *Workers and Intelligentsia in Late Imperial Russia*, edited by Reginald Zelnik. Berkeley, CA: International and Area Studies, University of California at Berkeley.

Semyonov, Alexander, and Jeremy Smith. 2017. "Nationalism and Empire before and after 1917." *Studies in Ethnicity and Nationalism* 17(3): 369–80.

Seton-Watson, Hugh. 1964. *Nationalism and Communism: Essays, 1946–1963*. London Methuen.

———. 1967. *The Russian Empire, 1801–1917*. Oxford: Clarendon.

Severin, N. A. 1956. *Otechestvennye puteshestvenniki i issledovateli*. Moscow: Gosudarstvennoe uchebno-pedagogicheskoe izdatel'stvo ministerstva prosveshcheniia RSFSR.

Shaumian, Stepan. 1978. *Izbrannye proizvedeniia v dvukh tomakh*. Moscow: Politizdat.

Sheĭnis, Z. 1989. *Maksim Maksimovich Litvinov: revoliutsioner, diplomat, chelovek*. Moscow: Izd-vo polit. lit-ry.

Shelokhaev, V. V. (Ed.). 1996. *Politicheskie partii Rossii, konets XIX—pervoi tret' XX veka: entsiklopediia*. Moscow: ROSSPEN.

Shen, Ziqiang (Ed.). 1990. *Zhejiang yishi fengchao*. Hangzhou: Zhejiang daxue chubanshe.

———. 2014. *E luo si jie mi dang an xuan bian: zhong su guan xi*. Shanghai: Zhong guo chu ban ji tuan dong fang chu ban zhong xin.

———. 2015. "Jin richeng zoushang quanli dingfeng: qingchu yiji." *Er shi yi shi ji* 151(10): 68–85.

———. 2020. *Lengzhan de zhuanxing zhongsu gongmeng jianli yu yuandong geju bianhua*. Beijing: Jiuzhou chubanshe.

Sheng, Renxue. 1985. *Zhang guotao nianpu ji yanlun*. Beijing: Jie fang jun chubanshe.

Shestakov, Andrei Vasil'evich. 1955. *Istoriia SSSR kratkii kurs uchebnik dlia 4 klassa*. Moscow: Uchpedgiz.

Shevzov, Vera. 2020. "The Orthodox Church and Religion in Revolutionary Russia, 1894–1924." In *The Oxford Handbook of Russian Religious Thought*, edited by Caryl Emerson, George Pattison, and Randall A. Poole, 39–60. Oxford: Oxford University Press.

Shi Ou, Zhang Zengtian, and Wu Xiao'ou. 2015. *Xinzhongguo zhongxiaoxue jiaokeshu tuwenshi*. Guangzhou: Nanfang chubanshe.

Shkandrij, Myroslav. 2001. *Russia and Ukraine: Literature and the Discourse of Empire from Napoleonic to Postcolonial Times*. Montreal: McGill-Queen's University Press.

Shlestov, Dmitrii. 1990. *Vremia Alekseia Rykova*. Moscow: Progress.

ShShDY, Shanghai shiwei dangshi yanjiushi (Ed.). 2010. *Zhang Wentian shehuizhuyi lungao*. Beijing: Zhonggong dangshi chubanshe.

Shteppa, Konstantin F. 1962. *Russian Historians and the Soviet State*. New Brunswick, GA: Rutgers University Press.

Sidel, John. 2021. *Republicanism, Communism, Islam: Cosmopolitan Origins of Revolution in Southeast Asia*. Ithaca, NY: Cornell University Press.

Singh, Sudhir Kumar. 2015. "Colonialisms, Nationalism and Vietnam's Struggle for Freedom." *Proceedings of the Indian History Congress* 76: 620–30.

Sipovskii, V. D. 1884. *V pomoshch' uchashchimcia rodnaia starina: vypusk tretii* St. Petersburg: Izdanie poluboiarinova.

Sitao. 2010. *Liu Lantao shengping jishi*. Beijing: Zhongguo wenshi chubanshe.

Skocpol, Theda. 1979. *States and Social Revolutions: A Comparative Analysis of France, Russia and China*. Cambridge: Cambridge University Press.

Slater, Dan, and Nicholas Rush Smith. 2016. "The Power of Counterrevolution: Elitist Origins of Political Order in Postcolonial Asia and Africa." *American Journal of Sociology* 121(5): 1472–516.

Slezkine, Yuri. 1994. "The USSR as a Communal Apartment, or How a Socialist State Promoted Ethnic Particularism." *Slavic Review* 53(2): 414–52.

———. 2019. *The House of Government: A Saga of the Russian Revolution*. Princeton, NJ: Princeton University Press.

Smele, Jonathan. 2015. *The 'Russian' Civil Wars, 1916–1926: Ten Years That Shook the World*. New York, NY: Oxford University Press.

Smilga, Ivar. 1920. *K voprosy o stroitel'stve krasnoi armii*. Moscow: Literaturno-izdatel'skii otdel politicheskogo upravleniia revoliutsionnogo voennogo soveta respublik.

Smirnov, M. A. 1985. *O Viacheslave Menzhinskom vospominaniia ocherki stat'i*. Moscow: Politizdat.

Smith, C. Jay. 1955. "Russia and the Origins of the Finnish Civil War of 1918." *The American Slavic and East European Review* 14(4): 481–502.

Smith, Craig A. 2017. "China as the Leader of the Weak and Small: The Ruoxiao Nations and Guomindang Nationalism." *Cross-Currents: East Asian History and Culture Review* 6(November): 530–57.

Smith, Jeremy. 1999. *The Bolsheviks and the National Question, 1917–23.* New York, NY: St. Martin's Press.

Smith, S. A. 2008. *Revolution and the People in Russia and China: A Comparative History.* Cambridge: Cambridge University Press.

Sohrabi, Nader. 2018. "Reluctant Nationalists, Imperial Nation-State, and Neo-Ottomanism: Turks, Albanians, and the Antinomies of the End of Empire." *Social Science History* 42(4): 835–70.

Sokolob, Boris. 2007. *Budennyi: krasnyi miurat.* Moscow: Molodaia gvardiia.

Somin, Ilya. 1996. *Stillborn Crusade: The Tragic Failure of Western Intervention in the Russian Civil War, 1918–1920.* New Brunswick, NJ: Transaction.

Spillman, Lyn. 1996. "'Neither the Same Nation Nor Different Nations': Constitutional Conventions in the United States and Australia." *Comparative Studies in Society and History* 38(1): 149–81.

Stalin, Iosif. 2013. *Stalin Trudy (1894–1904).* Moscow: Prometei Info.

Startsev, V. I. 1970. "Rabota V. I. Lenina nad istochnikami po russkoi istorii." *Voprosy istorii* 4:152–64.

Stepanov, H. 1989. *Podvoiskii.* Moscow: Molodaia gvardiia.

Struve, Petr. 2000. *Patriotica: rossiia, rodina, chuzhbina.* St. Petersburg: RKhGI.

Stuart, Robert. 2006. *Marxism and National Identity: Socialism, Nationalism, and National Socialism in the French Sin de Siecle.* Albany, NY: State University of New York.

Stuart-Fox, Martin. 1983. "Marxism and Theravada Buddhism: The Legitimation of Political Authority in Laos." *Pacific Affairs* 56(3): 428–54.

Su Yu. 2005. *Su Yu zhanzheng huiyilu.* Beijing: Zhishi chanquan chubanshe.

Su Zhenlan. 2006. "Yao Zhe zhongjiang jianchi fenzhan daqingshan." *Dang shi bo cai* (06): 45–50.

Sultanbekova, B. F. 1992. *Tainy natsional'noi politiki TsK RKP stenograficheskii otchet sekretnogo IV soveshchaniia TsK PKP 1923 g.* Moscow: INSAN.

Sumner, William G. 1906. *Folkways.* Boston, MA: Ginn and Company.

Suny, Ronald Grigor. 1993. *The Revenge of The Past: Nationalism, Revolution, and the Collapse of the Soviet Union.* Stanford, CA: Stanford University Press.

Sverdlov, Iakov. 1957. *Izbrannye proizvedeniia.* Moscow: Izdatel'stvo politicheskoi literatury.

Swain, Geoffrey. 1992. "The Cominform: Tito's International?" *The Historical Journal* 35(3): 641–63.

Sypchenko, A. V., and K. N. Morozov. 2003. *Trudovaia narodno-sotsialisticheskaia partiia dokumenty i materialy.* Moscow: ROSSPEN.

Szporluk, Roman. 1988. *Communism and Nationalism: Karl Marx Versus Friedrich List.* New York, NY: Oxford University Press.

———. 1993. "Belarus', Ukraine and The Russian Question: A Comment." *Post-Soviet Affairs* 9(4): 366–74.

Tagore, Rabindranath. 2001. *Nationalism.* New Delhi: Macmillan.

Tan Shanxiang. 2010. *Teng Daiyuan zaoqi wenji.* Beijing: Renmin chubanshe.

Thompson, Ewa. 2000. *Imperial Knowledge: Russian Literature and Colonialism.* Westport, CT: Greenwood Press.

Tilly, Charles. 1985. "War Making and State Making as Organized Crime." In *Bringing the State Back In*, edited by Peter Evans, Dietrich Rueschemeyer, and Theda Skocpol, 169–91. New York, NY: Cambridge University Press.

———. 1994. "States and Nationalism in Europe 1492–1992." *Theory and Society* 23: 131–46.

Bibliography

Timasheff, Nicholas. 1948. *The Great Retreat: The Growth and Decline of Communism in Russia*. New York, NY: [s.n.].

Tishkov, A. 1985. *Dzerzhinskii*. Moscow: Molodaia gvardiia.

Tismaneanu, Vladimir. 2003. *Stalinism for all Seasons: A Political History of Romanian Communism*. Berkeley, CA: University of California Press.

Tito, Josip Broz. 1984. *Tie tuo xuan ji [Josip Broz Tito izabrana djela]*. Beijing: Renmin chubanshe.

Titov, A. S. 1981. *Bor'ba za edinyi front v Kitae 1935–1937*. Moscow: Nauka.

Todorova, Maria. 1992. "Historiography of the Countries of Eastern Europe: Bulgaria." *The American Historical Review* 97(4): 1105–17.

Tőkés, Rudolf L. 1967. *Béla Kun and the Hungarian Soviet Republic: The Origins and Role of the Communist Party of Hungary in the Revolutions of 1918–1919*. New York, NY: The Hoover Institution on War, Revolution, and Peace.

Tolz, Vera. 2011. *Russia's Own Orient: The Politics of Identity and Oriental Studies in the Late Imperial and Early Soviet Periods*. Oxford: Oxford University Press.

———. 2015. "The Eurasians and Liberal Scholarship of the Late Imperial Period: Continuity and Change across the 1917 Divide." In *Between Europe and Asia: The Origins, Theories, and Legacies of Russian Eurasianism*, edited by Mark Bassin, Sergey Glebov, and Marlene Laruelle, 27–47. Pittsburgh, PA: University of Pittsburgh Press.

Trencsényi, Balázs. 2010. "Writing the Nation and Reframing Early Modern Intellectual History in Hungary." *Studies in East European Thought* 62: 135–54.

Trofimova, L. I. . 1973. "Stranitsa diplomaticheskoi deiatel'nosti G. V. Chicherina" *Voprosy istorii*: 114–23.

Trotsky, Leon. 1937. *Revolution Betrayed: What is the Soviet Union and Where Is It Going?* www.marxists.org/archive/trotsky/1936/revbet/.

———. 1960. *My Life*. New York, NY: Grosset & Dunlap.

———. 2020 [1973]. *Problems of Everyday Life: Creating the Foundations for a New Society in Revolutionary Russia*. New York, NY: Pathfinder.

Tu, Xiaofei. 2019. "Between the Comintern, the Japanese Communist Party, and the Chinese Communist Party: Nosaka Sanzo's Betrayal Games." In *Left Transnationalism: The Communist International and the National, Colonial, and Racial Questions*, edited by Oleksa Drachewych and Ian McKay. Montreal: McGill-Queen's University Press.

Tudev, Lologiin. 1982. *Natsional'noe i internatsional'noe v Mongol'skoi literature*. Moscow: Izdatel'stvo Nauka glavnaia redaktsiia vostochnoi literatury.

Tumarkin, Nina. 1983. *Lenin Lives!: The Lenin Cult in Soviet Russia*. Cambridge, MA: Harvard University Press.

Turtsevich, Ar. 1913. *Kratkii uchebnik russkoi istorii*. Vil'na: Sed'moe izdanie bez peremen.

Uriabova, Anna. 2018. "Brestskii mir i russkaia porevoliutsionnaia emigratsiia." In *Bretskii mir. Istoriia i geopolitika. 1918–2018*, edited by E. A. Bondareva and E. H. Rudaia, 252–69. Moscow: Veche.

Vatlin, Aleksandr. 2009. *Komintern idei resheniia sud'by*. Moscow: ROSSPEN.

Venkov, A. V. 2000. *Belye generaly*. Rostov-na-Dony: Feniks.

Vitte, Sergei. 1960. *Vospominaniia*. Moscow: Izdatel'stvo sotsial'no-ekonomicheskoi literatury.

Vu, Tuong. 2016. "The Revolutionary Path to State Formation in Vietnam." *Journal of Vietnamese Studies* 11(3/4): 267–97.

Vujačić, Veljko. 2015. *Nationalism, Myth, and the State in Russia and Serbia: Antecedents of the Dissolution of the Soviet Union and Yugoslavia.* New York, NY: Cambridge University Press.

Walker, Lydia. 2022. "Minority Nationalisms in Postwar Decolonization." *American Historical Review* 127(1): 351–54.

Wan, Yi. 1998. *Wanyi jiangjun huiyilu.* Beijing: Zhonggong dangshi chubanshe.

Wang Binglin. 2021. *Zhonggong dangshi xueke jiben lilun wenti yanjiu.* Beijing: Beijing renmin chubanshe.

Wang, Chaoxing (Ed.). 1968. *Mao Zedong sixiang wansui.* Unpublished collection.

Wang, Jianying. 2007. *Minzhu geming shiqi lijie zhonggong zhongyang lingdao jiti shuping.* Beijing: Zhongguo dangshi chubanshe.

Wang, Jiping, and Qi Ruoxiong. 2004. "Lun zhonggong zhongyang lianluoyuan deng liqun zai xinjiang heping jiefang zhong de zuoyong." *Xinjiang shifan daxue xuebao* 25(3): 72–75.

Wang, Ke. 2001. *Min zu yu guo jia: zhong guo duo min zu tong yi guo jia de si xiang xi pu.* Beijing: Zhongguo she hui ke xue chubanshe.

Wang, Lingyun. 1986. *Guan Xiangying zhuan.* Zhengzhou: Henan renmin chubanshe.

Wang, Ming, and Xu Teli. 1940. *Tuopai zai zhongguo.* Chongqing: Xin zhongguo chubanshe.

Wang, Renshu. 1948. *Yinni shehui fazhan gaiguan.* Nanjing: Shenghuo shudian.

Wang, Shoukuan. 2020. *Zhongguo shaoshu minzu shixueshi.* Beijing: Huaxia chubanshe.

Warth, Robert D. 1967. "On the Historiography of the Russian Revolution." *Slavic Review* 26(2): 247–64.

Watenpaugh, Keith David. 2006. *Being Modern in the Middle East: Revolution, Nationalism, Colonialism, and the Arab Middle Class.* Princeton, NJ: Princeton University Press.

Weber, Eugen. 1964. "Nationalism, Socialism, and National-Socialism in France." *French Historical Studies* 2(3): 273–307.

———. 1976. *Peasants into Frenchmen: the Modernization of Rural France, 1870–1914.* Stanford, CA: Stanford University Press.

Weitz, Eric D. 1997. *Creating German Communism, 1890–1990.* Princeton, NJ: Princeton University Press.

Wen Shaohua. 1994. *Chen Gongbo zhuan.* Beijing: Dongfang chubanshe.

Westergard-Thorpe, Wayne. 2016. "Syndicalist Internationalism and Moscow, 1919–1922: The Breach." *Canadian Journal of History* 14(2): 199–234.

White, Elizabeth. 2011. *The Socialist Alternative to Bolshevik Russia: The Socialist Revolutionary Party, 1921–1939.* London: Routledge.

Whyte, Martin King. 2021. "From Physics to Russian Studies and on into China Research: My Meandering Journey Toward Sociology." *Annual Review of Sociology* 47: 1–15.

Wildman, Allan K. 1976. "The Bolsheviks of the Twelfth Army and Latvian Social Democracy." In *Reconsiderations on the Russian Revolution,* edited by Ralph Carter Elwood, 173–78. Cambridge, MA: Slavica.

Willett, Robert L. 2003. *Russian Sideshow: America's Undeclared War, 1918–1920.* Washington DC: Brassey's.

Wimmer, Andreas. 2018. *Nation Building: Why Some Countries Come Together while Others Fall Apart.* Princeton, NJ: Princeton University Press.

Wright, Alistair S. 2012. "The Establishment of Bolshevik Power on the Russian Periphery: Soviet Karelia, 1918–1919." PhD diss., University of Glasgow.

Bibliography

Wright, Mary C. 1962. "Debate: Revolution from Without?" *Comparative Studies in Society and History* 4(2): 247–52.

Wu, Jimin. 2008. *Lianyu zhongguo tuopai de kunan yu fendou*. Singapore: Bafangwenhua.

Wu, Lanfu. 1989. *Wu lanfu huiyilu*. Beijing: Zhonggong dangshi ziliao chubanshe.

Wu, Minxia, and Wang Zhiping. 2020. "Yan'an shiqi wodang shi ruhe peiyang shaoshu minzu ganbu de" *Dang shi wen hui* (12): 48–53.

Wu, Peng. 2020. "Hongqi budao bian tianya gudao fenzhan de qiongya zongdui." *Yan Huang Chun Qiu* (08): 19–23.

Wu Xiuquan (Ed.). 1998. *Wu Xiuquan jiangjun zishu*. Shenyang: liaoning renmin chubanshe.

Xie, Huaidan. 1991. *Sui yue qi hen: yi ge mo si ke zhong shan da xue nv sheng de hui yi*. Fuzhou: Fujian renmin chubanshe.

Xie, Juezai. 1984. *Xie juezai riji*. Beijing: Renmin chubanshe.

Xie, Shijin, and Qian Zhanyuan. 1988. *Neimenggu geming lishi wenjian huiji 1928–1937*. Huhehaote: Neimenggu zizhiqu dang'anguan.

Xinghuoliaoyuan (Ed.). 1995. *Jiefangjun jiangling zhuan*. Beijing: Jiefangjun chubanshe.

Xu, Aixian, and Li Baoping (Eds.). 1983. *Yang Xianzhen wenji*. Shijiazhuang: Hebei renmin chubanshe.

Xu, Linxiang, and Zhu Yu. 2003. *Li Kenong zhuan*. Hefei: Anhui renmin chubanshe.

Xu, Xiangqian. 1987. *Lishi de huigu*. Beijing: Jiefangjun chubanshe.

———. 2013. "Belonging Before Believing Group Ethos and Bloc Recruitment in the Making of Chinese Communism." *American Sociological Review* 78(5): 773–96.

Xu, Zehao (Ed.). 2001. *Wang Jiaxiang nianpu*. Beijing: Zhongyang wenxian chubanshe.

Xue, Nongshan. 1935 [1996]. *Zhongguo nongmin zhanzheng zhishi yanjiu*. Shanghai: Shanghai shudian chubanshe.

Ya, Yuanbo. 2017. *Donglan xian geming renwu zhi*. Nanning: Guangxi renmin chubanshe.

Yan, Fan (Ed.). 2017. *Zhongyang souq wenyi yanjiu lunji*. Wuhan: Changjiang wenyi chubanshe.

Yan, Shuming. 2015. "Lun Feng baiju zai qiongya kangzhan zhong de zhengzhi zhihui." *Zhonggong dangshi* (08): 18–20.

Yang, Benjamin. 1998. *Deng: A Political Biography*. Armonk, NY: M. E. Sharpe.

Yang, Kuisong. 2021. "Guanyu zaoqi gongchandang ren makesi zhuyi zhongguohua wenti." *Shilin* (1): 6–13.

Yang, Xiaozhe. 2020. "Li Jingquan shuaibu kaipi daqingshan kangri genjudi." *Dang shi bo lan* (9): 45–50.

Ye, Yonglie. 2016. *Chen Boda zhuan*. Chengdu: Sichuan renmin chubanshe.

Yilmaz, Harun. 2015. *National Identities in Soviet Historiography*. London: Routledge.

Yu, Hongjun. 2015. "Ma lai xi ya gong chan dang ji qi wu zhuang dou zheng de xing qi he chen ji." *Dang dai shi jie yu she hui zhu yi* 2: 42–51.

Yun, Daiying. 1927. *Zhongguo minzu geming yundong shi*. Guangzhou: Kaiming shudian.

Yun, Shui. 1996. *Chushi qiguo jishi: jiangjun dashi wang youping*. Beijing: Shijie zhishi chubanshe.

Zarnitskii, S., and A. Sergeev. 1966. *Chicherin*. Moscow: Molodaia gvardiia.

Zarrow, Peter. 1990. *Anarchism and Chinese Political Culture*. New York, NY: Columbia University.

248   *Revolution in China and Russia*

———. 2012. *After Empire: the Conceptual Transformation of the Chinese State, 1885–1924.* Stanford, CA: Stanford University Press.

Zhang, Chenchen. 2014. "Situated Interpretations of Nationalism, Imperialism, and Cosmopolitanism: Revisiting the Writings of Liang in the Encounter Between Worlds." *Journal of Historical Sociology* 27(3): 343–60.

Zhang, Guotao. 1991. *Wo de huiyi.* Shanghai: Dongfang chubanshe.

Zhang, Yue (Ed.). 2009. *Zhongguo shixueshi ziliaohuibian.* Beijing: Beijing shifan daxue chubanshe.

Zhao, Fushan (Ed.). 2003. *Xibaipo renwu.* Beijing: Zhongguo guoji guangbo chubanshe.

Zhao, Gang. 2006. "Reinventing China: Imperial Qing Ideology and the Rise of Modern Chinese National Identity in the Early Twentieth Century." *Modern China* 3(2): 3–30.

Zhao, Junqing. 2015. *Zhou Baozhong Zhuan.* Haerbin: Heilongjiang renmin chubanshe.

Zhelitski, B. I. 1989. "Bela Kun." *Voprosy istorii* 1:58.

———. 1997. "Postwar Hungary, 1944–1946." in *The Establishment of Communist Regimes in Eastern Europe, 1944–1949,* edited by Norman M. Naimark. Boulder, CT: Westview Press.

Zhitomir. 1928. *Istoriia 44-ogo artilleriiskogo polka.* Zhitomir: Izdanie politicheskogo otdela 44-oi divizii.

Zhonggong hainanqu dangwei dangshi bangongshi. 1988. *Feng Baiju yanjiu shiliao.* Guangzhou: Guangdong renmin chubanshe.

Zhou, Fohai. 2015. *Wang yi ji zhou fohai huiyilu.* Taibei: Xiuwei chubanshe.

Zhou, Li 1991. *Zhou li huiyilu.* Changsha: Hunan chubanshe.

Zhou, Luyang. 2018. "Boosting Nationalism with Non-Nationalist ideology: A Comparative Biographical Analysis of the Chinese Communist Revolutionaries." *Nations and Nationalism* 24(3): 767–91.

———. 2019a. "Historical Origins of the Party-Army Relations in the Soviet Union and China." *Communist and Post-Communist Studies* 52(3): 197–207.

———. 2019b. "Nationalism and Communism as Foes and Friends: Comparing the Bolshevik and Chinese Revolutionaries." *European Journal of Sociology* 60(3): 313–50.

Zhou, Weiren. 1992. *Jia Tuofu zhuan.* Beijing: Zhonggong dangshi chubanshe.

Zhou, Yiping. 2014. *Qu Qiubai yu zhonggong dangshi yanjiu.* Beijing: Shehui kexue wenxian chubanshe.

Zhou, Yongxiang. 1992. *Qu Qiubai nianpu xinbian.* Shanghai: Xuelin chubanshe.

Zhu, Hanguo, and Qun Yang. 2006. *Zhonghua minguoshi.* Chengdu: Sichuan renmin chubanshe.

Zhu, Zhenghui. 2000. *Lv Zhenyu xueshu sixiang pingzhuan.* Beijing: Beijing tushuguan chubanshe.

Ziesche, Philipp. 2006. "Exporting American Revolutions: Gouverneur Morris, Thomas Jefferson, and the National Struggle for Universal Rights in Revolutionary France." *Journal of the Early Republic* 26: 419–47.

Zubkova, Elena. 2004. "The Soviet Regime and Soviet Society in the Postwar Years: Innovations and Conservatism, 1945–1953." *Journal of Modern European History* 2(1): 134–52.

Zubok, V. M. 1996. *Inside the Kremlin's Cold War: From Stalin to Khrushchev.* Cambridge, MA: Harvard University Press.

Index

affirmative action empire 194
Allies' intervention 9
anarchists 16, 19, 59, 67, 74, 111, 139
    Chen, Gongbo 59
    Wang, Jingwei 60
    Zhou, Fohai 59
Anderson, Perry 2, 11, 32, 56, 135
annexations 55
    applications to join the Soviet
        Union 55
    Karelia 4, 55, 154–55
anti-cosmopolitan movement 162
anti-traditionalist-minded leadership 18
    despotism 79, 220
    "great tradition", not "little" one 80
    ignorance 79
    mobilizational scale 19, 79, 114, 123
    patriarchy 48, 79
    patron-clientism 79
    radical break with the past 80
anti-war socialist propaganda 46
    Valerian Kuibyshev 43, 150
Antonov-Ovseenko, Vladimir 149
April 12th Massacre 124
archeologists 86, 138, 220
Arjomand, Said 11, 13
Armenia 13, 152
    Dashnaktutiun 156
assimilationism 29, 58, 163, 168, 178,
    185–87, 211
atheists 87
    iconoclastic campaigns 87
    Pisarev, Dmitry 18, 87–88, 90
autonomous minority regimes 169
    Eastern Qian Committee 168
    Miao's and Yi's rights to separate
        from China 168

Tibetan state 167
Azerbaijan 53–55, 91, 109, 141, 152,
    156, 158

Baltic states 4, 18, 36, 55, 138
Bandung Conference 196
Baranskii, Nikolai 91
Basmachi rebellion 156
Beijing Mongolian–Tibetan Middle
    School 62, 173, 175
Beijing operas 119
Beiyang government 15, 218
    military unification 166
    warlordism 60, 167
Belarus 33, 55–56, 153, 154,
    159, 222
Belogurova, Anna 59
bilateral economic relationship 160
    Turkey 8, 17, 32, 54, 62, 67, 153,
        156, 158–60, 167, 183, 217
biography 23, 121–22, 130
Black American nationalism 196
Bo, Yibo 165
Bogdanov, Aleksandr 27, 93
Bolsheviks 2, 5–6, 8–9, 10–18, 20–26,
    29–35, 37, 40–54, 57
    Bolsheviks' citations of classical
        literature 139
    Bolsheviks' knowledge of the
        periphery 139
Boxer Rebellion 60, 164, 222
Brandenberger, David 9, 82,
    84, 142
Brest–Litovsk Peace 45
    Brest Peace 69, 148, 151
Brubaker, Rogers 77
Bubnov, Andrei 91, 151

250   *Index*

Budennyi, Semen 156
buffer state 155, 174, 182
Bukharin, Mikhail 46, 88–91, 93
bulletin dramas 116
   Li, Bozhao 116
Bund 52
Buryat–Mongolian nationalism 155

central committee members 26,
   28, 43
Cheka 45, 148, 159, 156–57
Chen, Boda 122–23, 183
Chen, Duxiu 9, 27, 111–12, 166
Chen, Geng 173
Chen Yun 165
Chiang Kai-shek 21
   China's Destiny 335
Chicherin, Georgi 27, 49–50, 92,
   154–55, 158, 184
Chinese Anti-Imperialist Alliance 59
Chinese Communist Party 2, 14, 32,
   42, 65, 125, 165
Chinese confederation 166
Chita 140
Closer to the People 97
commissar 49, 60, 98, 115, 118, 139,
   150–53, 162
Commissariat of Enlightenment 96
Communist historians 96, 121
   He, Ganzhi 120, 125
   Hou, Wailu 120–21
   Lv, Zhenyu 120–21
Confucian legacies 122
Congress of Far Eastern Laboring
   Nations 167
Constitution of 1923 159
cosmopolitans 16, 59, 67, 74
   Kamo 47
   Kun, Bela 48
   Kollontai, Alexandra 46, 48, 70,
      93, 184
   Radek, Karl 47, 69–70,
      93, 156
   weak state allegiance 42–43,
      60, 74
cultural nationalism 51, 78
   regeneration 78
   vernacularism 78
curse of the conqueror 107
   red scare 16, 36, 66, 74

Daqingshan guerrilla base 177
decolonization 3, 35, 50, 95, 131,
   205, 215
Deng, Liqun 27, 182–83
Deng, Xiaoping 165, 172
Deng, Zhongxia 124, 130, 173
diplomats 27, 49, 94, 147–48, 184, 220
Dong, Biwu 162

economic decolonization 25
elite-centered approaches 46
Empire's support for national
   liberation 39
Entente 45, 47, 49, 99, 137, 144,
   147–49, 153–54, 156
equalizing the economic foundation 30
Estonia 49, 148–49, 154, 162
ethnic Balkanization 7, 12, 17, 61, 63,
   74, 188
   China inland 74
   Eastern Turkestan Republic 73
   Korean borderland 61
   Mongolian belt 61
   Southeast Asian corner 61
   Three-Region Revolution 62, 72
ethnic mobilization 167, 198
ethnicity-dissolving Soviet identity 161
European socialists 10, 14–15, 41,
   45, 136
   Second International 41, 46, 57,
      107, 136
exile 139
   transethnic cooperation 140

Fan, Wenlan 27, 119–20, 123
Far Eastern Republic (DVR) 155
   overseas diaspora 58
   Pan-Asianism 58, 208
   small and weak nations 38, 167
Feng, Baiju 181
Feng, Yuxiang 173–74
fifth column 21, 134, 157, 188, 223
five major ethnic groups 163
forced assimilation 1–2, 127, 209
Frunze, Mikhail 140
   national armies 141

Gao, Gang 56, 72, 165, 176
   political equality plus economic
      aids 176

Gellner, Ernest 120
Genghis Khan 174
Gorky, Maxim 104
Granat 46, 51–53, 103
Great Hanism 30
Great Retreat 81–83, 129
Greater East Asian Co-Prosperity
    Sphere 209
Guangdong 17, 60, 65, 169, 171
guerrilla states 171, 173, 181, 195, 205
Guo, Huaruo 27
Guo, Moruo 120–21
    A Study of *China's Ancient
    History* 121
Gusev, Serge 153

Haimson, Leopoid 145
Hainan Island 22, 181
Hakka 170
Han Chinese 5, 7, 9, 11, 177
    Han-centric nation 127
Han Green riots 169
Hanized CCP elites 170
    Jiang, Hua 171
    Liao, Hansheng 170
    Su, Yu 170
    Teng, Daiyuan 170
He, Long 170
homegrown 80, 195, 204–6
homeland of all nationalities 105
Hroch, Miroslav 10, 78
Hu, Qiaomu 125
    *Thirty Years of the Chinese
    Communist Party* 125
Huangpu Academy 60
Hui 163, 167, 169, 171, 173–74,
    177–78

Iaroslavskii, Emel'ian 67, 140
imperial ethnicity 33
    imperial nations 33, 107
    nationalizing empires 33
indigenization 14, 51, 53, 155, 160,
    171, 210
indivisible Russia 143–44
in-group solidarity 134
Inner Mongolian communist group
    62, 175
    Ji Taiya 62, 175
    Kui Bi 62, 175

insurrectional groups 153
integration with Europe 15, 45, 48
    Joffe, Adolph 49
    Krasin, Leonid 46, 49, 70
    Litvinov, Maksim 46, 48–49,
        158, 184
interethnic amalgamation 127
internationalists 16–17, 45, 67, 69,
    115–18, 206
    mountainous Marxism 42
inter-revolution relation 35, 196
Istpart, Commission for the Collection
    and Study of Materials on
    the History of the October
    Revolution and the History of the
    Russian Communist Party 103
Iudenich, Nikolai 149

Jian, Bozan 27, 120
Jiangxi 19, 71, 169–71, 179

Kadets 143, 145, 218
Kai Feng 165
Kalinin, Mikhail 91, 141
Karelian Commune 154–55
Kirov, Seigei 91–92, 101, 141
KMT 9–10, 21–22, 26, 35, 37, 43–44,
    58, 60, 66
KMT–CCP civil war 10, 129, 149,
    175, 181
Kotovskii, Grigorii 45
Krasin, Leonid 46, 39, 70
Krasnoshchekov, Alexander 155
Krasnov, Petr 149
Krupskaya, Nadezhda 88, 93–94, 96, 99
    communist ethics 94
    productionism 94

Lachmann, Richard 24
late Qing state 163
    Qing citizens 163
Latvian Shooting Regiment 149
Latvian Social Democratic Party 53
League of Left-wing Writers 113
leisure reading 87
    revolutionary democrats 18, 88, 100
Lenin, Vladimir 6, 9, 16, 41, 43–44,
    46–48, 52, 55, 69
    historical test 87
    return to Lenin 92

Index

lessons from historical rebellions 19, 115
  Li, Zicheng 20, 115
  Taiping Tianguo 115
Li, Dazhao 27, 58, 111–12, 115, 165, 173
Li, Weihan 27, 177–78
  Outline of the Huihui Nationality Question 320
liberal monarchy 145
Lin, Boqu 66, 164
Liu, Shaoqi 168, 183
Long March (of the Chinese Red Army) 8, 70, 167–69, 173
Lunacharskii, Anatorii 27
  new citizen religion 89

Manchukuo 178–79, 209
Manchurians 59
  Guan, Xiangying 172
  Minority cadres from the Northeast 172
  Wan, Yi 172
Mann, Michael 11, 24
Mao, Zedong 63, 164, 168, 185
  Cultural Revolution 30, 41, 110–11, 126, 171, 183, 195, 202, 211
  self-governance in Hunan province 166
Marxist–Leninist 41, 113, 195, 204, 206–7
masculinization 186
mass journalism 97
May Fourth 20, 61, 115, 117, 166, 170
Mensheviks 102, 144–46, 148, 152, 155, 159
minzu 4, 127, 211
Molotov, Viacheslav 141
Mongolian People's Republic 62, 72
  Greater Mongolia 206
Moore, Barrington 23
Mudge, Stephanie 24–25
  refraction 25
multi-ethnic China 6, 14, 75, 126, 162, 164–65, 170, 181, 183
multinational China 62, 164–65, 175, 188
multinational Russia 90–91, 137–39, 143, 187
Muslim battalions 151

Narimanov, Nariman 50, 53–54, 156, 158
nation as a multilayer identity 21
national communists 64, 156, 206
national united front 75
  closed-doorism 76
neo-classicalism after 1949 119
neo-traditionalism 82
  Chineseness 4, 30, 36, 83, 111
  Dmitri Donskoi 84
  Russianness 4, 9, 83, 128, 144
  Timasheff, Nicolai 82
New Cultural Movement 82
Nogin, Victor 43, 141
nomads 22, 86, 176
Non-Aligned Movement 197
Northern Iran 54, 65
Northeast 10, 17, 22, 36–37, 56, 62, 73–74, 114, 119
  Manchuria 70–72, 164, 179
  Northeastern People's Revolutionary Army 179
  Zhou, Baozhong 27, 179, 180
  Zhu, Dehai 27, 63, 180

Octoberists 143, 147
Old-school historians 105–8
Ol'minskii, Mikhail 101
  State, Bureaucracy, and Absolutism in History of Russia 101
One-China framework 7, 21, 173–74, 176, 181–82, 212
"One-Russia" plan 159
  electrification 91, 157, 161
Ordzhonikidze, Grigorii 152–53

Pan-Slavism 54, 85–86
partition of China 164, 166
partitioning Russia 147
party schools in Paris and Capri 46
Piatakov, Grigorii 159
Plekhanov, George 6, 18, 89, 102, 123
Podvoiskii, Nikolai 27, 45
Pokrovsky, Mikhail 6, 18, 89
  Pokrovskii school 106
Political Department of the Red Army 95
popular democratic polities 71–72

Index

post-imperial nationalism 165
  disintegration of China 165–66
  federalism 53, 166–67
  Ming-dynasty domain 166
  provincial independence 166
Proletarian Culture School 88, 94, 166
propagandists 27, 36, 95, 100–1
prosopographic comparisons 29
protracted revolution 1, 8, 18, 75, 83
Provisional Government of 1917 35
Putin, Vladimir 31, 210

Qiao, Guanhua 27, 185
Qing Dynasty 6–7, 66, 110, 163
Qinghai 167, 177, 182
Qu, Qiubai 9, 59, 111, 113, 116, 125, 164
  Introduction of Social Science 113

radical Russian writers 94
Rakovskii, Christian 54, 158–59
Razin, Stepan 88, 161
Red Army 45, 95–98, 103, 106, 116, 140, 149–53, 155, 168–69
red cultural workers 99, 117–18
Rehe Autonomic Republic 72
reinventing China 130, 222
revenge from history 30
revolutionary literati 101, 107–8, 124, 126, 199
Revolutionary Russophobia 12, 36
Revolution–counterrevolution relations 35
Revolution–society relations 35
right-leaned centralists 147
Rozhkov, Nikolai 100, 102
  Russian History in Comparative Interpretation 102
Russian Civil War 14, 115–16, 144, 147, 153, 174
"Russian Highest School of Social Science" at Paris 139
Russian imperialism 53, 138
Russian nationalism 9, 84–85, 88, 90, 92–93, 103, 105–7, 142, 153
  disappointment with the tsar 143
  Eurasianism 85–86, 139
  separate Russia from tsardom 84
  Slavism 85–86

Russification 8–9, 17, 19, 92, 155, 157, 159–61, 210
  de-Russification 5, 30, 83, 86, 92
  linguistic Russification 8, 92
Russified internationalism 53
Russo–Japanese War 60, 163, 210
  Movement of Resisting Russia 164
Rykov, Aleksei 90
Ryskulov, Turar 54–55

Samara Steel Division 150–51
school textbooks (of the Soviet Union) 109
school textbooks (of Tsarist Russia) 106, 138–39
  Poles and other Western Slavic peoples 106
secessionist movement 1, 136, 168
  revolutionary separatism 144
  secessionism 21, 39, 127, 132, 134, 136–37, 183
self-determination 57, 95, 132, 137, 142, 153, 164–66, 168–69, 173–74
self-reliance 197
Shan'ganning border area 176
Shaumian, Stepan 53, 101, 159
  Evolutionism and Revolutionism in Social Science 101
Sheng, Shicai 55, 72, 182
Siberia 48, 55, 91–92, 138–39, 145, 147–48, 150, 155
Sino–Japanese War 6, 9, 20, 22, 60, 62, 70, 163–65, 175–79
Sino-Soviet split 6, 30, 73, 204
Skocpol, Theda 11, 23, 135–36
Slezkine, Yuri 5, 7, 87
socialism in one country 16, 42, 45, 47, 55–56, 95, 102
socialist realism 99
  folk style 99
  Shostakovich, Dmitrii 99
Socialist Revolutionaries 45, 145–46
  stateless world 58, 145
Soviet economic geographers 91
Soviet masters of cinema 97
Soviet men 99
Soviet patriotism 99, 108–9
  Siberian explorers 109

254 *Index*

Soviet-controlled nationalism 154
Soviet–German War 55, 104
Sovietization 72, 195, 205
Soviet–Polish pact 150
Stalin, Josef 9, 41, 50, 55–56, 61,
    70–73, 75, 95, 102
  Anarchism or Socialism? 101
  five-phrase formula 20, 120
  Marxism and Nationality
    Question 160
  nostalgia for the Georgian
    land 160
  Short Course 103, 125
  Stalinism 11, 83, 89, 108, 130
Stasova, Elena 87
state Russian nationalism 142
  autocracy 84, 137, 221–22
  demonization of the foe 85
  Ivan the Terrible 84, 139
  military expansion 84, 147
  Orthodox Church 84–85, 143
  patriotic education 109, 142
Struve, Peter 138
Stuchka, Peter 52
studying in Japan 59, 66, 112, 164
Sultan-Galiev, Mirsaid 156
Sun, Yat-sen 65, 185
  assimilated into Han 163
  model of the United States 163
Sverdlov, Iakov 139–40

Taiwan 28, 164–65, 181, 183
Tartar-Bashkir republic 160
Tibet 163, 165, 167–68, 177,
    181, 212
Transcaucasian Federation 4, 92, 141,
    153, 158
transnational and transethnic
    backgrounds 15
  Felix Dzerzhinskii 45, 50, 69, 90
  Soviet-selected non-Han or
    transethnic groups 14
Trotsky, Leon 46–47, 50–52, 59, 67,
    81, 89, 94–95, 102–3, 211
  *History of the Russian
    Revolution* 59
  Soviet-made internationalists 67
Trotskyists (of China), 16, 67–69,
    74–75, 123–24, 129

Trudniki (Labor Popular-Socialist
    Party) 144
  class mediation 144
Turkic socialist republic 55
"Twenty-first demands" of 1915 61

Ukrainian Bolsheviks 51
  leftist Ukrainians 152
  Skrypnik, Nikolai 51, 156
Ukrainian Jews 51
Ukrainian Skoropatskii state 149
Ulanhu (Wu Lanfu) 175
unified political and economic front 145
University of Resistance 165

Vitte, Sergei 147
Voroshilov, Kliment 148
Vrangel', Petr 149

Wang, Jiaxiang 70–71, 165
Wang, Ming 68–69
Warring-State school 186
Weber, Max 23, 84
Wei, Baqun 171
Wei, Guoqing 171
Westerners 92
Whites 99, 103, 105, 137, 148–50,
    152–53, 155, 159, 161
  chauvinism 4, 9, 88, 102, 106, 143,
    145, 159, 182
  Russocentric sentiment among the
    old officers 99
Wilsonism 13, 208
Work and Study 218
World War II 55, 195, 200, 205
Wu, Xiuquan 70
Wu, Yuzhang 66, 120, 164, 166

Xi, Jinping 31, 211–12
Xinjiang 31, 33, 36, 55, 61–65, 72–73,
    164–65, 167, 177
  Deng, Liqun 27, 182, 183
  Saifuding Aziz 27
Xuan, Xiafu 167, 173

Yan'an Rectification 50, 113
Yang, Du 163
Yang, Kuisong 61
Yuan, Shikai 66, 163

Yugoslav–Bulgarian Balkan socialist federation 197
Yun, Daiying 114, 130, 166

Zemstvo 44
Zhang, Guotao 167–68
Zhang, Wentian 70–71, 112

Zhang, Yunyi 172
Zhao, Shuli 118
Zhdanov-style discipline 199
Zhou, Enlai 66, 112, 168, 184–85
Zhuang 169, 171
Zubok, Vladislav 72